S. W. Christophers

The poets of Methodism

S. W. Christophers

The poets of Methodism

ISBN/EAN: 9783742837509

Manufactured in Europe, USA, Canada, Australia, Japa

Cover: Foto ©Andreas Hilbeck / pixelio.de

Manufactured and distributed by brebook publishing software (www.brebook.com)

S. W. Christophers

The poets of Methodism

[*Frontispiece.*

The dead are like stars by day,
  Withdrawn from mortal eye,
But not extinct ; they hold their way
  In glory through the sky.

THE POETS

OF

METHODISM,

BY THE REV. S. W. CHRISTOPHERS,

AUTHOR OF "HYMN WRITERS AND THEIR HYMNS," "HOMES OF OLD ENGLISH WRITERS," &C.

"When Poetry keeps its place, as the handmaid of Piety, it shall attain, not a poor perishable wreath, but a crown that fadeth not away."—*John Wesley.*

LONDON:
HAUGHTON & CO., 10, PATERNOSTER ROW.

1875.

CONTENTS.

	PAGE
FRONTISPIECE.—(*Page Illustration.*)	
PREFACE	vii

CHAPTER I.
INTRODUCTORY CHAPTER 1

CHAPTER II.
FATHERS OF POETS 20

CHAPTER III.
THE EPWORTH SINGERS 41

CHAPTER IV.—(*Page Illustration.*)
OTHERS OF THE EPWORTH SINGERS 61

CHAPTER V.
TWO BROTHERS IN SONG 90

CHAPTER VI.
MORE ABOUT SONGS FROM THE BROTHERS . . . 113

CHAPTER VII.
OTHER PSALMS FROM THE BROTHERS IN SONG . . 135

CHAPTER VIII.
CLERICAL SONG-MASTERS 160

CHAPTER IX.
MORE CLERICAL SONG-MASTERS 179

CHAPTER X.—(*Page Illustration.*)
ITINERANT MINSTRELS 200

CHAPTER XI.
A CONTROVERSIAL SONGSTER 219

CONTENTS.

CHAPTER XII.
Three Lay Singers 241

CHAPTER XIII.
A Choir of Holy Women 262

CHAPTER XIV.
Poetical Divines, Father and Son 284

CHAPTER XV.
Two Poetic Metaphysicians 305

CHAPTER XVI.
Later-Day Clerical Hymnists 324

CHAPTER XVII.
A Poetical Satirist 344

CHAPTER XVIII.
The Tuneful Son of a Prophet 366

CHAPTER XIX.—(Page Illustration.)
An Inspired Young Maiden 388

CHAPTER XX.
A Bard from the Mine 412

CHAPTER XXI.
A Kentish Lyric 434

CHAPTER XXII.
Three Poetic Voices from the West . . . 454

CHAPTER XXIII.
Some of the Latest Sons of Song . . . 478

Index to Hymns, with Authors' Names . . 499

   ,,   Names, Places, etc. . . . 508

PREFACE.

IT is not intended, in this volume, to give full biographies of all "the Poets of Methodism." In most cases, enough is said, it is hoped, to show where, when, and amidst what surroundings, the Methodist Poets lived. Every possible care has been taken to secure accuracy as to dates and chronological order; while all available means have been used to preserve the sketches of life and character from any shade or colouring of untruthfulness. The reader has before him every name of worthy poetic genius and taste with which the writer has become acquainted, during a quiet and patient research into all accessible Methodist chronicles, dating from the times of Wesley to the present day. If the volume should appear chargeable with omissions, the author has only to say that no place has been given to some worthy names, such as Miles Martindale and J. W. Etheridge, for lack of timely access to their poetic remains. In other instances, the claims to notice have seemed too doubtful, or the names had fallen into too deep an obscurity.

CONTENTS.

CHAPTER XII.
Three Lay Singers 241

CHAPTER XIII.
A Choir of Holy Women 262

CHAPTER XIV.
Poetical Divines, Father and Son 284

CHAPTER XV.
Two Poetic Metaphysicians 305

CHAPTER XVI.
Later-Day Clerical Hymnists 324

CHAPTER XVII.
A Poetical Satirist 344

CHAPTER XVIII.
The Tuneful Son of a Prophet 366

CHAPTER XIX.—(*Page Illustration.*)
An Inspired Young Maiden 388

CHAPTER XX.
A Bard from the Mine . . . . . 4••

CHAPTER XXI.
A Kentish Lyric 434

CHAPTER XXII.
Three Poetic Voices from the West . . . 454

CHAPTER XXIII.
Some of the Latest Sons of Song . . . 478

Index to Hymns, with Authors' Names . . 499

„ Names, Places, etc. . . . 508

PREFACE.

IT is not intended, in this volume, to give full biographies of all "the Poets of Methodism." In most cases, enough is said, it is hoped, to show where, when, and amidst what surroundings, the Methodist Poets lived. Every possible care has been taken to secure accuracy as to dates and chronological order; while all available means have been used to preserve the sketches of life and character from any shade or colouring of untruthfulness. The reader has before him every name of worthy poetic genius and taste with which the writer has become acquainted, during a quiet and patient research into all accessible Methodist chronicles, dating from the times of Wesley to the present day. If the volume should appear chargeable with omissions, the author has only to say that no place has been given to some worthy names, such as Miles Martindale and J. W. Etheridge, for lack of timely access to their poetic remains. In other instances, the claims to notice have seemed too doubtful, or the names had fallen into too deep an obscurity.

Grateful acknowledgments are due to the authors of several papers on "Hymns and their Writers," in the *Wesleyan Times*. In particular the author's thanks are tendered to Mr. W. M. Symons, of Vauxhall, for a sight of his valuable collection of MSS. and printed notes on "Methodist Hymn-Writers and their Hymns"; also to the Rev. Messrs. Benjamin Gregory and F. F. Woolley, Mr. Benjamin Gough, Mr. James Smetham, and Mr. C. L. Ford, for permission to use the verses which he has given in association with their names.

The main object of these pages is to afford occasional opportunities of agreeable communion with a few hallowed and gifted spirits who have "served their generation, by the will of God," in holy song and psalmody. And if any reader's soul should be brought to realise a happier tone of thought and feeling, while taking a passing glance at the persons of Methodist Poets, or should gain, at any leisure moment, a pleasant insight into their hearts, habits, and homes, while he is under the charm of their musical variations in verse, the author's recompense will be full.

S. W. C.

Redruth, 1874.

THE POETS OF METHODISM.

INTRODUCTORY CHAPTER.

> The *Christian* bard has, from a *real* spring
> Of inspiration, other themes to sing;
> No vain philosophy, no fabled rhyme,
> But sacred story, simple and sublime,
> By holy prophets told; to whom belong
> The subjects worthy of the pow'rs of song.

THERE is sometimes a striking similarity between what is said or done at a particular point in one man's history, and words or actions at a remarkable turn in the life of another. The actions or words seem, indeed, to repeat themselves like times in the personal experience of very different men. So it would appear to be in the lives of Charles Wesley and Lord Byron. "What, would you have me to be a saint all at once"? said Charles Wesley, when he was a sprightly young Oxford student, and his brother John spoke to him about religion. Charles did become saintly, however, and was a Methodist rather earlier than his brother.

"Would you have me turn Methodist?" said Byron once to Walter Scott, when, like a true friend, the poetic novelist had spoken plainly to him about the claims of personal piety. "Methodist!" replied Scott, "no, I cannot think of you as a Methodist; but I can conceive of your being a catholic Christian." Had Byron asked his friend to define the term 'catholic Christian,' we should have had a definition of Christian piety such as the mind of Scott conceived to be proper for a poet like Byron. His catholic Christianity would probably be broad, artistic, and gorgeous enough to allow entire freedom to the play of the poet's genius. In outward grandeur of forms, influence, and power, it must be favourable to the unchecked supremacy of his imagination and poetic passion. There must be full licence for pride of intellect to live under the semblance of severe devotion. It must be rather ritualistic than spiritual; more sensuous than heartfelt; and all its requisitions must leave the poet free to make poetic fame and success the commanding objects of his life. Romish pomp, or Greek ceremonial splendour, or even the show of Anglo-Catholicism, might suit a catholic Christian such as Scott wished Byron to be. From his point of sight, perhaps, the great novelist saw that Methodism would be too bald in its forms, too simple in its aim, too unadorned in its style, too primitive in its discipline, and too absorbing in its one pursuit, to fit a genius whose only ambition was poetic glory. Scott, it may be, did not look deep enough into Methodism to see that its standard of spiritual piety was such as would not permit the mere culture of intellect, or the exercise of poetic genius alone, to be the one absorbing action or object of life.

It has been said by some, "How gloriously would Byron have shone as a poet, had he been a Christian!" He might possibly have shone had he been a Christian in the popular sense: a Christian chiefly in creed, or ritual, or even in spirit, according to the general notion of a Christian spirit; but would his poetic powers have been so gloriously exhibited had he become a Christian after St. Paul's style, or St. John's type, or one in accordance with the original standard of the Divine Master? Probably not. It is a question whether any man, whatever his genius may be, can become a poet of the first order in the estimation of the mere intellectual world, without proving that the main purpose and leading motives of his life have checked the cultivation of that pure, Christ-like unselfishness which the New Testament calls the Christian to attain. But it is not a question whether the Christian who is wholly bent on holiness of heart carries his life's aim far beyond the successes and rewards of mere intellect or genius. Nor can it be doubted that the pure principles of spiritual Christian life, in their commanding influence over the "whole spirit and soul and body," though they may bring every natural gift into full exercise for the glory of Christ, always carry the hallowed man above the desire of devoting his powers to any service that is not purely for Christ's glory; certainly saving him from devotion to anything that glorifies self.

New Testament Christianity is in conformity with the truth, " Ye are not your own, for ye are bought with a price: therefore glorify God in your body and in your spirit which are God's." The genuine Christian serves Christ " in spirit " ; not merely in his "soul and body," but " in spirit." His higher powers, his 'spirit,' his religious faculty, his "inner man," which communes with "the Father and the Son and the Holy Spirit," enables him to realize St. Paul's experience, "we walk by faith, not by sight." The world of sense does not engage us, the region of mere intellect does not detain us. Men of lower views and narrower aims mind the "things that are seen," the things which their thinking faculty, their unhallowed genius and passions, may deal with; but we have eyes for "things that are not seen." Our spiritual sight is not so bent beneath and around us; it is rather turned forward and upward. God has brought us around to Himself and His kingdom; and now we walk with our eyes on Him and His "heavenlies." "I am crucified with Christ; nevertheless I live; yet not I, but Christ liveth in me; and the life which I now live in the flesh, I live by the faith of the Son of God, who loved me and gave Himself for me." " Ye are dead," says the same apostle to Christians "and your life is hid with Christ in God." You are dead to all glory but His. For " He died for all, that they which live should not henceforth live unto themselves but unto Him which died for them and rose again."

Paul was a man of noble gifts. His acute and powerful understanding, his imagination, his genius and taste, his depths of feeling, his powers of expression, and his varied attainments, might have secured distinguished honours; but the moment he became a Christian, every thing which he possessed or could command was unreservedly devoted to his Lord's service and glory. His talents were improved and employed to the uttermost; but never so as to let 'self' seek or share any honour that belonged to his Master alone. "What things were gain to me," says he, "those I counted loss for Christ. Yea doubtless and I count all things but loss for the excellency of the knowledge of Christ Jesus my Lord; for whom I have suffered the loss of all things and do count them but dung, that I may win Christ, and be found in Him." There have been souls, since Paul's time, who have caught his spirit, and with simplicity and meek unselfishness have kept Christ's glory before them, forgetting their own, and calling all their genius, or science, or learning, or philosophy into full action, have done all for Christ's glory. Like "wise men," they have been led to Jesus by every new "star" they have discovered; and have laid all their 'opened treasures,' the rich fruits of their thought and toil, at His feet, their "gold, and frankincense, and myrrh." And so the Christian who is gifted with poetic genius, if he follow Paul as Paul followed Christ, will, for Christ's sake, improve his talent and exercise his gift, not "to be seen of men," not merely to excel as a poet, or to "please men," or to immortalize his own name, but, as Paul would say, to honour Him "whose I am and whom I serve." The poetry of such a man would please his neighbour "for his good to edification." It would never be inconsistent with Christian purity of thought and feeling. It would accord with the finely expressed feeling of a young modern poet, " I wish to be less a popular than a religious poet. My desire is to write only Christian poetry— praise to Christ, my Lord and Saviour, and to leave popular and general themes to those who can succeed in them far better than I. I would have Redemption for my song; and though mine may not be the Muse for the million, yet, if her voice may rise sweetly in the ear of Jesus, and find an echo in His disciples' hearts, how high will be my honour!" or, as she devoutly expresses herself to God,

> O Thou whose poetry and love in one,
> Walk forth where'er Thou art, and hand in hand
> Encircle heaven and earth, Thou above praise
> Exalted infinitely; O great God!
> Hear me, and make *me* a pure golden harp
> For Thy soft finger. Might I be Thy bird,
> Hidden from all, singing to Thee alone.

"I would have no poetry but such as *Christ* can *smile* on," said this same sweet singer; "oh, may I write no other!"

Such is the poetry which holy men of God used to utter in the fulfilment of their Divine mission. Their psalms and hymns, odes and visions, which have come down to us, show how rich and rare were the natural gifts which they employed in declaring the will of Him to whom they ceaselessly rendered homage as the Author and End of all their endowments. With all the simple majesty of their odes, the ringing harmony of their anthems, the grandeur and beauty of their hymns, the awful glories of their dreams and visions, the rich simplicity of their pastorals, and the chaste, impressive, and thrilling music of their illustrations, all of surpassing excellence—yet self is never seen. They never decline from their lofty aim. Their aim is God. Their work is to declare His will, to proclaim His Messiah, to sustain His worship, to issue His warnings and teachings, and to record the truth which is to make "men wise unto salvation." They are true poets, though they never show poetry to be their object. Theirs is no mere intellectual calling. Theirs is a work of sublime faith; faith in the Unseen. They might be unconscious of their own poetic spirit and power, so void are they of any apparent thought about themselves. If they speak of themselves, it is only to make God's will more clear and impressive. There is no evident effort, no straining for effect, no design to show their wealth of material, no apparent wish to startle by sudden brilliancy or happy turns. The reader never smells the writer's lamp. Nor, indeed, does a breath escape them which might serve to indicate the loss of their Divine purpose amidst cherished thoughts about their own inner selves or their personal reputation. They are careless of their own names as poets; and have no concern about leaving a memorial. Indeed, they never speak as professional poets. Poetry is not their profession. They are simply prophets, ambassadors, voices; and if they psalm it, they chant to bewail their sins, to glorify God for their deliverance, or, as humble and happy saints, to declare what God had done for their souls. Their standard of piety was too high, too God-like, to allow their poetry to be anything but purely devotional, anything that did not most certainly tend to God's glory. And while their standard is maintained by men of poetic genius, poetry will take the same character, and be mainly such as will purify the tone of human intellect, and, above all, awaken the human spirit to the duties and joys of Christian worship.

> Though now there seems one only worthy aim
> For poet—that my strength were as my will!
> And which renounce he cannot without blame—
> To make men feel the presence of his skill,
> Of an eternal loveliness; until
> They faint with love, and longing for their home,
> Yet not the less be strengthened to fulfil
> Their work on earth, that they may surely come
> Unto the Land of Rest, who here as exiles roam.

Those who are not under the sacred control of the Holy Ghost in a way analogous to that in which inspired writers were, will of course feel more deeply the difficulty of exercising their conscious poetic power consistently with that thorough unselfishness which pure Christianity demands. And their difficulty will be the greater in proportion to the strength of their conviction, that self must be ignored if they would glorify Christ by full conformity to His mind. Charles Wesley felt this difficulty at first; and has recorded his deep sense of it in a hymn of touching plaintiveness, warm pathos, and vigorous harmony of expression—

> Where shall I lay my weary head?
> Where shall I hide me from my shame?
> From all I feel, and all I dread,
> And all I have and all I am!
> Swift to outstrip the stormy wind,
> And leave this cursed *self* behind.
>
> O the intolerable load
> Of nature, waken'd to pursue
> The footsteps of a distant God,
> Till faith hath form'd the soul anew!
> 'Tis death, 'tis more than death to bear—
> I cannot live till God is here.
>
> Give me Thy wings, celestial Dove,
> And help me from myself to fly;
> Then shall my soul far off remove,
> The tempest's idle rage defy,
> From sin, from sorrow, and from strife
> Escaped, and hid in Christ, my Life.
>
> Stranger on earth, I sojourn here:
> Yet, O, on earth I cannot rest
> Till Thou, my hidden Life, appear,
> And sweetly take me to Thy breast:
> To Thee my wishes all aspire,
> And sighs for Thee my whole desire.
>
> Search and try out my panting heart:
> Surely, my Lord, it pants for Thee,
> Jealous lest earth should claim a part:
> Thine, wholly Thine I gasp to be.
> Thou know'st 'tis all I live to prove;
> Thou know'st I only want Thy love.

The hymnist here discloses the struggle in the soul of a poet who admits the supreme claim of Christ to all that a Christian has and is, and who is fixed in his purpose and desire of realizing entire consecration of his powers to the Divine service; while he yet feels the effort of self against the sacrifice of all which the pride of intellect and conscious genius would contend for on their own behalf.

The standard of Christian holiness which Charles Wesley set before himself was that which he and his brother John set before themselves and the people called Methodists. It was the standard of that perfect love to Christ which constrains him who realizes it to fulfil the apostolic injunction, "I beseech you therefore, brethren, by the mercies of God, that ye present your bodies a living sacrifice, holy, acceptable unto God, which is your reasonable service. And be not conformed to this world: but be ye transformed by the renewing of your mind, that ye may prove what is that good, and acceptable, and perfect will of God." To be a holy people in this sense of living for Christ alone, and so, in the spirit of self-sacrifice to "spread scriptural holiness over the land," was the principle and purpose of the Methodists; and faithfulness to this standard of piety would admit of no self-seeking, no proud aspirations of mere intellect, no pandering to the worshippers of mind, no mode of limiting the pursuits of life to the regions of either sense, or genius, or passion, or intellectual power. Whatever efforts the poetic genius of a consistent Methodist might put forth, they must necessarily be such, and such only, as are in keeping with unreserved devotion to Christ alone.

A young Methodist poet beautifully represents the temptation which may assail conscious genius in its first essays to devote itself entirely to Christ; and shows the spirit in which the temptation is to be met and overcome. The tempter is symbolized by

>A giant flower
>Whose cup turned upward.

And he speaks to the tempted who is figured by

>A lily of the vale without a spot.

>"Rise," he said,
>"Thou pretty, timorous spirit; wherefore hide
>Such matchless beauty; I, not half so fair,
>Lift up my head and live: I am a king,
>And Genius is my name; and on the stem
>Of pride do I sit royally, and gaze
>On the broad universe—that mirror spread
>For gods and me—wherein I read my form
>Glassed out in glory; tall as the night heavens,
>And broader than the ocean. Rise too
>Thou white Humility, darling of heaven,
>Give me thy hand; I'll teach thee how to soar,

> And thou shalt be a queen, if thou but turn
> Thy bells this way. See what a world of light
> Stands o'er thee!"
>   "Nay, I must not," said the flower;
> " I have commandment ever to rise up,
> And ever to look down ;—this law is given
> To keep my robe snow-white."

Methodism proper, then, could never be expected to number among its members such poets as live by choice among the intellectual gods. Byron could not be Byron the poet and Byron the Methodist all under one. Nor could a genuine Methodist gifted with poetical powers ever be a poet of Byron's class. The same thing may be said of others who have lived to be poets, poets by profession, and nothing higher. "They," as was once said, "do not comprehend the deep and lofty mysteries of Poetry. They have not dwelt in her heart, nor known what it is to feel her power burning in every pulse of the spirit, and drawing the curtain from heaven, earth, and ocean, to show the resplendent omnipresence of beauty and love beaming from the face of God over them all. Poetry covered them with her flowers, buried them in showers of gems, but sealed from their eyes that one simple magic pearl of white, immortal truth, which God has set in her bosom as the richest of all caskets. Some of them with half-open eyes, pore dreamily over the great secret, or seem to have their finger trembling on the very spring of that portal, which but once opened, admits the true poet to gaze upon the universal landscape as with angel's eyes." Some poets show large Christian knowledge and reverent feeling; and yet for them to have conformed to the principles, the simple aim, and spiritual pursuits of Methodism would probably have been to put a final check to that wide expatiation of genius, that undevout indulgence of imagination, and that morbid intercourse with self which have secured for them all their distinction. No, Methodism, while she is faithful to her first principles and one design, can never boast of any poets but such as sing to help her devotion, or serve to illustrate her rule of holiness, or to inspirit her in her labours, or to console her by unfolding the beauty of her prospects and the consummation of her design. The poets of Methodism are mostly of this class. And it may be said that the fruits of her consecrated genius are mainly such as might come from spirits who have been able to adopt as their own the motto of a reverend "pilgrim" "I have nothing, I am nothing, I desire nothing but Jesus and Jerusalem"; or the tuneful words which have been accepted by Methodist hymnists from the songs of a saintly French woman—

> Henceforth may no profane delight
> Divide this consecrated soul;
> Possess it Thou who hast the right,
> As Lord and Master of the whole.
>
> Thy gifts, if call'd for, I resign,
> Pleased to receive, pleased to restore:
> Gifts are Thy work; it shall be mine
> The Giver only to adore.

Let it not be thought that these remarks on Methodist poets in general are in any way intended to form an apology for them in the presence of poets of another class. Poetry like theirs needs no apology, at least among Christians. If on a review of their works all varieties of poetic power are found; if the highest degree of that power sometimes makes itself felt; if all the essentials of poetry show themselves; if the distinctive genius and spirit, the imagination and fancy, the facility and flexibility of thought and language, the deep sympathy with nature, the instinctive insight into the depths of human feeling, the order, taste, sense of beauty and of music, the spirit of harmony, and precise but full and various expression — if all these manifest themselves as they do among the poets of Methodism, these poets may take their stand among their peers without any further introduction. But if all these qualities are theirs; and, combined in fair proportions, have been faithfully used as God's gifts in promoting the spiritual holiness, the mental renovation, the social purity, and the final triumphs of Christ's kingdom; the Divine sanctions add dignity to their charms. Their poetry, so largely devotional, has put forth its beauty and life under an inspiration which associates it with the happiest thoughts of daily Christian life, the deepest joys, the richest grace, and the most jubilant victories of individual saints and Christian churches throughout the world. If true "Poetry is the religious idea incarnate in the beautiful," then the poets of Methodism may take a high rank among true poets.

"But have the Methodists ever written anything but hymns?" Yes, some of them have. And what, if they had written nothing but hymns? Their hymns, in many cases, have become world-wide in their influence, and find a welcome from growing numbers of cultured minds and pure hearts. "Anything but hymns!" Why, none but a true poet could produce a true hymn. A genuine hymn is a thing of beauty and diffusive life; and nothing short of hallowed poetic genius could bring it into being. A hymn of the highest order, most instinct with devout life, requires, however, more than mere poetic genius to give it birth. It requires that spiritual taste, that sympathy with Heaven, that pure love of truth, and that holy familiarity with the Divine source of inspiration, without which the hymn will lack the undying impress of the Blessed Spirit. For lack of all this not even Milton could secure for his psalms a permanent life among Christian songs. His great hymn, the "Nativity Hymn," had so much of *Milton* in it that it failed to fulfil the purpose of a hymn, as it fails to engage Christian hearts in pure and unchecked adoration of the Incarnate One. Methodist poets have not always been happy as hymnists. Some of their hymns take a lead in holy song. Others were sung for the last time when their authors first chanted them to themselves. But, on the whole, the devotional and Godward poetic utterances of Methodism promise to live permanently among the things which reverent genius, pure taste, and truthful hearts will ever appreciate and enjoy.

"The poets of Methodism! Do you include the little rhyme factors and makers of jingling ditties which have sprung up and given voice now and then in the course of the Methodist history?"

Certainly not. Though even these may have a passing notice as amusing phenomena. The "poetry" pages of the old Methodist magazines were not always free from verses whose only virtue was the ring of their rhyme. The editors were, perhaps, at times too indulgent to their contributors—more tender over young essayists in verse than careful of their own reputation for taste, although, it may be, these very rhymes served to increase the popularity which distinguished the original Methodist serial. The earlier issues were certainly more suited to the Methodist multitude, and were more enjoyed by the many than the modern continuation of the periodical seems to be.

More or less of oral rhyme, too, has always been afloat among Methodists. Now and then some zealous, though uncultured, brother or sister has been known to start up under rhyming inspiration and set all like-minded fellow-worshippers a singing at the poet's dictation. Many a ditty never submitted to an "editor" has become more popular in its oral form than it would have been as shut up in print. We once attended service in a little rural chapel on a Devonshire moorland. At the close of the sermon, just as the preacher was about to give out the last hymn, a good woman, taken with the spirit of spontaneous song, rose to her feet, and shouted—

" Long metre!

> "There's bread and fish for you and me,
> And plenty more for two and three ;
> Your empty baskets you may bring,
> And gather all the fragments in."

" Long metre!"

The preacher sat down and patiently waited till the ode, of about twelve verses, was sung through, with swelling effect, under the guidance of the enthusiastic woman. The first verse was by no means an unfair specimen of the many which followed.

Not very far from the scene of this inspiring performance, a still more stirring ditty and chorus had served to move the spiritual warriors to the combat "against principalities and powers," as if they battled with "flesh and blood." "Come, neighbours!" was the war song,

> Come, neighbours, with your sticks and stones,
> And break the Devil's back and bones,
> And send him to hell with bitter groans,
> And we shall gain the union.

After all, this fondness for rude, ringing rhymes and jingling choruses may be the lingering taste which has been begotten and cherished by Church authority. Sternhold and Hopkins taught their generation to sing,

> When Israel by God's command
> From Pharaoh's land was bent;
> And Jacob's home the strangers left
> And in the same tram went.

"The Epworth people," said their Rector, Samuel Wesley, "must be contented with their present parochial way of singing. Indeed they must also be content with their Grandsire Sternhold. Bishop Beveridge declared that the common people could understand the psalms of Sternhold better than those of Tate and Brady. And there may be truth in this, for the common people have a strange genius for understanding nonsense."

But David was done into English metre by other hands, still more rude. Grave and educated congregations used to psalm it thus—

> 'Tis like the precious ointment
> Down Aaron's beard did go;
> Down Aaron's beard it downward went
> His garment skirts unto.

Or thus—

> Why dost thou hold thine hand aback
> And hide it in thy lap?
> O pluck it out and be not slack
> To give thy foes a rap.

Solomon as well as David has been made to foot it to Church music, so—

> The race is not for ever got
> By him who fastest runs;
> Nor the battle by the people
> Who shoot the longest guns.

Dr. Belcher, an American authority in psalm literature, says, "From the hymns in use before the days of Watts, here is a specimen verse; and though our readers may smile at it, their fathers did not—

> "Ye monsters of the bubbling deep,
> Your Maker's praises shout;
> Up from the sands, ye codlings, peep,
> And wag your tails about."

Dr. Watts seems to have been the first to break in upon this serio-comic style of devotional song; and, in his own way, to lead Christian voices up into nobler and sweeter harmonies. Yet, for a long time those voices were loth to sacrifice the old measures in favour of the new ones. Attempts were occasionally made, in America at least, to improve on Watts by bringing him back into something like conformity to old fashions. An old correspondent from Connecticut tells us that the leading singer in one of the churches thought he could better the music and the poetry of their psalms. He set Watts's ninety-second psalm to music of his own; but found that to make the music and the verse accord, he must substitute his own *finer* lines for those of Watts—

> Oh, let my heart in time be found
> Like David's harp of solemn sound.

He waited on the Pastor to submit his improved version and music, and proposed to sing—

> Oh, may my heart be tuned within
> Like David's sacred violin.

The Pastor, who was a little waggish, found his gravity severely tested; but, maintaining a becoming dignity, he suggested an improvement even on the singer's '*great* improvement.' "Pray let me hear what you propose," said the flattered poet. The minister scribbled two lines for him, thus—

> Oh, may my heart go diddle, diddle,
> Like uncle David's sacred fiddle.

Watts was rescued; and the would-be restorer of old

metrical psalmody was content for the future to allow that the new rhyming was better than the old.

Doggrel, then, is not peculiar to Methodism. It was patronized in the Church of England, the Kirk of Scotland, and among English Presbyterians long before Methodism began her songs. Methodism, at all events, has never patronized or sanctioned the use of doggrel in worship. Never, we say; but just now one verse occurs which may be deemed an exception. A Methodist preacher, in the use of his authorized "Hymn Book," may call on his congregation to glorify their Divine Master by singing—

>No matter how dull
>The scholar that He
>Takes unto His school
>And gives him to see—

John Wesley sanctioned this by issuing it for Methodist use. But there was always a redeeming provision. Should there be a bald place in the hymn, or a rhyme so homely as to be akin to doggrel, he always secured music of sufficient spirit and power to carry the singing multitude above any feeling of weakness. This redeeming provision, however, is not always to be found associated with more modern Church doggrel. Even those who affect the highest culture of choral harmony may be found singing—

>My God, I love Thee, not because
>I hope for heaven thereby,
>Nor yet because who love Thee not
>Must burn eternally—

and rendering such rhymes, too, in tunes or dronings so expressionless that the choir might seem

>to lie in shady cloister mew'd
>Chanting faint hymns to the cold, fruitless moon.

While in another quarter, in a manner neither "ancient" nor "modern," people have been heard singing by the water-side—

>O tarry not—your Lord obey;
>And be baptized without delay:
>Nor ever think of coming here
>Unless you are a volunteer.

Methodism, then, is not to be the scape-goat. All the halting verses and ragged rhymes are not to be considered as the burden of her tongue. If some of her simple, warm-hearted people have, now and then, given out such utterances, it has been generally by the bye, and on their personal responsibility. And if they have been personally happy under such inspirations, or if their rhymes have chimed in with their fellow-worshippers' taste and feeling for the time, it has only served to remind us that unsophisticated human nature, when most excited, always shows itself ready to throw out its expressions of passion in some rhythmical or metrical form. The rhymes, however rude, show that the original gift of poesy continues to be represented among men, and sometimes gives signs of life even where there is the least culture. It doubtless helps to solace the poor rhymer when he finds his measures flowing in spite of circumstances; and where the rhyming power is turned to the service of religion, the solace is all the more sweet, and is not only innocent, but mentally and morally beneficial.

While John Wesley was conducting public worship in one of his chapels, his ear became uneasy under the discordant voice of an old woman who was, in her way, singing with the congregation. The fine-eared Methodist apostle stopped at length, and gently said, "My good sister, you are singing out of tune." "My heart is singing, sir!" was the prompt reply. "Then, sing on, my sister!" was the final decision of the preacher. Rude rhymes may provoke the smile of finely-tuned people, or prove instruments of passing torture to others; but better let the rhymers "sing on" than let them lose the joy of singing in the best way they can. If jingling ditties form their highest and happiest mode of expressing their devotion, let them rhyme it, till they rhyme it better in a better world.

In the course of her history, however, Methodism has had poets, as courtesy has called them, or as they have thought themselves to be — spirits of higher pretensions than the mere impromptu authors of oral psalms or hymns. "Poems" have now and then been issued, "Chimes" have been set a going; and on these some well-meaning but mistaken souls have staked their mental and literary character. An interview with one of these line-stringers, some years ago, will never be forgotten. It was an evening gathering of friends, some of whom were distinguished for learning, intellectual power, and refined taste. The inspired or rather inflated poetizer had just sent his book into the world; and now he was evidently disposed to press his effusions on the attention of the guests. He began by claiming acquaintance with a venerable literary man, and first throwing a glance around, and then giving the old student a significant look, he said, in a tone which rose above all other voices,

"When I returned from my journey to the tropics, I presented a native-grown stick to Mr. ——— accompanied with verses expressive of my esteem; did I not, Sir? do you remember?"

"Yes," said the fine old man with a waggish look, "I remember, it was a very pretty *stick!*"

Not feeling this stroke, or, if feeling it, not discouraged, he turned to another who was near him, a man of remarkable taste, massive in his knowledge, and a deep thinker,

"Have you seen my volume of poems?"

"No, sir."

"I should like your opinion of it. Will you let me give you a bit by way of sample?"

"Yes; but you must speak up; I am rather deaf."

The poet began, and his voice swelled as his spirit kindled with the measure

> Oh she's dead!—but she's gone to the home of the good,
>   She dwells in a palace royàl,
> O'er-past has her spirit cold Jordan's flood,
>   And escaped from the land of triàl.

"Stay!" said the listener, "before you go on, tell me what poetry is."

There was silence.—The poet had never defined to himself what he affected to produce. He was evidently at a loss. But before he could well recover himself, the other continued, "If you cannot tell me what poetry is, I am sure it is not for me to define it to you; but listen, I will give you a specimen of true poetry."—Then with beautiful intonation and touching emphasis he quoted—"Consider the lilies of the field, how they grow: they toil not, neither do they spin. And yet I say unto you that even Solomon in all his glory was not arrayed like one of these."—"Now, Sir," he added, "that is poetry; compare that with your own, and say no more."

The rebuke was effective, and the hush that followed gave birth to thoughts and feelings which have been fruitful to this day.

And, yet, mere rhymers and chimers have continued to give voice from time to time. A check upon one does not hush the voice of another. Now, we have the affectation of a lengthy "Poem" on "the Birth of Christ," for instance, "that the virtuous, or at least the young," as the author says, may be benefited by hearing him tell how the Saviour

> Should lift the captive from the dungeon up,
> And rescue all the prisoners of hope!

And then, from another quarter we have tender tinklings, as sweetly innocent of poetic genius as the pretty chimes from a country church tower on a Sabbath morning—sound —imitative sound—with no living native breath of harmony, proving by its freshness that it is the gush of a poet's own life. But, after all, Methodism has its genuine poets; that is to say, men and wómen of original and originating genius, whose music, though not, in some cases, without discords, has life in it which will continue to awaken answering harmonies when oblivion has for ever covered those who end as well as

> begin with their Jingle (or Rattle
> As some of them call it) the delicate battle.

It is hoped that the following pages may serve to lead their readers into pleasant communion with true Methodist Bards, and help to make them happily familiar with "Fathers of Poets," "Epworth Singers," "Brothers in Song," "Clerical Song-Masters," "Itinerant Minstrels," "Lay Singers," "Choirs of Holy Women," "Poetical Divines," "Tuneful Metaphysicians," "Latter-day Clerical Hymnists," "Poetical Satirists," "Musical Sons of Prophets," "Inspired Young Maidens," "Bards of Cornwall and Kent," "Some of the Latest Sons of Song," and, indeed, all that are fairly known as "The Poets of Methodism."

CHAPTER II.

FATHERS OF POETS.

> To unseen realms the elders urge their flight,
> And prophets vanish in a car of light;
> Yet still the plenteous unction ceaseless flows,
> Jehovah's hand the needful gift bestows.

"MAN is, what he knows." This may mean not only that the kind and degree of man's knowledge gives a shaping to his character, but that the measure of one man's real knowledge is the standard of his value and use to another. Something like an illustration of this lives among recollections of early travels. It was early on a spring morning. The "Guard" cried, "take your seats, gentlemen!" as he stood ready to take his. Another moment, and we were off; not on the rails, no, but behind the beautiful team of a fast coach which then ran from Exeter through Dorset. As we left the suburbs of the old city, the merry tramp of the horses was cheerily in tune, as a kind of castanet accompaniment, to the music of the Guard's bugle. We dashed along gaily through rich variations of scene. Now, standing, as the coach reached the pitch of the hill above Honiton, to look back on the lovely vale in which so many fair lace-makers once plied their skilful hands at their cottage doors; and now, stopping to salute old Axminster dreamily reposing by the side of her own little river. At length we crossed the border into Dorset. Among the travellers, there was one to whom, up to this time, it seemed in vain to appeal. He was muffled up; and was evidently indisposed to respond to any remark or question from a fellow traveller. No fine turn of the road, no sudden unfolding of prospect, no bit of flowery hedge-row, no charm of cottage home or village had any attractive power for him, as far as could be seen. A short "Yes," or "No" was his only word. There was a cold and somewhat forbidding look of absence, passing, at times, into an expression of pain or distress. He seemed to know nothing. And it was silently decided, at last, that he was nothing, nothing of any worth to his companions on the coach, at all events. For it must be remembered that coach travelling was a far more sociable and conversational thing than our present mode of getting conveyed, like goods and chattels, by rail. It allowed people, too, to hear one another's natural voice. So that a coach traveller could scarcely maintain a persistent silence without danger of being thought too ignorant, too rude, too stupid, or too contemptibly proud to speak. Our road now began to decline from the heights above Lyme Regis; and it was evident, from the prospect which was opening beneath, that our way down would be steep and critical. Just at this point, however, our muffled mope who had been so impenetrably entrenched within himself gave signs of change. His face more fully disclosed itself; a little freshness seemed to spring up and pass over it; the rigidity left his lips; and it was felt that his eye seemed ready to speak before his tongue gave voice. Indeed there was a kindling light in his eye which awakened a wish to hear him speak. The coach was now requiring all the skill and power of the driver to guide it down into the depth which yawned beneath us.

One who sat next to the strangely quickened traveller cried at length, "Where in the world are we going?"

"Going!" said the one whose mouth was now open as well as his face, "we are going down into the hole which so very nearly proved a trap-hole for that runaway ragamuffin, Charles Stuart, the Second. It is a hallowed spot, sir. It would have been more sacred to England, perhaps, had it witnessed the handcuffing rather than the escape of the graceless fugitive. Nevertheless, it is a hallowed spot. That," continued he, pointing to a village rising from the base of the hill, "that is 'the hole of the pit' whence was dug that gifted and divinely marked family for which England and the world owes God an ever accumulating debt of gratitude. That is Charmouth, sir; the earliest home, as far as we can trace, of the Wesley family."

By this time, we had reached the bottom of the hill, and had pulled up in front of the little rustic inn. And now our friend with the loosened tongue became enthusiastic.

"It was near this spot, I suppose," said he, "that the wretched Charles, under the care of his companion, Lord Wilmot, spent the night in watching for the arrival of the boat that was to take them from the creek below to the craft bound for the French coast. And up there in the village must have been the little chapel into which he sneaked to prevent suspicions, and where he heard Bartholomew Wesley hold forth in what a rollicking royalist called, 'his long-breathed devotions and bloody prayers.' That Bartholomew Wesley was the 'puny parson of the place,' as some called him; true to his post; ready to feed his flock as a pastor, or to work at the spinning wheel, as St. Paul did at tent-making, to eke out his pittance, by making home-spun hose and doublets for himself. The village smith had reported that the strangers' horses were shod in a foreign style, and the parson thought that one rider, at least, must be the proscribed Stuart; and, as in duty bound, he left his chapel service to catechise the inn-keeper. But, alas! it was too late; the game was gone. It was a pity. But with all his alleged puritanical gravity, he had good humour enough to joke over it. 'I am sure,' said he to a friend, 'that if ever the king come back he will be certain to love long prayers; for if I had not been at that time longer than ordinary at devotion, I should surely have snapt him.'"

"What would have come of it, if the parson had 'snapt him'?" asked one of the travellers. "Into what groove would the history of England have run? Would your Wesley family ever have been 'divinely marked'? Would they have appeared at all? Would they have placed 'England and the world under a debt of gratitude to God'?"

"I can't tell," was the reply, "how mysteriously the course of human generations have been made to hang upon a few minutes continuation of prayer, or upon the fitting of a horse-shoe a few minutes sooner or later; I think, however, that if that heartless prince had been 'snapt' by Bartholomew Wesley, neither the good Rector nor his son John would have had to endure so much bitter suffering from the Church which acknowledged Charles Stuart at its head."

Just at this moment there came an old man asking the coach passengers to buy his prawns which he held out temptingly on a plate.

"Oh," said our now interesting companion, "this is the place for prawns. They were coming to this creek long before Bartholomew Wesley was made Rector in 1640; and they have been coming ever since; affording meals to many a cottage home from generation to generation. John Wesley, the grandfather of the great Oxford Methodist, must have been a boy running about here soon after 1640; and I dare say, like many a boy used to catching prawns in the tidal pools, he used to prove himself equal to the task of garnishing the poor Rector's table, now and then in the season, with a little dish-full quite as large and delicious as these."

The prawns were demolished, and as the coach crept up the opposite hill, one traveller, at least, was trying to get at the secret of this wonderful change in the manner of the gentleman who had so long shut himself up within himself. The problem was at last good-naturedly solved. The man in his unaccountable mood had been undergoing a kind of periodical attack of physical suffering, which was intensely aggravated by the necessary effort to conceal his agony. The paroxysm had passed just as the coach crossed the border of Dorset; and the restored freedom of body and mind had resulted in the fresh flow of spirits with which he entered on the historical associations of Charmouth. In Devon, he was accounted nothing, and had credit for knowing nothing. In Dorset, his knowledge, and his pleasant mode of using it, made him every thing to his fellow travellers for the rest of the journey. So that, after all, "man is what he knows." A lesson had been given to some, at all events, on the duty of abstaining from hasty judgment as to the character and knowledge of those who may sometimes be silent fellow travellers.

"I should like to know a little more about the Wesleys of Charmouth," some one said, as we approached the top of the hill.

"Well, it is a story that can be but partly told, for much of it is lost," said the oracle of the party, calling us to look back a moment or two. "You have seen the hamlet in the valley; yonder on the hill is another of Bartholomew Wesley's pastorates, Catherston, which was given him in charge about 1650. In these parishes he served, using great plainness of speech, and edifying his flock without any sparkle of what is called popularity. He lived there to see his son John pass through his university training in Oxford; undergo his examination successfully before the Parliamentary 'Triers'; enter on his work as a preacher among the villages on the coast yonder, near Weymouth; take the pastoral charge of Winterborn-Whitchurch; become a companion with himself in tribulation under the Act of Uniformity, on Bartholomew day 1662; and then pass away in comparatively early life, worn out by persecution, privation, sorrow, and toil. The old man never entirely threw off the painful effect of his bereavement. The law would not allow him to preach; but he seized every opportunity of fulfilling his sacred mission; while to gain a livelihood he practiced physic, calling into exercise, at last, the knowledge which he had gathered as a medical student at Oxford. He did not live long to endure the disabilities and oppressions to which he and his nonconforming neighbours were cruelly subjected. He soon met his martyred son again in their new inviolable home. Charles Wesley might have felt something like an inherited share in his great grandfather's latest thoughts and feelings, when he wrote one of his hymns on 'Preparation for Death.' The plaintive desire for rest, and the longing hopefulness of the old weary confessor are finely uttered—

> "Hide me by Thy presence, Lord,
>   From the dire infectious race,
> From the men Thou call'st Thy sword,
>   From the gale of bitterness,
> From the strife of tongues conceal,
> Tongues inflamed with fire of hell.
>
> In Thy tabernacle keep
>   Till I bow my weary head
> Close my eyes in lasting sleep
>   Sink among the quiet dead,
> Where the world no more molest,
> Where the weary are at rest.
>
> Weary of contention here
>   Saviour, to Thy arms I fly.
> Save Thine aged messenger,
>   Bid me get me up and die,
> Die out of a world of strife,
> Die into immortal life.
>
> Made by pure consummate love
>   Meet and ready to depart,
> Gladly would I now remove,
>   See Thee, Saviour, as Thou art,
> Cherished in Thy loving breast
> Lull'd to everlasting rest."

About the harvest time of the year 1683, a young man footed it into Oxford from London. He was rather short in stature, but of well formed and muscular figure. His face would be thought handsome. It was alive with genius, humour, and intelligence. It bore the stamp of calm thought and strong decision. And an observer who saw him tramping over the bridge which spanned the Charwell, with all his little store of worldly goods on his back, would have seen in his earnest look, the will and the power to bend himself successfully to his chosen life-task. Under the vigorous Vice Chancellorship of Dr. John Owen, the old seat of learning was, by this time, recovering from the effect of civil war. Broken trees were removed; trampled down gardens were putting forth new beauty; broken windows and shattered roofs and walls were repaired; and public and private ways were again free from their overgrowth of bramble and weed. Things seemed to be put somewhat in order for the admission of Bartholomew Wesley's grandson, Samuel, who, without a friend in the city, and scarcely one any where else, was come with his fortune of forty five shillings in his pocket, resolved to work his way to academic honour, or to perish in the struggle. When but an infant on his mother's breast, he was driven from his birth-place, Winterborn Whitechurch in Dorset, out of the pastoral care of which his persecuted nonconformist father, John Wesley, was cast by the act of uniformity in 1662. His parents, by and by, notwithstanding their straits and perils, managed to secure for him the full advantage of the Dorchester Grammar School. On the premature death of his father, he had been admitted to a dissenting academy in London, first at Stepney and then at Newington Green; where, in learning to defend the ecclesiastical system of Nonconformity, he learnt to prefer the polity of the Church of England. And now, having broken away from his dissenting friends, the poor fatherless lad paced the "stream-like windings of the beautiful High Street of Oxford, beautiful then it must have been. Did he linger to look at that remarkable porch of St. Mary's then of recently gained significance, with its virgin and child, set up by the obsequious chaplain of the unhappy Laud, in time to help towards relieving his master of his imponderous head? Wesley must have heard the story from his mother. Did he think while looking up at that porch and tower, for the first time, that he was looking at the church in which the voices of his sons would be lifted up with such power and effect? Did he stop to regale his spirits with a draught from the quaint old Carfax Conduit, which then stood at the corner of High Street, where it had served to adorn and refresh the city ever since 1590? However that might be, he found his way to Exeter College, and entered it, perhaps with something before him like a prophetic looming of future success, such as is sometimes caught by the eye of conscious genius, while as yet it is unseen by all others. He had passed over the threshold of a College which was divided by a narrow lane only from Lincoln, in which his son was to attain academic distinction, and from which that son was to go prepared to face at once the cultured and the unlearned world in fulfilling the apostolic mission of his life. How mysteriously places are sometimes linked at certain points in their history! and how close though subtle may be the relations between the turns in a father's life and the bent and issues of his children's action!

Samuel Wesley began his college life at the right point,—the lowest! acting on the wise maxim of the old Jack-tar, who seeing, for the first time, a messmate getting into an omnibus of modern style, cried, "Jack, you are wrong! you are getting in at the stern! Get in at the bows, I say, and work your way up to the quarter deck!" Young Wesley got in at the bows; and worked his way up. He was admitted as *pauper scholaris;* and became a serving man to his richer fellow students, that he might get bread for his outer man, while his inner man fed on the learning afforded him in the schools. He could assist those who were willing to pay for learning; or lift those into place who found it more easy to pay for being lifted than to put themselves to climbing work. There are always men enough in Oxford who have more money than wit. Wesley's poverty was perhaps a blessing. It was more of a stimulus than a check.

> "Sweet are the uses of adversity,
> Which, like the toad ugly and venomous,
> Wears yet a precious jewel in his head."

Necessity threw him upon his own resources. He remembered his school-day essays in rhyme; and feeling that there was power within him still, he put it forth, and produced what he hoped would help to enrich his pocket, while it challenged the world's estimate of his genius. His first little volume appeared as, "Maggots; or, Poems on several

Subjects never before handled; by a Scholar." The volume had a portrait of the author, represented as crowned with laurel, but with a maggot on his brow, and an explanatory verse beneath,

> In his own defence the author writes,
> Because when this foul maggot bites,
>   He ne'er can rest in quiet:
> Which makes him make so sad a face,
> He'd beg your worship, or your grace,
>   Unsight, unseen, to buy it.

This first outbreak of genius showed, for the most part, the mere playful and witty side of the poet's character; and is valuable chiefly as shewing the sprightly elements of his power. He proves himself capable of scorching satire against the fashionable vices of his times; though he conforms too frequently to the fashion himself, by using unchaste words in reproving unchaste actions. But what can be expected from "Maggots"? True, they are, as he tells us, his "first formed birth, the natural issue of his own brain pan, born and bred there, and only there;" yet, the breed would not naturally find very general entertainment, though some of them appeared under curious titles. "A Ginger-bread Mistress"; "A Covetous old Fellow"; "A Bear-faced Lady"; "A Tame Snake in a box of Bran"; "A Certain Nose"; "A Leather Bottle"; "A Cow's Tail"; and "A Tobacco Pipe," might be rare specimens of "Maggots"; but probably most critics will think that they were not least kindly thought about when they were thought to have found a home in Pope's "Dunciad."

> Here she beholds the chaos dark and deep,
> Where nameless somethings in their causes sleep,
> 'Till genial Jacob, or a warm third day
> Calls forth each mass, a poem or a play.
> How hints, like spawn, scarce quick in embryo lie!
> How new-born nonsense first is taught to cry!
> *Maggots* half form'd, in rhyme, exactly meet,
> And learn to crawl upon poetic feet!
> Here one poor word a hundred clench'es makes,
> And ductile dulness new meanders takes;
> There mothy images her fancy strike,
> Figures ill-pair'd, and similes unlike.

Samuel Wesley's first volume was published by the crack-brained genius and book-worm, Dunton, whose publishing shop, near the Exchange, bore the sign of "The Black Raven." He gave to the world a flattering description of his own person and character, telling us that his modesty was more than usually great, and then saying, " I have all those good qualities that are necessary to render me an accomplished gentleman." He fell out with Samuel Wesley, however, after the death of his beautiful wife, who was Mrs. Wesley's sister; and then turned the laugh against his brother-in-law, telling the world that he had "got his bread by the 'Maggots.'" The " Maggots " seem, therefore, to have been rather prolific than barren. One of the poetic pieces in the volume was called " A Tobacco Pipe," and it appears to indicate the young poet's early devotion to the pipe. He versifies the usual vapoury arguments in its favour, and then sings

> Surely when Prometheus climb'd above the poles,
> Slyly to learn their art of making souls,
> When of his fire he fretting Jove did wipe,
> He stole it thence in a tobacco pipe;
> Which, predisposed to live, as down he ran,
> By the soul's plastic power, from clay was turn'd to man.

This would have been an important hint for Darwin. The tobacco pipe would, perhaps, be more popular than the ape as an ancestral type. And smokers especially may be glad to know of what clay they are made, and to what form of clay they may return. Did the father's confirmed habit of smoking and snuff-taking beget that aversion to tobacco and snuff which his son John so strongly expresses in a letter to somebody in Ireland ? " Use all diligence to be clean.

> " Let thy mind's sweetness have its operation
> Upon thy person, clothes, and habitation.

Use no tobacco—it is an uncleanly and unwholesome self-indulgence. Use no snuff. I suppose no other nation in Europe is in such vile bondage to this silly, nasty, dirty custom as the Irish are. But let Christians be in this bondage no longer." Was it his father's habit that awakened John

Wesley to the importance of prohibiting the use of snuff and tobacco to his preachers? That, probably, it was which moved Samuel Wesley's sister in law to prompt the poetical pen of his son Samuel and to bring out those sarcastic lines

> The snuff-box first provokes our just disdain,
> That rival of the fan and of the cane,
> Your modern beaux to richest shrines intrust
> Their worthless stores of fashionable dust.
> Strange is the power of snuff, whose pungent grains
> Can make fops speak, and furnish beaux with brains;
> Nor care of cleanliness, nor love of dress,
> Can save their clothes from brick-dust nastiness.
> Some think the part too small of modish sand
> Which at a niggard pinch they can command;
> Nor can their fingers for that task suffice,
> Their nose too greedy, not their hands too nice;
> To such a height with these is fashion grown,
> They feed their very nostrils with a spoon.
> One, and but one degree is wanting yet,
> To make our senseless luxury complete;
> Some choice regale, useless as snuff and dear
> To feed the mazy windings of the ear.

This satire would have been more complete had it included smoking, the more intrusively offensive form of selfishness.

The young author of "Maggots" felt as if a kind of apology were needed for productions which some called "light, vain, frothy, and below the gravity of a man, at least of a Christian." In a style as playful as the poems he calls on the objector to lend him a handful of beard, and to be at the charge of grafting it on, and then he will promise reformation. He pleads, too, the necessity for recreation as well as work, and thinks that as recreation for his pen, his "Maggots" give "neither his readers nor himself any reason to blush." Many, perhaps, might doubt his judgment, while they allowed his plea for recreation.

> Sweet recreation barr'd what doth ensue,
> But moody and dull melancholy,
> Kinsman to grim and comfortless despair;
> And at her heels, a huge infectious troop
> Of pale distemperatures, and foes to life?

His recreations prepared him for more serious and voluminous work. It is interesting and instructive, too, to visit, if it be only in imagination, the spot where a remarkable man did some of his best work and realized some of the sweetest pages of his life. A traveller on horseback jogging from Spilsby in Lincolnshire towards Louth about the year 1692, and passing through Harrington would, just beyond Brinkhill, descend into a pleasant valley, and find himself in a little picturesque village, with low mud-built and thatched cottages here and there on the right and the left, by the way side. A primitive old farm house on one hand, and on the other, on what, there, would be called a hill, the old Church looking down kindly upon the graves of generations who had once gathered under its roof, and offering friendly shelter to the lowly home of its parson; while it claimed spiritual superiority to the Hall whose surrounding woods served to grace the borders of God's acre. There he would have found Samuel Wesley with his wife and first boy living on fifty pounds a year in a style which he himself poetically describes—

> In a mean cot, composed of reeds and clay,
> Wasting in sighs the uncomfortable day;
> Near where the inhospitable Humber roars,
> Devouring, by degrees, the neighbouring shores.
> Let earth go where it will, I'll not repine,
> Nor can unhappy be, while heaven is mine.

This was South Ormsby, in the gift of his friend the Marquis of Normanby. The young parson was as active as he was content, and as happy as he was active. Happy, at all events, he was in his wife, and happy he must have been in himself while he could beautify his poetic pages with portrait illuminations of such loveliness and virtue as hers. He has immortalized her character thus—

> She graced my humble roof, and blest my life,
> Blest me by a far greater name than wife;
> Yet still I bore an undisputed sway,
> Nor was't her task, but pleasure to obey;
> Scarce thought, much less could act, what I denied,
> In our low house there was no room for pride;
> Nor need I e'er direct what still was right,
> She studied my convenience and delight.

> Nor did I for her care ungrateful prove,
> But only used my power to show my love.
> Whate'er she asked I gave, without reproach or grudge,
> For still the reason asked, and I was judge.
> All my commands, requests at her fair hands,
> And her requests to me where all commands.
> To others' thresholds rarely she'd incline,
> Her house her pleasure was, and she was mine;
> Rarely abroad, or never, but with me,
> Or when by pity called, or charity.

The woman who thus gave joy to his home was the well-trained Susannah, daughter of the saintly nonconformist minister of London, Dr. Annesley, and sister to the wife of Dunton, who published Wesley's first volume; and who after the death of his own beautiful wife, revenged himself, it may be, for Wesley's expression of pain at his haste to marry again, by issuing the satirical verse·

> Poor harmless Wesley, let him write again;
> Be pitied in his old heroic strain;
> Let him in reams proclaim himself a dunce,
> And break a dozen stationers at once.

This sneer is directed chiefly, perhaps, at the parson's Poem on "The Life of Christ," in folio. There is, however, in one of the poet's contributions to the "Athenian Gazette," which, for a long time, he so largely and with so much learning helped Dunton to keep up, a passage which with more correct severity reflects upon the defects of his own poem. "A young poet," says he, "should never be ambitious of writing much, for a little gold is worth a great head of lead ... to be a perfect poet, a man must be a general scholar, skilled both in the tongues and sciences, and must be perfect in history and moral philosophy." Many will differ from him in his estimate of the learning necessary to a poet. As highest class poetic genius and passion may be found without much of such learning as he requires. If such learning were a main qualification, he would have been nearer to perfection as a poet; but his fault was that which he himself condemns. He wrote too much, too fast, and too carelessly to write well; the fault, in a less degree, into which, some think, his son Charles fell after him. But his poem was more mercilessly dealt with, long after he had left this world, and that under the guise of friendliness.

"I have been for a long time looking out for a copy of Samuel Wesley's Poem on the 'Life of our Lord and Saviour Jesus Christ,'" said a book-worm, the other day, as he sat in a friend's library, "but my search has been in vain."

"There is one here," was the reply; and a thick little duodecimo volume was produced, which proved to be Dr. Coke's edition. The book-worm rejoiced at a sight of the treasure. But, alas for him! and alas for the poet! and alas for the little doctor! On opening to the preface, there were the following utterances—" Each book of the poem (except the 6th) has an addition of many lines, some as many as hundreds—on the whole, not less than two thousand, besides those which supply the places of those lopped off.—Besides lines additional, others new. . . . Few of the original lines are now standing. The versification may be said to be new—an old poem cast in a new model. The writer flatters himself that on a comparative estimate they will be found not unworthy of regard. But he does not profess himself to be a particular favourite of the Muses. Parnassus is a mount which he never intended to ascend. His tale on the present occasion is short and simple. He saw this poem of Mr. Wesley, the plan and design of which he thought to be excellent, but the lines appeared to be very bad. He has therefore endeavoured to mend what he has preserved, and to supply what he thought to be deficient."

"What do you think of that, for a little doctor?" cried the book-worm, "a man who 'never intended to ascend Parnassus'! One who never 'thought himself a favourite with the Muses.' For him to undertake to mend every line of Samuel Wesley's which he thought worthy of his touch! To supply what he 'thought to be deficient' after he had 'lopped off' most of the book as redundant! No! no!

my little doctor! You were a glorious missionary hero; but you should have let alone 'commentary' making; and as to clipping and botching Samuel Wesley, neither 'Parnassus' nor the 'Muses' ever gave you licence or power!"

The thick little volume was flung down in disappointment; and no wonder! Some of Wesley's best passages had been marred and 'mended.' Among these, one or two are remarkable for their original pure lyric beauty and power. One to the glory of God the Father—

> Before this beauteous world was made,
> Before the earth's foundations laid,
> He was, He ever is, we know not how!
> No mean succession His duration knows,
> That spring of being neither ebbs nor flows:
> Whatever was, was God, ere time or place;
> Endless duration He, and boundless space,
> Fill'd with Himself, wherever thought can pierce,
> He fill'd Himself alone, the universe.

Another, in celebration of the Divine Son—

> The Father's image He, as great as bright,
> Closed in the same insufferable light;
> More closely join'd, more intimately one
> With His great Father, than the light and sun.
> Equal in goodness and in might,
> True God of God, and Light of Light;
> Him, with the Father, we adore;
> There is no after, or before.

But some of the poet's smaller detached pieces are among his more polished gems. So his sons, John and Charles, thought when they gave prominence to one or two of them in their first volume of "Hymns and Sacred Poems." One piece was declared by an able critic to be "the finest poem on the subject in the English language." The poet heads the verses with what he supposes to be, "Part of a (new) dialogue between Plato and Eupolis the poet"; at the close of which Eupolis gives his "Hymn to the Creator"—

> Author of Being, Source of Light,
> With unfading beauties bright,
> Fullness, Goodness, rolling round
> Thy own fair orb without a bound:

Whether Thee Thy suppliants call
Truth, or Good, or One, or All,
Ei or *Jao*; Thee we hail
Essence that can never fail,
Grecian or *Barbaric* name,
Thy steadfast Being still the same.

Thee, when morning greets the skies
With rosy cheeks and humid eyes:
Thee, when sweet declining day
Sinks in purple waves away;
Thee will I sing, O Parent *Jove*,
And teach the world to praise and love.

Yonder azure vault on high,
Yonder blue, low, liquid sky,
Earth on its firm basis placed,
And with circling waves embraced,
All, Creating Power confess,
All their mighty Maker bless.
Thou shak'st all Nature with Thy nod,
Sea, earth, and air confess Thee God:
Yet does Thy powerful hand sustain
Both earth and heaven, both firm and main.

Scarce can our daring thought arise
To Thy pavilion in the skies;
Nor can *Plato's* self declare
The bliss, the joy, the rapture there.
Barren above Thou dost not reign,
But circled with a glorious train,
The Sons of God, the Sons of Light,
Ever joying in Thy sight
(For Thee their silver harps are strung):
Ever beauteous, ever young,
Angelic forms their voices raise,
And through heaven's arch resounds Thy praise.

The feather'd souls that swim the air,
And bathe in liquid ether there;
The lark, preceptor of their choir,
Leading them higher still and higher,
Listen and learn; the angelic notes
Repeating in their warbling throats;
And ere to soft repose they go,
Teach them to their lords below:
On the green turf, their mossy nest,
The evening anthem swells their breast
Thus like Thy golden chain from high
Thy praise unites the earth and sky.

Source of Light, Thou bid'st the sun
On his burning axles run;

The stars like dust around him fly,
And strew the area of the sky.
He drives so swift his race above,
Mortals can't perceive him move;
So smooth his course, oblique or straight,
Olympus shakes not with his weight.
As the queen of solemn night
Fills at his vase her orb of light,
Imparted lustre; thus we see
The solar virtues shine by Thee.

Eiresione we'll no more,
Imaginary Power, adore;
Since oil, and wood, and cheering wine,
And life-sustaining bread is Thine.

Thy herbage, O great *Pan*, sustains
The flocks that graze our *Attic* plains;
The olive with fresh verdure crown'd,
Rises pregnant from the ground;
At Thy command it shoots and springs,
And a thousand blessings brings.
Minerva, only is Thy mind,
Wisdom and bounty to mankind.
The fragrant thyme, the bloomy rose,
Herb and flower and shrub that grows
On *Thessalian Tempe's* plain,
Or where the rich *Sabeans* reign,
That treat the taste or smell or sight,
For food, for medicine, or delight;
Planted by Thy parent care,
Spring and smile and flourish there.

O ye nurses of soft dreams,
Reedy brooks and winding streams,
Or murmuring o'er the pebbles' sheen,
Or sliding through the meadows green,
Or where through matted sedge you creep,
Travelling to your parent deep:
Sound His praise by whom you rose,
That Sea which neither ebbs nor flows.

O ye immortal woods and groves,
Which the enamour'd student loves;
Beneath whose venerable shade,
For thought and friendly converse made,
Famed *Hecadem*, old hero, lies,
Whose shrine is shaded from the skies,
And through the gloom of silent night
Projects from far its trembling light;
You, whose roots descend as low
As high in air your branches grow;

Your leafy arms to heaven extend,
Bend your heads, in homage bend :
Cedars and pines that wave above,
And the oak beloved of *Jove*.

  Omen, monster, prodigy,
Or nothing are, or, *Jove*, from Thee ;
Whether various Nature play,
Or re-inversed Thy will obey,
And to rebel man declare
Famine, plague, or wasteful war.
Laugh, ye profane, who dare despise
The threatening vengeance of the skies,
Whilst the pious, on his guard,
Undismay'd is still prepared :
Life or death, his mind's at rest,
Since what Thou send'st must needs be best.

  No evil can from Thee proceed :
'Tis only suffer'd, not decreed.
Darkness is not from the sun,
Nor mount the shades till he is gone :
Then does night obscure arise
From *Erebus*, and fills the skies,
Fantastic forms the air invade,
Daughters of nothing and of shade.

  Can we forget Thy guardian care,
Slow to punish, prone to spare ?
Thou brak'st the haughty *Persian's* pride,
That dared old ocean's power deride ;
Their shipwrecks strew'd the *Eulæan* wave,
At *Marathon* they found a grave.
O ye blest *Greeks* who there expired,
For *Greece* with pious ardour fired,
What shrines or altars shall we raise
To secure your endless praise ?
Or need we monuments supply
To rescue what can never die ?

  And yet a greater Hero far
(Unless great *Socrates* could err)
Shall rise to bless some future day,
And teach to live and teach to pray.
Come, unknown Instructor, come !
Our leaping hearts shall make Thee room ;
Thou with *Jove* our vows shalt share,
Of *Jove* and Thee we are the care.

  O Father King, whose heavenly face
Shines serene on all Thy race,
We Thy magnificence adore,

> And Thy well-known aid implore:
> Nor vainly for Thy help we call;
> Nor can we want: for Thou art All!

The author of this hymn was remarkable for the versatility of his talents; and though there was much in his hastily-written pages that occasionally provoked the satirical powers of contemporary genius, yet there was much of suggestive thought underlying his unpolished material; and sometimes, it may be, the suggestions were used by those who repaid the benefit with a laugh. Wesley's " Epistle to a Friend concerning Poetry" may have suggested the notion of Pope's "Dunciad," if not of Byron's "English Bards and Scotch Reviewers." It is without the bad feeling which breathes in these productions, but is distinguished by much critical acumen, just thought, and fair judgment; while it evidences, here and there, fine poetic ingenuity.

Samuel Wesley would have done better as a poet had he adopted the German motto and kept to both its terms—" Never haste, never rest." He never rested; but he was too hasty. His verse-making was ceaseless; but his verses could not always mature themselves for haste. So it was in his last volumes, " The History of the Old and New Testament, attempted in verse; and adorned with three hundred and thirty sculptures."

But in the estimation of good Methodists, and, indeed, of all Christian people throughout the world, one hymn of Samuel Wesley's will ceaselessly shed balm on his memory.

"Among my recollections," says a Sunday-school teacher, "is the image of a gentle girl who was missed from the school but one Sabbath; and then we heard that Sarah was no more. In her short illness, while she was able to express herself, she spoke of happy days in the school. 'Mother,' said she, ' find me that hymn beginning with

> " ' Behold the Saviour of mankind
> Nail'd to the shameful tree!
> How vast the love that Him inclined
> To bleed and die for thee!'

"Her mother read the entire hymn, and the happy girl responded, 'Now, mother, mind the line

"'To bleed and die for—*me!*
Yes! He did! for *me!* for *me!* He calls me home!'

"It was her last word. She had left her mother behind to 'mind the line'—

"To bleed and die for thee!"

"Good Friday! O how I love the return of Good Friday!" said a silver-haired, saintly woman, as she sat with a friend at the door of her cottage in the evening light of that Christian memorial day. Her eyes looked as if they were reflecting holy light from the mysterious cross; and her voice was tremulous with sacred feeling as she spoke. "It was on a Good Friday evening that my heart, while yet young, was first broken, as I listened to the story of the cross; and then healed, as the music of the hymn seemed to come direct with life from heaven in those words—

"O Lamb of God! was ever pain,
Was ever love like Thine!

O how precious has that hymn been to me ever since! It is, indeed, my Good Friday hymn. This day's return is always sweet. And that hymn is my heart's music throughout the day, and will be till I go to see Him!"

Among the few things saved from the fire when the Epworth Parsonage was burnt, and the child John Wesley was so marvellously preserved, was this same precious "Good Friday hymn."

Behold the Saviour of mankind
Nail'd to the shameful tree!
How vast the love that Him inclined
To bleed and die for thee!

Though far unequal our low praise
To Thy vast sufferings prove,
O Lamb of God, thus all our days,
Thus will we grieve and love.

Hark, how He groans! while nature shakes,
And earth's strong pillars bend!
The Temple's veil in sunder breaks,
The solid marbles rend.

'Tis done! the precious ransom 's paid;
"Receive my soul," He cries:
See where He bows His sacred head!
He bows His head and dies.

But soon He'll break Death's envious chain,
And in full glory shine!
O Lamb of God, was ever pain,
Was ever love like Thine!

Thy loss our ruins did repair,
Death by Thy death is slain;
Thou wilt at length exalt us where
Thou dost in glory reign.

Were this all that the elder Samuel Wesley ever left us, it would be sufficient to establish his claim in our hearts as a father of Methodist poetry, and a worthy head of "the Epworth singers."

CHAPTER III.

THE EPWORTH SINGERS.

From yon lonely roof, whose curling smoke
O'ermounts the mist, is heard at intervals
The voice of psalms—the simple song of praise.

VERY remarkable manifestation of Christ appears to be heralded and ushered in by newly inspired song. The mystery of the holy Incarnation was preceded by successive strains of prophetic poesy. Those who were sent to proclaim the Saviour's personal approach were inspired bards. Every Messianic prophet was a poet; and every sacred poem was a prophecy. When the prophetic promises were fulfilled in Christ's visible presence among men, heaven opened its harmonies in accordance with inspired human voices—the poetic utterances of hallowed genius below melted into the swell of anthems from above—the poetry of inspired men was felt to be akin to that which belongs to heaven, the home and source of all pure poetic life. "And suddenly there was with the angel a multitude of the heavenly hosts praising God," and

>   . . . sudden blaze of song
>   Spreads o'er the expanse of Heav'n;
>   In waves of light it thrills along,
>   Th' angelic signal given—
> " Glory to God!" from yonder central fire
> Flows out the echoing lay beyond the starry quire:
>
>   Like circles widening round
>   Upon a clear blue river,
>   Orb after orb the wondrous sound
>   Is echoed on for ever:
> " Glory to God on high, on earth be peace,
> And love towards men of love—salvation and release."

So in the following "days of the Son of Man," when He comes in the power of His truth, and in fresh manifestations of His Spirit, to assert His claims anew as the Saviour and Mediatorial Lord of mankind, it would seem that His approach awakened the powers of song, and called human genius to consecrate its powers to the celebration of His Pentecostal glory. We may not, in such cases, hear the harmony above as shepherds once did, for

> Whilst this muddy mixture of decay
> Doth grossly close us in, we cannot hear it—

but He calls up tuneful human voices to hail each mightier coming of the Spirit of Truth; to marshal the powers and spread the joys of His saving grace. Indeed, those who devoutly study the history of the Christian religion will now and then find themselves pleasantly arrested by periodic swells in the tide of holy song; the Church will be seen to have its "times and seasons" of new poetic inspiration: "times of refreshing from the presence of the Lord." And it is happily instructive to observe that these fresh breathings of spiritual music from above are so timed as to provide Christ's people with enlarged means of expression, as, by turns, they are called to the joys of victory, and to "glory in tribulation." Beautiful illustrations of this are to be found in the annals of Christianity on the Continent.

The well-timed rise in succession of the "Minne Singers," the "Mystic Hymnists," the "Master Singers," and the tuneful "Bohemian Brethren," shows how graciously hallowed poetic and musical genius has been made to minister to Christ's spiritual household at each crisis in its history. The mighty Comforter, who, by the ministry of Luther, called such multitudes in Germany into newness of life, spoke by him, too, when he summoned forth new powers of spiritual song, and opened a new era in the history of tuneful worship. "I would fain," says Luther, "see all arts, especially music, in the service of Him who has given and created them. It is my intention, after the example of the prophets and ancient fathers, to make German psalms for the people; that is, spiritual songs, whereby the Word of God may be kept among them by singing. We seek therefore everywhere for poets." Nor did he seek in vain. Poets arose under an inspiration which seemed to be given for the occasion. And the Spirit's work in the psalmody of Luther's time bore fruit and fulfilled its purpose, until—a Romanist being witness—"the whole people were singing themselves into this Lutheran doctrine." The succession of devout poets continued; and the great work of the Reviving Spirit issued in the opening of a new era of spiritual life, until the consecrated poetic genius of Germany seemed to become the connecting link between holy reformation on the Continent and the spiritual awakening under the Wesleys and their companions in England. The name of Epworth appears to be naturally associated with the rise of what may be called the Methodist school of psalmody.

At the most north-western point of Lincolnshire, on the westerly bank of the river Trent, there was a tract of land which, towards the close of the seventeenth century, was still, for the most part, a low marsh. Even the few raised portions of it were overflown on the rise of the waters. "I and my company have been confined to an upper chamber," says an eye-witness, "and seen no dry land for the space of these seven days.. I did see the mothers, Pyrrha-like, trudging middle-deep in water with theire infants hanging upon theire breastes; and the fathers, Deucalion-like, bearinge theire children upon theire shoulders, to seek higher ground for theire succour. All sorts of people in pitifull distress; some to save theire lives, some theire goods and cattle, some to get food for theire hungrie bodies." The district formed an island between three rivers and an old dyke, known as the "Isle of Axholme." About the centre of the province, on a swell that rose above the fen, was the ancient Heapeurde, or "the Hill Farm," afterwards known as Epworth. From the church on this comparatively high ground, the eye might range over the swampy flats and throw its glance around from Kirton on the Lincolnshire side, down to Nottinghamshire, and with a sweep to the west into Yorkshire, until it reached up to the Northern Wolds. To this "farm on the rising ground" Samuel Wesley came, during the year 1696, by such roads only as led across the partially cultured flax and barley fields. Here he found a rectory described as a dwelling of "five baies, built all of timber and plaister, and covered all with straw thatche, the whole building being contrived into three stories, and disposed into seven chiefe rooms, namely—a kitchinge, a hall, a parlour, a butterie, and three large upper rooms; besydes some others of common use; and also a little garden impailed, betweene the stone wall and the south. The horne-stall, or scite of the parsonage, situate and lyenge betweene the field on the east, and Lancaster Lane on the west, and abuttinge upon the High Street on the south, and of John Maw—sonne of Thomas—his tenement, and a croft on the north. By estimation three acres. One barn of six baies, built all of timber and clay walls, and covered with straw thatche; and outshotts about it, and free house therebye. One dovecoate of timber and plaister covered with straw thatche; and one hempkiln, that hath been useallie occupied for the parsonage ground, adjoyning upon the south."

The Rector and his exemplary wife brought four children to this Epworth home—Samuel, who was born in London, and three girls, Emilia, Susanna, and Mary. This Epworth parsonage became the birth-place of six more children, succeeding one another, as, Mehetabel, Anne, John, Martha, Charles, and Kezia. Thus was formed the remarkable family of ten, all more or less gifted with poetic power, and several of whom have been immortalized as what may be called the family of Epworth singers.

The influence which this family has had on so many following generations, and its still widening power for good over families and populations throughout the world, are largely owing to their sanctified training in that Epworth home. Where has not the accumulated fruit of the saintly mother's deeds been seen and felt? When will the good inherited from the learning, genius, and steadfast godliness of the venerable head of that Epworth household die out from human life? "Though," says that faithful mother, "the education of so many children must create abundance of trouble, and will perpetually keep the mind employed as well as the body; yet consider 'tis no small honour to be entrusted with the care of so many souls. And if that trust be but managed with prudence and integrity, the harvest will abundantly recompense the toil of the seed-time; and it will be certainly no small accession to the future glory to stand forth at the last day and say, 'Lord, here are the children which Thou hast given me, of whom I have lost none by my ill example, nor by neglecting to instil into their minds, in their early years, the principles of Thy true religion and virtue.'" The woman who held this principle duly worked it out. She aimed at educating each child's "whole spirit and soul and body"; bringing all and each under such physical discipline as best to promote health and strength, training and instructing their intellect to mental vigour and intelligence; and, above all, leading them to act on religious principle, and to form habits of devout acquaintance with the Divine will. Their genius and poetic passion were inherited from the father; but the gracious exercise of their genius, and the fine balance of their various powers and gifts, they owed to the character and oversight of the devoted mother. Her mode of home training was somewhat shaped, it may be, by the peculiarities of her first boy's case. The young Samuel's "hearing was acute and perfect; his intellect apparently keen and active; but there was no power of speech. He never uttered an intelligible word until he was nearly five years old; and his parents began to fear that he was hopelessly dumb. Having been missed longer than usual on one occasion, his mother sought him in different parts of the house, but without success. Becoming alarmed, she called him loudly by name, and to her joyful surprise he answered from under a table, in a clear, distinct voice, ' Here I am, mother!' Suddenly, and without any assignable reason or effort, he had gained the use of speech. This early infirmity in the case of her first-born prevented Mrs. Wesley beginning to teach him, had she been so disposed, before he was five years old. He now learned with great rapidity," and soon amply repaid her care. The cheering success of this her first attempt at teaching probably fixed her plans for the future. "The school always opened and closed with singing a solemn psalm;" and nothing was permitted to disturb this order. This regulated system of psalm-singing may have done much to tune the native powers of song which were more or less peculiar to every member of the household.

Samuel was about six years old when brought to Epworth, and after due preparation was sent to Westminster School in his thirteenth or fourteenth year. As the hope of his father and the object of loving solicitude to his mother, he had the benefit of their written advice and warning and teaching. The influence of the father may be traced in its distinctness from that of the mother in their correspondence; while the beautiful harmony of parental feeling is equally clear. The child of such parents, the scholar from such a parental school, if possessed of any genius or heart, might be expected to do, or to say, or to be, something that would graciously associate him with the happiness and welfare of future generations. And so it was. Samuel Wesley, as the eldest-born of the Epworth singers, has, by the exercise of his hallowed poetic power, become for ever one with the most tender and holy sympathies of Christian life. A single hymn of his was enough to effect this. What wonder is awakened in the soul when it seeks to trace the innumerable linkings of things in the kind works of Providence and saving grace! How mysteriously one person is found to be related to another, though far apart both as to space and time: and how delicate is the tie which sometimes binds the action of one to the ever unfolding destinies of many! One word in conversation, one sentence in a sermon, or one verse of a hymn, is, in some cases, immortally connected with the salvation of ever-expanding multitudes of souls.

"God has given you many spiritual children," said one Christian minister to another, as they walked and talked about Divine things, "and you have the joy of knowing that your children in the Gospel are among those 'chosen pilgrims of the dispersion,' who, like the 'elect strangers' to whom Peter wrote, are maintaining and spreading spiritual life in almost all parts of the world where English-speaking people are found. It seems to me that the prolific power of your ministry is found in that realization of unseen and eternal things which you seem to have in yourself while you speak, and which, by the grace of the Blessed Spirit, your words appear to awaken in those who hear you."

"It may be so," was the answer, "and if so, it is 'according to His abundant mercy'; for I can trace that sense of Divine reality in the spiritual and unseen to one point in my early course, when it was so called into life as never to lose its power. Soon after my conversion, I was taken to see a young woman who was at the point of death. She had been a fellow-teacher with me in the Sunday-school; but in spite of all holy influences, examples, warnings, and prayers, she had given her heart to the vain world, and had accepted the homage which it paid to her beauty. I looked at her now—beautiful still; and while my venerable companion was tenderly pressing the claims of Jesus on her heart, I was rehearsing to myself those exquisite lines—

> "Or worn by slowly-rolling years,
> Or broke by sickness in a day,
> The fading glory disappears,
> The short-lived beauties die away.

In my youthful hopefulness, I hoped for her, and inwardly pursued the happier strain—

> "Yet these, new rising from the tomb,
> With lustre brighter far shall shine;
> Revive with ever-during bloom,
> Safe from diseases and decline.

But I had scarcely finished the verse in my thought, before a cast of inexpressible horror was on her face, and in answer to an invitation to Christ from my friend, she shrieked, as she tore her hair, 'Too late!'—and was gone! I hurried from that room feeling that there were terrible realities in the unseen world around me. That feeling remained till I myself, to all human appearance, was close on the end of my mortal life. The solemn blessedness of that night still impresses me. My friends standing around in that silent chamber; the grave calmness of the old physician by my side; the loss, on my part, of all power to utter even a whisper; the keen sensitiveness of my spirit as it seemed to be moving peacefully—oh, how peacefully!—towards some Divine region—then it was that I had that hallowed realization of the spiritual world in its nearness, which has given a tone to my views and feelings ever since. That realization was given to me by what appeared to be a sweetly-toned, heavenly breathing into my soul of a favourite verse,

> "Let sickness blast, and death devour,
> If heaven must recompense my pains;
> Perish the grass and fade the flower,
> If firm the word of God remains.

That rich inward intonation of those lines floats to my spirit's ear even now. And I often think whether what I felt then of the power and meaning of the lines were anything like a spiritual reflection of the author's own thought and feeling when he wrote them. If so, he must have been 'in the heavenlies with Christ' when his soul first uttered that hymn. How fine and touching is its music, rising so calmly as it does, from melting plaintiveness to bright and even triumphant assurance! It was written 'on the death of a Young Lady,' and is a paraphrase of Isaiah's poetic verse, 'All flesh is grass, and all the goodliness thereof is as the flower of the field.'

> "The morning flowers display their sweets,
> And gay their silken leaves unfold,
> As careless of the noontide heats,
> As fearless of the evening cold.
>
> Nipt by the wind's unkindly blast,
> Parch'd by the sun's directer ray,
> The momentary glories waste,
> The short-lived beauties die away.

> So blooms the human face divine,
>   When youth its pride of beauty shows:
> Fairer than spring the colours shine,
>   And sweeter than the virgin rose.
>
> Or worn by slowly rolling years,
>   Or broke by sickness in a day,
> The fading glory disappears,
>   The short-lived beauties die away.
>
> Yet these, new rising from the tomb,
>   With lustre brighter far shall shine;
> Revive with ever-during bloom,
>   Safe from diseases and decline.
>
> Let sickness blast, and death devour,
>   If heaven must recompense my pains;
> Perish the grass, and fade the flower,
>   If firm the word of God remains.

"Blessings for ever on the memory of Samuel Wesley, junior!"

"Yes," said the minister's companion, "and blessings upon that name will come from many others, from me among the rest. But from how many, many besides! From all those, indeed, your children in the Gospel, whose spiritual birth and growth, and fruitfulness, and immortal victories, are for ever in mysterious relationship to the hymn which the Holy Ghost used in preparing you for preaching, during so many years, within the light of "things unseen," and with accumulative results! Endless are the living associations which I see gathering around that hymn and its glorified author."

Samuel Wesley, junior, could never be strictly called a Methodist. He was from the first, and ever remained, what, in his times, might be considered a High Churchman; and yet, as a poet, his hymns give him an immortal connection with the Epworth singers and with the poets of Methodism. His talents as a wit and literary genius, brought him into companionship and friendliness with the leading geniuses of his times, such as Lord Orford, Pope, and Atterbury. His close friendship with Atterbury cost him the loss of Robert Walpole's good-will; and probably resulted in his quiet settlement at Tiverton in Devon, as the master of Blundell's Grammar School. He did not shrink from the free exercise of his sarcastic powers against those who differed from him and his friend in politics. Hence the biting verses on his sordid opponent, Walpole—

> A Steward once, the Scripture says,
> When ordered his accounts to pass,
> To gain his master's debtors o'er,
> Cried, " For a hundred write fourscore."
>
> Near as he could, Sir *Robert* bent
> To follow Gospel precedent:
> When told a hundred late would do,
> Cried, " I beseech you, sir, take two."
>
> In merit which would we prefer,
> The Steward or the Treasurer?
> Neither for justice car'd a fig,
> Too proud to beg, too old to dig;
> Both bountiful themselves have shown,
> In things that never were their own :
> But here a difference we must grant—
> One robb'd the rich to keep off want;
> T'other, vast treasures to secure,
> Stole from the public and the poor.

How often, when walking up the old avenue to the unpretending door-way of ancient Tiverton's " Free Grammar School," have we thought of Peter Blundell's, the poor clothier, who, at the end of the sixteenth century, by industry and uprightness rose to the dignity of a rich merchant, and secured honour for his own memory by saying that, "though he was no scholar himself, he would be the means of making many!" And how often have our thoughts about his good purpose been associated with the name of Samuel Wesley, as one of the most efficient instruments in fulfilling the good man's design! Never have we looked upon that speaking portrait of the " Master " which is still preserved in the school, without thinking of that master's faithful and affectionate observance of his father's request—" Endeavour to repay your mother's prayers for you by doubling yours for her; and, above all things, to live such a virtuous and religious life that she may find that her care and love have not been lost upon you, but that we may all meet in heaven. In short, reverence and love her as much as you will, which I hope will be as much as you can. For though I should be jealous of any other rival in your heart, yet I will not be jealous of her; the more duty you pay her, and the more frequently and kindly you write to her, the more you will please your affectionate father."

The master of Blundell's School entered on his work about the year 1732; having for many years proved himself ready for ruling and training others by setting an example of tender obedience to the command, "Honour thy father, and thy mother." Gentle warmth, simplicity, and keen, sarcastic force, were combined in his character as a poet. These features of his character are found embalmed in verse, each in its own shrine. And sometimes, when side by side, they strikingly show the diversity of his powers. Now, his child-like simplicity and gentleness breathe in an "Epitaph on an Infant"—

> Beneath, a sleeping infant lies;
> To earth whose ashes lent
> More glorious shall hereafter rise,
> Though not more innocent.
> When the Archangel's trump shall blow,
> And souls and bodies join,
> What crowds will wish their lives below
> Had been as short as thine!

And now, he reflects on the erection of a monument to the author of "Hudibras" in Westminster Abbey, with a sarcastic force which, like forked lightning, leaves its impress burnt into the object which it smites—

> While Butler, needy wretch! was yet alive,
> No generous patron would a dinner give;
> See him, when starved to death and turn'd to dust,
> Presented with a monumental bust!
> The Poet's fate is here in emblem shown—
> He asked for Bread, and he received a Stone.

But it is in his hymns that the human lovableness and the high-toned piety and devotion of Samuel Wesley, still live to bless the spiritual descendants of the Epworth Singers.

Two friends once stood side by side, during the Sunday service, in Westminster Abbey. Their devotion was aided by the chant and song which arose swelling and melting by turns, and which, to them, was so new and fresh that it might seem to be the approaching music of an immortal Sabbath. Little did one of them think that so soon from that time the music of an immortal Sabbath would fill the departed soul of his companion; but so it was. Years afterwards, when far away from Westminster Abbey, while he " went through the cornfields on the Sabbath day," the music of that self-same Westminster Abbey chant seemed to come flowing to his ear, though no choristers were to be seen. From whencesoever it came, it touched a chord in his soul, for he had some " music in himself," and he sang in response—

> " The Lord of Sabbath let us praise,
>   In concert with the blest,
> Who joyful in harmonious lays
>   Employ an endless rest.
> Thus, Lord, while we remember Thee,
>   We blest and pious grow;
> By hymns of praise we learn to be
>   Triumphant here below.
>
> On this glad day a brighter scene
>   Of glory was display'd,
> By God, th' eternal Word, than when
>   This universe was made.
> He rises, who mankind has bought
>   With grief and pain extreme:
> 'Twas great to speak a world from naught:
>   'Twas greater to redeem!"

It was not until a few years after this responsive song in the cornfield that the singer knew the hymn to be a Sabbath utterance of one who, a century and half ago, caught inspiration amidst the Sabbath harmonies of old Westminster Abbey. While Samuel Wesley was as yet but a pupil at Westminster, his father said to him in a letter from Epworth, " I hope you understand the Cathedral service—I mean, understand what they sing and say. If we do understand the service, and go along with it, we shall find Church music a great help to our devotion... We are not to think God has framed man in vain an harmonious creature; and surely music cannot be better employed than in the service and praises of Him who made both the tongue and the ear." This appeal could not be in vain to one who inherited his father's musical as well as poetic taste. Cathedral music was a devout joy to him, and when, as an usher in Westminster School, his genius became mature, it was under the inspiration of Sabbath music in the old Abbey that his poetical soul concentrated, in that one short, tuneful hymn, its own harmonized thoughts on the Divine reason, authority, blessed associations, and sanctifying influence of the Christian Sabbath.

The quietness of old Twyford, or Tiverton, reposing on its southern slope between the Devonian streams of the Exe and the Loman, and the rich beauty of its surroundings, were more akin, it may be, to the poet's taste and powers than the dim cloisters of Westminster. Here, it is certain, his genius gave out some of its sweetest and holiest music. No one who loves his memory and breathes the spirit of his hymns can approach the richly sculptured southern porch of the parish church without picturing the intellectual-looking head master, with his usher and one hundred and fifty foundation boys, passing into the fine old sanctuary, in observance of "Fast" or "Festival." And it might be that as the bells from that lofty tower ceased their tuneful call, in the solemn silence which fell on the worshippers before the opening sentences of the service, Samuel Wesley would come under that thrilling sense of the Divine Father's presence which he has so grandly expressed in the Methodist hymn—

> Hail, Father, whose creating call
> Unnumber'd worlds attend;
> Jehovah comprehending all,
> Whom none can comprehend!
> In light unsearchable enthroned,
> Whom angels dimly see;
> The Fountain of the Godhead own'd,
> And foremost of the Three.

From Thee, through an eternal now,
  The Son, Thine Offspring flow'd;
An everlasting Father Thou,
  An everlasting God.
Nor quite display'd to worlds above,
  Nor quite on earth conceal'd;
By wondrous, unexhausted love,
  To mortal man reveal'd.

Supreme and all-sufficient God,
  When nature shall expire;
And world's created by Thy nod,
  Shall perish by Thy fire.
Thy name, Jehovah be adored
  By creatures without end;
Whom none but Thy essential Word
  And Spirit comprehend.

Nor would any reverent Christian who had entered into the doctrine of the cross deeply enough to be free from modern heathenism in the observance of Good Friday ever move up, on that memorial day, between the fine clustered columns of the spacious nave towards the chancel of St. Peter's, Tiverton, without being solemnized at the thought of one who used to worship there; and who, on a Good Friday about the year 1734, kindled there into the spirit of a hymn in which an apostolic intensity of devotion to the Crucified wraps the worshipper in holy wonder at the mystery, the agony, the joy of the cross—

From whence these dire portents around,
  That heaven and earth amaze?
Wherefore do earthquakes cleave the ground?
  Why hides the sun his rays?

Not thus did Sinai's trembling head
  With sacred horror nod,
Beneath the dark pavilion spread
  Of legislative God.

Thou Earth, thy lowest centre shake,
  With Jesus sympathize!
Thou Sun, as hell's deep gloom be black:
  'Tis thy Creator dies!

See, streaming from the accursèd tree,
  His all-atoning blood!
Is this the Infinite?—'Tis He!
  My Saviour and my God!

> For me these pangs His soul assail,
> For me the death is borne;
> My sins gave sharpness to the nail,
> And pointed every thorn.
>
> Let sin no more my soul enslave;
> Break, Lord, the tyrant's chain;
> O save me, whom Thou cam'st to save,
> Nor bleed nor die in vain!

The amiable and gifted hymnist, so graciously trained at Epworth, departed to his rest from Tiverton, Nov. 6, 1739, aged forty-nine.

In thinking of the Epworth singers, a regretful thought must be given to the eldest daughter of the house, Emilia. The thought must be regretful both on her account and our own. We are sorry to find so little remaining fruit of her poetic passion; while it must be deplored that seemingly unhappy circumstances should ever have crossed or embittered the thought and feeling of so gifted a woman. She had been brought from her birth-place, South Ormsby, to Epworth while but a child. Her parents bestowed special care on her training. She became a thoroughly intellectual and educated woman, with an exquisite taste for the beautiful, especially in poetry and music. Her brother John, of whom she was passionately fond, declared that she was the best reader of Milton he had ever heard. She loved her mother with intense affection; while in occasional sharpness' of temper and impatience of opposition, she reflected her father's infirmities, showing, at the same time, that she inherited his energy, perseverance, imperious will, and noble courage. Some time before she became Mrs. Harper, and while she was residing at Wroote, her sister Hetty, then Mrs. Wright, tuneful and elegant amidst all her sorrows, sent her the following lines illustrative of her personal character and surroundings—

> My fortunes often bid me flee
> So light a thing as Poetry;
> But stronger inclination draws,
> To follow Wit and Nature's laws—

Virtue, Form, and Wit, in thee
Move in perfect harmony;
For thee my tuneful voice I'll raise,
For thee compose my softest lays;
My youthful muse shall take her flight,
And crown thy beauteous head with radiant beams of light.

True Wit and sprightly Genius shine
In every turn, in every line—
To these, O skilful Nine, annex
The native sweetness of my sex;
And that peculiar talent let me show
Which Providence divine doth oft bestow
On spirits that are high, with fortunes that are low.

Thy virtues and thy graces all,
How simple, free, and natural!
Thy graceful form with pleasure I survey;
It charms the eye, the heart, alway.—
Malicious Fortune did repine,
To grant her gifts to worth like thine!

To all thy outward majesty and grace,
To all the blooming features of thy face,
To all the heavenly sweetness of thy mind,
A noble, generous, equal soul is joined,
By reason polished, and by arts refined.
Thy even, steady eyes can see
Dame Fortune smile or frown at thee;
At every varied change can say, "It moves not me!"

Fortune has fixed thee in a place
Debarred of Wisdom, Wit, and Grace.
High births and virtue equally they scorn
As asses dull, on dung-hills born:
Impervious as the stones, their heads are found;
Their rage and hatred steadfast as the ground.
With these unpolished wights thy youthful days
Glide slow and dull, and Nature's lamp decays:
O what a lamp is hid, 'midst such a sordid race!

But though thy brilliant virtues are obscured,
And in a noxious, irksome den immured,
My numbers shall thy trophies rear,
And lovely as she is, my Emily appear.
Still thy transcendent praise I will rehearse,
And form this faint description into verse;
And when the Poet's head lies low in clay,
Thy name shall shine in words which never can decay.

An interesting and somewhat amusing indication of her character is given in one of her letters to her favourite brother

John. It would appear that John, while at Oxford, was disposed to introduce priestly confession, among the other High Church practices which he so diligently pursued, before he found the enjoyment of salvation in Christ. He must have proposed the plan to Emilia; and she proves herself more than an equal, even for him, in strong sense, and free, vigorous thought. "To lay open the state of my soul to you, or any of our clergy, is what I have no inclination to at present; and I believe I never shall: I shall not put my conscience under the direction of any mortal man, frail as myself. To my own Master I stand or fall. Nay, I scruple not to say that all such desire in you, or any other ecclesiastic, seems to me like Church tyranny, and assuming to yourselves a dominion over your fellow-creatures which was never designed you by God." Well done, Emilia! Would to God that the youthful mind of England may prove equally free and powerful to resist the new generation of unfledged priests who seek to insinuate themselves into mastery over young women's consciences! Had this eldest daughter of the Epworth home thrown her clear, strong thoughts about clerical pretensions into verse, we might have had something that would even more than rival the lines of her brother Charles in his poetical epistle to his brother John as to the Church—

> But should the bold usurping spirit dare
> Still higher climb, and sit in *Moses*' chair,
> Power o'er my faith and conscience to maintain,
> Shall I submit, and suffer it to reign?
> Call it *The Church*, and darkness put for light,
> Falsehood with truth confound, and wrong with right?
> No: I dispute the evil's haughty claim,
> The spirit of the world be still its name,
> Whatever called by man, 'tis purely evil,
> 'Tis Babel, Antichrist, and Pope, and Devil.

Emilia Wesley's memory is closely associated with a remarkable occurrence in the history of the Epworth family. In a letter to her brother Charles, she says, respecting the extraordinary supernatural disturbances in the new parsonage—"I am so far from being superstitious, that I was too much inclined to infidelity; and I therefore heartily rejoice at having such an opportunity of convincing myself, past doubt or scruple, of the existence of some beings besides those we see." So, in this case, there was an object accomplished fully adequate to the mysterious magnitude of the means. Whatever the spiritual agency was, it found Emilia a doubting genius, and it left her as true a believer as her brother, who as one article of his Christian creed sang—

> Bound in chains of hidden night,
>   Stragglers from the infernal pit,
> Devils cannot wreak their spite,
>   'Till our sovereign Lord permit:
>
> Jesus covers us and ours,
>   Who on His great name depend,
> Limits hell's malicious powers,
>   Saves His people to the end.

Did it ever occur to Emilia Wesley, or to anybody else, that the machinations of human malice might be permitted for some purposes to continue their operation by unseen agency, from the region where malicious souls are suffering their reward? Was there no connection between the unearthly distractions in the new rectory at Epworth and the wicked persecutions which had been consummated in the burning of the old parsonage? Was there no relation between the mortal overthrow of the leading persecutors of the Rector's household and the fiendlike intrusions on that household's peace and devotion? Among the bitterest enemies of the godly Rector there was one pre-eminent villain, the horrid circumstances of whose death, after his last desperate act of malice, seemed to symbolize his destiny under a retributive Providence. This was Robert Darwin; one of the richest, but one of the most abandoned parishioners. The name, curiously enough, appears, as a matter of course, to call up Isaac Taylor's mode of accounting for the disturbances in Epworth Parsonage. "Around us," says he, "as most believe, are beings of a high order, whether good or evil, and yet not cognizable by the senses of men. But the analogies of the visible world favour the supposition that, besides these, there are orders, or species, of all grades, and some, perhaps, not more intelligent than apes or pigs. That these species have no liberty, ordinarily, to infringe upon the solid world, is manifest; nevertheless, chances or mischances, may, in long cycles of time, throw some—like the Arabian locust—over his boundary, and give him an hour's leave to disport himself among things palpable." May there be some truth in this? May the truth that is in it be reconcilable with the notion that the monster Darwin and his companions may have been permitted still to manifest, for a time, their despairing malice in their now dark spiritual style? The name of Darwin has often, since then, been identified with queer minglings of species, and mysterious alliances between human beings and other orders of life, "not more intelligent than apes or pigs"! Such associations of thought may be distinctive of some family lines. We can afford to wait for more light in such matters.

It is clear, in the meantime, that Emilia Wesley needed an impressive lesson on unseen realities, and that, with other members of her family who became so mighty in dealing with "things that are eternal," she manifested in her character the saving design of the extraordinary teaching. She lived to realize the Christian's openness to the good influences of the spirit-world as well as to its powers of evil; to the joys of its ministerial guardianship as well as to its readiness for mischief. And after all her trials she could sing in harmony with her musical brother—

>   Angels, where'er we go, attend
>   Our steps, whate'er betide,
>   With watchful care their charge attend
>   And evil turn aside.
>
>   But thronging round with busiest love,
>   They guard the dying breast;
>   The lurking fiend far off remove,
>   And sing our souls to rest:

> And when our spirits we resign,
> On outstretch'd wings they bear,
> And lodge it in the arms Divine,
> And leave for ever there.

This eldest sister of the Epworth group lived nearly to her eightieth year. Her beloved brother John provided a retreat for her, during the time of her widowhood, in the chapel-house of West Street, Seven Dials, London; and there, in the use of the religious services, her enjoyment of truth deepened until her course was peacefully finished. The only specimen of her verse that remains is in a few lines, "written under a portrait of John Wesley"—

> His eyes diffuse a venerable grace;
> And charity itself is in his face.
> Humble and meek, learn'd, pious, prudent, just,
> Of good report, and faithful to his trust:
> Vigilant, sober, watchful of his charge,
> Who feeds his sheep, and doth their folds enlarge.

To feel in such a scene and hour,
  Mid all that each discloses,
The presence of that viewless power
  On whom the world reposes :

This to the heart is more than all
  Mere beauty can bring o'er it :
Thought, feeling, fancy, own its thrall,
  And joy is hushed before it.

CHAPTER IV.

OTHERS OF THE EPWORTH SINGERS.

Say, what is life? A mystery! most to them
  Who strive to fathom its still changeful deep;
Who fain exultingly the tide would stem
  That human bosoms in dim woe doth steep:
Who soar aspiringly, yet still must weep;
  On towering pinions, chain'd to earthly coil;
Intensely questioning the vast, the deep,
  The gem enshrined within its mortal foil;
The ethereal spark bedimm'd by sorrow and turmoil.

THERE is much mystery about what one may call the particular fate by which some families are followed. Distinguished as the household may be for gifts and culture, each member in succession appears, in some cases, to take the same unhappy turn at some one point in their course. So it was with the Wesleys. With but few exceptions, the Epworth family were either crossed in love, or proved unhappy in their wedded life. One of the exceptions was the beautiful little Mary; with a diminutive and somewhat deformed figure, there was an exquisite charm of countenance, sweetly expressive of the lovely temper and gracefulness of her soul. With the approbation of all her family, she became the much loved and loving wife of John Whitelamb, who, from humble birth and charity-school training, rose, under the care of Mary's father, to a successful college life, and to the pastoral charge of Wroote, a neighbouring parish to Epworth. The conjugal joys of the little rude primitive parsonage among the fens were broken up, however, in twelve months. Mary and her first infant were buried together in the rural grave-yard of her husband's first parish. Her sister, Mehetabel, wrote this beautiful " Epitaph on Mrs. Mary Whitelamb,"—

> If highest worth, in beauty's bloom,
> Exempted mortals from the tomb,
> We had not round this sacred bier
> Mourned the sweet babe and mother here,
> Where innocence from harm is blest,
> And the meek sufferer is at rest!
> Fierce pangs she bore without complaint,
> Till heaven relieved the finished saint.
>
> If savage bosoms felt her woe,
> (Who lived and died without a foe),
> How should I mourn, or how commend,
> My tenderest, dearest, firmest friend?
> Most pious, meek, resigned, and chaste,
> With every social virtue graced!
>
> If, reader, thou would'st prove, and know,
> The ease she found not here below;
> Her bright example points the way
> To perfect bliss and endless day.

The same gifted sister shows herself to be the brightest poetical genius of the Epworth Singers in another tribute to Mary's memory: a poem which immortalizes the loveliness and virtue of the departed, while it touchingly associates the poet's tender recollections of her sister's beauty of character with plaintive allusions to the springs of her own sorrow—

> If blissful spirits condescend to know,
> And hover round what once they loved below;
> Maria! gentlest excellence! attend
> To her, who glories to have called thee friend!
> Remote in merit, though allied in blood,
> Unworthy I, and thou divinely good!
> Accept, blest shade, from me these artless lays,
> Who never could unjustly blame, or praise.
> How thy economy and sense outweighed
> The finest wit in utmost pomp displayed,
> Let others sing, while I attempt to paint
> The god-like virtues of the friend and saint.
>
> With business and devotion never cloyed,
> No moment of thy life passed unemployed,
> Well-natured mirth, mature discretion joined,
> Constant attendants of the virtuous mind.
> From earliest dawn of youth, in thee well known,
> The saint sublime and finished Christian shone.

Yet would not grace one grain of pride allow,
Or cry, "Stand off, I'm holier than thou!"
A worth so singular since time began,
But one surpassed, and He was more than man.
When deep immersed in griefs beyond redress,
And friend and kindred heightened my distress,
And with relentless efforts made me prove
Pain, grief, despair, and wedlock without love,
My soft Maria could alone dissent,
O'erlooked the fatal vow, and mourned the punishment.
Condoled the ill, admitting no relief,
With such infinitude of pitying grief,
That all who could not their demerit see,
Mistook her wond'rous love for worth in me;
No toil, reproach, or sickness could·divide
The tender mourner from her Stella's side ;
My fierce inquietude, and maddening care,
Skilful to soothe, or resolute to share!

Ah me! that heaven has from this bosom tore
My angel friend, to meet on earth no more;
That this indulgent spirit soars away,
Leaves but a still, insentient mass of clay ;
Ere Stella could discharge the smallest part
Of all she owed to such immense desert ;
Or could repay with aught but feeble praise
The sole companion of her joyless days ;
Nor was thy form unfair, though heaven confined
To scanty limits thy exalted mind.
Witness thy brow serene, benignant, clear,
That none could doubt transcendent truth dwelt there ;
Witness the taintless whiteness of thy skin,
Pure emblem of the purer soul within :
That soul, which tender, unassuming, mild,
Through jetty eyes with tranquil sweetness smiled.
But ah! could fancy paint, or language speak,
The roseate beauties of thy lip or cheek,
Where nature's pencil, leaving art no room,
Touched to a miracle the vernal bloom.
(Lost though thou art) in Stella's deathless line,
Thy face immortal as thy fame shall shine.

To soundest prudence (life's unerring guide),
To love sincere, religion without pride ;
To friendship perfect in a female mind,
Which I nor hope nor wish on earth to find ;
To mirth (the balm of care) from lightness free,
Unblemished faith, unwearied industry ;
To every charm and grace combined in you,
Sister and friend!—a long, a last adieu!

Of the seven Epworth daughters, the only other exception,

as a case of comfortable married life, was that of Anne, sometimes at home familiarly called Nancy, or Nan. She makes no figure in the records of the family; and no notice is given of her person, except it may be in her brother Samuel's playful allusion to his father at Wroote—

> Methinks I see you striving all
> Who first shall answer to his call,
> Or lusty Nan, or feeble Moll,
> Sage Pat, or sober Hetty;
> To rub his cassock's draggled tail,
> Or reach his hat from off the nail,
> Or seek the key to draw his ale,
>   When damsel haps to steal it;
> To burn his pipe, or mend his clothes,
> Or nicely darn his russet hose,
> For comfort of his aged toes,
>   So fine they cannot feel it.

"Lusty Nan" has left no memorial of her mind's character. Her marriage to John Lambert, a land surveyor in Epworth, brought from her eldest brother some verses, the good sense, wisdom, and piety of which may have been reflected in her domestic character and life, while they were exemplified in the anthor's own home experience—

> No fiction fine shall guide my hand,
>   But artless truth the verse supply;
> Which all with ease may understand,
>   But none be able to deny.
>
> Nor, sister, take the care amiss
>   Which I, in giving rules employ
> To point the likliest way to bliss,
>   To cause as well as wish you joy.
>
> Let love your reason never blind,
>   To dream of paradise below;
> For sorrows must attend mankind,
>   And pain, and weariness, and woe!
>
> Though still, from mutual love, relief
>   In all conditions may be found:
> It cures at once the common grief,
>   And softens the severest wound.
>
> Through diligence and well-earned gain
>   In growing plenty may you live!
> And each in piety obtain
>   Repose that riches cannot give!

If children e'er should bless the bed,
  Oh, rather let them infants die
Than live to grieve the hoary head,
  And make the aged father sigh!

Still duteous, let them ne'er conspire
  To make their parents disagree;
No son be rival to his sire,
  No daughter more beloved than thee!

Let them be humble, pious, wise,
  Nor higher station wish to know;
Since only those deserve to rise
  Who live contented to be low.

Firm let the husband's empire stand,
  With easy but unquestioned sway;
May HE have kindness to command,
  And THOU the bravery to obey!

Long may he give thee comfort, long
  As the frail knot of life shall hold!
More than a father when thou'rt young,
  More than a son when waxing old.

The greatest earthly pleasure try,
  Allowed by Providence Divine;
Be still a husband, blest as I,
  And thou a wife as good as mine!

To Nan's educated, well-read husband we owe the careful preservation of his father-in-law's early publications, many of which happily illustrate the character of the venerable parent of our Epworth Singers.

Pitiable, indeed, is the marriage story of the other sisters. Of Susanna, lovely in form and face, of lively, strong, and cultured intellect, her mother writes to an uncle, who had failed to fulfil his promise of providing for his niece, "My second daughter, Sukey, a pretty woman, and worthy a better fate, when, by your unkind letters, she perceived all her hopes in you were frustrated, rashly threw herself upon a man,—if man he may be called that is little inferior to the apostate angels in wickedness,—that is not only her plague, but a constant affliction to the family."

Martha, still more unhappy, was miserably bound to

> The vilest husband, and the worst of men,

who, in his last hour of penitence, cried, "I have injured an angel! An angel that never reproached me!" "Sister Patty was always too wise to be witty," said Charles, her brother. She was intellectual and accomplished; well read, and gifted with conversational powers which made Dr. Samuel Johnson value her society. Her poetic taste was equal to her memory, which enabled her to quote freely and at large from the best English poets. The man she married was as "unstable as water"; was first betrothed to her; then courted her younger sister Kezia; again returned, and fulfilled his promise to Martha; plunging her, at length, into the miseries of a home polluted and cursed by an infidel and licentious apostate; and casting a blight upon her forsaken sister, of whom, in her thirty-first year, Charles Wesley says, "Yesterday (March 9, 1741) Sister Kezzy died in the Lord Jesus. He finished his work, and cut it short in mercy."

Hetty, or Mehetabel Wesley, was the first child of the family born in Epworth, and was, perhaps, the first in poetic rank of the Epworth Singers. She was a gay sprightly child, overflowing with fun, good nature, and wit. Warm fancy, sparkling genius, delicate sensitiveness, and petulant temper soon made themselves known and felt in the handsome girl. Her vigorous poetic talent was quite equalled by her early capacity for polite and substantial learning. And though her lighter disposition and temper sometimes gave uneasiness to her parents, her keen appreciation of various knowledge promised ample returns for their careful culture of her powers. She owed much, as to education, to her father's brother, Matthew Wesley, a London physician. He did a great deal to bring out her distinctive faculties, by making her his pet companion during his hours of leisure; and, it may be, helped too fully to intensify the warmth of a nature naturally conscious of superior ability and genius. It was under his care that her fine taste had its first excitements and enjoyment. She never forgot to sing,—

'Twas owing to his friendly care
I breathed at ease the rural air,
Her ample bounds where Reading spreads,
Where Kennett winds along the meads,

> Where Thompson the retreat approves,
> By streams refreshed and gloomed with groves,
> Where, from Cadogan's lofty seat,
> Our view surrounding landscapes meet.
> 'Twas there he made my leisure blest,
> There waked the muse within my breast.

Her susceptibility to tender impressions was soon apparent; and to the pressure of parental checks, especially on the part of her father, we owe some of the first outflowings of her tuneful feeling and wit. One of her early notes in verse has been found in her father's handwriting, and marked by her brother John among his papers as "Hetty's Letter to her Mother." It tells its own love tale,—

> Dear Mother,
> You were once in the ew'n,
> As by us cakes is plainly shewn,
> Who else had ne'er come after.
> Pray speak a word in time of need,
> And with my sour-looked father plead
> For your distressed daughter!

Her early wit was often sportive, and was sometimes indulged in a way which indicated her power, taste, elegant turn of mind, and readiness to give others a share of her own innocent literary pleasure. She would sometimes supply the " Gentleman's Magazine " with

A RIDDLE.

> I am an implement that's common,
> Much occupied by man and woman;
> Not very thick nor very long,
> Yet tolerably stiff and strong.
> If inches twelve may give content,
> That measures much about my stint.
> Sometimes I'm only used for pleasure,
> And then I'm jaded out of measure;
> If a young vigorous bard employs me,
> Egad, e'en to the stumps he tries me;
> A parson to get one in ten,
> In private plies me now and then;
> The lawyer, and the doctor too,
> For fees will wear me black and blue.
> I have a dribbling at the nose,
> Which leaves a stain where'er it goes,

> And yet the fairest nymph will use me,
> The queen herself will not refuse me.
> I'm used by members of all arts,
> Who would be reckoned men of parts;
> And none esteems a lady polished
> Who has not often me demolished;
> And let me tell you, by the by,
> A minute's labour drains me dry;
> I'm now exhausted, so have done;
> Now who or what I am make known.

While she could thus ingeniously furnish a riddle on "A Pen," she was equally prepared to utter a tuneful laugh at the old philosophy of Metempsychosis, or transmigration of the soul. Somebody, whom she calls her sister Sukey's idol, had seemed disposed to assert this pagan doctrine, and she writes:—

> The period fast comes on when I
>   Must to an oyster turn
> (Unless my Sukey's idol lie);
>   Nor will I grieve or mourn.
>
> Welcome my transmigrated state!
>   I'll for the worst prepare:
> *Think* while 'tis given to *think* by fate;
>   Then like a *log* must bear.
>
> These eyes, I feel, will soon depart
>   (Else Hettie should not write);
> Their balls will to such pearls convert
>   As ladies wont delight.
>
> The *pineal gland*, from whence, some say,
>   Man thinks, reflects, and knows
> Whate'er is best,—perhaps it may
>   The *oyster's head* compose.
>
> Or coarse or curious be the mould,
>   Whate'er its form contains;
> That small peninsula may hold
>   My few but *working* brains.
>
> My *fingers* may the *striæ* make,
>   The *shell* my parched *skin*;
> My *nerves* and *bones* with palsies shake
>   The *white* reverse within.
>
> Perhaps at *tide-time* I may wake,
>   And sip a little moisture;
> Then to my pillow me betake,
>   And sleep like brother *oyster*.

What shall I dream? or what compose?
  Some harmless rhymes like these;
Below the *wits*, above the *beaux*,
  Which Poll and Kez may please.

A dubious being, hardly life;
  Yet sensible of woe;
For when Death comes with rusty knife,
  But few will meet the blow.

Which sure my heart, though once 'twas strong,
  Will then nor fly nor choose;
The pulpy substance will not long
  The *coup de grâce* refuse.

My loving oyster-kins, which sit
  So fast to native shell,
Must then some other harbour get,
  Or in wide ocean dwell.

And since this sensible must fail,
  I feel it bend and sink,
Come age, come death, you'll soon prevail,
  I'll wait you on the brink.

But is there not a *something* still
  Sprung from a nobler race,
Above the passions and the will,
  Which lifts to heaven its face?

There is—I feel it upward tend,
  While these weak spirits decay,
Which sighs to meet its Saviour—Friend,
  And springs for native day.

When all its organs, marred and worn,
  Let *Locke* say what he can
'Twill act still round itself—turn,—
  The *mind* is still the man:

Which, if fair virtue be my choice,
  Above the stars shall shine;
Above want, pain, and death rejoice,
  Immortal and divine.

Alas, that this brilliant playful genius should become melancholy and plaintive amidst the miseries of ill-fated wedlock! Yet so it was.

A venerable country pastor some years ago, on returning from a pastoral round, said to a friend, " Among the daughters of that home on the hill yonder, there was one in whom, somehow, I became deeply interested. There was a peculiar charm about her person and manners; and I found her mind finely cultured. She had travelled; was intelligently acquainted with several parts of Europe, and was familiar with their language and literature. I observed, however, that she wore a marriage ring; though it was evident that all allusion to her husband was carefully avoided by the family; and from the cast of melancholy which was occasionally apparent on her countenance and even in the tone of her voice, I began to suspect that there was some sorrowful element in her history. Do you know any thing about her?"

"Yes," said the friend, "I never look at her without grief. I believe I am correct in saying that she was crossed in her first love by the interference of her family, and in her vexation vowed that she would marry the next man who made advances, whoever or whatever he might be. The next man was a rude, uncultured, ill-savoured sot. She kept her vow. With him she went to a distant part of the kingdom; suffered all the miseries of union with an utterly uncongenial and repulsive person, whose treatment of her was in keeping with his own selfish nature. He is now wandering somewhere; and she, having buried her only child, finds a temporary refuge in the home of her girlhood."

"Poor girl!" was the pastor's reply, "how things seem to repeat themselves. Your account appears to be very nearly a repetition of Hetty Wesley's case. She too vowed rashly when crossed in her first choice. It was, either that she would never marry another, or, that she would take the first man that might offer, whose suit her parents should approve. Her father urged her marriage with Mr. Wright, and was inexorable; while she was doubly bound by her filial duty, and her vow. The ill-sorted marriage took place, and the husband's character and conduct broke the wife's heart."

The tale is a sad one. Who can read Hetty's letter to her father soon after this fatal knot was tied without thinking and feeling that, in such cases, there has not been fair and proper respect to the mutual choice of young hearts; and that violence has been done to nature under colour of parental prudence and care? Who can see genius and beauty thus sacrificed without a tear? How deeply the heart is moved to hear a sensitive poetic soul appealing to a vulgar sottish husband in a strain like this—

> If e'er thou didst in Hetty see
> Aught fair, or good, or dear to thee,
> If gentle speech can ever move,
> The cold remains of former love,
> Turn thee at last—my bosom ease,
> Or tell me why I cease to please.
>
> Is it because revolving years
> Heart-breaking sighs, and fruitless tears,
> Have quite deprived this form of mine
> Of all that once thou fanciedst fine?
> Ah no! What once allured thy sight
> Is still in its meridian height:
> These eyes their usual lustre show,
> When uneclipsed by flowing woe.
> Old age and wrinkles in this face
> As yet could never find a place:
> A youthful grace informs these lines,
> Where still the purple current shines,
> Unless by thy ungentle art
> It flies to aid my wretched heart;
> Nor does this slighted bosom shew
> The thousand hours it spends in woe.
>
> Or is it that, oppressed with care,
> I stun with loud complaints thine ear;
> And make thy home, for quiet meant,
> The seat of noise and discontent?
> Ah no! Those ears were ever free
> From matrimonial melody:
> For though thine absence I lament
> When half the lonely night is spent,
> Yet when the watch or early morn
> Has brought me hopes of thy return,
> I oft have wiped these watchful eyes,
> Concealed my cares, and curbed my sighs,
> In spite of grief, to let thee see
> I wore an endless smile for thee.
>
> Had I not practised every art
> T' oblige, divert, and cheer thy heart,
> To make me pleasing in thine eyes,
> And turn thy house to paradise;

I had not asked, "Why dost thou shun
These faithful arms, and eager run
To some obscure, unclean retreat,
With fiends incarnate glad to meet,
The vile companions of thy mirth,
The scum and refuse of the earth;
Who when inspired by beer can grin
At witless oaths and jests obscene,
Till the most learned of the throng
Begins a tale of ten hours long;
While thou, in raptures, with stretched jaws
Crownest each joke with loud applause?"

Deprived of freedom, health, and ease,
And rivalled by such things as these;
This latest effort will I try,
Or to regain thy heart, or die.
Soft as I am, I'll make thee see
I will not brook contempt from thee!

Then quit the shuffling doubtful sense,
Nor hold me longer in suspense;
Unkind, ungrateful as thou art,
Say, must I ne'er regain thy heart?
Must all attempts to please thee prove
Unable to regain thy love?

If so, by truth itself I swear,
The sad reverse I cannot bear:
No rest, no pleasure, will I see;
My whole of bliss is lost with thee!
I'll give all thoughts of patience o'er
(A gift I never lost before);
Indulge at once my rage and grief,
Mourn obstinate, disdain relief,
And call that wretch my mortal foe
Who tries to mitigate my woe;
Till life, on terms severe as these,
Shall, ebbing, leave my heart at ease;
To thee thy liberty restore
To laugh when Hetty is no more.

Alas, for the woman who could make such an appeal to her husband in vain! It was in vain. Nor was this all. She saw her children wither and die one after another under the unhealthy fumes which pervaded their close dwelling in connection with Wright's lead works; and seemed to mix themselves with the effects of his influence for fatal mischief on the spirits and health of his accomplished wife. In a dim chamber in dingy Frith Street, London, amidst the network of close dwellings below Soho Square, with unwholesome smells of paint and putty and whitelead finding their way into the scene of affliction, there is the worn mother in confinement, languishing in weakness, and looking in helpless sorrow on her dying infant; until her overflowing soul calls on her stupefied husband to write from her lips her finely tuned and melting utterance to the departing babe—

> Tender softness! infant mild!
> Perfect, purest, brightest child!
> Transient lustre! beauteous clay!
> Smiling wonder of a day!
> Ere the last convulsive start
> Rends thy unresisting heart;
> Ere the long enduring swoon
> Weigh thy precious eyelids down;
> Ah, regard a mother's moan,
> Anguish deeper than thy own.
>
> Fairest eyes, whose dawning light
> Late with rapture blest my sight,
> Ere your orbs extinguished be,
> Bend their trembling beams on me!
>
> Drooping sweetness! verdant flower!
> Blooming, withering in an hour!
> Ere thy gentle breast sustains
> Latest, fiercest, mortal pains,
> Hear a suppliant! let me be
> Partner in thy destiny!
> That whene'er the fatal cloud
> Must thy radiant temples shroud;
> When deadly damps, impending now,
> Shall hover round thy destined brow,
> Diffusive may their influence be,
> And with the blossom blast the tree.

These exquisite lines were put on paper by her amanuensis in a style as rude as the hand that used the pen; and were enclosed in a note equally barbarous, addressed to the Rev. Mr. John Wesley. To think of such a correspondent as the husband of John Wesley's elegant and accomplished sister is to be prepared for tender sympathy with the forlorn woman, when, "in deep anguish of spirit," she wrote:—

Oppressed with utmost weight of woe,
  Debarred of freedom, health, and rest;
What human eloquence can show
  The inward anguish of my breast!

The finest periods of discourse
  (Rhetoric in all her pompous dress
Unmoving) lose their pointed force,
  When griefs are swelled beyond redress.

Attempt not then with speeches smooth
  My raging conflicts to control;
Nor softest sounds again can soothe
  The wild disorder of my soul!

Such efforts vain to end my fears,
  And long-lost happiness restore,
May make me melt in fruitless tears,
  But charm my tortured soul no more.

Enable me to bear my lot,
  O Thou who only canst redress!
Eternal God, forsake me not
  In this extreme of my distress.

Regard Thy humble suppliant's suit;
  Nor let me long in anguish pine,
Dismayed, abandoned, destitute
  Of all support but only Thine!

Nor health, nor life, I ask of Thee;
  Nor languid nature to restore:
Say but "A speedy period be
  To these thy griefs,"—I ask no more!

Nor will any mother's heart, especially a heart bereft of its children, ever fail to weep with her that wept, while it tries to sing her plaintive yet hopeful verses on the death of her children,—

Though sorer sorrows than their birth
  Your children's death has given,
Mourn not that others bear for earth,
  While you have peopled heaven!

If now so painful 'tis to part,
  O think, that, when you meet,
Well bought with shortly fleeting smart
  Is never-ending sweet!

What if those little angels, nigh
  T' assist your latest pain,
Should hover round you when you die,
  And leave you not again!

> Say, shall you then regret your woes,
>   Or mourn your teeming years?
> One moment will reward your throes,
>   And overpay your tears.
>
> Redoubled thanks will fill your song;
>   Transported while you view
> Th' inclining, happy, infant throng;
>   That owe their bliss to you!
>
> So moves the common star, though bright
>   With simple lustre crowned;
> The planet shines, with guards of light
>   Attending it around.

The gifted woman's sorrows constrained her, at last, to turn to Him whose gentle, loving heart is always open to the weary child of affliction. In the course of 1743, in a touching letter to her brother John, she tells the story of her espousals to Jesus and records her new-born joys of Christian hope. From an allusion in this letter, she seems to have escaped from among the oppressive fumes of Frith Street to the leafy heights of Stanmore, looking out, near Edgware, upon the rich inland landscapes of Buckinghamshire, and, on the other hand, towards the waters of the German Ocean. Stanmore will be all the more sacred to the country rambler who has been touched by the music of Mrs. Wright's genius. Mr. Duncombe, author of "The Feminead," in which he celebrates the character of several eminent women, Mrs. Wright among the rest, in one of his letters to Mrs. Elizabeth Carter, says of the poet, " Mr. Highman, who knew her when she was young, told me she was very handsome. When I saw her, she was in a languishing way, and had no remains of beauty, except a lively piercing eye. She was very unfortunate, as you will find by her poems, which are written with great delicacy, but so tender and affecting they can scarce be read without tears. I am told she wrote some hymns for the Methodists, but I have not seen any of them. It affected me too much to view the ruins of so fine a frame; so I only made her three or four visits."

The allusion to hymns which she was said to have

"written for the Methodists" affords additional reason for classifying this unfortunate but finely gifted poet with the poets of Methodism. And that her talent was equal to hymn writing, as well as other forms of poetry, may be seen and felt in her hymn entitled " The Resignation : a penitent heart hoping in God."—

> Great Power! at whose almighty hand
>   Vengeance and comfort ever wait;
> Starting to earth at Thy command,
>   To execute Thy love or hate.
>
> Thy indignation knits Thy brow
>   On those who dare to sin give way ;
> But who so perfect, Lord, below
>   As never from Thy word to stray ?
>
> But when Thy mighty laws we break,
>   And after do our guilt deplore ;
> Thou dost the word of comfort speak,
>   And treasure up our crimes no more.
>
> O Thou, Thy mighty grace display,
>   And Thy offending servant spare;
> With pain my body wastes away,
>   My weakened limbs with constant care.
>
> Grief has my blood and spirits drunk,
>   My tears do like the night-dew fall ;
> My cheeks are faded, eyes are sunk,
>   And all my draughts are dashed with gall.
>
> Thou canst the heavy hand withdraw
>   That bends me downward to the grave,
> One healing touch my pain can awe,
>   And Thy declining servant save.
>
> But if Thy justice has decreed
>   I still must languish out my days;
> Support me in the time of need,
>   Patient to bear these slow decays.
>
> Lo ! to Thy dreadful will I bow,
>   Thy visitations still to prove ;
> Thy judgment do Thy mercies show,
>   Since, Lord, Thou chastenest in Thy love.

The plaintive devotion of these verses indicates her approach towards rest from sorrow. That rest came in due time. For several years before her death, she lost the easy use of her pen. Among her last efforts, however, her " Farewell to the World" has touching revelations respecting herself, and is full of exquisite feeling in its allusion to her loved and lovable little sister Mary :—

> While sickness rends this tenement of clay,
> Th' approaching change with pleasure I survey;
> O'erjoyed to reach the goal, with eager face,
> Ere my slow life has measured half its race.
> No longer shall I bear, my friends to please,
> The hard constraint of seeming much at ease;
> Wearing an outward smile, a look serene,
> While piercing racks and tortures work within.
> But let me not, ungrateful to my God,
> Record the evil, and forget the good:
> For both I humble adoration pay,
> And bless the Power who gives and takes away.
> Long shall my faithful memory retain
> And oft recall each interval of pain.
> Nay, to high Heaven for greater gifts I bend;
> Health I've enjoyed, and I had once a friend!
> Our labour sweet, if labour it might seem,
> Allowed the sportive and instructive scene.
> Yet here no lewd or useless wit was found;
> We poised the wavering sail with ballast sound.
> Learning here placed her richest stores in view,
> Or winged with love, the minutes gaily flew.
> Nay, yet sublimer joy our bosoms proved,
> Divine benevolence, by heaven beloved.
> Wan meagre forms, torn from impending death,
> Exulting, blest us with reviving breath.
> The shivering wretch we clothed, the mourner cheered,
> And sickness ceased to groan when we appeared.
> Unasked, our care assists with tender art
> Their bodies, nor neglects the immortal part.
> Sometimes in shades unpierced by Cynthia's beam,
> Whose lustre glittered on the dimpled stream,
> We wandered innocent through sylvan scenes,
> Or tripped like fairies o'er the level greens.
> From fragrant herbage decked with pearly dews,
> And flowerets of a thousand different hues
> By wafting gales the mingling odours fly,
> And round our heads in whispering breezes sigh.
> Whole nature seems to heighten and improve
> The holier hours of innocence and love.
> Youth, wit, good-nature, candour, sense combined
> To serve, delight, and civilize mankind;
> In wisdom's love we every heart engage,
> And triumph to restore the Golden Age!
>
> Nor close the blissful scene, exhausted muse,
> The latest blissful scene that thou shalt choose;

> Satiate with life, what joys for me remain,
> Save one dear wish, to balance every pain,—
> To bow my head, with grief and toil opprest,
> Till borne by angel-bands to everlasting rest!

"It is but justice to her memory," says her brother John, "to observe that she was at 'rest' before she went hence, being for some years a witness of 'that rest' which remains even here, 'for the people of God.'" On the 5th of March, 1750, "I prayed by my sister Wright," says her brother Charles, "a gracious, tender, trembling soul; a bruised reed which the Lord will not break." On the 14th of the same month, "I found her," he says, "very near the haven; and again, on the 21st, at four I called on my brother Wright, a few minutes after her spirit was set at liberty. I had sweet fellowship with her in explaining at the chapel those solemn words, 'Thy sun shall no more go down, neither shall thy moon withdraw itself; for the Lord shall be thine everlasting light, and the days of thy mourning shall be ended.' All present seemed partakers both of my sorrow and my joy.—Monday, March 26th, I followed her to her quiet grave, and wept with them that wept." Where that "quiet grave" is, none can now tell.

Of the three brothers in the Epworth group, John Wesley was, remarkably enough, like the majority of his sisters in this, that he was crossed, and more than they, crossed and crossed again in his earlier approaches towards wedded life; and found, at last, that a marriage of mere convenience is close enough upon evil to prove, sometimes, as in his case, the greatest cross of all. A gay and sprightly young Oxford student, given to wit and humour, when just twenty-one, "appearing," as a contemporary said, "the very sensible and acute Collegian, a young fellow of the finest classical taste, of the most liberal and manly sentiments," might be expected to show himself open to tender impressions; and if his genius were poetic, his first tuneful effusions would shew his heart's susceptibility. His wit and taste would take a gentle turn. So it was with the young Oxonian; and there is a pleasant naturalness of humour in a letter of his to his brother Samuel, who had unfortunately broken his leg, while in the attached verses he shows himself capable of giving expression to a quiet laugh in a musical and elegant way. "I believe," says he, "I need not use many arguments to show I am sorry for your misfortune, though at the same time I am glad you are in a fair way of recovery. If I heard it from any one else, I might probably have pleased you with some impertinent consolations; but the way of your relating it is a sufficient proof that they are what you don't stand in need of. And, indeed, if I understand you rightly, you have more reason to thank God that you did not break both, than to repine because you have broke one leg. You have undoubtedly heard the story of the Dutch seaman, who, having broke one of his legs by a fall from the main-mast, instead of condoling himself, thanked God that he had not broken his neck. I scarce knew whether your first news vexed me, or your last news pleased me more: but I can assure you that though I did not cry for grief at the former, I did for joy at the latter part of your letter. The two things which I most wished for of almost anything in the world, were to see my mother and Westminster once again, and to see them both together was so far above my expectations that I almost looked upon it as an impossibility. . . Since you have a mind to see some of my verses, I have sent you some which employed me above an hour yesterday in the afternoon. There is one, and I am afraid but one, good thing in them, that is, they are short.

"FROM THE LATIN.

As o'er fair Cloe's rosy cheek
 Careless a little vagrant pass'd,
With artful hand around his neck
 A slender chain the virgin cast.

As Juno near her throne above,
 Her spangled bird delights to see;
As Venus has her fav'rite dove,
 Cloe shall have her fav'rite flea.

> Pleased at his chains, with nimble steps
>   He o'er her snowy bosom stray'd :
> Now on her panting breast he leaps,
>   Now hides between his little head.
>
> Leaving at length his old abode,
>   He found, by thirst or fortune led,
> Her swelling lips that brighter glow'd
>   Than roses in their native bed.
>
> Cloe your artful hands undo,
>   Nor for your captive's safety fear,
> No artful bands are needful now
>   To heed the little vagrant here.
>
> Whilst on that heav'n 'tis giv'n to stay
>   (Who would not wish to be so blest),
> No force can draw him once away,
>   'Till death shall seize his destin'd breast."

On March 17th, 1726, the young poetical student was elected Fellow of Lincoln College, and grave work awaited him. He acted on his good mother's advice, however. "I would not have you leave off making verses, rather make poetry sometimes your diversion, though never your business." In a letter to his brother soon after his election to the Fellowship, he writes, "The most tolerable of my own verses you probably received from Leyburn. Some of those I had besides I have sent here ; and shall be very glad if they are capable of being so corrected as to be of any service to you." Though sent in their rough as the amusement of a leisure hour, they are evidence enough of his native poetic talent. One is after Horace.

> Integrity needs no defence ;
> The man who trusts to innocence,
> Nor wants the darts *Numidians* throw,
> Nor arrows of the *Parthian* bow,
>
> Secure o'er *Lybia's* sandy seas,
> Or hoary *Caucasus* he strays,
> O'er regions scarcely known to fame,
> Wash'd by *Hydaspes'* fabled stream.
>
> While void of cares, of naught afraid,
> Late in the *Sabine* woods I stray'd ;
> On *Sylvia's* lips while pleas'd I sung
> How love and soft persuasion hung !

A rav'nous wolf intent on food
Rush'd from the covert of the wood;
Yet dar'd not violate the grove
Secur'd by innocence and love.

Nor *Mauritania's* sultry plain,
So large a savage does contain;
Nor e'er so huge a monster treads
Warlike *Apulia's* beechen shades.

Place me where no revolving sun
Does o'er this radiant circle run;
Where clouds and damp alone appear,
And poison the unwholesome year:

Place me in that effulgent day
Beneath the sun's directer ray;
No change from its fix'd place shall move
The basis of my lasting love.

The elegant young scholar who thus sang of love was not to be without heart experience of its charms. But he was seemingly fated to be held in check, or left defeated in his hopes. His tender correspondence with Betsy, the sister of his friend Robert Kirkham, was interrupted. His pleasant intercourse with the beautiful and accomplished Mary Granville, afterwards Mrs. Delany, quietly ceased. His subsequent expectations of happiness in union with Sophia Christiana Hopkey, in Georgia, were cut off. And, to his bitter disappointment in later life, as to marriage with Grace Murray, we owe the outflowing of his feeling in characteristic verse,—

O Lord! I bow my sinful head!
  Righteous are all Thy ways with man!
Yet suffer me with Thee to plead,
  With lowly reverence to complain;
With deep unutter'd grief to groan;
Oh! what is this that Thou hast done?

. . . .

Unsearchable Thy judgments are,
  O Lord, a bottomless abyss;
Yet sure Thy love, Thy guardian care,
  O'er all Thy works extended is,
Oh! why didst Thou the blessing send?
Or why thus snatch away my friend?

> What Thou hast done, I know not now,
> Suffice I shall hereafter know,
> Beneath Thy chastening hand I bow;
> That still I live, to thee I owe.
> Oh! teach thy deeply-humbled son
> To say, "Father, Thy will be done."
>
> Teach me from every pleasing snare
> To keep the issue of my heart;
> Be Thou my Love, my Joy, my Fear;
> Thou my Eternal Portion art.
> Be Thou my never-failing Friend,
> And love, oh, love me, to the end.

It is pleasant to see so much of human naturalness in one the sacred and happy results of whose life and labours invest his name with ever brightening honours. Had his affections been happily met, had his heart found repose in a worthy "help-meet," would such permanent honour and blessing have illuminated his memory? Who can tell? Though in his college days, when his classical knowledge gave polish and elegance to his effusions, John Wesley amused himself with sprightly composition, his finely balanced character would find opportunity for giving tuneful utterance to graver thought and devout feeling. Just as he came of age, he wrote an imitation of the 65th Psalm, which secured the approval of his tasteful and venerable father. "I like your verses," said the venerable poet, "and would not have you bury your talent." His talent was not buried. Poetic inspiration came upon him in his birthplace in 1726. He had spent the summer in the old seat of the Epworth Singers, and amidst the first-fruits of the harvest in the old farm on the hill, he began his fine metrical paraphrase on the first eighteen verses of the 104th Psalm, and proved by his faithfulness to the inspired version, the beauty, strength, and harmony of his English verse, that he was a worthy member of that remarkable family choir of Psalmists. This is the most finished of John's early songs:—

> Upborne aloft on venturous wing,
> While spurning earthly themes I soar
> Through paths untrod before,
> What god, what seraph shall I sing?

Whom but Thee should I proclaim,
Author of this wondrous frame;
  Eternal, uncreated Lord,
  Enshrin'd in glory's radiant blaze!
    At whose prolific voice, whose potent word
Commanded Nothing swift retir'd, and worlds began their race.

Thou, brooding o'er the realms of night,
  Th' unbottom'd, infinite abyss,
  Bad'st the deep her rage surcease,
  And said'st, "Let there be light!"
  Ethereal Light Thy call obey'd,
  Glad she left her native shade,
Through the wide void her living waters past;
  Darkness turn'd his murmuring head,
  Resign'd the reins, and trembling fled;
The crystal waves roll'd on, and filled the ambient waste.

In light, effulgent robe, array'd,
  Thou left'st the beauteous realms of day;
  The golden towers inclin'd their head,
  As their Sov'reign took his way.
  The all-encircling bounds (a shining train,
  Minist'ring flames around Him flew)
Through the vast profound He drew,
  When, lo! sequacious to His fruitful hand,
Heaven o'er the uncolour'd void her azure curtain threw.

Lo! marching o'er the empty space,
  The fluid stores in order rise,
  With adamantine chains of liquid glass,
  To bind the new-born fabric of the skies.
  Downward th' Almighty Builder rode,
  Old *Chaos* groan'd beneath the God,
  Sable clouds His pompous car,
    Harness'd winds before Him ran,
    Proud to wear their Maker's chain,
And told, with hoarse-resounding voice, His coming from afar.

Embryon earth the signal knew,
And rear'd from night's dark womb her infant head,
Though yet prevailing waves her hills o'erspread,
  And stain'd their sickly face with pallid hue.
But when loud thunders the pursuit began,
Back the affrighted spoilers ran;
In vain, aspiring hills opposed their race,
  O'er hills and vales with equal haste,
  The flying squadrons past,
Till safe within the walls of their appointed place:
There firmly fix'd, their sure enclosures stand,
Unconquerable bounds of ever-during sand!

He spake! From the tall mountain's wounded side,
Fresh springs roll'd down their silver tide:
　O'er the glad vales the shining wanderers stray,
Soft murmuring as they flow,
While in their cooling wave inclining low,
　The untaught natives of the field their parching thirst allay.
High seated on the dancing sprays,
　Chequering with varied light their parent streams,
The feather'd choirs attune their artless lays,
　Safe from the dreaded heat of solar beams.

　　Genial showers at His command,
　　Pour plenty o'er the barren land:
　　Labouring with parent throes,
　　See! the teeming hills disclose
　　A new birth; see cheerful green,
　　Transitory, pleasing scene,
　　O'er the smiling landscape glow,
　　And gladden all the vale below.
　　Along the mountain's craggy brow,
　　Amiably dreadful now!
　　See the clasping vine dispread
　　Her gently-rising verdant head;
　　See the purple grape appear,
　　Kind relief of human care!

　　Instinct with circling life, Thy skill
　　　Uprear'd the olive's loaded bough;
　　What time on *Lebanon's* proud hill,
　　　Slow rose the stately cedar's brow.
　　Nor less rejoice the lowly plains,
　　　Of useful corn the fertile bed,
　　Than when the lordly cedar reigns,
　　　A beauteous, but a barren shade.
　　While in His arms the painted train,
　　　Warbling to the vocal grove,
　　Sweetly tell their pleasing pain,
　　　Willing slaves to genial love.
　　While the wild-goats, an active throng,
　　　From rock to rock light-bounding fly,
　　Jehovah's praise in solemn song
　　　Shall echo through the vaulted sky.

About five years after the birth of John Wesley, a little puny thing was "born out of due time" in the old Epworth Parsonage. Its eyes were as yet shut against the light. It gave no voice, and, scarcely betokening much life, it was kept nestled in soft wool till its natural birthday, when its eye-lids were lifted, and its first cry was given. Who would have ventured to prophesy that those eyes would be so alive to beauty for nearly eighty years, and that that voice would, through a long life, pour forth a continuous succession of holy songs from the depths of a consecrated musical soul ? Yet so it happened with Charles Wesley. The delicate child grew, under parental care and discipline, and became, by-and-by, the rollicking young student at Oxford. His poetical passion sometimes became a frenzy. In the rage of composition he would, at times, commit sad breaches on his brother John's order and method ; talking incoherently, while his inner genius was at work ; overturning the study table, by suiting his action to his thought ; spouting a few lines, and then scattering the books, so as to turn the retreat of learning into a chaos, while he was conceiving his harmonies of rhyme and rhythm. Nothing of the early outflowings of his soul remains but the burning, torturing satire which he sent to his sister Martha on her marriage with Mr. Hall. Charles knew that the wretched Hall had promised to marry his younger sister, Kezia, but had no knowledge of Martha's previous betrothal to him ; so that when he heard of the marriage of Hall and the elder sister, he charged her with guilty union with Kezia's affianced husband. He was hasty, and, in the heat of the moment, sent her a poetic epistle, the closing lines of which are enough to show its character and to prove his early poetic power :—

> No—wert thou as thou wast, did heaven's first rays
> Beam on thy soul, and all the Godhead blaze,
> Sooner shall sweet oblivion set us free
> From friendship, love, thy perfidy and thee ;
> Sooner shall light in league with darkness join,
> Virtue and vice, and heaven and hell, combine,
> Than her pure soul consent to mix with thine ;
> To share thy sin, adopt thy perjury,
> And damn herself to be revenged on thee ;
> To load her conscience with a sister's blood,
> The guilt of incest, and the curse of God.

The poet retained this capacity for scathing satirical verse to the last. It was put forth now and then. Nor could age chill this vein of satire. Only four years before his death, he pictures " The Man of Fashion."

What is a modern man of fashion?
A man of taste and dissipation;
A busy man, without employment;
A happy man, without enjoyment;
Who squanders all his time and treasures
In empty joys, and tasteless pleasures;
Visits, attendance, and attention,
And courtly arts too low to mention;
In sleep, and dress, and sport and play,
He throws his worthless life away;
Has no opinion of his own,
But takes from leading beaux the *ton*;
Born to be flatter'd, and to flatter,
The most important *thing* in nature,
Wrapt up in self-sufficient pride,
With his own virtues satisfied;
With a disdainful smile or frown
He on the riffraff crowd looks down;
The world polite, his friends and he,
And all the rest are—nobody.

Taught by the great his smiles to sell,
And how to write, and how to spell,
The great his oracles he makes,
Copies their vices and mistakes,
Custom pursues, his only rule,
And lives an ape, and dies a fool!

Charles Wesley, however, had higher work than mere satire, which, after all, he indulged in but seldom. His conversion, by the instrumentality of a good Moravian woman, turned all his powers into a devotional current, and hymn-writing became the business and joy of his life. On the third day from that of his first joy in Christ, "I waked," says he, "under the protection of Christ, and gave myself up, soul and body, to Him. At nine I began a hymn upon my conversion, but was persuaded to break off, for fear of pride. Mr. Bray coming, encouraged me to proceed in spite of Satan. I prayed to Christ to stand by me, and finished the hymn." The spiritual song, thus composed under the tremulous sensitiveness of "first love," was soon taken up by joyful voices in celebration of his brother John's new birth. On the very evening after it was composed, "towards ten," he says, "my brother was brought in triumph by a troop of our friends, and declared, 'I believe.' We sang the hymn with great joy."

Where shall my wondering soul begin?
  How shall I all to heaven aspire?
A slave redeem'd from death and sin,
  A brand pluck'd from eternal fire,
How shall I equal triumphs raise,
And sing my great Deliverer's praise?

O! how shall I the goodness tell,
  Father, which Thou to me hast show'd?
That I, a child of wrath and hell,
  I should be call'd a child of God!
Should know, should feel my sins forgiven,
Blest with this antepast of heaven!

And shall I slight my Father's love,
  Or basely fear His gifts to own?
Unmindful of His favours prove?
  Shall I, the hallow'd cross to shun,
Refuse His righteousness to impart,
By hiding it within my heart?

No! though the ancient dragon rage,
  And call forth all his hosts to war;
Though earth's self-righteous sons engage;
  Them, and their god, alike I dare;
Jesus, the sinner's Friend, proclaim;
Jesus, to sinners still the same.

Outcasts of men, to you I call,
  Harlots, and publicans, and thieves!
He spreads His arms to embrace you all;
  Sinners alone His grace receives:
No need of Him the righteous have,
He came the lost to seek and save.

Come, all ye *Magdalens* in lust,
  Ye ruffians fell in murders old;
Repent, and live; despair and trust!
  Jesus for you to death was sold:
Though hell protest, and earth repine,
He died for crimes like yours—and mine.

Come, O my guilty brethren, come,
  Groaning beneath your load of sin!
His bleeding heart shall make you room,
  His open side shall take you in.
He calls you now, invites you home:
Come, O my guilty brethren, come!

For you the purple current flow'd
  In pardons from His wounded side:
Languish'd for you the eternal God,
  For you the Prince of Glory died.
Believe, and all your guilt's forgiven;
Only believe—and yours is heaven.

What a flood of spiritual song followed that remarkable conversion hymn!

Charles Wesley's disposition, temper, training, and accomplishments, as well as his distinctive genius and taste, prepared him for his life-task as a hymnist. His Biblical knowledge and his elegant classical learning were always under command in the pursuit of his great object, and were sometimes amusingly made to serve his humour in self-defence or self-control. His brother's turbulent wife once succeeded in entrapping him and John in a room from which, for the time, there was no escape, and there she opened on them a running volley of complaints. The poet called Virgil to his help, and kept up so vehement and rapid a rehearsal of Latin verse as to "tame the shrew," and constrain her to give them freedom. He was little in stature like his brother; but he could make himself felt, especially by those who were forward, self-complacent, or pert. His reproofs could be hard and sharp. Hypocrisy and affectation always felt his frown. But he was frank, generous, and steady as a friend; was pleasing, instructive, and cheerful as a companion, humorous, witty, and good. His powers of expression, whether in the pulpit, or by the pen as a hymnist, were marked by simplicity and energy. He went on his way hymning through life. And his name is balmy and immortal, not only because of his multitude of songs, but for the beautiful completeness and rich variety of his rhyme, the pleasant variations of his metre, his happy union of strong argument and melodious diction, and his genuine and tasteful setting of evangelical truth. Hymns broke from his finely tuned soul wherever he moved. Inspiration was often caught in the saddle. That mode of travel seemed favourable to his creation of harmony; though sometimes it had its disadvantages. "Near Ripley," says he in the May of 1743, "my horse threw and fell upon me .... which spoiled my making hymns, or thinking at all, till the next day." The dear old poet used to be seen, when he was near eighty, riding about in London on a little old grey pony;

and now and then, as he jogged along, his inward melodies would rise, and then out would come a small card from the well-stored pocket, and there would be pencil short-hand jottings by the way. As soon as City Road was reached, the honoured nag was left to ruminate in front, while its master, with a soul bubbling up with rhyme and rhythm, would call for pen and ink, that the full measure of his devotional music might find permanent life. Just before he departed to the home of poetry and music, he breathed out his last prayerful lines—

> In age and feebleness extreme,
> Who shall a helpless worm redeem?
> Jesus! my only hope Thou art,
> Strength of my failing flesh and heart;
> Oh! could I catch one smile from Thee
> And drop into eternity!

The songs of his pilgrimage ceased on the 29th of March, 1788, and in the old graveyard of St. Marylebone an epitaph, which he had written on the death of a good Moravian minister, was put on his own sepulchre stone, by those who felt that it was beautifully appropriate to the author himself:—

> With poverty of spirit bless'd,
> Rest, happy saint, in Jesus rest;
> A sinner saved, through grace forgiven,
> Redeem'd from earth to reign in heaven!
> Thy labours of unwearied love,
> By Thee forgot, are crown'd above;
> Crown'd, through the mercy of thy Lord,
> With a free, full, immense reward!

CHAPTER V.

TWO BROTHERS IN SONG.

> Give me thy hand, brother—give me thy hand,
>   But not as our fathers did, dropping with gore;
> Dash down the gauntlet, and shiver the brand,
>   But not in the fashion they did so of yore;
> Throw away war's array, and come, let us prove
> Which has the heart that is strongest in love.

THAT spiritually minded and exemplary Christian, whose devout diary has so often aided the pious soul, Joseph Williams of. Kidderminster, once visited Bristol, and had an interview with Charles Wesley. It was on October 8th, 1739, when Wesley " preached the word of reconciliation at the brickyard."

"Hearing," says Williams, "that Mr. Charles Wesley would preach in the afternoon, just out of the city, I got a guide, and went to hear him. . . . I then went with him to a religious society, which met about seven in the evening. . . . . Never did I hear such praying or such singing. . . . Their singing was not only the most harmonious and delightful I ever heard, but, as Mr. Whitefield writes in his Journals, they 'sang lustily, and with a good courage.' I never so well understood the meaning of that expression before. . . . If there be such a thing as heavenly music upon earth, I heard it there." The secret of that charm which Primitive Methodist singing had for the soul of this good man was found in the fine adaptation of the tunes to the spirit, power, and music of the hymns; and in the naturalness, spiritual harmony, devout warmth, and oneness of the singers. It was genuine praise, words, tones, and feeling, all in harmony, after the manner of Charles Wesley's inspiring version of the 150th Psalm :—

> Publish, spread to all around
>   The great Jehovah's name;
> Let the trumpet's martial sound
>   The Lord of Hosts proclaim.
> Praise Him in the sacred dance,
>   Harmony's full concert raise;
> Let the virgin-choir advance,
>   And move but to His praise.
>
> Celebrate th' Eternal God
>   With harp and psaltery;
> Timbrels soft, and cymbals loud,
>   In His high praise agree.
> Praise Him every tuneful string,
>   All the reach of heavenly art;
> All the power of music bring,
>   The music of the heart.

There are tokens that such singing as Williams heard at Bristol is passing away from Methodism; passing away in favour of the soft, nerveless, soulless, namby-pamby toning, fashionable, now-a-day, among those who utter their hymns both "Ancient and Modern," as if they were

> Chanting faint hymns to the cold fruitless moon.

The clarion ring of early Methodist voices, the joyful swing and swell and expressive repeat; now from men, and now from women, are becoming things of the past. Such singing, indeed, must die out from among those who are losing the singing power, as they fall into pitiable dependence on organs and choirs. This change may be the rather deplored in that the declension of Methodist music is accompanied by a declining taste for the spiritual intensity and lofty heavenliness of original Methodist hymns. An unhealthy taste for mere artistic sounds is symptomatic of a lowered tone of spiritual life. The two brothers in song, the Wesleys, ceaselessly aimed at keeping up a consistent accordance between the spirited, earnest, and triumphant devotion of their hymns and the music to which they were set and sung. They had fine taste and warm love for music; and knew how to employ it to the glory of Him from whom all music comes. Nor, with their musical bent, could they always abstain from tuneful satire even when charity prompted them to "an apology for the enemies of music." So Charles sings:—

> Men of true piety, they know not why
> Music with all its sacred powers decry,
> Music itself (not its abuse) condemn,
> For good or bad is just the same to them.
> But let them know they quite mistake the case,
> Defect of nature for excess of grace;
> But whilst they reprobate the harmonious art, }
> Blamed we excuse, and candidly assert }
> The fault is in their ear, not in their upright heart. }

The brothers availed themselves of musical composition from any and every source; so that the people might be suitably and largely supplied with "Service of Song." These supplies sometimes came in a way beautifully illustrative of the harmony between the Divine Grace which they preached and the Divine Providence which guided their steps, their voices, and their pens. On March 29th, 1746, Charles Wesley jots in his diary: "I passed the afternoon at Mrs. Rich's, where we caught a physician by the ear, through the help of Mr. Lampe and some of our sisters. This is the true use of music." This little record gives an insight into the way in which early Methodists made their private social gatherings subservient, at once, to their own cultivation in psalmody and the spiritual benefit of casual visitors; while it affords a clue to some of the first retired springs of Methodist hymn-tunes. Mr. Rich was the lessee of Covent Garden Theatre. His wife, a beautiful and accomplished actress, had, on one occasion, found her way into West Street Chapel, where Charles Wesley preached. She was arrested by the Word, gave herself to the pursuit of Divine mercy, and found the joys of salvation. Now came the conflict. Her husband required her usual presence on the stage; but, though enduring painful persecution, she firmly refused to appear, unless it were to bear public testimony against theatrical amusements. She conquered. Her husband soon left her a rich widow;

and under her roof her spiritual father always found a welcome. In her home it was that Charles Wesley met with Frederick Lampe, a German musician, who was engaged by Mr. Rich as a composer of dramatic music. For many years he had been a Deist; but on reading John Wesley's "Earnest Appeal to Men of Reason and Religion," he, too, became a hearty believer in Christ; and consecrated his musical talent by setting tunes to many of the hymns of his now beloved friends, the Wesleys. The interesting relations between the members of this remarkable group are seen in happy light from a letter of Mrs. Rich's to Charles Wesley on Nov. 27th, 1746, during her husband's life :—"Dear and Rev. Sir,—I am infinitely obliged to you for your kind letter. It gave me great comfort, and at a time I had much need of it; for I had been very ill both in body and mind. Some part arose from my poor partner, who, I fear, has in a great measure stifled his convictions which God gave him.

"As to myself, God has been pleased to show me so much of my own unworthiness and helplessness that the light has almost broken my heart; and I might truly be called a woman of a sorrowful spirit.

"O think what it is to be obliged to conceal this from the eyes of those who know nothing of these things, but call it all madness! The Lord teach them better : at whose table I have been greatly strengthened, and through His grace I still hope to conquer all the enemies of my soul.

"I gave a copy of the hymn to Mr. Lampe, who, at the reading, shed some tears, and said he would write to you: for he loved you as well as if you were his own brother. The Lord increase it; for I hope it is a good sign.

"The enclosed is a copy of a song Mr. Rich has sung in a new scene, added to one of his old entertainments, in the character of *Harlequin Preacher*, to convince the town he is not a Methodist. Oh, pray for him, that he may be a Christian indeed, and then he will be no more concerned about what he is called, and for me. Your unworthy daughter in Christ."

The hymn, which brought tears from the musician's eyes, and elicited his expression of love for the man whose hymns he helped the Methodists to sing, was one in which the happy change in the gifted tune-maker is charmingly sung, while the musician's hopes of future harmonies swell into longing ecstacy :—

> Thou God of harmony and love,
> Whose name transports the saints above,
>   And lulls the ravish'd spheres—
> On Thee in feeble strains I call,
> And mix my humble voice with all
>   The heavenly choristers.
>
> If well I know the tuneful art
> To captivate a human heart,
>   The glory, Lord, be Thine;
> A servant of Thy blessèd will,
> I here devote my utmost skill
>   To sound the praise Divine.
>
> With *Tubal's* wretched sons no more
> I prostitute my sacred power
>   To please the fiends beneath;
> Or moderate the wanton lay,
> Or smooth with music's hand the way
>   To everlasting death.
>
> Suffice for this the season past—
> I come, great God, to learn at last
>   The lesson of Thy grace;
> Teach me the new, the Gospel song,
> And let my hand, my heart, my tongue,
>   Move only to Thy praise.
>
> Thine own musician, Lord, inspire,
> And let my consecrated lyre
>   Repeat the Psalmist's part;
> His Son, and Thine, reveal in me,
> And fill with sacred melody
>   The fibres of my heart.
>
> So shall I charm the listening throng,
> And draw the living stones along
>   By Jesus' tuneful name;
> The living stones shall dance, shall rise,
> And form a city in the skies—
>   The *New Jerusalem*.

> Oh! might I with Thy saints aspire—
> The meanest of that dazzling choir—
>   Who chant Thy praise above;
> Mix'd with the bright musician-band,
> May I a heavenly harper stand,
>   And sing the song of love.
>
> What ecstacy of bliss is there,
> While all the angelic concert share,
>   And drink the floating joys!
> What more than ecstacy when all,
> Struck to the golden pavement, fall
>   At Jesus' glorious voice!
>
> Jesus—the heaven of heaven He is—
> The soul of harmony and bliss;
>   And while on Him we gaze,
> And while His glorious voice we hear,
> Our spirits are all eye, all ear,
>   And silence speaks His praise.
>
> Oh, might I die that awe to prove,
> That prostrate awe which dares not move
>   Before the great Three-One;
> To shout by turns the bursting joy,
> And all eternity employ
>   In songs around the throne!

Lampe's tunes became popular. In a letter to his wife, Charles Wesley asks—"How many of Lampe's tunes can you play?" and in an epistle from Newcastle to his friend Blackwell, the good London banker, he says—"His tunes are universally admired here among the musical men, and have brought me into high favour with them." Like many a pious musician, Lampe must have found it difficult to maintain the public exercise of his profession. It was more easy to throw his heart into a Methodist hymn-tune than to entertain the musical multitude. In October, 1748, he was in Dublin, and his friend Wesley says:—"I met at Mr. Lunell's an old Dutch Quaker, who seemed to have deep experience of the things of God. At two Mr. Lampe and his wife called, and were overjoyed to see me. I cannot yet give up my hope that they are designed for better things than feeding swine—that is, entertaining the gay world."

What curious associations are sometimes around these

brothers in song!—an old Dutch Quaker and a converted German musician and Methodist tune-maker! The tune-maker realized his poetic friend's hope at last. His work of "feeding swine" was over—he got something better in the music way more to his taste, and that for ever! With what a swell of poetic music and heavenward affection Wesley sings at his upward flight!—

> 'Tis done! The Sovereign will's obey'd,
> The soul, by angel-guards convey'd,
>   Has took its seat on high;
> The brother of my choice is gone
> To music sweeter than his own,
>   And concerts in the sky.
>
> His spirit, mounting on the wing,
> Rejoiced to hear the convoy sing
>   While harping at his side;
> With ease he caught their heavenly strain,
> And smiled and sung in mortal pain—
>   He sung, and smiled, and died.
>
> Enroll'd with that harmonious throng,
> He hears th' unutterable song,
>   Th' unutterable Name;
> He *sees* the Master of the choir,
> He bows, and strikes the golden lyre,
>   And hymns the glorious Lamb.
>
> He hymns the glorious Lamb *alone*,
> No more constrain'd to make his moan
>   In this sad wilderness:
> To toil for sublunary pay,
> And cast his sacred strains away,
>   And stoop the world to please.
>
> Redeem'd from earth, the tuneful soul,
> While everlasting ages roll,
>   His triumph shall prolong;
> His noblest faculties exert,
> And all the music of his heart
>   Shall warble on his tongue.
>
> Oh, that my mournful days were past!
> Oh, that I might o'ertake at last
>   My happy friend above!
> With him the Church triumphant join,
> And celebrate in strains divine
>   The majesty of love!

> Great God of Love! prepare my heart,
> And tune it now to bear a part
>   In heavenly melody;
> "I'll strive to sing as loud as they
> Who sit enthroned in brighter day,"
>   And nearer the Most High.
>
> Oh, that the promised time were come!
> Oh, that we all were taken home,
>   Our Master's joy to share!
> Draw, Lord, the living, vocal stones,
> Jesus, recall Thy banish'd ones,
>   To chant Thy praises there.
>
> Our number and our bliss complete,
> And summon all the choir to meet,
>   Thy glorious throne around;
> The whole musician-band bring in,
> And give the signal to begin,
>   And let the trumpet sound.

The "two brothers in song" began their issue of "Hymns and Sacred Poems" in 1739, and continued, at intervals, to supply Christian singers for half a century. Thirty-eight publications appeared, one after the other; now under the name of one brother, now under that of the other; some with both names, and others nameless. The two hymnists appear to have agreed that, in the volumes which bore their joint names, they would not distinguish their hymns. They left those who read and sang them to detect, if they could, the severer taste, the stronger style, and the clearer precision of John; or the bolder flights, the more glowing fancy, the more various harmony, and the more diffuse, flowing diction of the younger poet. Most of the hymns commonly attributed to John are translations, but his stamp may be found upon a larger number of the original Methodist songs than tradition or custom has allowed; and, perhaps, had his distinctive claims been more fairly put in from the beginning, the Methodists would have found their indebtedness to him for his part in their doctrinal standards and ecclesiastical discipline far more nearly balanced than it now is by their obligations to him for his share in their service of psalmody. At all events, the hymns which bear his name are ever living things. Much of their life is owing

H

to the living impressions made on the author's soul by important facts in his personal history. It was so with both brothers. One part of their education at home, under the regulated and prayerful oversight of their devoted mother, evidently influenced their devotional thought and action through life. They were instructed, as soon as they could speak, to give utterance to any feeling of devotion that might rise in their minds, in short and simple prayers. The Lord's Prayer was rightly adopted as at once the most simple and awe-inspiring form of prayerful words which human language could afford, and they were therefore made to say it at rising in the morning and on retiring at night. Both John and Charles give out their poetical paraphrases on that prayer with a loving reverence and a simple, warm, intense devoutness which indicate the still fresh influence of impressions in childhood.

Charles, in his rhyme and rhythm, is beautifully childlike; but John's hymn excels in a becoming harmony of grandeur, condensed power, and tender warmth.

> Father of all, whose powerful voice
>   Call'd forth this universal frame—
> Whose mercies over all rejoice,
>   Through endless ages still the same;
> Thou by Thy word upholdest all,
>   Thy bounteous love to all is show'd,
> Thou hear'st Thy every creature's call,
>   And fillest every mouth with good.
>
> In heaven Thou reign'st, enthroned in light,
>   Nature's expanse beneath Thee spread;
> Earth, air, and sea before Thy sight,
>   And hell's deep gloom, are open laid.
> Wisdom, and might, and love are Thine—
>   Prostrate before Thy face we fall,
> Confess Thine attributes Divine,
>   And hail Thee Sovereign Lord of all.
>
> Thee, Sovereign Lord, let all confess,
>   That moves in earth, or air, or sky,
> Revere Thy power, Thy goodness bless,
>   Tremble before Thy piercing eye.
> All ye who owe to Him your birth,
>   In praise your every hour employ;
> Jehovah reigns! be glad, O Earth,
>   And shout, ye Morning Stars, for joy.

Son of Thy Sire's eternal love,
   Take to Thyself Thy mighty power;
Let all earth's sons Thy mercy prove,
   Let all Thy bleeding grace adore.
The triumphs of Thy love display;
   In every heart reign Thou alone,
Till all Thy foes confess Thy sway,
   And glory ends what grace begun.

Spirit of grace, and health, and power,
   Fountain of light and love below,
Abroad Thine healing influence shower,
   O'er all the nations let it flow.
Inflame our hearts with perfect love,
   In us the work of faith fulfil;
So not Heaven's host shall swifter move
   Than we on earth to do Thy will.

Father, 'tis Thine each day to yield
   Thy children's wants a fresh supply;
Thou cloth'st the lilies of the field,
   And hearest the young ravens cry:
On Thee we cast our care; we live
   Through Thee, who know'st our every need;
O feed us with Thy grace, and give
   Our souls this day the living bread.

Eternal, spotless Lamb of God,
   Before the world's foundation slain,
Sprinkle us ever with Thy blood;
   O cleanse, and keep us ever clean.
To every soul (all praise to Thee)
   Our bowels of compassion move,
And all mankind by this may see
   God is in us, for God is love.

Giver and Lord of life, whose power
   And guardian care for all are free,
To Thee in fierce temptation's hour
   From sin and Satan let us flee.
Thine, Lord, we are, and ours Thou art,
   In us be all Thy goodness show'd;
Renew, enlarge, and fill our heart
   With peace, and joy, and heaven, and God.

Blessing and honour, praise and love,
   Co-equal, co-eternal Three,
In earth below, and Heaven above,
   By all Thy works, be paid to Thee.
Thrice Holy, Thine the kingdom is,
   The power omnipotent is Thine;
And when created nature dies,
   Thy never-ceasing glories shine.

Nearly half a century ago, on a Sunday morning, an old Methodist preacher preached in a village on the heights above Marazion, in Cornwall, near St. Hilary Downs. After the service, he was invited to dine with a member of the congregation. The table was somewhat richly laden. For a minute or two he seemed to hesitate in his chair, and at length said—

"Isn't this the place where John Wesley sat in the saddle and dined on blackberries from the hedge for want of a better inner?"

"Yes," it was replied.

"Then," said he, "forbid that I should indulge in this plenty, or eat or drink in this place. Where Wesley had not a morsel of bread offered him, I will not feast. In honour of his memory I will go out on the downs and fast and pray."

The stalwart old pilgrim stalked away, singing—

> His happiness, in part, is mine,
> Already saved from self-design,
> From every creature-love!
> Bless'd with the scorn of finite good,
> My soul is lighten'd of its load,
> And seeks the things above.

Some would think that this came too near to the ascetic; but the old man was a sturdy representative of that early class whose veneration for John Wesley and whose love for his work and their own were master feelings. He was one of the few who could appreciate John Wesley's hymn for "The Pilgrim," and consistently sing it throughout. He was, too, in built and appearance, in physical constitution, mental character, and intensity of devotion, something like a copy of the man who recorded Wesley's pilgrim experience on St. Hilary Downs—John Nelson; and, like Wesley's vigorous companion, could say from his heart, "By the grace of God I love every man, but fear no man." Nelson gives us his vivid recollections:—"When I had been out a week, I returned to St. Ives. . . . All that time Mr. Wesley and

I lay on the floor, he had my great-coat for his pillow, and I had Burkett's 'Notes on the New Testament' for mine. After being here near three weeks, one morning, about three o'clock, Mr. Wesley turned over, and finding me awake, clapped me on the side, saying, 'Brother Nelson, let us be of good cheer. I have one whole side yet, for the skin is off but one side.' We usually preached on the commons, going from one common to another, and it was but seldom any one asked us to eat or drink. One day we had been at St. Hilary Downs, and Mr. Wesley had preached from Ezekiel's vision of dry bones, and there was a shaking among the people as he preached. As we returned, Mr. Wesley stopped his horse, to pick the blackberries, saying, 'Brother Nelson, we ought to be thankful that there are plenty of blackberries; for this is the best country I ever saw for getting a stomach, but the worst that ever I saw for getting food.' 'Do the people think we can live by preaching?' I said; 'I know not what they may think, but one asked me to eat something as I came to St. Just, when I ate heartily of barley-bread and honey.' He said, 'You are well off; I had a thought of begging a crust of bread of the woman where I met the people at Morva, but forgot it till I had got some distance from the house.'"

In the light of this record of a week's adventures in the pilgrim-poet's life, his hymn appears in all its distinctive beauty and singular appropriateness. Follow the man from Oxford to Georgia; watch him amidst the disappointments of his love, the falling away of weak friends; his perils in the distant wilderness, his perils in the deep, his perils at home amidst hostile mobs, his single-handed defensive battles against all classes of foes to truth, his continuous rounds of missionary travel, his ceaseless variety of company and accommodation, and his untiring efforts to bless the world; see him "in stripes, in tumults, in labours, in watchings, in fastings; as poor, yet making many rich; as having nothing, and yet possessing all things;" look at him, as to this world fortuneless, homeless, with his back on things that are seen, his whole soul bent on eternal life; a lone man still, an apostolic pilgrim, lingering on the open Western common to feed on wild berries, and thinking of begging a crust from a poor woman; look at him, and then listen, as he pours forth a jubilant song from his heart—his pilgrim's song:—

> How happy is the pilgrim's lot,
> How free from every anxious thought,
>   From worldly hope and fear!
> Confined to neither court nor cell,
> His soul disdains on earth to dwell—
>   He only sojourns here.
>
> His happiness in part is mine,
> Already saved from self-design,
>   From every creature-love!
> Bless'd with the scorn of finite good,
> My soul is lighten'd of its load,
>   And seeks the things above.
>
> The things eternal I pursue,
> A happiness beyond the view
>   Of those that basely pant
> For things by nature felt and seen
> Their honours, wealth, and pleasures mean,
>   I neither have, nor want.
>
> I have no sharer of my heart,
> To rob my Saviour of a part,
>   And desecrate the whole;
> Only betroth'd to Christ am I,
> And wait His coming from the sky
>   To wed my happy soul.
>
> I have no babes to hold me here,
> But children more securely dear
>   For mine I humbly claim;
> Better than daughters, or than sons,
> Temples divine of living stones
>   Inscrib'd with Jesus' name.
>
> No foot of land do I possess,
> No cottage in this wilderness—
>   A poor wayfaring man;
> I lodge awhile in tents below,
> Or gladly wander to and fro,
>   Till I my *Canaan* gain.
>
> Nothing on earth I call my own—
> A stranger to the world unknown,
>   I all their goods despise;
> I trample on their whole delight,
> And seek a country out of sight,
>   A country in the skies.

There is my house and portion fair,
My treasure and my heart is there,
　And my abiding home:
For me my elder brethren stay,
And angels beckon me away,
　And Jesus bids me come.

I come, thy servant, Lord, replies;
I come to meet Thee in the skies,
　And claim my heavenly rest:
Now let the pilgrim's journey end,
Now, O my Saviour, Brother, Friend,
　Receive me to Thy breast.

A Methodist preacher, travelling in the United States of America, found his way into Indiana. He and his family suffered deep poverty. A settler who loved him, being a large landholder, presented him with a title-deed of very many acres. He went home glad at heart, in freedom, as he thought, from his difficulties. Three months after this he came to his friend, the kind-hearted settler. He was welcomed; but he soon drew out the parchment.

"Here, sir," said he, "I want to give you back your title-deed."

"What's the matter?" said the other; "any flaw in it?"

"No."

"Isn't it good land?"

"Good as any in the State."

"Do you think I repent the gift?"

"I have not the slightest reason to doubt your generosity."

"Why don't you keep it, then?"

"Well, sir," said the preacher, "you know I am very fond of singing, and there is one hymn in my book, the singing of which is one of the greatest comforts of my life. I have not been able to sing it with my whole heart since I have been here. A part of it runs this way:—

"No foot of land do I possess,
No cottage in this wilderness,
　A poor, wayfaring man,

I lodge a while in tents below,
Or gladly wander to and fro,
　Till I my *Canaan* gain,

> There is my house and portion fair,
> My treasure and my heart is there,
> And my abiding home.

"Take your title-deed," he added; "I would rather sing that hymn than own America."

He went his way, and sang his hymn, fulfilling his ministry, and confiding in Him to whose service he had sacrificed himself. Nor did he or his family ever lack bread. He is gone now to his "abiding home."

"When you have a trouble that haunts you," said one friend to another, as they sat in the dusk, communing about their experience of life, "how it peers at you around every corner, and crosses your way at every turn! Some say that, in such cases, the time of nightfall is the worst, according to the old saying, 'Cares double at night;' and it is true that they come on, thickening the darkness, and taking multitudinous forms to the lone, sleepless sufferer. But to me, the moment of waking in the morning has often proved the worst; it used to seem as if I awoke under suffocating pressure, which made every nerve twitch and every pore weep. Relief, however—sweet relief—came to me. I prayed at night that I might have a peaceful and free awakening, and that God might be first in my morning thought and feeling. My prayer was answered. I fell off to sleep in hope, and I was seemingly called in the morning by the voice of a hymn which came with such freshness and power as if it were breathed into my soul by the spirit who first inspired the author. It was the hymn beginning with—

> "O God, my God, my all Thou art;
> Ere shines the dawn of rising day.

"My mornings from that time have been too bright for intrusive troubles. That is now my elect morning hymn. It is John Wesley's, I believe."

Well, he was the translator. The original was in the Spanish, and who its author was is not known. But though the thoughts were at first those of some saintly Spaniard, the English rendering is such as to show that John Wesley had a poet's appreciative talent, and a poet's beauty and power of expression; and the circumstances under which it came from his pen might prove that his experience, like your own, was a sympathetic reflection of what the Spanish hymnist was feeling when he wrote. The translation was probably made while Wesley was in Georgia. There he, too, was haunted by troubles. The violation of his conscientious Churchism, the vile machinations of his hostile parishioners, the vexatious results of his courtship, and the seeming failure of his loved mission work—all combined to darken his evening retrospects and to bedim the prospects of his early mornings. Under such circumstances, with a heart still set upon the good, and seeking refuge in God, with what appropriate and cheering light must this Spanish version of the 63rd Psalm have touched his soul, and how finely and with what unction he has uttered his own, as well as his author's, devout feeling!

> O God, my God, my all Thou art;
>   Ere shines the dawn of rising day,
> Thy sovereign light within my heart,
>   Thy all-enlivening power display.
>
> For Thee my thirsty soul doth pant,
>   While in this desert land I live;
> And hungry as I am, and faint,
>   Thy love alone can comfort give.
>
> In a dry land, behold, I place
>   My whole desire on Thee, O Lord;
> And more I pay to gain Thy grace
>   Than all earth's treasures can afford.
>
> In holiness within Thy gates
>   Of old oft have I sought for Thee;
> Again my longing spirit waits
>   That fulness of delight to see.
>
> More dear than life itself, Thy love
>   My heart and tongue shall still employ
> And to declare Thy praise will prove
>   My peace, my glory, and my joy.
>
> In blessing Thee with grateful songs
>   My happy life shall glide away;
> The praise that to Thy name belongs
>   Hourly, with lifted hands, I'll pay.

> Abundant sweetness, while I sing
>   Thy love, my ravish'd soul o'erflows ;
> Secure in Thee, my God and King,
>   Of glory that no period knows.
>
> Thy name, O Lord, upon my bed
>   Dwells on my lips, and fires my thought;
> With trembling awe, in midnight shade,
>   I muse on all Thy hands have wrought.
>
> In all I do I feel Thy aid,
>   Therefore Thy greatness will I sing,
> O God, who bid'st my heart be glad
>   Beneath the shadow of Thy wing.
>
> My soul draws nigh, and cleaves to Thee;
>   Then let or earth or hell assail,
> Thy mighty hand shall set me free:
>   For whom Thou sav'st, he ne'er shall fail.

This was one of the first hymns which John Wesley published on his arrival in England, and is among the first-fruits of his genius, brightened and hallowed as it was by sanctified trial and growing devotion to God's service.

When fully brought under the holy constraint of Christ's love, and unreservedly consecrated to the work of "spreading scriptural holiness over the land," John Wesley seems to have gone his rounds through the most western province of England in a spirit differing from that of some of his preachers—some of his own time, and some who have followed. Where he felt "all his patience put to the proof again and again," others have found it pleasant to dwell; and where he was disposed to "leap" under a sense of freedom, some of his modern representatives have grumbled as if amidst the hardships of banishment. One of his letters illustrates this. The letter was written in Redruth, a remarkable centre of Wesley's itinerant operations in Cornwall. About halfway down the steep, queer old street, at the back of a house, just below the broad space of the market, where he had often preached to the multitude, he sat in a little room over the side-passage, with its small window commanding the covered entrance from the street, as if it were a prophet's watch-tower. The nest was about fifteen feet square, with a kind of garret-like ceiling, and affording just room for a bed, table, and chair by the small fire-place in the corner near the window. It was on Sunday, September 31, 1755. On the evening before, he had preached in the street, though he had just arrived "extremely weary;" "and our friends," as he said, "were so glad to see me that none once thought of asking me to eat or drink. My weariness vanished when I began to speak." On the Sunday morning at eight, he was preaching again from "How shall I give up Ephraim?" "Many endeavoured, but in vain, to hide their tears." From the street service he walked off to church, where he was "agreeably surprised to hear the prayers read, not only with deliberation, but with uncommon propriety." At one o'clock he was once more preaching in the street to double as many as were there in the morning, "and all were still as night." At five in the afternoon there were to be thousands waiting to hear him in Gwennap; but within the short interval he retreated to his snug little lodging-hole, and wrote thus to his friend Blackwell, in London :—

Dear Sir,—Experience confirms your advice both ways. In my last journey into the North, all my patience was put to the proof again and again, and all my endeavour to please, yet without success. In my present journey, I leap, as broke from chains. I am content with whatever entertainment I meet with, and my companions are always in good humour, "because they are with me." This must be the spirit of all who take journeys with me. If a dinner ill-dressed, a hard bed, a poor room, a shower of rain, or a dirty road will put them out of humour, it lays a burden upon me, greater than all the rest put together. By the grace of God I never fret: I repine at nothing; I am discontented with nothing; and to have persons at my ear, fretting and murmuring at everything, is like tearing the flesh off my bones. I see God sitting upon His throne, and ruling all things well. Although, therefore, I can bear this also, to hear His government of the world continually found fault with (for in blaming the things which He alone can alter, we, in effect, blame Him), yet it is such a burden to me as I cannot bear without pain, and I bless God when it is removed.

The doctrine of a particular providence is what exceeding few persons understand; at least, not practically, so as to apply it to every circumstance of life. This I want—to see God acting in everything, and disposing all for His own glory and His creatures' good. I hope it is your continual prayer that you may see Him, and love Him, and glorify Him with all you are and all you have. Peace be with you all!

The opening sentences of this epistle contain healthy lessons for the more modern Methodist preachers; but the latter part is of beautiful interest in relation to one of John Wesley's most successfully translated hymns. It seems to be a record of the thought and feeling which the work of translating that hymn had permanently fixed in his soul. We are reminded of the evident connection between Donne's poetic riches, as amassed in his poems, and as laid out with taste in his sermons, and the clearly discoverable alliance between the imagery of Milton as an essayist and his wrought-up grandeurs and beauties as a poet. Wesley's letter is the prose form of that creed as to a ruling Providence which with such loving skill he had worked into tuneful English out of Paul Gerhardt's well-known hymn. No translator has equalled him in this for native ease, pure elegance, weight, inspiring force, and unction. His own genius was never put forth with more permanent and sacred effect than when he taught us to sing—

> Commit Thou all thy griefs
> And ways into His hands;
> To His sure truth and tender care,
> Who earth and Heaven commands.
>
> Who points the clouds their course,
> Whom winds and seas obey;
> He shall direct thy wandering feet,
> He shall prepare thy way.
>
> Thou on the Lord rely,
> So safe shalt thou go on;
> Fix on His work thy steadfast eye,
> So shall thy work be done.
>
> No profit canst thou gain
> By self-consuming care:
> To Him commend thy cause, His ear
> Attends the softest prayer.
>
> Thy everlasting truth,
> Father, Thy ceaseless love,
> Sees all Thy children's wants, and knows
> What best for each will prove.

And whatsoe'er Thou will'st,
　Thou dost, O King of Kings;
What Thine unerring wisdom chose
　Thy power to being brings.

Thou everywhere hast way,
　And all things serve Thy might;
Thy every act pure blessing is,
　Thy path unsullied light.

When Thou arisest, Lord,
　What shall Thy work withstand?
When all Thy children want Thou giv'st,
　Who, who shall stay Thy hand?

Give to the winds thy fears;
　Hope and be undismay'd;
God hears thy sighs and counts thy tears,
　God shall lift up thy head.

Through waves and clouds and storms,
　He gently clears thy way;
Wait thou His time, so shall this night
　Soon end in joyous day.

Still heavy is thy heart?
　Still sink thy spirits down?
Cast off the weight, let fear depart,
　And every care be gone.

What though thou rulest not?
　Yet Heaven and earth and hell
Proclaim, God sitteth on the throne,
　And ruleth all things well.

Leave to His sovereign sway
　To choose and to command;
So shalt thou, wondering, own His way,
　How wise, how strong His hand.

Far, far above thy thought
　His counsel shall appear,
When fully He the work hath wrought
　That caused thy needless fear.

Thou seest our weakness, Lord,
　Our hearts are known to Thee;
O, lift Thou up the sinking head,
　Confirm the feeble knee!

Let us in life, in death,
　Thy steadfast truth declare,
And publish with our latest breath
　Thy love and guardian care.

The gracious influence of this hymn on the thought, feeling, and character of Christians under the discipline of life might find unnumbered illustrations. One or two may be given from the recollections of an old observer. A venerable minister once said to him:—

"My first year after marriage was spent in the South of England, and then I was called to take a pastoral charge in South Wales. My income had been small, and my expenses somewhat large, so that when the time of starting came, I had not money enough to pay my way to our journey's end. We had done our best with the means we had, and were happily one in our repose on God's fatherly goodness. I believed that He would supply our need day by day as He had always done, and in that full trust we went off on the top of the coach. Those were old coaching days. We had got about halfway towards our destination, and when I had given the coachman and guard their fees, I had but twenty-pence left in my pocket. We were to go into the inn while the horses were changed, and had to be booked for the rest of the journey. Where the amount of our fare was to come from, I did not know; but still I rested on the promise of Divine help. As I got off the coach, that verse came freshly to my mind—

>"No profit canst thou gain
> By self-consuming care;
>To Him commend Thy cause, His ear
> Attends the softest prayer.

And I lifted up my heart to God in the language of the next verse—

>"Thy everlasting truth,
> Father, Thy ceaseless love,
>Sees all Thy children's wants, and knows
> What best for each will prove.

"As we walked through the lobby, I saw a paper on the floor, picked it up, and opened it. It was a ten-pound note. 'The help has come in time,' said I to myself. But putting the note in my pocket, I called the landlord, told him that I had found a note which I supposed somebody in the house had lost. If he could tell me the amount and the number of the note, I would let the owner have it. There was at once a hue and cry through the house, 'Who had lost a bank-note?' Nobody claimed it; nobody could describe it. The horn blew; the coach was to start; we could not stay; and hurriedly giving the landlord my address in Wales, and assuring him that I would remit the amount lost as soon as the owner of the note was identified, we took our seats, and, by-and-by, safely arrived at our new residence. No news of the person who had lost the note ever came, nor has any claim ever been made on me from that day to this. How ever some people may account for the fact, there it is; one of many instances in my life in which God has shown Himself near to help me in the time of need."

Another dear old friend used to tell a story of his mining days. He was a purser at a mine in the West of England. The road from the mine towards his home was dangerous in the dark, leading in and out among old mine pits and shafts. "It was almost dark one evening," said he, "before I left the counting-room, but my heart was always ready to sing—

> "Who points the clouds their course,
> Whom winds and seas obey;
> He shall direct thy wandering feet,
> He shall prepare thy way.

"I took a captain's candle to light me on my way, but somehow or other I got wrong in starting, and wandered on till I became thoroughly confused. Suddenly I felt a slight twitch of my fingers, and the candle I was holding was taken from me as by an unseen hand. It did not fall, neither was it put out immediately, but was borne on in front of me, and then slightly inclined to the left, and that sufficiently to discover to me a precipice. When I saw it, I knew my whereabouts, which had I not known, the next moment I should have been hurled into eternity. Immediately after the candle fell, and was extinguished. I stood still, and praised God for His great deliverance; then scrambling on my hands and knees, and feeling my way as I went from amidst the shafts and pits by which I was surrounded, I escaped to the turnpike road, and went home with a thankful heart. The next day I repaired to the memorable spot again, and thankfully surveyed the precipice of ruin where I stood the night before, but from which the kind overruling providence of God had delivered me.

> "Let us in life, in death,
> Thy steadfast truth declare,
> And publish with our latest breath
> Thy love and guardian care."

CHAPTER VI.

MORE ABOUT SONGS FROM THE BROTHERS.

> Thanks be to God ! His grace has shown
> How sinful man on earth
> May join the songs which round His throne
> Give endless praises birth.
> He gave His Son for man to die!
> He sent His Spirit from on high
> To consummate the scheme :
> O be that consummation blest !
> And let Redemption be confest
> A poet's noblest theme.

THE sanctified genius of Christianity has made the hills and valleys of the English-speaking world vocal with prayer and praise to "Jesus and Him crucified."

"It was nearly sunset," says a Western travelling preacher, "and a mellow light was upon the valley up which I was footing it towards a village chapel. The light seemed to hallow the balmy quietness around me. I came at length within sight of a group of tin-washers. They were mostly young women in their picturesque sun-bonnets and working dress. They were gracefully using their long-handled instruments in regulating the action of the water on the pounded tin ore, as it was carried over a succession of sloping boards, so as to allow the cleanly-washed tin to form a deposit beneath. They were singing in concert as they worked, and on passing the nearest point of the road to them, I caught some of the words of their evening song. The words came swelling up the valley—

> "Wash me, and make me thus Thine own,
> Wash me, and mine Thou art;

"It filled me with sacred feeling as I passed, and the softening music followed. It was an agreeable preparation for evening worship. The time of service arrived, and the same singers came with their parents, friends, and neighbours, all decently dressed for God's house, and true to the hour for prayer. I chose the same favourite hymn. New inspiration seemed to come upon them, and they made the sanctuary ring with their spirited, glowing harmony, as they sang:—

> "Jesu, Thou art my Righteousness,
>   For all my sins were Thine;
> Thy death hath bought of God my peace,
>   Thy life hath made Him mine.
>
> Spotless and just in Thee I am;
>   I feel my sins forgiven;
> I taste salvation in Thy name,
>   And ante-date my heaven.
>
> For ever here my rest shall be,
>   Close to Thy bleeding side;
> This all my hope, and all my plea,
>   For *me* the Saviour died.
>
> My dying Saviour, and my God,
>   Fountain for guilt and sin,
> Sprinkle me ever with Thy blood,
>   And cleanse and keep me clean.
>
> Wash me, and make me thus Thine own
>   Wash me, and mine Thou art;
> Wash me, but not my feet alone—
>   My hands, my head, my heart.
>
> Th' atonement of Thy blood apply,
>   Till faith to sight improve,
> Till hope shall in fruition die,
>   And all my soul be love.

"It was indeed a joy to hear this from the lips of so many happy young people who had known the washing of regeneration, and renewing of the Holy Ghost; and the joy became deeper as their faces brightened or their eyes sparkled through their tears as they listened to their preacher's address on the words of Jesus. 'If I wash thee not, thou hast no part with me.' Every feature of the eager, upturned countenances seemed to respond, 'Lord, not my feet only, but also my hands and my head.' Nor will that parting music ever be forgotten; for as they went off in groups from the service, I could hear them singing along the hill-side lane—

> "Wash me, and make me thus Thine own;
> Wash me, and mine Thou art;
> Wash me, but not my feet alone,
> My hands, my head, my heart."

Methodism owes it to Charles Wesley that its distinctive teachings are so embodied in the psalmody which the masses of its generations have formed the habit of singing, that it has been preserved in doctrinal integrity while some other communities have been " tossed to and fro, and carried about with every wind of doctrine." The doctrine, for instance, of the Holy Spirit's " witness " with the spirit of believers, that they " are the children of God," is so wrought into the very life of the Methodists' hymnology that their " service of song " has been an agreeable preservative from indistinct notions, mistiness of experience, and doubtful gloom.

"I used to go mourning for my sins all the day," said a tinner once, at a Methodist lovefeast, "and sometimes nearly all night, too. Now and then, it seemed as if I had

> " The tears that tell the sin forgiven,
> The sighs that waft the soul to Heaven;

And then I should again be in darkness and uncertainty. I was going over the down one day when the furze-blossom was ripening to seed, and I said within myself, ' If the Lord would make a furze seed-pod burst this moment, I would believe the sign that my sins were forgiven.' A seed-pod did burst with a crack, but I could not believe. ' Lord, try me again,' said I; and again a seed opened; but still I had no faith. I went home, determined that I would pray for the salvation of a friend, and if it came to pass within a fixed time, I thought I should be able to believe a sign like that. Within the time, the friend I prayed for was led to give his heart to Christ; but I was darker than ever. All at once the thought came, ' What am I doing? I am like the wicked Jews, I am looking for a sign to prove what the

Holy Ghost only can make known.' 'Lord,' said I, 'Thou wilt not give Thy glory to another. It is Thine to tell me of my acceptance.'

> " Spirit of faith, come down,
>   Reveal the things of God;
> And make to *me* the Godhead known,
>   And witness with the blood :
> 'Tis *Thine* the blood to apply
>   And give me eyes to see,
> Who did for every sinner die
>   Hath surely died for *me*.

"I will 'cast my soul on Jesus,' and wait. I did not wait long. The Blessed Spirit came, and oh, how clear it was then! Then I could sing, and hear the sweet meaning of the hymn :—

> " How shall a slave releas'd
>   From his oppressive chain
> Distinguish ease and rest
>   From weariness and pain?
> Can he his burden borne away
>   Infallibly *perceive?*
> Or I before the Judgment Day,
>   My pardon'd sin believe?
>
> Redeem'd from all his woes,
>   Out of his dungeon freed,
> Ask how the prisoner knows
>   That he is free indeed!
> How can he tell the gloom of night
>   From the meridian blaze?
> Or I discern the glorious light
>   That streams from Jesus' face?
>
> The gasping patient lies
>   In agony of pain!
> But see him light arise,
>   Restored to health again,
> And doth he *certainly* receive
>   The knowledge of his cure?
> And am I *conscious* that I live?
>   And is my pardon sure?
>
> A wretch for years consign'd
>   To hopeless misery,
> The happy change must find,
>   From all his pain set free :

> And must not I the difference know
>   Of joy and anxious grief,
> Of grace and sin, of weal and woe,
>   Of faith and unbelief?
>
> Yes, Lord, I now perceive,
>   And bless Thee for the grace
> Through which, redeem'd, I live
>   To see Thy smiling face.
> Alive I am who once was dead,
>   And freely justified;
> I *know* Thy blood for me was shed,
>   I feel it *now* applied.
>
> By sin no longer bound,
>   The pris'ner is set free,
> The lost again is found
>   In Paradise in Thee:
> In darkness, chains, and death I was,
>   But, lo! to life restored,
> Into Thy wondrous light I pass,
>   The freeman of the Lord.
>
> In comfort, power, and peace,
>   Thy favour, Lord, I prove,
> In faith, and joy's increase,
>   And self-abasing love;
> Thou dost my pardon'd sin reveal,
>   My life, and heart renew;
> The pledge, the witness, and the seal
>   Confirm the record true.
>
> The Spirit of my God
>   Hath certified Him mine,
> And all the tokens show'd
>   Infallible, Divine;
> Hereby the pardon'd sinner knows
>   His sins on earth forgiven,
> And thus my Saviour *shows*
>   My name inscribed in Heaven."

Nothing but clearly defined spiritual life, and certain joyfulness in God, could be expected in the experience of people whom Charles Wesley taught to sing of salvation. Some of his hymns on a present sense of pardon and adoption are most jubilant, and have furnished means of expression to happy souls without number. Under one date, in the narrative of the ill-fated Patagonian Mission, it is recorded: "Found Mr. Williams and Badcock to-day very ill, the latter beyond the hope of recovery. He is most patient, and leaning upon his Saviour." John Badcock was a pious Cornish fisherman—a Methodist. He had devoted himself to the mission as a boatman, and now he was lying in the "Speedwell's cabin, in Terra del Fuego, starving to death, and awaiting his end." At eleven o'clock that same evening he died. As the end approached, he requested Mr. Williams to join him in singing a hymn, and having repeated it, he then sang the whole with a loud voice:—

> Arise, my soul, arise,
>   Skake off thy guilty fears ;
> The bleeding sacrifice
>   In my behalf appears;
> Before the throne my Surety stands,
> My name is written on His hands.
>
> He ever lives above
>   For me to intercede,
> His all-redeeming love,
>   His precious blood to plead ;
> His blood atoned for all our race,
> And sprinkles now the throne of grace.
>
> Five bleeding wounds He bears,
>   Received on *Calvary;*
> They pour effectual prayers,
>   They strongly speak for me.
> Forgive him, O forgive! they cry—
> Nor let that ransom'd sinner die !
>
> The Father hears Him pray,
>   His dear Anointed One;
> He cannot turn away,
>   The presence of His Son;
> His Spirit answers to the blood,
> And tells me I am born of God.
>
> My God is reconcil'd,
>   His pardoning voice I hear,
> He owns me for His child,
>   I can no longer fear;
> With confidence I now draw nigh,
> And Father, Abba, Father, cry !

His voice fell, and in a few minutes after his spirit joined the choir above.

Charles Wesley was as warm and correct in most of his songs about entire holiness as he was about the evidence of adoption, though he was somewhat tinged now and then by the morbid mysticism to which he had shown an early proneness.

An aged Congregational minister and his wife, who resided in a retired North Devon village, used occasionally to visit a Methodist home in which the services of the Society were held. While they were sitting in the parlour one day, the old man took up a book from the table, and, looking at the title, threw it down, saying, "There is no such thing in this world." It was John Wesley's "Plain Account of Christian Perfection." The old lady took up the rejected volume, and opening about the middle (as those who are not habitual readers are apt to do), her eye fell upon a passage which arrested her. "Why," said she, "is this perfection? Why, John?" she cried to her husband, "is this perfection? Listen to this. I have enjoyed this for many years. Is this perfection, as the Methodists call it? Then I have got it! It is possible in this world, John. It is to be enjoyed even here. This blessing God gives me from day to day. Listen to this"; and she read from one of Wesley's pages. Her husband was silent, until the Methodist mother of the house opened an old hymn-book, and asked whether they could not both join her in singing a hymn of Charles Wesley's, which expressed the same spiritual experience as John Wesley described, in a manner more tuneful, but not with less precision. "Can't you sing this from your hearts?" said she, repeating verse after verse.

"Yes," they said.

"Well, then, we will sing together." And the good Methodist woman, and the old veteran theologue, and his venerable, warm-hearted wife, sang :—

> O for a heart to praise my God,
> A heart from sin set free,
> A heart that always feels Thy blood,
> So freely spilt for me!

A heart resign'd, submissive, meek,
  My dear Redeemer's throne,
Where only Christ is heard to speak,
  Where Jesus reigns alone.

A humble, lowly, contrite heart,
  Believing, true, and clean,
Which neither life nor death can part
  From Him that dwells within.

A heart in every thought renew'd,
  And full of love Divine,
Perfect, and right, and pure, and good,
  A copy, Lord, of Thine.

Thy tender heart is still the same,
  And melts at human woe;
Jesus, for Thee distrest I am,
  I want Thy love to know.

My heart, Thou know'st, can never rest
  Till Thou create my peace,
Till of my *Eden* repossest,
  From self and sin I cease.

Fruit of Thy gracious lips, on me
  Bestow that peace unknown,
The hidden manna, and the tree
  Of life, and the white stone.

Thy nature, dearest Lord, impart,
  Come quickly from above,
Write Thy new name upon my heart,
  Thy new, best name of Love.

Among the multitude of Charles Wesley's hymns, the one hundred and sixty-six spiritual songs which he issued under the title of "Hymns for a Family" have a peculiar charm. A venerable man, remarkable for his brilliant wit and cultured taste, and to whom Charles Wesley was known, once said of these hymns:—"Such accumulated strength and beauty of expression, in presenting the daily wants, pains, trials, and embarrassments of a family to the God of the families of the whole earth, surely never before was presented to the suffering children of men." The poet's experience of family life, and his inspiration as a family hymnist, may be said to have begun on his own wedding-day. He remained single nearly forty years, that he might give himself to evangelical work; but then there arose the thought,

"How know I whether it is best for me to marry or not? Certainly, better now than later; and, if not now, what security have I that it shall not be then? It should be now or not at all." While this thought was working, he found his way to a small village in Wales, where he was welcomed by a respectable and pious family. There was a lovable daughter who arrested his heart. He consulted his brother and his friend Perronet, pondered much, waited, expressed himself to God in hymns, and, at last, proposed, was accepted, and ere long came the wedding-day. What a wedding-day was that! "Saturday, April 8, 1749," says the bridegroom—

> "Sweet day! so cool, so calm, so bright,
> The bridal of the earth and sky.

"Not a cloud was to be seen from morning till night. I rose at four; spent three hours and a half in prayer, or singing, with my brother, with Sally, with Beck. At eight I led My Sally to church. Her father, sisters, Lady Rudd, Grace Bowen, Betty Williams, and, I think, Billy Tucker and Mr. James, were all the persons present. At the church door, I thought of the prophecy of a jealous friend, 'that if we were even at the church door to be married, she was sure, by revelation, that we could get no farther.' We both smiled at the remembrance. We got farther. Mr. Gwynne gave her to me (under God); my brother joined our hands. It was a most solemn season of love! Never had I more of the Divine presence at the sacrament. My brother gave out the following hymn—

> "Come, Thou everlasting Lord,
> By our trembling hearts adored;
> Come, Thou heaven-descended Guest,
> Bidden to our marriage feast;
> Jesus, in the midst appear,
> Present with Thy followers here,
> Grant us the peculiar grace,
> Show us all Thy smiling face.

Now the veil of sin withdraw,
Fill our souls with sacred awe,
Awe that dares not speak or move,
Deepest awe of humble love;
Love that doth its Lord descry,
Ever intimately nigh,
Sees the Invisible in Thee,
Fulness of the Deity.

Let on us Thy Spirit rest,
Enter each devoted breast,
Still with Thy disciples sit,
Still Thy works of grace repeat:
Now the former wonder show,
Manifest Thy power below,
Earthly souls exalt, refine,
Turn the water into wine.

Stop the hurrying spirit's haste,
Change the soul's ignoble taste;
Nature into grace improve,
Earthly into heavenly love:
Raise our hearts to things on high,
To our Bridegroom in the sky,
Heaven our hope and highest aim,
Mystic marriage of the Lamb.

O might each obtain a share
Of the pure enjoyments there!
Now, in rapturous surprise,
Drink the wine of Paradise;
Cry, amidst the rich repast,
Thou hast given the best at last,
Wine that cheers the Host above,
The best wine of perfect love.

"He then prayed over us in strong faith. We walked back to the house, and joined again in prayer. Prayer and thanksgiving was our whole employment. We were cheerful without mirth, serious without sadness. . . . My brother seemed the happiest person among us."

Family life begun in this style promised to be a life of family prayer and praise amidst all the vicissitudes to which it would necessarily be subject. And so it was. About four months after marriage we have an insight into the household order of the Methodist hymnist. On a September morning there was a record made. "We had family prayer at eight. I began the New Testament. I passed the hour of retirement in the garden, and was melted into tears by the Divine goodness." On the next day but one: "I rose with my partner at four," says the husband. "Both under the Word, and among the select band, we were constrained to cry after Jesus with mighty prayers and tears. We sang this hymn in my family—

> "God of faithful *Abraham*, hear
>   His feeble son and Thine,
> In Thy glorious power appear,
>   And bless my just design.
> Lo! I come to serve Thy will,
>   All Thy blessed will to prove;
> Fired with patriarchal zeal,
>   And pure primeval love.
>
> Me and mine I fain would give
>   A sacrifice to Thee,
> By the ancient model live,
>   The true simplicity;
> Walk as in my Maker's sight,
>   Free from worldly guile and care,
> Praise my innocent delight,
>   And all my business prayer.
>
> Whom to me Thy goodness lends
>   Till life's last gasp is o'er,
> Servants, relatives, and friends,
>   I promise to restore;
> All shall on Thy side appear,
>   All shall in Thy service join,
> Principled with godly fear,
>   And worshippers Divine.
>
> Them, as much as lies in me,
>   I will through grace persuade;
> Seize and turn their souls to Thee,
>   For whom their souls were made;
> Bring them to th' atoning blood
>   (Blood that speaks a world forgiven),
> Make them serious, wise, and good,
>   And train them up for Heaven."

No family, however holy, is free from affliction; and, indeed, sometimes the weight of affliction seems to rise with the measure of holiness. Charles Wesley's wife was attacked with small-pox, and, for a time, the disease threatened to be fatal. Nevertheless, she was spared; but while yet trembling under the effects of the trial, their first-born, a boy of uncommon promise, was cut down by the disease which had weakened and sadly changed the mother. The poet felt the stroke keenly, but maintained his power to minister comfort to his wife. He wrote a hymn for her, entitled "A Mother's Act of Resignation on the Death of a Child." It was sweet, soothing, and full of spiritual comfort. Its influence has hushed many a sorrowing mother since then.

"In the course of pastoral visitation," says a city pastor, "I found my way once into a cellar, in one of the crowded suburbs of Manchester. There was a comparatively young couple, in miserable poverty, partly resulting from the affliction of the husband, who was evidently dying of consumption. He sat in moody silence over a low fire. The poor mother was on the end of a ragged couch, bending in anguish over the dead body of her child, which looked beautiful in death. I sat down, and tried first to console the woman; then, turning to the father, I said, 'There is bright and certain hope, you know, in the departure of a little one.' 'I *don't* know,' was the curt reply. 'That is my library,' he added, pointing to a shelf, on which there were a few volumes of modern infidel authors; 'you may know now what my opinions are.' 'Yes; but you know,' I replied, 'that such opinions are no help to you now. They don't supply you with one comfortable answer to the cravings of your soul as it is moving towards another world. You want something to clear your prospects. I am not going to dispute with you; but I want to tell you that I have a wife, and that we have known what it is to lose a child—a lovely boy. My wife was reconciled to her loss by thinking of what her child had gained; and she was helped to this sweet resignation by a hymn which I read to her. It was a hymn written by a bereaved father like you and I, and written for the comfort of his wife under the trial, such as your wife is now suffering. Come, I will give you the hymn as well as I can.' I then rehearsed Charles Wesley's verses, known as 'A Mother's Act of Resignation.'

> "Peace, my heart, be calm, be still,
> Subject to my Father's will;
> God in Jesus reconciled
> Calls for *His* beloved child;
> Who on me Himself bestow'd
> Claims the purchase of His blood.
>
> Child of prayer, by grace Divine,
> Him I willingly resign,
> Through his last convulsive throes
> Borne into the true repose,
> Borne into the world above,
> Glorious world of light and love!
>
> Through the purple fountain brought,
> To his Saviour's bosom caught,
> Him in the pure mantle clad,
> In the milk-white robe array'd,
> Follower of the Lamb I see;
> See the joy prepared for me.
>
> Lord, for this alone I stay;
> Fit me for eternal day;
> Then Thou wilt receive Thy bride
> To the souls beatified,
> Then with all Thy saints I meet,
> Then my rapture is complete.

"As I closed I saw the poor mother's face gathering calmness, and there was a tear in the dying father's eye. I invited them to join me in prayer. There were sobs; and on rising from our knees, the woman's face had brightened, though wet with tears. 'I will follow my child to Jesus,' said she. 'And so will I,' sobbed the broken-hearted man. The end was happy. The wife found a heavenly Friend under her greater bereavement. She lost her husband; but the sceptic was saved."

Charles Wesley had deep and universal sympathy with suffering human nature. His loving heart led him into all accessible scenes of mental conflict, bodily anguish, and perplexity and pressure of circumstances. Indeed, he was more marvellously gifted with insight into varieties of human misery and trial than any other of our hymnists. And it is to his experience as a sufferer in Christian fellowship with sufferers that we owe some of his most touching, consoling, and richly fruitful hymns.

It is refreshing in this mortal life to fall in, here and there, with a pilgrim so anointed with the heavenly Spirit as to rise fairly above the sufferings incidental to human nature. One such instance can never be forgotten. The man, a strong robust man, had rheumatic fever in a cottage-chamber under the shelter of Mount Edgecumbe, at the mouth of the Tamar. He was a good man. For several days there had been an agonising struggle to "let Patience have her perfect work." But, when his pastor called, he was really triumphing with "joy unspeakable and full of glory;" literally "glorying in tribulation." There were shouts and songs by turns. As the visitor entered the room, he was singing, with a clear, ringing voice—

> This is the straight and royal way
>   That leads us to the courts above;
> Here let me ever, ever stay,
>   Till, on the wings of perfect love,
> I take my last triumphant flight
> From *Calvary's* to *Sion's* height!

In answer to a question as to his spiritual comfort, he said, "I had been lying here for several days, suffering as I never thought my poor body could suffer. But for some time the Lord kept me in patience, until I began to feel that I could not stand it much longer. I was afraid that, after all, I should murmur against the Lord. 'Lord,' said I, 'keep me!' Then I began to think about the martyrs. I had read that some of them sang in the fire; and I said, 'Why shouldn't I sing?' It seemed to be said to me, 'You are not a martyr, and you can't look for such joy.' 'I am not a martyr,' said I to myself, 'though I am called to suffer perhaps as much as if I had been in the fire. My God who appoints me to this suffering is the same God as called the martyrs to theirs. He is as able to help me as He was to help them, and as willing too. Lord,' I cried, 'give me the victory! I believe Thou wilt   Thou dost!' I shouted, for in a moment there was a light upon my soul, a joy within me that was like heaven in the midst of my pain. The pain was not gone, but it was over-balanced by the joy; and I said, 'If the joy cannot stay without the pain, let the pain stay, Lord!' Then I knew what that verse meant, and could sing it—

> "When my sorrows most increase,
>   Let Thy strongest joys be given:
> Jesus, come with my distress,
>   And agony is heaven.

Nor have I been able ever since to keep myself from singing another hymn—that beautiful hymn for 'believers suffering.' Come, sing it with me." The song was raised; and never did that hymn appear so full of holy music, deep meaning, and heavenly refreshment, as when the pastor's voice fell into harmony with that of the agonising man, in singing:—

> Saviour of all, what hast Thou done,
>   What hast Thou suffer'd on the tree?
> Why didst Thou groan Thy mortal groan,
>   Obedient unto death for me?
> The mystery of Thy passion show,
> The end of all Thy griefs below.
>
> Thy soul for sin an offering made,
>   Hath clear'd this guilty soul of mine;
> Thou hast for me a ransom paid,
>   To change my human to Divine
> To cleanse from all iniquity
> And make the sinner all like Thee.
>
> Pardon, and grace, and heaven to buy,
>   My bleeding *Sacrifice* expired:
> But didst Thou not, my *Pattern*, die,
>   That, by Thy glorious Spirit fired,
> Faithful to death I might endure,
> And make the crown by suffering sure?
>
> Thou didst the meek example leave,
>   That I might in Thy footsteps tread;
> Might, like the Man of Sorrows, grieve,
>   And groan, and bow with Thee my head;
> The dying in my body bear,
> And all Thy state of suffering share.
>
> Thy every perfect servant, Lord,
>   Shall as his patient Master be,
> To all Thy inward life restored,
>   And outwardly conform'd to Thee;
> Out of Thy grave the saint shall rise
> And grasp, through death, the glorious prize.

> This is the straight and royal way
>   That leads us to the courts above;
> Here let me ever, ever stay,
>   Till, on the wings of perfect love,
> I take my last triumphant flight
> From *Calvary's* to *Sion's* height!

The spirit in which this sufferer sang must have been the spirit of many among the suffering early Methodists; and from some of the hymns which Charles Wesley wrote "For the Brotherhood," it is evident that in their "brotherhood" of suffering they often mutually stimulated one another to "rejoice in tribulation." This is strikingly shown in the fact that, from the beginning, and for many generations, one favourite hymn was always swelling from the harmonised voices of the societies. It was a joy which might make one forget the distress of life, to hear the old Methodists sing:—

> Come on, my partners in distress,
> My comrades through the wilderness,
>   Who still your bodies feel;
> Awhile forget your griefs and fears,
> And look beyond the vale of tears
>   To that celestial hill.
>
> Beyond the bounds of time and space,
> Look forward to that happy place,
>   The saints' secure abode;
> On Faith's strong eagle pinions rise,
> And force your passage to the skies,
>   And scale the mount of God.
>
> See where the Lamb in glory stands,
> Encircled with His radiant bands,
>   And join th' angelic powers;
> For all that height of glorious bliss
> Our everlasting portion is,
>   And all that Heaven is ours.
>
> Who suffer for our Master here,
> We shall before His face appear,
>   And by His side sit down:
> To patient faith the prize is sure,
> And all that to the end endure
>   The Cross shall wear the crown.

> Thrice blessèd bliss-inspiring hope!
> It lifts the fainting spirits up,
>   It brings to life the dead:
> Our conflicts here shall soon be past,
> And you and I ascend at last,
>   Triumphant with our Head.
>
> That great mysterious Deity
> We soon with open face shall see:
>   The beatific sight
> Shall fill the heavenly courts with praise,
> And wide diffuse the golden blaze
>   Of everlasting light.
>
> The Father shining on His throne,
> The glorious co-eternal Son,
>   The Spirit One and Seven,
> Conspire our rapture to complete;
> And, lo! we fall before His feet,
>   And silence heightens Heaven.
>
> In hope of that ecstatic pause,
> Jesus, we now sustain Thy cross,
>   And at Thy footstool fall,
> Till Thou our hidden life reveal,
> Till Thou our ravished spirits fill,
>   And God is all in all.

Every verse of this exalted and exalting song has had its numerous illustrations from year to year—now one, and now another—now in this scene of life, and now in that. A young man who was born blind in Tewkesbury, rather more than fifty years ago, was brought from spiritual darkness to light while a mere boy. He soon became known as a kind of walking Bible, and had stored his sanctified memory with at least five hundred of Wesley's hymns. Of these, one seemed to be ever rising in his soul with saving freshness, as, in his seventeenth year, he neared the land of immortal light. He had a foresight of his last mortal day, as that day approached; and when it came, a day of suffering, his father said, "O, my dear boy, you are called to suffer!" He answered, in a song—

> Who suffer with our Master here,
> We shall before His face appear,
> And by His side sit down.

And, after a moment or two, the blind, but happy young saint sang again—

> Thrice blessèd bliss-inspiring hope!
> It lifts the fainting spirits up,
> It brings to life the dead:
> Our conflicts here shall soon be past,
> And you and I ascend at last
> Triumphant with our Head.

It was his last song as a sufferer. His head fell on the pillow, and his final "conflict" was "past."

Another young devoted Methodist passed away from Ebchester once, with portions of the same hymn on her lips. A witness says:—"On the day of her departure, sitting in her chair, as she had done for some time both night and day, she broke out into singing with a loud voice. Her friends were startled, for she had spoken but in whispers for several weeks. They gathered around and listened. She kept up her songs for half an hour, and then requested that they would sing with her—

> Come on, my partners in distress.

She struck in here and there with great earnestness, now and then saying, "Sing on!—sing on!" They sang—

> To patient faith the prize is sure,
> And all who to the end endure
> The Cross shall wear the crown.

She asked for the window to be opened, and, as if talking to spiritual attendants, she said, "Stay, stay; I am not yet ready!" Her sight now became dim, and she called us to come nearer to her, and sing on—

> Tha great mysterious Deity
> We soon with open face shall see:
> The beatific sight
> Shall fill the heavenly courts with praise,
> And wide diffuse the golden blaze
> Of everlasting light.

She waved her hands, and sang with deep feeling—

> And, lo! we fall before His feet
> And silence heightens Heaven.

There was silence; she was at the feet of her visible Master.

There are some hymns which make themselves felt at once—as soon as they fall on the ear—hymns which never lose their freshness and power, never cease to widen their influence until they are acknowledged as things of life, by all souls, in all lands, and over all seas. Such a hymn is one of Charles Wesley's—a hymn whose music is kept up on both sides of the Atlantic. It has often been on the lips of departing saints in this land, when, as an old saint said, "They see their native land in the distance, and the sea intervening—a sea which none is able to cross unless borne by the Cross of Christ." One hymn has often helped them to "cling to the wood and cross the sea." Thousands have been aided as the venerable John Lomas, of Manchester, was, who, after more than forty years of Methodist pilgrimage and faithful service, came to the flood in 1854, "clung to the Cross, and crossed the sea," uttering his favourite hymn with his latest breath—

> Jesus, Lover of my soul,
> Let me to Thy bosom fly,
> While the nearer waters roll,
> While the tempest still is high.

This was the first verse of the Methodist poet's immortal hymn to be sung "In Temptation." Its living music has passed over the great waters into the land where the poet put forth the first efforts of his genius as a hymnist. Dr. Belcher says, "Mr. Gould mentions the influence of singing on the mind of a minister in Vermont. He was a stranger called to officiate for a Sabbath in a cold and dreary church. When he entered it, the wind howled, and loose clapboards and windows clattered. The pulpit stood high above the first floor. There was no stove, but a few persons in the church, and those few beating their hands and feet to keep them from freezing. He asked himself, 'Can I preach? Of what use can it be? What shall I do? Can these two or three singers in the gallery sing the words if I read a hymn? I concluded to make a trial, and read—

> "Jesus, Lover of my soul,
>   Let me to Thy bosom fly,
> While the nearer waters roll,
>   While the tempest still is high:
> Hide me, O my Saviour, hide,
>   Till the storm of life is past;
> Safe into the haven guide,
>   O, receive my soul at last.
>
> Other refuge have I none,
>   Hangs my helpless soul on Thee:
> Leave, ah! leave me not alone,
>   Still support and comfort me.
> All my trust on Thee is stay'd,
>   All my help from Thee I bring;
> Cover my defenceless head
>   With the shadow of Thy wing.
>
> Wilt Thou not regard my call?
>   Wilt Thou not accept my prayer?
> Lo! I sink, I faint, I fall—
>   Lo! on Thee I cast my care:
> Reach me out Thy gracious hand!
>   While I of Thy strength receive,
> Hoping against hope I stand,
>   Dying, and, behold, I live!
>
> Thou, O Christ, art all I want,
>   More than all in Thee I find;
> Raise the fallen, cheer the faint,
>   Heal the sick and lead the blind.
> Just and holy is Thy name,
>   I am all unrighteousness;
> False and full of sin I am,
>   Thou art full of truth and grace.
>
> Plenteous grace with Thee is found,
>   Grace to cover all my sin:
> Let the healing streams abound,
>   Make and keep me pure within.
> Thou of life the Fountain art;
>   Freely let me take of Thee,
> Spring Thou up within my heart,
>   Rise to all eternity!

"They commenced, and the sound of a single female voice has followed me with an indescribable, pleasing sensation ever since, and probably will while I live. The voice, intonation, articulation, and expression seemed to me perfect. I was warmed inside and out, and for the time was lost in rapture. I had heard of the individual and voice before; but hearing it in this dreary situation made it doubly grateful. Never did I preach with more satisfaction to myself. And from this incident I learned a lesson: never to be discouraged from unfavourable appearances, but, where duty calls, go to work cheerfully, without wavering.'"

The beautiful hymn, thus sung with such power and happy effect in Vermont, has served in other instances to melt American life into the life of Heaven.

A fine, intelligent Virginian young man, while residing in the West, became an infidel and a blasphemer of the name of God. From this state he was delivered by reading the work of Soame Jenyns; but, while he acquiesced in the truth of revelation, he yet did not feel its power. He was attacked by a lingering and fatal disease, which led him to reflection and prayer, but often made it difficult for him to converse. Three Christian friends sometimes visited him, to beguile the tedious hours by singing. They one day entered his room, and, almost without any previous remarks, began the hymn—

> There is a fountain filled with blood;

And then—

> The voice of free grace cries escape to the mountain.

He then said to them, "There is nothing I so much delight to hear as the first hymn you ever sang to me—

> "Jesus, Lover of my soul."

They began to sing it to the tune *Martyn*, and found the solemnity which had reigned in the little circle while singing the two former hymns began to be changed to weeping. They struck the touching strains of the second stanza, and the weeping became loud; the heart of him who had reviled Christ broke, and they feared that to sing the remaining stanzas would be more than he could bear. When singing in his room after this, he said, "I don't think I shall ever hear

"Jesus, Lover of my soul,

sung again. It so excites me that my poor body cannot bear it."

That "poor body" now waits for the awakening. The rescued spirit has met the author of his loved hymn, and in the same Paradise sings, without weeping—

Jesus, Lover of my soul!

CHAPTER VII.

OTHER PSALMS FROM THE BROTHERS IN SONG.

> Spirit of God! whose glory once o'erhung
>   A throne, the Ark's dread cherubim between,
>   So let Thy presence brood, though now unseen,
> O'er those two powers by whom the harp is strung—
> Feeling and thought!—till the rekindled chords
> Give the long-buried tone back to immortal words.

WHILE the Wesleys met all varieties in the condition and experience of religious societies by their successive issue of hymns for Christian "Fasts and Festivals," for "Times of Trouble and Persecution," on "Preparation for Death," and "Funeral Hymns," "Hymns for Families," for "Christian Friends," and for "Children," "Hymns on God's Everlasting Love," and for all "Seekers of Redemption," there never was any startling or stirring event in the natural world or in national history, but they were ready with suitable songs, turning all passing circumstances to account for the good of the people. They gave out hymns for "Times of Tumult," "On the Earthquake," "Hymns for the Nation," hymns of "Intercession" in times of danger to the throne and to English hearths and altars. Charles produced hymns faster and more freely than John could select, or abridge, or revise. The pre-eminent Methodist poet was too full of feeling to allow his pen to cease its action: that ready pen, so vigorous, so free, so easy, so full of fine English harmonies, so happily consecrated to Christian holiness. The poet never lacked inventive power; but in his eagerness to press everything into his Master's cause, he would now and then seize the expressed thoughts of others, and weave them into the texture of his devotional verse; ever, with beautiful simplicity and unselfishness, pouring out his soul in numbers to edify the Church, and to supply Christian homes and congregations with suitable songs for all occasions and through all times.

There is a beautiful entry in his journal marking the birth-time of one of his hymns of triumph in tribulation. "May 20th, 1743, I got once more to our dear colliers of Wednesbury.... I preached in a garden on the first words I met (1 Cor. ii. 1). While I spoke of His sufferings, He looked upon us, and made us look upon Him and mourn. ... I saw a piece of ground given us by a Dissenter to build a preaching-house upon, and consecrated it by a hymn. I walked with many of the brethren to Walsall, singing. We were received with the old complaint: 'Behold, they that turn the world upside down are come here also.' I walked through the town amidst the noisy greetings of our enemies, and stood on the steps of the market-house. An host of men were laid against us. The floods lifted up their voices and raged horribly. I opened the book on the first presented words, Acts xx. 24. The street was full of fierce Ephesian beasts (the principal man setting them on), who roared, and shouted, and threw stones incessantly. Many struck without hurting me. I besought them in calm love to be reconciled to God in Christ. While I was departing, a stream of ruffians was suffered to bear me from the steps. I rose, and having given the blessing, was beat down again. So the third time, when we had returned thanks to the God of our salvation. I then from the steps bade them depart in peace, and walked quietly through the thickest of the rioters. They reviled us, but had no commission to touch a hair of our heads."

The song of "Thanks to the God of our Salvation" broke for the first time like trumpet-notes of victory:—

Worship, and thanks, and blessing,
  And strength ascribe to Jesus !
    Jesus alone
    Defends His own
  When earth and hell oppress us.
Jesus with joy we witness,
  Almighty to deliver;
    Our seal set to
    That God is true,
  And reigns a King for ever.

Omnipotent Redeemer,
  Our ransom'd souls adore Thee,
    Our Saviour Thou,
    We find it now,
  And give Thee all the glory.
We sing Thine arm unshorten'd,
  Brought through our sore temptation,
    With heart and voice
    In Thee rejoice,
  The God of our salvation.

Thine arm hath safely brought us
  A way no more expected
    Than when Thy sheep
    Pass'd through the deep,
  By crystal walls protected.
Thy glory was our reward,
  Thine hand our lives did cover,
    And we, even we,
    Have walked the sea
  And march'd triumphant over.

Thy works we now acknowledge,
  Thy wondrous loving-kindness,
    Which held Thine own
    By means unknown,
  And smote our foes with blindness.
By Satan's host surrounded,
  Thou didst with patience arm us,
    But would'st not give
    The *Syrians* leave,
  Or Sodom's sons, to harm us.

Safe as devoted Peter,
  Betwixt the soldiers sleeping,
    Like sheep we lay,
    To wolves a prey,
  Yet still in Jesus' keeping.

> Thou from th' infernal *Herod*
>   And Jewish expectation
>   Hath set us free;
>   All praise to Thee,
>   O God of our salvation!
> The world and Satan's malice,
>   Thou, Jesus, hast confounded;
>   And by Thy grace,
>   With' songs of praise,
>   Our happy souls resounded.
> Accepting our deliverance,
>   We triumph in Thy favour,
>   And for the love
>   Which now we prove
>   Shall praise Thy name for ever.

This song became a favourite form of thanksgiving amidst the joys of deliverance from persecutors. A few months later the evangelizing poet was again among the Wednesbury lions. "I found the brethren assembled, standing fast in one mind and spirit, in nothing terrified by their adversaries. The word given me for them was, 'Watch ye, stand fast in the faith, quit yourselves like men, be strong.' Jesus was in the midst, and covered us with a covering of His Spirit. Never was I before in so primitive an assembly. We sang praises lustily and with a good courage, and could all set our seal to the truth of our Lord's saying, 'Blessed are they that are persecuted for righteousness' sake.' We laid down and slept, and rose up again, for the Lord sustained us. We assembled before day to sing hymns to Christ as God. And again, there, before day, was the victorious shout—

> "Worship, and thanks, and blessing."

A series of alarming events opened with earthquake shocks in London during 1750. The genius of the heavenly-minded poet seems to have risen with the occasion. "This morning," he tells his brother, "at a quarter after five, we had another shock of an earthquake, far more violent than that of February 8th. I was just repeating my text, when it shook the Foundry so violently that we all expected it to fall upon our heads. A great cry followed from the women and children. I immediately cried out, 'Therefore will we not fear, though the earth be moved, and the hills be carried into the midst of the sea; for the Lord of Hosts is with us; the God of Jacob is our refuge.' He filled my heart with faith, and my mouth with words, shaking their souls as well as their bodies." The tokens of judgment followed each other until 1756. There were fears of invasion, and the kingdom was kept in painful excitement. John Wesley made his appeal to his countrymen in "Serious Thoughts" about the Lisbon earthquake. "How many hundred thousand men," says he, "have been swept away by war, in Europe only, within half a century! How many thousands, within little more than this, hath the earth opened her mouth and swallowed up! . . . Is there not a God that judges the world? and is He now making inquisition for blood? . . . It has been the opinion of many that even this nation has not been without some marks of God's displeasure. Has not war been let loose even within our own land, so that London itself felt the alarm? Has not a pestilential sickness broken in upon our cattle, and, in many parts, left not one of them alive? And, although the earth does not yet open in England or Ireland, has it not shook and reeled to and fro like a drunken man? and that not in one or two places only, but almost from one end of the kingdom to the other?"

At the same time, amidst the "rumours of wars," Charles Wesley went up and down faithfully, warning the guilty, and singing with the faithful in hope of final victory. "At Nottingham I warned them," he says, "of the impending judgments. . . . My subject, both at night and in the morning, was, 'I will bring the third part through the fire.' It was a time of solemn rejoicing." On October 8, 1756, he was in company with his friend, the saintly Grimshaw, of Haworth. His record is: "We spent an hour in intercession for the Church and nation. I exhorted the many persons present to continue instant in prayer, and mark the answer and the end." After another week, he tells us:—" I preached a second time at Haworth (Mr. Grimshaw reading prayers), from Psalm xlvi. 8. My mouth was open to declare the approaching judgments, and the glory which shall follow, when the Lord is exalted in all the earth. . . . After an hour's interval we met again, as many as the church walls would contain, but twice the number stood without till the prayers were over. Then I mounted a scaffold, and, lifting up my eyes, saw the fields white unto harvest. We had prayed for a fair day, and had the petitions we asked. The churchyard, which will hold thousands, was quite covered. God gave me a voice to reach them all. I warned them of those things which shall come to pass, and warmly pressed them to private, family, and public prayer; enlarged on the glorious consequences thereof, even deliverance from the last plagues, and standing before the Son of Man. I concluded and began again, for it was an accepted time. I do not remember when my mouth has been more opened, or my heart more enlarged."

It was amidst excitements, labours, and triumphs of faith like these that the consecrated powers of the happy poet rose into their grandest flights; and amid the darkling surroundings of the hymnist, his voice swells with the more impressive and awe-inspiring majesty, as he sings:—

> Righteous God, whose vengeful vials
>   All our fears and thoughts exceed,
> Big with woes and fiery trials,
>   Hanging, bursting o'er our head:
> While Thou visitest the nations,
>   Thy selected people spare,
> Arm our cautioned souls with patience,
>   Fill our humbled hearts with prayer.
>
> If Thy dreadful controversy
>   With all flesh is now begun,
> In Thy wrath remember mercy,
>   Mercy first and last be shown;
> Plead Thy cause with sword and fire,
>   Shake us till the curse remove,
> Till Thou com'st, the world's Desire,
>   Conquering all with sovereign love.

> By the signals of Thy coming
>   Soon, we know, Thou wilt appear,
> Evil with Thy breath consuming,
>   Setting up Thy kingdom here:
> Thy last heavenly revelation
>   These tremendous plagues forerun,
> Judgment ushers in salvation,
>   Seats Thee on Thy glorious Throne.
>
> Earth unhinged, as from her basis,
>   Owns her great Restorer nigh,
> Plunged in complicate distresses,
>   Poor distracted sinners cry:
> Men, their instant doom deploring,
>   Faint beneath their fearful load;
> Ocean working, rising, roaring,
>   Claps his hands to meet his God.
>
> Every fresh alarming token
>   More confirms Thy faithful word,
> Nature (for its Lord hath spoken),
>   Must be suddenly restored:
> From this national confusion,
>   From this ruin'd earth and skies,
> See the times of restitution,
>   See the new creation rise!
>
> Vanish then this world of shadows,
>   Pass the former things away;
> Lord, appear, appear to glad us
>   With the dawn of endless day:
> O conclude this mortal story,
>   Throw this universe aside,
> Come, eternal King of Glory,
>   Now descend, and take Thy bride.

John Wesley could sometimes use the pruning knife with good effect, and here and there, by a delicate touch or two, he has certainly improved the beauty of his brother's verses; but some of his rearrangements and efforts at abridgment prove that he was not always to be trusted. Charles's hymn, "After Preaching in a Church," has been unhappily dealt with. John's selection from it is in the "Methodist Hymn Book," beginning with—

> Jesus, the Name high over all;

but the abridgment of the original hymn impairs its strength, breaks its unity, and mars its grandeur. With what clarion-like music Charles's own song rings through the soul, especially when sung with the spirit which fired its author:—

> Jesus, accept the grateful song,
>   My Wisdom and my Might,
> 'Tis Thou hast loosed the stammering tongue,
>   And taught my hands to fight.
>
> Thou, Jesus, Thou my mouth hast been;
>   The weapons of Thy war,
> Mighty through Thee, I pull down sin,
>   And all Thy truth declare.
>
> Not without Thee, my Lord, I am
>   Come up into this place,
> Thy Spirit bade me preach Thy name,
>   And trumpet forth Thy praise.
>
> Thy Spirit gave me utterance now,
>   My soul with strength endued,
> Harden'd to adamant my brow,
>   And arm'd my heart with God.
>
> Thy powerful hand in all I see,
>   Thy wondrous workings own,
> Glory, and strength, and praise to Thee
>   Ascribe, and Thee alone.
>
> Gladly I own the promise true,
>   To all whom Thou dost send,
> " Behold, I always am with you,
>   Your Saviour to the end."
>
> Amen, amen, my God and Lord,
>   If Thou art with me still,
> I still shall speak the Gospel Word,
>   My ministry fulfil.
>
> Thee I shall constantly proclaim,
>   Though earth and hell oppose,
> Bold to confess Thy glorious Name,
>   Before a world of foes.
>
> Jesus, the Name high over all
>   In hell, or earth, or sky,
> Angels and men before it fall,
>   And devils fear and fly.
>
> Jesus, the Name to sinners dear,
>   The Name to sinners given,
> It scatters all their guilty fear,
>   And turns their hell to Heaven.

Balm into wounded spirits it pours,
  And heals the sin-sick mind,
It hearing to the deaf restores,
  And eyesight to the blind.

Jesus the prisoners' fetters breaks,
  And bruises Satan's head,
Power into strengthless souls it speaks,
  And life into the dead.

O that the world might taste and see
  The riches of His grace!
The arms of love that compass me
  Would all mankind embrace.

O that my Jesus' heavenly charms
  Might every bosom move!
Fly sinners, fly into those arms
  Of everlasting love.

The lover of your souls is near,
  Him I to you commend,
Joyful the Bridegroom's voice to hear,
  Who calls a worm His friend.

He hath the bride, and He alone,
  Almighty to redeem,
I only make His mercies known,
  I send you all to Him.

Sinners, behold the Lamb of God!
  On Him your spirits stay;
He bears the universal load,
  He takes your sins away.

His only righteousness I show,
  His saving grace proclaim;
'Tis all my business here below
  To cry, " Behold the Lamb ! '

For this a suffering life I live,
  And reckon all things loss;
For Him my strength, my all I give,
  And glory in His cross.

I spend myself that you may know
  The Lord our righteousness;
That Christ in you may live and grow,
  I joyfully decrease.

Gladly I hasten to decay,
  My life I freely spend,
And languish for the welcome day
  When all my toil shall end.

> Happy if, with my latest breath,
> I might but gasp His name,
> Preach Him to all, and cry, in death,
> "Behold, behold the Lamb!"

The poet's joy seems to be all the more exalted because he once more preached the Gospel "in a church." The joy of dispensing the Gospel in such a place was, perhaps, becoming rare. As the thoughts and feelings unfold themselves from verse to verse, the poet's passion glows with greater warmth and rushes on its upward course, flashing with more and more of life, until it passes into a rapt devotion, as near as can be to that of a disembodied soul. How many a saint, both old and young, this hymn has cheered amidst his struggles to maintain his conflict with Satan, and with the latent unbelief of the heart. How many a minister of truth has gathered strength from it in his work of proclaiming his Master. And how many, who are now beholding the Lamb, crossed the Jordan into His presence with the inspiring tones of this hymn on their dying lips.

It has been with thousands as it was with Benjamin Edward Knowles, who, in 1841, fled from Birstal into Paradise. Wasted by consumption, he awaited his Lord's call. The night before his departure was, to his mother, a night of weeping; but seeing her tears, the happy young Christian said, "I can sing—

> "Jesus, the Name to sinners dear,
> The Name to sinners given,
> It scatters all their guilty fear,
> It turns their hell to Heaven!"

With his hand pressing his temples, he said, "O, this poor head! But, mother, it is not crowned with thorns, as His was—

> "Jesus the prisoners' fetters breaks,
> And bruises Satan's head,
> Power into strengthless souls it speaks,
> And life into the dead."

He asked his friends to cheer his last hours with singing;

and from the sound of those voices he passed within hearing of those who "sing the Lamb in hymns above."

To sing her favourite hymns was the life's joy of Elizabeth Lee, of Nottingham. She sank finally into mortal weakness when only eighteen years of age; but her passion still ruled her soul when her bodily powers refused to lift themselves in song. She burst into tears when thus made painfully sensible of her weakness, but with all her remaining strength cried—

> Happy if, with my latest breath,
> I might but gasp His name,
> Preach Him to all, and cry, in death,
> "Behold, behold the Lamb!"

"I shall go home to-day," said she; and as the evening came, she went into the presence of Him whose name hallowed her last mortal breath.

During the fatal illness of the late Rev. Robert Wood, some allusion was made to the "Great Exhibition" of 1851, in which he had always shown a great interest. A hope was expressed that in a short time his desire to visit it might be gratified. He shook his head and said, "No, I shall never see the 'Crystal Palace.' But reach me the Hymn Book, read the 73rd hymn, and you will see that I shall not lose much." That hymn is one of Charles Wesley's grandest effusions. It is among his "Funeral Hymns," but how exultant is its music! All the crystal palaces of earth are comparatively dim to the eye of those who, as "joint heirs with Christ," are "come unto the City of the Living God, the Heavenly Jerusalem," and who can sing, as the old Methodists used to sing :—

> Away with our sorrow and fear!
> We soon shall recover our home;
> The city of saints shall appear,
> The day of eternity come:
> From earth we shall quickly remove,
> And mount to our native abode,
> The house of our Father above,
> The palace of angels and God.

Our mourning is all at an end,
  When raised by the life-giving Word,
We see the new city descend,
  Adorn'd as a bride for her lord;
The city so holy and clean,
  No sorrow can breathe in the air;
No gloom of affliction or sin,
  No shadow of evil is there.

By faith we already behold
  That lovely *Jerusalem* here!
Her walls are of jasper and gold,
  As crystal her buildings are clear :
Immovably founded in grace,
  She stands as she ever hath stood,
And brightly her builder displays,
  And flames with the glory of God.

No need of the sun in that day
  Which never is followed by night,
Where Jesus's beauties display
  A pure and a permanent light;
The Lamb is their light and their sun,
  And, lo! by reflection they shine,
With Jesus ineffably one,
  And bright in effulgence Divine.

The saints in His presence receive
  Their great and eternal reward,
In Jesus, in Heaven they live,
  They reign in the smile of their Lord
The flame of angelical love
  Is kindled at Jesus's face,
And all the enjoyment above
  Consists in the rapturous gaze,

Some years ago, Mr. Brewster, a Methodist missionary, when travelling in Newfoundland, turned aside to visit an old settler whom he had heard of. He found him living with his daughters; and soon the talk turned upon the old country.

"And have you ever seen the Shannon?" said the old man; "and do ye know the river?"

"No," was the reply, "I don't know it."

The old man then told the story, how he had left the banks of the Shannon, and how, when all were sad and sighing as they parted from their friends, his little wife sang—

> Away with our sorrow and fear!
> We soon shall recover our home;

and then, how they started on their journey; how, when they came to the shore and were ready to embark and to leave the old country behind, the tears came, but his little wife sang again—

> Away with our sorrow and fear!

They dried their tears and were soon on board, By-and-by a storm came, and all was terror. The captain and sailors gave up all for lost. But the little wife, she was happy, and began to sing—

> Away with our sorrow and fear!

The captain plucked up courage; the sailors went to the pumps; the storm passed, and all was well. They landed at length; and when they found themselves left in the wilderness, their hearts were sad and heavy; but the little wife, she sang again—

> Away with our sorrow and fear!

and then they bestirred themselves; built their hut, and soon got over their difficulties. "But," said the old man, "and have you never seen the Shannon?"

The family grew up; and then "the little wife" sickened, and while they were around her dying bed, the hymn she loved so well was on her lips, and she died singing—

> Away with our sorrow and fear!
> We soon shall recover our home.

Among Charles Wesley's "Christian Festival Songs," his hymns for Whit Sunday are instinct with the true spirit of Pentecostal times. They have kept their life; and many times since his day have they served, not merely as celebrations of repeated Pentecosts, but as the happy means of kindling the spiritual devotion which always precedes the Holy Ghost's descent, and prepares the waiting multitude for His richer blessings. A Cornish minister, once visiting an old Methodist woman, who, in her ninety-sixth year, was waiting for her Lord in a cottage near the famous Gwennap Pit, said to the venerable pilgrim, "Well, Whit Monday comes next week when the preaching will be in 'the Pit'; you will not be able to join us, but your heart will sing with us, I am sure, though your voice will not be there."

"Ah," said the old saint, "I shall never forget the singing we had there on the Whit Monday after my conversion, which was in the great revival of 1814. O, what a Pentecost that was! 'Twas all over the country! and when the time for preaching in the Pit came round, O, what a gathering of happy souls there was! O, how the singing went up!"

"What did you sing—can you remember?"

"Yes, I can tell the first lines; but the hymn is in that little book in the window; the first lines were—

> "Father of everlasting grace,
> Thy goodness and Thy truth we praise,
> Thy goodness and Thy truth we prove."

"Shall I read the whole hymn to you?"

"O, I should like to hear it all once more. It will freshen up my soul, and make me feel as if I were converted over again, as if another Pentecost shower was coming down."

"Now then, this is the hymn :—

> "Father of everlasting grace,
> Thy goodness and Thy truth we praise,
> Thy goodness and Thy truth we prove :
> Thou hast, in honour of Thy Son,
> The Gift unspeakable sent down,
> The Spirit of life, and power, and love :
>
> Thou hast the Prophecy fulfill'd,
> The grand original compact seal'd
> For which Thy word and oath were join'd :
> The Promise to our fallen head,
> To every child of *Adam* made,
> Is now pour'd out on all mankind.
>
> The purchas'd Comforter *is* given,
> For Jesus is return'd to Heaven,
> To claim and then the Grace impart ;
> Our day of Pentecost is come,
> And God vouchsafes to fix His home
> In every poor expecting heart.

Father, on Thee whoever call
Confess Thy promise is for all,
  While everyone that asks receives,
Receives the Gift, and Giver too,
And witnesses that Thou art true,
  And in Thy Spirit walks, and lives.

Not to a single age confined,
For every soul of man design'd,
  O God, we now that Spirit claim:
To us the Holy Ghost impart,
Breathe Him into our panting heart,
  Thou hear'st us ask in Jesus' name.

Send us the Spirit of Thy Son,
To make the depths of Godhead known,
  To make us share the life Divine;
Send Him the sprinkled blood t' apply,
Send Him our souls to sanctify,
  And shew and seal us ever Thine.

So shall we pray and never cease,
So shall we thankfully confess
  Thy wisdom, truth, and power, and love;
With joy unspeakable adore,
And bless and praise Thee evermore,
  And serve Thee like Thy hosts above.

Till, added to that heavenly choir,
We raise our songs of triumph higher,
  And praise Thee in a bolder strain;
Out-soar the first-born seraph's flight,
And sing, with all our friends in light,
  Thine everlasting love to man."

"Bless the Lord! Bless the Lord!" cried the dear old woman. "Yes, that's it. It was such a blessed time when thousands of us took up those words,—

"And bless and praise Thee evermore,
  And serve Thee like Thy hosts above!

And then again, O my dear man, it seems to me as if I hear it now—

"Out-soar the first-born seraph's flight,
And sing, with all our friends in light,
  Thine everlasting love to man!

"Bless the Lord! 'Tis 'everlasting love!' 'everlasting love!'"

A lady writing on "The Wesleys and their Hymns," says, with truth and beauty :—" It was for the founders of Methodism to diverge so far from the staid nonconforming type of Watts and Doddridge as to show that the modern hymn was capable not only of paraphrasing Bible truths, but of uttering the most joyous as well as the most agonised feelings of the heart; to combine devout spiritual thought and personal experience with professed reverence and adoration, and so to bring the spirit of the old Hebrew poetry into harmony with the brighter songs of the New Covenant as to blend in one the voices of all who are by faith the children of faithful Abraham."

Charles Wesley's "Select Psalms" afford many rich and beautiful illustrations of these remarks. Of the hundred and nine Psalms which he rendered into English verse, there are some gems of superior value, while in most of the others he manages with great skill to unite faithfulness, strength, pathos, unction, and pleasantly appropriate music of expression. Who can chant his version of the sixth Psalm without feeling that his soul is brought into such tuneful sympathy with the plaintive, suffering, yet trustful " Singer of Israel " that the Hebrew Psalmist and the English Christian become one in the spirit of their song ?—

> In Thine utmost indignation,
>   Do not, Lord, Thine own chastise ;
> In Thine infinite compassion,
>   Hear my feeble, dying cries !
> Hear me, for my bones are vex'd ;
>   O forgive, forgive my sin !
> Sick I am, and sore perplex'd,
>   All a troubled sea within !
>
> Lord, how long shall Thy displeasure
>   Lengthen out my punishment ?
> O correct me, but in measure !
>   Let Thy yearning heart relent :
> Sinner's Friend, and kind Receiver,
>   Cast my sins behind Thy back :
> Turn me now, my soul deliver,
>   Save me for Thy mercy's sake !

O reverse the mortal sentence!
  Let me live to sing Thy grace:
After death is no repentance;
  Dead, I cannot sing Thy praise.
Spent I am with endless groaning,
  Wash with tears my sleepless bed;
Weary of my fruitless moaning,
  Send my gasping spirit aid!

Shorn of all my strength, I languish;
  See, I faint beneath my load!
Faint through deep distress and anguish,
  Faint into the arms of God!
God, to me, in great compassion,
  Doth a gracious token give;
I shall see His whole salvation,
  I shall all His love retrieve.

Leave me, then, to Jesus leave me,
  Ye that gloried in my fall!
Jesus' arms shall still receive me,
  He hath heard my mournful call:
He hath answered my petition,
  Show'd Himself the sinner's Friend,
Saved me in my lost condition,
  He shall save me to the end.

By a world of foes surrounded,
  By the hellish sons of night,
I shall see them all confounded,
  Put to everlasting flight.
He who hath my sins forgiven,
  All my sins to death shall doom,
Hence as by a whirlwind driven:—
  Come, my utmost Saviour, come!

Charles Wesley's "Short Hymns on Select Passages of the Holy Scriptures" were originally issued in 1762. In their modern form of publication they fill nearly five volumes. The poet spent many years, in later life, revising and enlarging them. This was a work of love, as the compositions were evidently favourites with him. The passages on which these hymns are founded range from the beginning of Genesis to the end of Revelation. His brother John says, "Many of these are little, if any, inferior to his former poems, having the same justness and strength of thought, with the same beauty of expression; yea, the same keenness of wit on proper occasions, as bright and piercing as ever." On a second reading, he adds, " Some are bad ; some mean ; some most excellently good. They give the true sense of Scripture, always in good English, generally in good verse." The poet's familiarity with Patristic modes of interpreting Scripture is evident in some of his hymns, and not unfrequently serves to give distinctive beauty to his verses. He confesses, too, his obligation to more modern commentators, whose thoughts he seems to set to music in a way that perhaps the grave authors could not anticipate. " Many of the thoughts," he says, " are borrowed from Mr. Henry's ' Commentary,' Dr. Gell on the Pentateuch, and Bengelius on the New Testament." So voluminous a poet, dealing with such a range of themes, could scarcely be free from inequality. But his pages are fairly begemmed with well-cut jewels. How happy is the turn he gives to Israel's prayer for Joseph's children, " And let my name be named on them "—

> My name be on the children ? No :
> But mark them, Lord, with Thine :
> Let all the heavenly offspring know
> By characters Divine ;
> Partakers of Thy nature make,
> Partakers of Thy Son,
> And then the heirs of glory take
> To Thine eternal throne.

Sentences in the sacred page which some would pass over, he is, now and then, arrested by ; and under his eye they become instinct with instruction and wisdom. The cry from the sons of the prophets, when they had tasted the poisoned pottage, " There is death in the pot ! " is made to suggest a beautiful lesson,—

> Death in the pot ! 'tis always there,
> The bane of all our food,
> When we partake it without fear,
> Without an eye to God ;
> Unless He sanctify the meat,
> And bless us from the sky,
> Unless we to his His glory eat,
> Our souls by eating die.

Job's melancholy wail, " I have made my bed in the darkness," is brought to melt into exquisite harmony of Christian hope :—

> Ready for my earthen bed,
> Let me rest my fainting head,
> Welcome life's expected close,
> Sink in permanent repose :
> Jesus' blood to which I fly
> Doth my conscience purify,
> Signs my weary soul's release,
> Bids me now depart in peace.
>
> Thus do I my bed prepare;
> O, how soft, when Christ is there,
> There my breathless Saviour laid,
> Turns it to a spicy bed ;
> Resting in His power to save,
> Looking now beyond the grave,
> Calm I lay my body down,
> Rise to an immortal crown.

Nothing can be more touching and instructive than the poet's efforts to maintain the exercise of his genius, as, in his latter days, he found his wings growing faint. Recollections of his own intense youthful zeal during the earlier times of his ministry, the readiness and impetuous force with which he pursued his holy calling, are followed by feelings of growing weakness, and deepening convictions that his period of action is passing into the season of calm submission, final weakness, and mental decay. A characteristic letter from his brother John affords an insight into his condition towards the close of his career. " Dear Brother,— You must go out every day, or die. Do not die to save charges. You certainly need not want anything as long as I live." The venerable poet, in his weakness, turned his thoughts on the Lord's address to Peter : " When thou wast young, thou girdedst thyself, and walkedst whither thou wouldest : but when thou shalt be old, thou shalt stretch forth thy hands, and another shall gird thee, and carry thee whither thou wouldest not." And catching inspiration, he gave utterance to his hymn entitled " A Retrospect."

When young, and full of sanguine hope,
    And warm in my first love,
My spirit's loins I girded up,
    And sought the things above;
Swift on the wings of active zeal
    With Jesus' message flew,
O'erjoy'd with all my heart and will
    My Master's work to do.

Freely where'er I would I went
    Through wisdom's pleasant ways,
Happy to spend and to be spent
    In ministering His grace:
I found no want of will or power,
    In love's sweet task employ'd,
And put forth every day and hour
    My utmost strength for God.

As strong and glorying in my might,
    I drew the two-edged sword,
Valiant against a troop to fight
    The battles of the Lord;
I scorn'd the multitude to dread,
    Rush'd on with full career,
And aim'd at each opposer's head,
    And smote off many an ear.

But now, enervated by age,
    I feel my fierceness gone,
And nature's powers no more engage
    To prop the Saviour's throne:
My total impotence I see,
    For help on Jesus call,
And stretch my feeble hands to Thee,
    Thou workest all in all.

Thy captive, Lord, myself I yield,
    As purely passive clay;
Thy holy will be all fulfill'd,
    Constraining mine t' obey:
My passions by Thy Spirit bind,
    And, govern'd by Thy Word,
I'll suffer all the woes design'd
    To make me like my Lord.

Wholly at Thy dispose I am,
    No longer at my own,
All self-activity disclaim,
    And move in God alone:
Transport, do what Thou wilt with me,
    A few more evil days,
But bear me safe through all to see
    My dear Redeemer's face.

The name of Charles Wesley can scarcely be mentioned without a thought about one hymn in which his hallowed genius rises even above itself. "Dr. Watts," John Wesley says, "did not scruple to say that that single poem, 'Wrestling Jacob,' was worth all the verses he himself had written." "Its wonderful conciseness," says Mr. John Kirk, with critical justness, "yet perfect and finished picturing of the scene on the Transjordanic hills, beyond the deep defile where the Jabbok, as its name implies, wrestles with the mountains through which it descends to the Jordan. The dramatic form, so singular in hymnic composition, shadowing forth the action of the conversation; the great force of its thoroughly English expression; the complete finish and rhythm of its verse; its straightforward ease without any straining at elegance; and the minuteness and general beauty of its application of the narrative, have won the commendations of all competent critics." The theme of this hymn was a favourite theme of the author's preaching. At Kingswood, on May 24, 1741, he says, "I preached on Jacob wrestling for the blessing. Many then, I believe, took hold on His strength, and will not let Him go till He bless them and tell them His name." Soon after he preached with similar effect in Cardiff. After the publication of the hymn, the power of his preaching seemed to grow. In London, June, 1744, he writes, "I preached on wrestling Jacob, and a glorious time it was. Many wept with the angel, and made supplication, and were encouraged to wait upon the Lord continually." And so again, again, and again at Bristol and Dublin. One would like to have heard the powerful preacher on those occasions give out his own hymn; to have seen the people as they kindled under its musical power and unction; and to have heard the ring and swell of their voices as they sang together—

> Come, O thou Traveller unknown,
> Whom still I hold, but cannot see,
> My company before is gone,
> And I am left alone with Thee;
> With Thee all night I mean to stay,
> And wrestle till the break of day.

I need not tell Thee who I am,
  My misery or sin declare,
Thyself has called me by my name,
  Look on Thy hands and read it there;
But who, I ask Thee, who art Thou?
Tell me Thy name, and tell me now.

In vain Thou strugglest to get free,
  I never will unloose my hold;
Art Thou the Man that died for me?
  The secret of Thy love unfold;
Wrestling, I will not let Thee go
Till I Thy name, Thy nature know.

Wilt Thou not yet to me reveal
  Thy new unutterable name?
Tell me, I still beseech Thee, tell;
  To know it now resolved I am;
Wrestling, I will not let Thee go
Till I Thy name, Thy nature know.

'Tis all in vain to hold Thy tongue,
  Or touch the hollow of my thigh;
Though every sinew be unstrung,
  Out of my arms Thou shalt not fly;
Wrestling, I will not let Thee go
Till I Thy name, Thy nature know.

What though my shrinking flesh complain,
  And murmur to contend so long,
I rise superior to my pain,
  When I am weak then I am strong;
And when my all of strength shall fail,
I shall with the God-man prevail.

My strength is gone, my nature dies,
  I sink beneath Thy weighty hand,
Faint to revive, and fall to rise;
  I fall, and yet by faith I stand—
I stand, and will not let Thee go
Till I Thy name, Thy nature know.

Yield to me now, for I am weak,
  But confident in self-despair;
Speak to my heart, in blessings speak,
  Be conquer'd by my instant prayer:
Speak, or Thou never hence shalt move,
And tell me if Thy name is Love?

'Tis Love! 'tis Love! Thou diedst for me;
  I hear Thy whisper in my heart;
The morning breaks, the shadows flee,
  Pure Universal Love Thou art;
To me, to all Thy bowels move—
  Thy nature and Thy name is Love.

My prayer hath power with God; the grace
  Unspeakable I now receive;
Through faith I see Thee face to face—
  I see Thee face to face and live;
In vain I have not wept and strove;
  Thy nature and Thy name is Love.

I know Thee, Saviour, who Thou art—
  Jesus, the feeble sinner's Friend;
Nor wilt Thou with the night depart,
  But stay and love me to the end;
Thy mercies never shall remove—
  Thy nature and Thy name is Love.

The Sun of Righteousness on me
  Hath rose with healing in His wings;
Wither'd my nature's strength, from Thee
  My soul its life and succour brings;
My help is all laid up above—
  Thy nature and Thy name is Love.

Contented now upon my thigh
  I halt, till life's short journey end;
All helplessness, all weakness, I
  On Thee alone for strength depend;
Nor have I power from Thee to move—
  Thy nature and Thy name is Love.

Lame as I am, I take the prey,
  Hell, earth, and sin with ease o'ercome;
I leap for joy, pursue my way,
  And as a bounding hart fly home,
Through all eternity to prove
  Thy nature and Thy name is Love.

The saintly poet had, at length, his own last wrestling. He left his brother John to give out the favourite hymn, and thousands whom he had taught to wrestle remained behind to sing of Israel's victory. About three weeks after his entrance into rest, his bereaved brother was at Bolton, in Lancashire. "I preached in the evening," says the veteran, "in one of the most elegant houses in the kingdom; and to one of the liveliest congregations. And this I must avow, there is not such a set of singers in any of the Methodist congregations in the three kingdoms. There cannot be, for we have near a hundred such trebles, boys and girls, selected out of our Sunday School and accurately taught, as are not found together in any chapel, cathedral, or music-room within the four seas. Besides the spirit with which they all sing, the beauty of many of them so suits the melody that I defy any to exceed it; except the singing of angels in our Father's house."

Mr. Haslam, of Markland Hill, near Bolton, was a Methodist of John Wesley's stamp, and a member of that "liveliest congregation" whose singing was so enjoyed by the venerable preacher. "Mr. Haslam told me," says one, "many years ago, while upon his death-bed, that he was present in the chapel at Ridgeway Gates when Mr. Wesley visited Bolton, just after his brother Charles's death. The venerable man, himself eighty-five years of age, commenced the service in the usual way, with singing and prayer; for the second hymn he selected 'Wrestling Jacob,' and gave out the first verse with peculiar emphasis. When he came to the words,

"My company before is gone,
And I am left alone with Thee,

his emotion became uncontrollable, and he burst right out into a flood of tears, and sat down in the pulpit, covering his face with both hands. The effect upon the congregation was such as might be expected—the people ceased to sing, and, in many parts of the chapel, sat down weeping and sobbing aloud. The congregation was very large, Saturday night though it was; and, said Mr. Haslam, the place was like a Bochim. After a while, Mr. Wesley recovered himself, arose, and gave out the lines again; 'and then there was such singing,' said the good old man, 'as I never heard before; it seemed as if the sound would lift the roof off the building.' A sermon followed, remarkable for the holy influence attending the delivery, and the deep impressions it seemed to make on the multitude of people."

That multitude of singers has passed away. The aged weeping preacher has had all tears wiped from his eyes. He is in immortal companionship with his brother poet. The brothers are gone from our sight, but they are brothers in song still. Their songs remain to be taken up by generations of happy singers on earth; while they "rest from their labour, and their works do follow them."

CHAPTER VIII.

CLERICAL SONG-MASTERS.

> He came to earth :—From eldest years,
>   A long and bright array
> Of prophet-bards and patriarch-seers
>   Proclaimed the glorious day :
> The light of Heaven in every breast,
>   Its fire on every lip,
> In tuneful chorus on they prest,
>   A goodly fellowship.

WHAT varieties of mighty but sweet life-giving influence may spring in combination from one small source, to unfold and spread themselves for ever and ever! It is so in material nature; and so in the region of Divine Providence and Grace. These outflowings of power and influence for good in human life are prepared and arranged and timed by the same ruling Wisdom and Rectitude as "appointed the ordinances of heaven and earth." The secret processes of their preparation are unobservable by man :

> Deep in unfathomable mines
>   Of never-failing skill,
> He treasures up His bright designs,
>   And works His sovereign will.

And even when they first spring into human sight, it proves impossible for us to foresee or anticipate the modes or results of their expansion,—

> Blind unbelief is sure to err,
>   And scan His work in vain :
> God is His own interpreter,
>   And He will make it plain.

CLERICAL SONG-MASTERS.

In the course of the year 1733 a few young collegians of Oxon might be found together, of an evening, in the chamber of one of the Fellows of Lincoln College. For a time they were on their knees at prayer. Then they joined at their evening meal, and after supper, one who seemed to be the acknowledged leader, having in his very face something of authority, happily mingled with modest gentleness, would conduct the friendly intercourse by reading, and eliciting expressions of thought from his companions, guiding them in a review of their day's work, and aiding in the formation of pious and charitable plans for the future. This was "The Holy Club," as the mass of candidates for "Holy Orders" called them with a devout sneer. The "chief manager" was John Wesley, followed with fraternal deference by his cheerful, open-hearted, free, and practically kind brother Charles. There was the high-toned ritualistic William Clayton; the philosophic and dreamy John Gambold; the stirring and successful evangelist, Benjamin Ingham; the contemplative and graceful James Hervey; the eloquent, apostolic George Whitfield; and a few others of like spirit, though of less prominent name. For some time, these variously gifted human spirits held together in a combination which appeared almost too sacred to be dissolved by circumstances. They might be looked at as

> A band of love, a threefold cord,
> Which never could be broke.

But the band was melted by and by. The powers and influences that had risen to the light in beautiful oneness began to fall off into different channels, and the members of the Holy Club went, each his own way, to fill his own place, and to do his own work. One fact courts deep attention. Those of the band whose memory has proved most lasting, and whose work has been most permanently fruitful, added to their powers and graces as evangelists, teachers, and pastors, the gifts of poetic genius and taste. So that while, by the ministry of the Word, they were the means of gathering multitudes into Christ's fold, they were prepared for guiding the devotions of the flock, and for providing them with "psalms and hymns and spiritual songs." Though some of them ceased, at length, to follow the old leader of the club, John Wesley, and even loosened their fellowship with his genial brother Charles, yet, as one after another they realized the spirituality and freedom of true believers in Christ, they continued to preach the same Saviour, and to consecrate their powers of song to the service of the same Lord. They were Methodists still, as, for a time, they still had the honour of being reviled as Methodist parsons; while in spirit, and by the law of original Methodist brotherhood, they were fairly classed among the "Poets of Methodism." When the Wesleys broke away from the Moravians, or were excluded from those among whom they first found the joy of salvation by faith in Christ alone, their friend and brother, Gambold, chose Moravian fellowship, and eventually became a Moravian bishop. His poetic genius, however, still kept identity with early Methodism in its first issue of "Hymns and Sacred Poems;" and for several generations the Methodists learnt to quote his lines as recommended for their devout use by John and Charles Wesley.

A preacher, one of early Methodism's "sons of thunder," seems to have stored his mind with poetic forms of expression suitable to every emergency. On one occasion, Gambold's poem, "To a Friend in Love," furnished the timely passage. There had been one of those remarkable visitations of the Blessed Spirit which some modern Methodists, as well as worldlings, fail to understand, and during the graciously repeated Pentecost, large numbers of both young and old people were made partakers of Divine life, under marvellous manifestations of spiritual power. When the excitement had been somewhat hushed, the preacher alluded to, on coming out from one of the public services, saw one or two of the young men walking off, each in company with a young woman. "There! see!" said he, "the courting devil is got among them already!"

> What art thou, Love? thou strange mysterious ill,
> Whom none aright can know, though all can feel.
> From careless sloth thy dull existence flows,
> And feeds the fountain whence itself arose;
> Silent its waves with baleful influence roll,
> Damp the young mind, and sink th' aspiring soul,
> Poison its virtues, all its powers restrain,
> And blast the promise of the future man.

It may be questioned whether Gambold, or the Wesleys, who published his verses, intended them to be applied with indiscriminate harshness. If, however, the earlier Methodists excelled their nominal descendants in intensity of spiritual devotion, they were certainly less guarded against ascetic extremes. The philosophic turn of Gambold's mind, his doubtful style of thought, his mystic dreaminess, and his tendency to unreal views of human life, all fitted him for a place among the Moravians of his day, rather than among the Methodists. His genius is seen at its best, and he is most agreeable as a poet, when he sings on "The Mystery of Life":—

> So many years I've seen the sun,
>   And call'd these eyes and hands my own,
> A thousand little acts I've done,
>   And childhood have and manhood known:
> O what is Life? and this dull round
> To tread, why was a spirit bound?
>
> So many airy draughts and lines,
>   And warm excursions of the mind,
> Have fill'd my soul with great designs,
>   While practice grovell'd far behind:
> O what is Thought? and where withdraw
> The glories which my fancy saw?
>
> So many tender joys and woes
>   Have on my quivering soul had power;
> Plain life with heightening passion rose,
>   The boast or burden of their hour:
> O what is all we feel? why fled
> Those pains and pleasures o'er my head?
>
> So many human souls divine,
>   Some at one interview display'd,
> Some oft and freely mix'd with mine,
>   In lasting bonds my heart have laid:
> O what is Friendship? why imprest
> On my weak, wretched, dying breast?

> So many wondrous gleams of light,
>   And gentle ardours from above,
> Have made me sit, like seraph bright,
>   Some moments on a throne of love :
> O what is Virtue? Why had I,
> Who am so low, a taste so high?
>
> Ere long, when Sovereign Wisdom wills,
>   My soul on unknown paths shall tread,
> And strangely leave, who strangely fills
>   This frame, and waft me to the dead:
> O what is Death?—'tis life's last shore,
> When vanities are vain no more;
> Where all pursuits their goal obtain,
> And life is all retouch'd again;
> Where in their bright result shall rise
> Thoughts, virtues, friendships, griefs, and joys.

The life which seemed such a mystery to Gambold was begun in South Wales. He was the son of an English clergyman; was born at Puncheston, in Pembrokeshire, April 10, 1711. His home training was truly Christian, and his preparation for college was complete when he was fifteen. At that age he entered Christchurch, Oxford; and there came into association with the Wesleys. Though that association was afterwards broken, the poet's beautiful testimony to its gracious influence on him remains on record. "Mr. Wesley, late of Lincoln College, has been the instrument of so much good to me that I shall never forget him. Could I remember as I ought, it would have very near the same effect as if he was still present; for a conversation so unreserved as his, so zealous in engaging his friends to every 'instance of Christian piety,' has left nothing now to be said, nothing but what occurs to us as often as we are disposed to remember him impartially. . . . . One time he was in fear that I had taken up notions that were not safe, and pursued my spiritual improvement in an erroneous, because inactive, way. So he came over and stayed with me near a week. He accosted me with the utmost softness, condoled with me the incumbrances of my constitution, heard all I had to say, endeavoured to pick out my meaning, and yielded to me as far as he could. I never saw more humility in him than at this time. It was enough to cool the warmest imaginations that swell an overweening heart." It was, indeed, his custom to humble himself most before the proud,—not to reproach them; but in a way of secret intercession to procure their pardon. While the poet was still in the border-land between Methodism and Moravianism, he wrote a drama, "The Martyrdom of Ignatius: a Tragedy." It was never intended for the stage. Nor, as a written drama, would it be a model; but, as a poem, it is valuable as a thoughtful embodiment of those religious views which formed the permanent point of unity between him and Methodism. He was one with the Wesleys in "holding the Head," and in maintaining the principle of salvation by faith in Christ alone, His own experience constrained him to sing—

> Come hither ye whom from an evil world
> The name of Jesus draws! You count him sweet,
> And great, and mighty, by that glimm'ring light
> Your novice minds have gained. You venerate
> That full acquaintance and that vital union
> Whereby the faithful know Him; and to this
> You now aspire. But can you then let go
> Your manly wisdom, and become as babes,
> To learn new maxims and the mind of Christ?
> Can you forsake your former ease and sunshine,
> To associate with a poor afflicted people,
> The scorn of all mankind? Can you the weight
> Of your whole souls, with all your hopes of God,
> Rest on a long-past action; and that such
> As your Lord's mystic but opprobrious death?

Both the poet and his old friend Wesley had learnt to forsake all for Christ and His afflicted people. They were ever one in this. What a pity that Wesley should ever have had to say, "Who but Count Zinzendorf could have separated such friends as we were? Shall we never meet again?" Never in this world! While the one was proving how a well-filled life of active zeal can permanently bless the entire world, the other, for seventeen years, timorously bore the honours of episcopacy; by turns preaching and retiring into stillness; doing homage with voice and pen to "The most dear and paternal heart of Papa Zinzendorf," and singing the brethren's fond doggrel hymns. He sang at the Lord's Supper, weak and wasted with suffering, five days before his departure, and was heard to say, as his sufferings closed, "Dear Saviour, remember my poor name, and come, come soon!" He quitted his mortal pastorate on September 13th, 1771, having written his own epitaph, and left it as one of his purest poetic gems:—

> Ask not who ended here his span;
> His name, reproach, and praise was man.
> Did no great deeds adorn his course?
> No deed of his but show'd him worse.
> One thing was great, which God supplied,
> He suffer'd human life—and died.
> What points of knowledge did he gain?
> That life was sacred all—and vain;
> Sacred how high, and vain how low,
> He knew not here, but died to know.

Gambold, during the college days of the Holy Club, writes to a friend respecting one of their number, "He is a man of surprising greatness of soul; and if you look for his virtues, you will not be able to discover them one by one, but you will see that he walks before God with a reverence and alacrity which includes them all." This was James Hervey, a native of Hardingstone, near Northampton. Like several of his devoted companions, he was the son of a country parson. His connection with the little Methodist knot in Oxford began in 1733, when he was about nineteen. "His character and career" have been described as "a contrast to those of Whitfield and Wesley. He was essentially contemplative; they were eminently practical. His mission was to sanctify the sentimentalism of the day. In him the breath of life did not blow, as in Wesley, in a strong, steady, all-pervading current; or, as in Whitfield, like a rushing and restless wind; but in a gentle zephyr, toying with the tresses of the trees, shaking the petals of the flowers and grasses of the grave, yet the minister of convalescence, and the messenger of peace." He may be classed among the poets of Methodism; his soul's life was poetic; his prose was poetry; the flowing harmony of his distinctive style showed the native tunefulness of his genius. The few remains of his versified fragments awaken regret that he should have yielded to the scrupulous feeling once expressed to his sister—" I am so far from carrying on my versifying designs that I heartily wish I had never conceived any; that those lines I sent to my cousin had either never been made, or that I had never heard them commended. Pride and vanity are foolish and unreasonable in dust and ashes, and, which is worse, odious and detestable before infinite perfection and infinite power." His hallowed talent might furnish the church with many a spiritual song. One of his has often been sung; and continues graciously to aid devout observers of the inspired wise man's counsel, " In all thy ways acknowledge Him."

> Since all the downward tracts of time
> God's watchful eye surveys,
> Oh, who so wise to choose our lot,
> And regulate our ways?
>
> Since none can doubt His equal love,
> Unmeasurably kind,
> To His unerring, gracious will,
> Be every wish resigned.
>
> Good when He gives, supremely good,
> Nor less when He denies;
> E'en crosses, from His sovereign hand,
> Are blessings in disguise.

It is his poetic vein that supplied the charm to the pages of "Meditations" which for so many generations aided the devout thought of the Christian multitude. All that is most precious in the memory of Hervey is associated with his early sojourn in the West of England.

"Dear old Hartland!" cried a Western pilgrim, "many fond memories cluster around thee: were it only the memory of the day-dreams, and the tranquillizing thoughts at night, which have come to me in her quiet lanes, and wooded slopes, and seaward tracks, the name of Hartland must ever awake pleasant echoes in my heart. It seems but yesterday since I was rambling down the narrow valley along by the stream which goes onward to the sea, beguiling its way by enticing the pensile woods to whisper responses to its music; or looking at what remains of St. Nectan's Abbey; or mounting the broad steps of the path from the abbey to the parish church, and listening to the local tradition about the tall lord of the manor, who used to take two of the steps at an upward stride on his way to the Sunday Service; or trying to picture the delicate form of Hervey trying to keep up with his friend Orchard, the long-striding saintly master of Hartland Abbey; or calling up the devout poet's description of his retreat. The house is situate in a fine vale. It is an ancient structure, built for the use of religious recluses, and has an antique, grave, and solemn aspect; before it is a neat spot of ground, set apart for the use of a garden enriched with fruits, and beautified with flowers. This leads into a curious sort of artificial wilderness made of elms and limes, planted in rows, cut into form, and uniting their branches. In the midst is a fountain large enough to swim in, and a little engine playing the waters. On each side are arbours for shade; in various parts seats for rest; on the right hand runs, parallel to it, a clear purling brook replenished with trout; on the left a thick grove hanging from the side of a hill; the one serves for a watery mound, the other is a leafy shelter from the north wind, and both, I think, greatly ornamental. This you will say is pleasant; but how unworthy to be compared with those blissful mansions fitting up for the righteous in the Heaven of heavens! I write this in a pleasure-house upon a high cliff, on the very edge of the sea. On one side a vast tract of land extends itself, finely diversified by stately trees, floating corn, and pasturage for cattle. On the other side rolls the great and wide sea. Which way soever I look, I meet with footsteps of the Divine immensity..... I have been about twenty, or twenty-six miles into *Cornwall,* and seen wondrous workmanship of the All-creating God; ragged rocks, roaring seas, frightful precipices, and dreadfully steep hills."

He had gone from Bideford to Kilkhampton, in North Cornwall. That journey has often been enjoyed by others since then. One who has gone over the ground says:—

"Many, many a Sabbath sun has set on Kilkhampton since that evening,

.... Most calm, most bright,

When I jogged into it for the first time, half plaintive, half jubilant, as I saw the people passing the graves of their forefathers on their way to the House of God. I thought of Hervey, when I saw the noble old parish church, whose fine Anglo-Norman doorway still invited the steps of the pilgrim who loves to commune with God amidst the crumbling memorials of departed men. I lingered long before that altar-piece, and turned again and again to gaze on the elaborate monument of Sir Bevil Grenville; feeling as if the ground were the holier because there Hervey conceived the thoughts which, in their embodiment, have improved the hearts of more than one generation." It was with the image of this Grenville monument before his mind that the meditative poet says, "As to such earthly memorials, yet a little while, and they are all obliterated. But as many names as are enrolled 'in the Lamb's Book of Life,' they shall never be blotted out from those annals of eternity."

> Make the extended skies your tomb;
> Let stars record your worth:
> Yet know, vain mortals, all must die,
> As nature's *sickliest birth.*
>
> Would bounteous Heav'n indulge my pray'r,
> I frame a nobler choice;
> Nor living, wish the pompous pile;
> Nor dead regret the loss.
>
> In Thy fair *Book of Life* divine,
> My God, inscribe my name,
> There let it fill some humble place,
> Beneath the slaughter'd Lamb.
>
> Thy saints, while ages roll away,
> In endless fame survive;
> Their glories, o'er the wrongs of time,
> Greatly triumphant, live.

Hervey's health was so far improved by his sojourn at Hartland that he undertook the duties of a curate at Bideford. He began his work there in the enjoyment of that "peace with God through our Lord Jesus Christ" which had inspired his old Oxford companions, too, with power to exercise their saving ministry. Like a true Methodist, he formed a religious society in Bideford, even before Methodism under Wesley had taken its society form. But that which distinguished his life at Bideford was the composition of his "Reflections on a Flower Garden." This work was partly done among the flowers, as he sat in the summer-house of a garden attached to the house in which he lodged. To the pleasant inspirations which came upon him there, we owe the verses which he has modestly thrown into the margin of his page of reflection on the inspired utterance, "All flesh is grass, and all the goodliness thereof is as the flower of the field"; as if he would apologize for associating poetic rhyme with his poetic prose, he says, "The reader will excuse me if I imitate rather than translate Theocritus; if I vary one image, add another, and give a new turn to the whole."

> When snows descend, and robe the fields
> In *winter's* bright array;
> Touch'd by the sun, the lustre fades,
> And weeps itself away.
>
> When *spring* appears; when violets blow,
> And shed a rich perfume;
> How soon the fragrance breathes its last!
> How short-lived is the bloom!
>
> Fresh in the morn, the *summer* rose
> Hangs with'ring ere 'tis noon;
> We scarce enjoy the balmy gift,
> But mourn the pleasure gone.
>
> With gliding fire, an evening star
> Streaks the *autumnal* skies;
> Shook from the sphere, it darts away,
> And, in an instant, dies.
>
> *Such* are the charms that flush the cheek,
> And sparkle in the eye:
> *So*, from the lovely finish'd form,
> The transient graces fly.
>
> To this the *seasons*, as they roll,
> Their attestation bring:
> They warn the fair; their every round
> Confirms the truth I sing.

Hervey was more happy in "Meditations" than in theological discussion. His attachment to John Wesley, as an Oxford Methodist, had been warm and tender. "Shall I call you," said he, once, "my father or my friend? for you have been both to me. I heartily thank you, as for all other favours, so especially for teaching me Hebrew. I have cultivated the study again according to your advice; I never can forget that tender-hearted and generous Fellow of Lincoln who condescended to take such compassionate notice of a poor undergraduate, whom almost everybody contemned, and when no man cared for my soul." After this it is lamentable that difference of theological opinion should result in estrangement. In the year 1755 Hervey issued his greatest book, "Theron and Aspasia"; in which doctrinal truth is wrought up with descriptive passages in the style of his "Meditations." Wesley said of the work, "Most of the grand truths of Christianity are herein explained and proved with great strength and clearness." At the same time, there were a few things to which he took exception, and on which he gave the author his private criticisms. Hervey not only treated his repeated communications with silence, but, under an unhappy influence, prepared an answer to them, and unfortunately submitted his sheets to the inspection of others. On this, Wesley published his strictures. His last letter to Hervey is touching. "O leave not your old well-tried friends! The new are not comparable to them. I speak not this because I am *afraid* of what anyone can say or do to *me*; but I am really concerned for *you*. An evil man has gained the ascendant over you; and has persuaded a dying man, who had shunned it all his life, to enter into controversy as he is stepping into eternity! Put off your armour, my brother! You and I have no moments to spare. Let us employ them all in promoting peace and goodwill among men. And may the peace of God keep your heart and mind in Christ Jesus." Hervey did not live to publish the response to his old friend's criticisms. Six years after he was gone, it was issued in a stealthy way by a disguised hand. Then it was published under the sanction of William Hervey, the deceased's brother. There was a spirit in it unlike that of Wesley's old friend. But Wesley's charity did not fail. "And is this thy voice, my son David?" said he, plaintively. "Is this thy tender, loving, grateful spirit? No; the hand of Joab is in all this." The "generous Fellow of Lincoln" was willing to believe that Hervey's posthumous letters had been tampered with. To believe that the bitter parts of these letters were written by the dying man so close upon his last moments, would be to have the pain of thinking that "good Mr. Hervey died cursing his spiritual father." God forbid! The spiritual father and his tender, loving, contemplative, and poetical son in the Gospel have met long since, in reconciliation and peace.

Hervey became his father's curate at Weston Favel in the year 1743. On his father's departure, he became the rector; and so, for fifteen years of rural retirement, he spent a contemplative, literary, and pastoral life.

> How full of Heaven his latest word!
> "Thou bid'st me now in peace depart;
> For I have known my precious Lord,
>   Have clasped Thee, Saviour, in my heart;
> My eyes Thy glorious joys have seen!"
> He spake, he died, and entered in.

Thus Charles Wesley sang on the news of his old companion's upward flight.

Another member of the original Holy Club, George Whitfield, had kept in closer bonds with Hervey, as having entire sympathy with his doctrinal notions, as well as with his poetic genius and taste. "And is my dear friend indeed about to take his last flight?" he asks, in a letter, just before Hervey's correspondence on earth ceased. "Farewell! my dear, dear friend! F-a-r-e-w-e-ll! Yet a little while and we shall meet

> Where sin, and strife, and sorrow cease,
> And all is love, and joy, and peace!"

The meditative poet, though so strangely fearful of indulging vanity by putting his poetic thoughts into rhyme, had sent hymns occasionally to Whitfield; and these were associated, by the great preacher, with spiritual songs of his own, for purposes of public and social worship. Whitfield had poetry enough in his soul to make hymns now and then; and some of these serve to illustrate his own character; while they have graciously aided many a Christian in expressing devout feeling amidst the discipline of life. Scarcely anything could be more interesting than to find the man who moved up and down shaking the multitudes, and thrilling the consciences of the polite few, by his thundering appeals, occasionally retiring to supply the quiet scenes of social and family life with a peculiarly suitable little psalm. It was something deeply touching to a soul susceptible of home tenderness when, on entering the cottage of a pious young couple, once, the mother was found gently rocking in the nursing chair by the hearth, with her first baby at her breast, and singing in a sweet undertone—

> Lo! from the borders of the grave,
> Jesus, Thy hand is strong to save;
> And thou hast made it bare!
> In deep distress thine handmaid prayed,
> And thou hast interposed Thine aid
> In answer to her prayer.
>
> Oft was her soul depressed with fear,
> As the expected hour drew near,
> And greatly did she mourn;
> But now her gloomy fears depart,
> And smiling mercy melts her heart,
> And former joys return.
>
> Thus favoured in the time of need,
> Her eyes behold her infant seed,
> And praises fill her tongue;
> Her husband of the joy partakes,
> And now his happy soul awakes,
> To join the grateful song.

The same tuneful hymnist had furnished a working-man with devout beguilement of his way to and from his scene of daily toil.

"You seem to be in good spirits, friend," said one who knew the singer. "It is a happy thing for a man who has family cares like yours to be able to march to the music of his own voice when on the way to labour."

"Yes, so it is," was the reply; "we are not without cares, you may be sure, with a family of twelve children, especially as some of them are of an age to make us think about how they will get on in life. But my wife has often said, and so say I, that though we have a home full, there's not one too many. I believe God will bless them and provide for them, and save them; as he did with my father before me, and with me and my wife. But I think my heart is kept up often, when otherwise it would go down, by my way of singing on the road. It is always one song with me, and one prayer. But the Lord, I believe, never gets tired of hearing; and I am sure while I keep from being tired of singing, he'll answer me and bless my children. This is my song:—

> "Thou who a tender parent art,
>   Regard a parent's plea;
> My offspring, with an anxious heart,
>   I now commend to Thee.
>
> My children are my greatest care,
>   A charge which Thou hast given;
> May grace their every heart prepare
>   To seek the joys of Heaven.
>
> If a Centurion could succeed
>   Who for his servant cried,
> Wilt thou refuse to hear me plead
>   For those so near allied?
>
> Almighty Father, God of grace,
>   Be to my children kind;
> Among thy saints give them a place,
>   And leave not one behind."

This was one of Whitfield's hymns, and happy even in Paradise would he be to know that his hymn-making faculty had borne fruit as well as his preaching power.

In the first band of Methodist collegians, none was more earnest and devout than Benjamin Ingham. And when, like his brethren, he at length found the spiritual freedom and power of God's adopted sons, he appeared as "a burning and shining light." There was a saving power in his early ministry which brought multitudes to repentance and peace. Swayed, however, by Moravian influence, he turned, by and by, from his Methodist companions, and became a centre of Moravian action in the North of England. His ministry had been hallowed to several in high rank of life. One of his titled converts was united to him in marriage; and in association with "honourable women," his influence widened its range. Then he separated himself from the Moravians; ordained preachers; and acted as bishop over the large societies which he had formed. Seduced now by the dim uncertainties of the Sandemanian faith, or no faith, he lived to see the results of his labours melt away. He, too, was gifted as a song-master; issued a Hymn Book for the use of "The Societies," and taught his converts how to sing the songs which he and some of his old friends composed. But his Societies, for the most part, broke away from him. His Hymn Book fell into disuse; and his poetic contributions to it passed into oblivion with the voices which used to sing them. The handsome but somewhat erratic evangelist and hymnist finished his career in his native county, Yorkshire, at the age of sixty, not very long after his loving and beloved Lady Ingham had entered into rest.

An interview once with a "widow indeed" is never to be forgotten. It was on a summer afternoon in the country, when everything felt quiet and cool after a refreshing shower. In a retired villa a few miles out of London, amidst fruit-trees, roses, honeysuckles, and jasmine, there was a summer-like drawing-room looking out, on one side, upon a lawn bounded by stately trees and fringed with flowers, and on the other, opening into a little paradise of a conservatory; there the dear old woman sat in a small elbow chair, and looked like a pattern of antique simplicity and gracefulness. She was dressed in a black silk gown, open at the neck so as to show a snowy neckerchief folded and pinned under the chin; with a small neatly fringed, cream-coloured shawl brought over the shoulders and fastened at the waist in front, with its corners falling over a white muslin apron. She wore a mobbed cap, with a modest crown, and a neat close border, yet not so close as to hide a clear, open brow, beautiful still; and it seemed more sweetly beautiful with its silvered locks than when it had been more richly adorned in the prime of womanhood. The charming old saint's face inspired loving veneration—a fair complexion, beautifully touched with fresh colour. Her eyes revealed a spiritual depth of kindness and peace. Her features combined to express power, perspicacity, gentleness, repose, and love. And there was something in the expression which inspired the thought of a transforming process already begun between mortal age and immortal youth. In opinion, taste, and feeling, she was an amiable representative of the last century; used to close and acute observation, well informed, remarkable for good sense, with a tenacious memory, and pleasant command of her native English; she was one of the few gifted elders who can really help a later generation to realize the life of older times. Dear old saint! she soon left her earthly paradise. Not long after an interesting chat with her, in which she seemed more at home with Wesley and Romaine than with the visible things of my own generation, she was called for from above. She had lived nearly a century; but her mind was as clear as an evening in spring. To her faith, unseen things were visible realities. One who sat quietly in her chamber could hear her whispering to her Saviour with holy familiarity. "It was," she said, "as if He talked with me." And then as she lay murmuring a song in sweet undertones, it was asked, "What are you singing—shall I join you?" "I was singing," said she,—

"When I tread the verge of Jordan,
Bid my anxious fears subside;
Death of death, and hell's destruction,
Land me safe on Canaan's side:
Songs of praises
I will ever give to Thee!"

Her love was perfect. Her tuneful spirit caught a higher strain, and took its part in the harmonies of Paradise.

The old saint's last song on earth was the closing verse of William Williams's beautiful hymn, as rendered in English—

> Guide me, O Thou great Jehovah!
>   Pilgrim through this barren land;
> I am weak, but Thou art mighty,
>   Hold me with Thy powerful hand;
>   Bread of heaven,
>   Feed me till I want no more.
>
> Open Thou the crystal fountain,
>   Whence the healing streams do flow:
> Let the fiery, cloudy pillar
>   Lead me all my journey through.
>   Strong Deliverer,
>   Be Thou still my strength and shield.
>
> When I tread the verge of Jordan,
>   Bid my anxious fears subside;
> Death of death, and hell's destruction,
>   Land me safe on Canaan's side:
>   Songs of praises
>   I will ever give to Thee.

Williams has been called "the last Lyric poet of South Wales," in that the utterances of his music were among the last pure, or comparatively incorrupt, specimens of native Welsh song. In his "Hosannah to the Son of David," "Gloria in Excelsis," and other pieces, much poetic originality and force are apparent, even where to an English ear there may be a lack of harmony. The poet is deeply spiritual, warmly devout, and has genius which sometimes flashes and glows. His hymns are often impassioned, and must always be useful and popular as aids to devotion. The poet was born in Carmarthenshire in 1717, and was at first educated for the medical profession; but his deep and alarming convictions of sin, and the jubilant sense of spiritual deliverance which followed, resulted in his consecration to the work of an evangelist. He was ordained a Deacon in the Church of England; but being refused Priest's orders, he was persuaded by Whitfield and the Countess of Huntingdon to become an itinerant minister among the Calvanistic Methodists. He was among the hero pioneers of Methodism in Wales. For just forty-five years he travelled forty or fifty miles a week; zealously preaching, praying, and hymning it up and down among his countrymen. His last illness resulted from intense study, while preparing a volume on

"A View of the Kingdom of Christ." When speech failed, his inward Heaven was still apparent. He had a joyful finish in the year 1791. As a preacher, he was a truly primitive Methodist itinerant; and as a hymnist, he may be properly classed among the early Methodist clerical song-masters. Indeed, among all the early Methodist poets, no one more deeply breathed the true missionary spirit, or more happily anticipated the missionary action and success of Methodism, than did William Williams in his favourite hymn—

> O'er the gloomy hills of darkness,
>   Look, my soul, be still, and gaze:
> All the promises do travail
>   With a glorious day of grace:
>   Blessed jubilee!
>   Let thy glorious morning dawn.
>
> Let the Indian, let the Negro,
>   Let the rude barbarian see
> That divine and glorious conquest
>   Once obtained on Calvary:
>   Let the Gospel
>   Loud resound from pole to pole.
>
> Kingdoms wide, that sit in darkness,
>   Grant them, Lord, Thy glorious light
> And, from eastern coast to western,
>   May the morning chase the night;
>   And Redemption,
>   Freely purchased, win the day.
>
> May the glorious day approaching,
>   On their grossest darkness dawn;
> And the everlasting Gospel
>   Spread abroad Thy holy Name,
>   O'er the borders
>   Of the great Immanuel's land.
>
> Fly abroad, thou mighty Gospel,
>   Win and conquer, never cease;
> May thy lasting wide dominion
>   Multiply and still increase:
>   Sway Thy sceptre,
>   Saviour, all the world around.

CHAPTER IX.

MORE CLERICAL SONG-MASTERS.

> Obedient to His Father's will
>   He came—He lived—He died ;
> And gratulating voices still
>   Before and after cried—
> From ages past descends the lay
>   To ages yet to be,
> Till far its echoes roll away
>   Into eternity.

WHILE the trained staff of College Methodists went out from Oxford, distributing themselves hither and thither, according to their several gifts, each in his own line, and all with a holy purpose, every tuneful genius exercising his talent and all singing to the same Divine Name, they were met almost at every turn by auxiliary forces coming from outlying parishes of the land, prepared, amidst their parochal duties, by the same awakening and sanctifying spirit, for aiding in the diffusion of Gospel truth and grace. Some of them were tuneful souls ; and "every one" of these "had a psalm," as well as a "doctrine," and a "tongue." It seemed as if, from every point, God had chosen evangelists who could be song-masters as well as preachers. The whole land was to be taught to sing as well as to watch and pray. One of the early poetic companions of the Wesleys was in the Methodist Chapel in London one evening when John Wesley was preaching. The preacher saw him, and, without asking consent, announced that he would preach there on the next morning at five o'clock. Wesley had long wished to hear him preach, and now he thought he had secured an opportunity. The preacher, thus announced, would not say nay, lest he might disturb the public worship; and because, too, he could not well seem to oppose Mr. Wesley's wish. At five o'clock in the morning he was in the pulpit, believing, of course, that Wesley would be somewhere among his hearers. After singing and prayer, he said that as he had been called before them contrary to his own wish, his consent to preach never having been asked, and that as he had done violence to his own feelings in deference to Mr. Wesley, and was now expected to preach, weak and inadequate, and unprepared as he was, he should give them the best sermon that ever had been delivered. Then opening the Bible, he read our Lord's Sermon on the Mount, and without a single word of his own in the way of note or comment, he closed the service with singing and prayer. The effect was deeply impressive. This was Edward Perronet, the brother of Charles, and the son of the Reverend Vincent Perronet of Shoreham, between whose family and the Wesleys there were close bonds of Christian affection.

"Mr. Perronet," says Charles Wesley, in a letter to a friend, "joins in hearty love and thanks for your kind concern for him. He grows apace, is bold as a lion, meek as a lamb, and begins to speak in this Name to the hearts of sinners." A proof of his boldness and meekness in the service of his Divine Master was seen on October 15th, 1746. "It was past eight," says Charles Wesley, "when we came to Penkridge.... We were hardly set down when the sons of Belial beset the house, and beat at the door. I ordered it to be set open, and immediately they filled the house. I sat still in the midst of them for half an hour. Edward Perronet I was a little concerned for, lest such rough treatment at his first setting out should daunt him; but he abounded in valour, and was for reasoning with the wild beasts before they had spent any of their violence. He got a deal of abuse thereby, and not a little dirt, both which he took very patiently." A week after this the same journal records, "I set out with Edward Perronet, and reached

Newcastle by Saturday noon. On Sunday my companion was taken ill of a fever. We prayed for him in strong faith, nothing doubting. Monday and Tuesday he grew worse and worse. On Wednesday the small-pox appeared; a favourable sort. Yet on Thursday evening we were much alarmed by the great pain and danger he was in. We had recourse to our never-failing remedy, and received a most remarkable answer to our prayer. The great means of his recovery was the prayer of faith. A fortnight from this recovery, I was sensible," says Wesley, " of the hard frost in riding to Burnup Field; but did not feel it while calling a crowd of sinners to repentance. At my return I found Edward Perronet rejoicing in the love of God." This cheerful spirit of the young poetic evangelist was kept up, for his Methodist friend and companion in travel put a jotting in his note-book about three years afterwards, "I set out for London with my brother and Ned Perronet. We were in perils of robbers, who were abroad, and had robbed many the night before. We commended ourselves to God, and rode over the heath singing." The happy trio could, each and all, write hymns as well as sing them. Perronet's poetic talent was faithfully consecrated to his Divine Master's service, and was so exercised as to furnish holy excitement to a tuneful adoration of the glorified Redeemer from every following generation of spiritual Christians.

About forty years ago, William Dawson, a Methodist local preacher, a farmer, but an original genius, and striking and popular speaker, was preaching in London on the Divine offices of Christ. After setting Him forth as the great Teacher and Priest, he showed Him in His glory as the King of Saints. He proclaimed Him as King in His own right, and then proceeded to the coronation. His ideas were borrowed from scenes familiar to his hearers. The immense procession was marshalled. Then it moved towards the grand temple to place the insignia of royalty upon the King of the universe. So vividly was all this depicted, that those who listened thought they were gazing upon the long line of patriarchs.

kings, prophets, apostles, martyrs, and confessors of every age and clime. They saw the great temple filled; and the grand and solemn act of coronation was about to be performed. By this time the congregation was wrought up to the highest pitch of excitement, and while expecting to hear the pealing anthem rise from the vast assembly upon which they seemed to gaze, the preacher lifted up his voice and sang—

> All hail the power of Jesu's name!
>   Let angels prostrate fall;
> Bring forth the royal diadem,
>   To crown Him Lord of all!

The effect was overwhelming. The crowd sprang to their feet, and sang the hymn with a feeling and a power which seemed to swell higher and higher at every verse. It was a jubilant multitude paying harmonious homage to their Sovereign Lord and Saviour.

Their hymn was that which had first appeared without a name in the "Gospel Magazine" during 1780, and five years afterwards was known to be Edward Perronet's. A volume of "Occasional Verses, Moral and Sacred," had been issued. The poet acknowledged this volume as his own, though it had no author's name. Among the "occasional verses" was the well-known spirited and inspiriting hymn in its original form—

> All hail the power of Jesu's name!
>   Let angels prostrate fall;
> Bring forth the royal diadem,
>   To crown Him Lord of all!
>
> Let high-born seraphs tune the lyre,
>   And as they tune it, fall
> Before His face who tunes their choir,
>   And crown Him Lord of all!
>
> Crown Him, ye morning stars of light,
>   Who fixed this floating ball;
> Now hail the strength of Israel's might,
>   And crown Him Lord of all!
>
> Crown Him, ye martyrs of your God,
>   Who from His altar call:
> Extol the stem of Jesse's rod,
>   And crown Him Lord of all!

> Ye seed of Israel's chosen race,
>   Ye ransom'd of the fall,
> Hail Him who saves you by His grace,
>   And crown Him Lord of all!
>
> Hail Him, ye heirs of David's line,
>   Whom David Lord did call,
> The God incarnate, Man divine,
>   And crown Him Lord of all!
>
> Sinners, whose love can ne'er forget
>   The wormwood and the gall,
> Go, spread your trophies at His feet,
>   And crown Him Lord of all!
>
> Let every tribe and every tongue
>   That bound creation's call,
> Now shout in universal song,
>   The crownèd Lord of all.

Perronet was for a time associated with the Wesleys. His doctrinal views subsequently became more accordant with those of the Countess of Huntingdon; and in connection with her society he laboured at Canterbury, Norwich, and other places, with zeal and success. His notions respecting the Church of England, by and by, became such as he expressed in an anonymous poem called "The Mitre," said to be one of the most cutting satires on the Established Church that was ever written. It was suppressed, after it was in print, by the influence of John Wesley, it is thought, though he himself, in later life, said, "For forty years I have been in doubts concerning that question, 'What obedience is due to heathenish priests and mitred infidels?'" Charles Wesley was shocked at the poem, and declared it to be lacking in wit, and of insufferable dulness; but his feeling as a churchman may have dimmed his sight as a critic. Perronet is severe. But, in his day, there was too much to provoke his satirical genius. He saw what he thought to be reason for saying of the system against which he launched his satire—

> To what compare thy fertile womb?
> A den, a cavern, or the tomb?
>   Why not compare to all?
> Dark, hollow, teeming, large, and deep;
> Or wild, or dead, or fast asleep;
>   And stubborn as a wall.

> Or like a *mart*, high vending place,
> Open for every age and face
>   Who loiter, steal, or range;
> Or like the common road or street,
> Where knaves, as honest, walk or meet,
>   As *Albion's* grand *Exchange*.
>
> In short, thou'rt like a common sewer,
> Filling and emptying—never pure
>   From pride, or pomp, or sin;
> That (speak they truth who say they know),
> With all thy *scavengers* can do,
>   They cannot keep thee clean.

And perhaps some may think that there is appropriateness to modern development as well as sharp poetic point in the prophetic part of his effusion—

> Permit me to foretell thy doom,
> (Which has in *part* been that of *Rome*,)
>   Thou wilt be clean abhorred;
> The *nation* will expose thy shame,
> Cast out as dung thy putrid name,
>   The vengeance of the Lord!
>
> For while her *orders* and her *rules*
> Are made the standard of thy schools,
>   And all besides of blame,
> What other portion canst thou hope,
> But that the wise should give thee up,
>   Her *ape*—without her *name?*

Perronet's feeling towards the Episcopal Church was so far from being agreeable to Lady Huntingdon that his connection with her was severed, and he finished his days as the minister of a dissenting congregation. His mortal course came to an end in Canterbury, January 2nd, 1792, and he departed crying, "Glory to God in the height of His divinity! Glory to God in the depth of His humanity! Glory to God in His all-sufficiency! And into His hands I commend my spirit!"

The contemporary song-masters of early Methodism were so distributed by their Divine Master over the field, that to pass from the place where one sang was soon to come within the sound of another's voice.

One day, in the course of December 1776, two old friends met in the vicarage of a parish in Bedfordshire, not having seen each other for sixteen years. One was a tall man, lusty, but well-formed and of good bearing, agreeable, and somewhat majestic, with a face in which gravity, thoughtfulness, kindness, jollity, and fun were curiously blended into consistent unison; while in his address there was a mingling of solemnity, ease, and tenderness. The other had something more of the ethereal about him. His person was striking. He was evidently one whose looks were often

> Commercing with the skies,
> His rapt soul sitting in his eyes.

Deep thought, language, philosophy, divinity, and holy imagination seemed to speak in his features; while his face appeared to give forth reflections of a spiritual world. There was sweetness even in his manifest languor; and, indeed, to see him and to hear his voice was to receive an impression which disposed the soul to divine pursuits. The last time these two friends met, they were alike in their theological views; now they came together knowing that they had become dissimilar. But doctrinal notions were as nothing before the warmth of their mutual love. Each saluted the other as brother; and they embraced with tears of brotherly affection. "We left them together," says an eye-witness, "for two hours, and when we returned we found them still consulting how they might be useful to the Church of Christ. They were now to part. The worn and languid one showed tokens of decay, and as he did not expect to see the other again, it was the more solemn. They invited us who were present, and also called in the servants, to join them in a parting address to the throne of grace. The invalid prayed fervently and affectionately, and having concluded, all were about to rise from their knees, when the other began to pray in language equally warm and loving with that of his dear brother. Their parting was such as might be expected after such a meeting. Their conduct reminds me of the saying of the persecutors of the primitive Christians—'See how these Christians love one another!'"

This parting scene was in the vicarage of Everton, and the two friends were the vicar himself, John Berridge, and John Fletcher of Madeley. When the loving vicar saw his saintly friend depart, never, probably, to enter that house of prayer again, he might have had thoughts and feelings like those which he threw into devout verse on the final departure of Whitfield, another of his evangelical co-workers. His hymn was founded on the Psalmist's prayer, " Help, Lord ; for the godly man ceaseth ; for the faithful fail from among the children of men."

    Send help, O Lord, we pray,
    And Thy own Gospel bless ;
    For godly men decay,
    And faithful pastors cease;
 The righteous are removed from home,
 And scorners rise up in their room.

    While Satan's troops are bold,
    And thrive in number too,
    The flocks in Jesu's fold
    Are growing lank and few.
 Old sheep are moving off each year,
 And few lambs in the fold appear.

    Old shepherds, too, retire,
    Who gather'd flocks below,
    And young ones catch no fire,
    Or worldly prudent grow ;
 Few run with trumpets in their hand,
 To sound alarms by sea and land.

    O Lord, stir up Thy power,
    To make the Gospel spread ;
    And thrust out preachers more,
    With voice to raise the dead,
 With feet to run where Thou dost call,
 With faith to fight and conquer all.

    The flocks that long have dwelt
    Around fair Sion's hill,
    And Thy sweet grace have felt,
    Uphold and feed them still;
 But fresh folds build up everywhere,
 And plenteously Thy truth declare.

    As one Elijah dies,
    True prophet of the Lord,
    Let some Elisha rise
    To blaze the Gospel Word ;
 And fast as sheep to Jesus go
 May lambs recruit his folds below.

The Wesleys and their Oxford companions had gone out from college, and were in their various positions, working out their Christian plans, when Berridge, at the age of nineteen, began his course of preparation for his great life-task at Clare Hall, Cambridge. Born at Kingston in Nottinghamshire, the son of a farmer, he was destined by his father to succeed him on the soil. But John had no capacity for calculating the worth of bullocks, and the disappointed parent declared he should go to college "to be a light to the Gentiles." The example of a pious boy-neighbour, and the religious influence of a tailor, sometimes employed in the house, led him to take a religious turn. With a mind well trained and largely furnished, he served as a curate for some years, and in 1755 was admitted to the vicarage of Everton. After a year or two of unsatisfactory labour, he was led to a clear discovery of the way of salvation by faith; and his ministry at once became living and fruitful. The first fruits were characteristic. One of his flock came to inquire for him. "Well, Sarah?" said he. "Well!" was the reply; "well, not so well, I fear!" "Why, what's the matter, Sarah?" "Matter? why I don't know what's the matter. These *new sermons!* I find we are all to be lost now; I can neither eat, drink, nor sleep; I don't know what's to become of me!" The number of such inquirers rapidly increased. Mr. Hicks, a neighbouring clergyman, was one of his converts. At length Wesley and the vicar met; and an alliance was formed.

"I was informed," says John Wesley, in November, 1758, "that Mr. Berridge desired I would come to him as soon as possible. I set out for Everton. Mr. B. was just taking horse; I rode on with him, and in the evening preached at Wrestlingworth, in a large church well-filled with serious hearers. We lodged at Mr. Hicks's, the vicar, a witness of the faith which once he persecuted. . . . . But a few months ago Mr. Berridge was thoroughly convinced that 'by grace' we are 'saved, through faith.' Immediately he began to proclaim aloud the redemption that is in Christ Jesus; and God confirmed His own word exactly as He did at Bristol, in the beginning, by working repentance and faith in the hearers, and with the same violent outward symptoms." The wonderful effects of Berridge's preaching are described by Wesley, who was an eye-witness. On Saturday 14th of July, 1749, he says: "While Mr. B. preached in the church, I stood with many in the churchyard to make room for those who came from far; therefore I *saw* little, but *heard* the agonizing of many panting and gasping after eternal life. In the afternoon Mr. B. was constrained, by the multitude of people, to come out of the church, and preach in his own close. Some of those who were here pricked to the heart were affected in an astonishing manner. The first man I saw wounded would have dropped, but others, catching him in their arms, did, indeed, prop him up, but were so far from keeping him still that he caused all of them to totter and tremble. His own shaking exceeded that of a cloth in the wind. It seemed as if the Lord came upon him like a giant, taking him by the neck, and shaking all his bones in pieces. One woman tore up the ground with her hands, filling them with dust, and with the hard trodden grass, on which I saw her lie, with her hands clenched, as one dead, when the multitude dispersed. Another roared and screamed in a more dreadful agony than ever I heard before. I omitted the rejoicing of believers, because of their number and the frequency thereof, though the manner was strange; some of them being quite overpowered with Divine love, and only showing enough of natural life to let us know they were overwhelmed with joy and life eternal."

Scenes like these opened everywhere in rapid succession. Under the ministry of Berridge's neighbour, Hicks, and himself, about four thousand souls were brought to seek God in the space of twelve months. He entered now on a course of itinerancy. He went through all the surrounding counties; preached ten or twelve sermons every week, travelling on horseback in that time about one hundred miles. It was in the spirit of this missionary work that he wrote his hymn on "Thy kingdom come :"—

> O Father, let Thy kingdom come,
>   Thy kingdom built on love and grace ;
> In every province give it room,
>   In every heart afford it place ;
> The earth is Thine, set up Thy throne,
> And claim the kingdoms as Thine own.
>
>   Still nature's horrid darkness reigns,
>   And sinners scorn the check of fear,
> Still Satan holds the heart in chains,
>   Where Jesu's messengers appear ;
> We pray that Christ may rise and bless
> The world with truth and righteousness.
>
>   Bid war and wild ambition cease,
>   And man no more a monster prove ;
> Fill up his breast with heavenly peace,
>   And warm it well with heavenly love ;
> To Jesus bid the people go,
> And Satan's kingdom overthrow.
>
>   More labourers in the vineyard send,
>   And pour Thine unction on them all ;
> Give them a voice to shake and bend
>   The mountains high and cedars tall ;
> That flocks of sinners, young and old,
> May shelter seek in Jesu's fold.

Berridge was thoroughly adapted for his work. Robust in form and constitution, firm and undaunted in spirit, fearless of men, unwavering in faith, with a mind well furnished, a heart glowing with zeal, a voice loud and strong, and perfectly under command, with never-failing power of expression, he was verily a "son of thunder." At times, when he spoke, Sinai seemed to thunder and flash ; while that same voice would become tremulous and melting while he wept over those to whom he preached a Saviour. Persecution of no kind checked him; though, for nearly thirty years, the enemies of truth would know him by no other title than "The Old Devil." His humility was deep and pure. The expression of his feelings respecting himself as an itinerant was sometimes in amusing accordance with his character. In a letter to the Countess of Huntingdon, he says, "I am one of those strange folks who set up for journeymen without knowing their business, and offer many precious wares to sale without understanding their full value. I have got a Master, too, a most extraordinary person, whom I am supposed to be well acquainted with, because He employs me as a riding pedlar to serve nearly forty shops in the country, besides my own parish; yet I know much less of my Master than I do of His wares." He was once on his way to a visitation when a strange clergyman joined him. After some chat, the stranger said, "Do you know one Berridge in these parts? he is a very troublesome, good-for-nothing fellow, they tell me." " Yes, I know him," said Berridge, "and I assure you that one half his wickedness has not been told you." The stranger was surprised, and begged to have the wicked fellow pointed out to him when they came to the church. Other talk followed, until they arrived at the place of meeting. Berridge's companion then reminded him of his promise to show him this Berridge. "My dear sir," said he, "I am John Berridge." "Is it possible?" cried the other; "and can you forgive me? Will you honour me with your acquaintance? Will you admit me to your house?" "Yes," was the old man's reply, "and to my heart."

The true simplicity of the hymnist's character, and his genuine lowliness of mind, are put forth in his best hymn style in his verses on "My Soul is even as a Weaned Child."

> Dear Jesus, cast a look on me,
> I come with simplest prayer to Thee,
>   And ask to be a child;
> Weary of what belongs to man,
> I long to be as I began,
>   Infantly meek and mild.
>
> No wild ambition I would have,
> No worldly grandeur I would crave,
>   But sit me down content;
> Content with what I do receive,
> And cheerful praises learn to give,
>   For all things freely sent.
>
> Well weanèd from the world below,
> Its pining care and gewgaw show,
>   Its joy and hope forlorn;
> My soul would step, a stranger, forth,
> And, smit with Jesus' grace and worth,
>   Repose on Him alone.

> I would love Him with all my heart,
> And all my secret thought impart,
>   My grief, and joy, and fear;
> And while the pilgrim life shall last,
> My soul would on the Lord be cast,
>   In sweet believing prayer.
> His presence I would have each day,
> And hear Him talking by the way
>   Of love, and truth, and grace;
> And when He speaks and gives a smile,
> My soul shall listen all the while,
>   And every accent bless.

He had learnt the lesson of his Lord's active service, and then was called to the suffering which was necessary to complete his character. He was for a time laid aside from work; and it was during this trial that he composed the hymns contained in his volume of "Sion's Songs." He had previously compiled and issued a collection of Divine songs designed chiefly for the religious societies of churchmen in the neighbourhood of Everton. It contained some originals; "but," says he, "I was not wholly satisfied with it. The bells indeed had been chiefly cast in a celebrated foundry, and in ringing were tuneable enough, none more so; but a clear Gospel tone was not found in them all." He alludes to the hymns of the Wesleys, from whose doctrinal notions, once his own, he had now somewhat swerved. "Sion's Songs," however, were Berridge's own. "Ill health, some years past, having kept me from travelling or preaching, I took up the trade of hymn-making, a handicraft much followed of late, but a business I was not born or bred to, and undertaken chiefly to keep a long sickness from preying on my spirits, and to make tedious nights pass over smoothly. Some tinkling employment was wanted, which might amuse and not fatigue me." He wanted "tinkling employment," and some of his hymns are certainly curious tinkling productions; but others are more worthy of a man who, on the testimony of those who knew him best, "possessed a strength of understanding, a quickness of perception, a depth of penetration, a brilliancy of fancy, and a fund of prompt wit, beyond most men." The peculiar balance of humour and gravity in his character is seen in the prayer with which he closes the preface to his hymn-book: "My Saviour and my God, accept this mite of love, which is cast into Thy treasury. Give it a blessing, and it shall be blessed. What is water in the hymns turn into wine; by giving them a charge to enliven the hearts of the children, and stir up the wills of aliens to seek Thy salvation. Only attend them with an unction of Thy spirit, and whatever be the hymns, Thy glory shall be promoted by them. Amen."

But his humour, and what may be called his grave waggery, often found vent in his letters and in his intercourse with friends. He was never married, and it is very curious to find him most free to joke and be serious by turns on the question of wedlock in his epistles to the Countess of Huntingdon.

MY LADY,—Before I parted with honest Glascott, I cautioned him much against petticoat snares. He had burnt his wings already; sure he will not imitate a foolish gnat, and hover again about the candle. If he should fall into a sleeping-lap, he will soon need a flannel night-cap, and a rusty chain to fix him down like a Church Bible to the reading-desk. No trap so mischievous to the field preacher as wedlock, and it is laid for him at every corner. Matrimony has quite maimed poor Charles, and might have spoiled John and George, if a wise Master had not graciously sent them a brace of ferrets. Dear George has now got the liberty again, and he will escape well if he is not caught by another tenter-hook. Eight or nine years ago, having been grievously tormented with housekeepers, I truly had thought of looking out for a Jezebel for myself. But it seemed needful to ask advice of the Lord; so falling down on my knees before a table, with a Bible between my hands, I besought the Lord to give me a direction.

The first sign he tells us was not satisfactory. Another trial brought up the passage, "Thou shalt not take thee a wife," &c. These words he took, as he says, "not only as a rule of direction, but as a promise of security," *Thou shalt not take a wife*, that is, I will keep thee from taking one.

In his sitting-room at Everton, he had several portraits of pious men hanging on the walls in small frames; and over the mantel-piece there was a looking-glass of the same size in a similar frame. A clergyman who paid him a visit for the first time looked at the pictures one after another. "That," said Berridge, "is Calvin, and that Luther; and that," pointing to the glass over the fireplace, " is the Devil ! " The visitor stepped quickly to look at it, and saw his own face. " Is it not," cried Berridge, " a striking likeness of his Satanic majesty ? "

Probably he sometimes felt that he was treading on snares when indulging this waggish mood, and might seem to be giving himself a caution and a check in his hymn on " I said of laughter, it is mad ; and of mirth, what good doeth it ? "

> But, oh, thou man of God,
> This empty mirth beware ;
> March off, and quit this giggling road ;
> No food for pilgrims there.
>
> It checks the Spirit's aid,
> And leaves the heart forlorn,
> And makes them look as Sampson did,
> When all his locks were shorn.
>
> May Jesus be my peace,
> And make up all my joy ;
> His love can yield me serious bliss,
> And bliss that will not cloy.

But the way in which he uses his faculty of merry quaintness in giving sharp point to moral and religious truth in his " Christian World Unmasked," and in his epistolary recommendation of " Cheerful Piety," gives a pleasant impression of consistency, and finely balanced intellect and affections. The closing verses of one of his best hymns breathe the spirit in which he waited for his Lord's coming—

> Leaning on Thy loving breast,
> Where a weary soul may rest ;
> Feeling well the peace of God,
> Flowing from Thy precious blood.
>
> In this posture let me live,
> And hosannas daily give ;
> In this temper let me die,
> And hosannas ever cry.

One who was near him at the last, said, " The Lord has enabled you to fight a good fight." " Blessed be His name for it," was the response. " Jesus will soon call you up higher," it was said again. " Ay, ay, ay," he cried, " higher !

higher! higher! Yes, and my children, too, will shout and sing, 'Here comes our father!'" This was his last voice on earth. He "fell asleep in Christ," January 22, 1793.

How difficult it is, at times, to prove a man's identity. The changes wrought in him and his surroundings during an interval of some years' absence, render it hard to say whether the person you see now is the same as you looked at then. A difficulty somewhat analogous to this occurs sometimes in fixing the authorship of a hymn. The lapse of a few years only since the death of the author so mystifies his claims, as to make it by no means easy for some people to be sure whether the hymn was written by him or by somebody else. So it seems to have been with that widely-known and soul-kindling hymn—

> Jesus, Thy blood and righteousness
> My beauty are, my glorious dress.

It was certainly issued by the Wesleys among their "Hymns and Sacred Poems," in 1740, and given as "from the German;" and seems to have been a rendering of one of Count Zinzendorf's hymns by John Wesley. Nevertheless, it has subsequently been ascribed to John Cennick, whose talent and taste as a hymnist are placed beyond a doubt by compositions which are certainly his, and need no sustenance from doubtful claims.

"To me," says an old psalm-singer, "there is one hymn which is always associated with my first insight into a happy future, and my earliest expressions of Christian hope. Long before I knew who wrote it, that hymn, whenever I heard it sung, used to melt and exhilarate me by turns, as it excited thoughts of going up amidst brightening multitudes and choral harmonies to meet the Saviour. I am not sure whether it was the hymn alone that awakened the feelings I speak of. The music of the finely adapted tune may have had something to do with it; for that music seems even now to rise within me in harmony with the thoughts, rhyme, and rhythm of the verses. However that may be, a deep chord is always touched in my soul when I read or hear John Cennick's spiritual song—

> Thou dear Redeemer, dying Lamb!
>   We love to hear of Thee;
> No music's like Thy charming name,
>   Nor half so sweet can be.
>
> O may we ever hear Thy voice
>   In mercy to us speak;
> And in our Priest we will rejoice,
>   Thou great Melchisedek.
>
> Our Jesus shall be still our theme,
>   While in this world we stay!
> We'll sing our Jesu's lovely name,
>   When all things else decay.
>
> When we appear in yonder cloud,
>   With all the ransom'd throng,
> Then will we sing more sweet, more loud,
>   And Christ shall be our song.

Cennick's doctrinal course was a wavering one; and but for the soundness of his conversion, and for the genuine groundwork of piety in his heart, it might have been unhappy. He had warmth, fancy, and tunefulness of poetic spirit as a hymnist; but as a divine he lacked discrimination, and as an evangelist his judgment was not always sound. His parents were Quakers; though he soon learnt to make hymns and to sing them. He was taught at home to pray if not to sing. It was soon seen that trade was not his calling.

For a time, he showed a proneness to gaiety. But in 1735 he was convinced of sin while walking in Cheapside; and at once his vain songs, and cards, and theatrical amusements were cast aside. Sometimes he wished to go into a Popish monastery to spend his life in devout retirement. At other times he would fain live in a cave, sleeping on fallen leaves, and feeding on forest-fruits. He fasted long and often, and prayed nine times every day. He lived in fear of departed spirits; and trembled lest he should meet the devil. Dry bread was too great an indulgence for such a sinner; and he began to feed on potatoes, acorns, crabs, and grass; and often wished he could live upon roots and herbs. He would have been a distinguished brother of the *Boskoi*, the grass-eating monks in the fields of old Mesopotamia. But he was saved from all this by the manifested peace of God which he received on September 6th, 1737. His course was now one of freedom and joy. He became at once a preacher of salvation through faith in Christ. His public Methodist action began in association with the Wesleys. On Friday, March 1739, "I came to Reading," says John Wesley, "where I found a young man who had in some measure known the powers of the world to come. I spent the evening with him and a few of his serious friends, and it pleased God much to strengthen and comfort them." This young man was Cennick. He worked as a lay-helper with the Wesleys nearly two years, preaching and making hymns. Charles Wesley sympathized with him as a hymn writer, and corrected his verses for the press. Like all those who took an active part in early Methodism, he had experienced spiritual conflict in the first pursuit of Christian peace; and had been led through a course of vain efforts into the great secret of salvation by faith in Christ alone. One of his best hymns may be taken as a record of his own first happy introduction to Jesus as "the way, the truth, and the life"—

> Jesus, my all, to heaven is gone;
> He whom I fix my hopes upon:
> His track I see, and I'll pursue
> The narrow way till Him I view.
>
> The way the holy prophets went—
> The road that leads from banishment—
> The King's highway of holiness—
> I'll go; for all His paths are peace.
>
> This is the way I long had sought,
> And mourned because I found it not;
> My grief and burden long had been
> Because I could not cease from sin.
>
> The more I strove against its power,
> I sinned and stumbled but the more;
> Till late I heard my Saviour say,
> Come hither, soul, I am the way.

> Lo! glad I come! and Thou, blest Lamb,
> Wilt now receive me as I am!
> My sinful self to Thee I give:
> Nothing but love shall I receive.
>
> Then will I tell to sinners round
> What a dear Saviour I have found;
> I'll point to Thy redeeming blood,
> And say—Behold! the way to God.

It was not long, however, before the young hymning evangelist began to show tokens of change. On Nov. 4, 1740, Charles Wesley writes: "At Kingswood, while I was testifying Christ died for all, Mr. Cennick, in the hearing of many, gave me the lie. I calmly told him afterwards, 'If I speak not the truth as it is in Jesus, may I decrease and you increase.'" About a month after this, John Wesley had to share with his brother the consequences of Cennick's changed disposition. He preached at Kingswood on the afternoon of Tuesday, December 16, 1740, from "Let patience have her perfect work;" and then his own patience was put to the test. "The next evening," says he, "Mr. Cennick came. I was greatly surprised when I went to receive him, as usual, with open arms, to observe him quite cold; so that a stranger would have judged he had scarce ever seen me before." The doctrinal differences between these good men soon became associated with warm feeling, until the spirited young hymnist declared that while connected with the Wesleys he was "in the midst of the plague;" and both in private and public denounced his old companions as preachers of Popery. Wesley quietly pursued his way, but grieved over the results. "Twenty years afterwards," he says, "I visited the classes at Kingswood. Here only there is no increase; and yet, where was there such a prospect till that weak man, John Cennick, confounded the poor people with strange doctrines? We see no end of it to this day."

There is, perhaps, a still more lasting effect of Cennick's public teaching in Ireland, at least. A few years ago, a lover of Goldsmith's poetry, on his way from Athlone to

"Sweet Auburn," saw a small unpretending chapel by the wayside, and inquired of the car-driver to what people it belonged. "To the Swaddlers," was the sneering reply. The traveller was interested and amused to find that the term of reproach still lived on Popish lips; and a passage from Charles Wesley's journal naturally occurred, illustrating the origin of the term. He was in Dublin on September 10th, 1747; and "at five," he says, "all was quiet within doors; but we had men, women, and children upon us as soon as we appeared in the streets. One I observed crying, 'Swaddler, Swaddler!' (our usual title here), who was a young Ishmael indeed, and had not long learned to speak. I am sure he could not be four years old. We dined with a gentleman, who explained our name to us. It seems we are beholden to Mr. Cennick for it, who abounds in such expressions as, 'I curse and blaspheme all the gods in heaven, but the Babe that lay in the manger, the Babe that lay in Mary's lap, the Babe that lay in swaddling clouts.' Hence they nick-named him 'Swaddler,' or 'Swaddling John'; and the word sticks to us all, not excepting the clergy." The man who declaimed in this style about the "Babe in the manger," could, however, sing more reverently to the Incarnate One whom God "exalted with His right hand":—

> We sing to Thee, Thou Son of God,
>   Fountain of life and grace;
> We praise Thee, Son of Man, whose blood
>   Redeemed our fallen race.
>
> Thee we acknowledge God and Lord,
>   The Lamb for sinners slain;
> Thou art by Heaven and earth adored,
>   Worthy o'er both to reign.
>
> To Thee all angels cry aloud,
>   Through Heaven's extended coasts;
> Hail! Holy, Holy, Holy Lord
>   Of glory and of hosts.
>
> The prophets' goodly fellowship,
>   In radiant garments drest,
> Praise Thee, Thou Son of God, and reap
>   The fulness of Thy rest.

> The apostles' glorious company
>   Thy righteous praise proclaim;
> The martyred army glorify
>   Thine everlasting Name.
> Throughout the world Thy Churches join
>   To call on Thee, their Head,
> Brightness of Majesty Divine,
>   Who every power hast made.
> Among their number, Lord, we love
>   To sing Thy precious blood;
> Reign here, and in the worlds above,
>   Thou holy Lamb of God.

When Cennick drew back from companionship with the Wesleys, he attached himself to Whitfield, whose theological notions he took to be more akin to his own. But after a time there was another shift, and he closed his earthly career in communion with the Moravians, and in the ranks of their ministry. He has again joined those with whom he began his Methodist itinerancy, and in union with whom he had his first inspirations as a hymnist. Those early poets of Methodism sing together now, and Cennick has left one of his immortal songs to aid those who are following him to the pilgrim's home:—

> Children of the Heavenly King,
> As ye journey, sweetly sing;
> Sing your Saviour's worthy praise,
> Glorious in His works and ways.
>
> Ye are travelling home to God,
> In the way the fathers trod;
> They are happy now, and ye
> Soon their happiness shall see.
>
> O ye banished seed be glad,
> Christ our Advocate is made;
> Us to save our flesh assumes,
> Brother to our souls becomes.
>
> Shout, ye ransomed flock, and blest,
> You on Jesu's throne shall rest;
> There your seat is now prepared,
> There your kingdom and reward.
>
> Fear not, brethren, joyful stand
> On the borders of your land;
> Jesus Christ, your Father's Son,
> Bids you undismayed go on.
>
> Lord, submissive may we go,
> Gladly leaving all below;
> Only Thou our Leader be,
> And we still will follow Thee.

CHAPTER X.

ITINERANT MINSTRELS.

It is once an age two hearts are set
So well in unison, that not a note
Jars in their music; but a skilful hand
Slurs lightly over the discordant tones,
And wakens only the full power of those
That sound in concord.
         Happy, happy those,
Who thus perform in the grand concert-life.

WHAT a chronicle of providences might be made from the early lives of that generation of Methodist preachers which sprang up in England during the first age of Methodism! For variety of origin, difference of mental constitution and culture, unlikeness of home training, and dissimilarity of appearance and manners, the men who laboured and suffered with the Wesleys in their evangelizing movement were most remarkable. Nor were ever such human varieties made so thoroughly one in heart and purpose as they. One secret of this was that deep and commanding sense of the living reality of unseen and Divine things. Hence their intense earnestness and full abandonment to their spiritual calling. The invisible was open to them. They lived more in "the heavenlies" than in the earthly world. They "walked by faith, not by sight." Those of them who sprang up from among the Cornish mines were distinguished in this respect. One reason may be found in their early introduction to dark, deep, and mysterious scenes of danger, and solemn momently nearness to death. When the miner's habit of companionship with awful uncertainty and unearthly imaginations becomes hallowed by living faith in the presence of Him to whom all worlds are subject, the Christian character

Perhaps in this neglected spot is laid
  Some heart once pregnant with celestial fire ;
Hands that the rod of empire might have swayed,
  Or waked to ecstasy the living lyre.

CHAPTER X.

ITINERANT MINSTRELS.

It is once an age two hearts are set
So well in unison, that not a note
Jars in their music; but a skilful hand
Slurs lightly over the discordant tones,
And wakens only the full power of those
That sound in concord.
  Happy, happy those,
Who thus perform in the grand concert-life.

WHAT a chronicle of providences might be made from the early lives of that generation of Methodist preachers which sprang up in England during the first age of Methodism! For variety of origin, difference of mental constitution and culture, unlikeness of home training, and dissimilarity of appearance and manners, the men who laboured and suffered with the Wesleys in their evangelizing movement were most remarkable. Nor were ever such human varieties made so thoroughly one in heart and purpose as they. One secret of this was that deep and commanding sense of the living reality of unseen and Divine things. Hence their intense earnestness and full abandonment to their spiritual calling. The invisible was open to them. They lived more in "the heavenlies" than in the earthly world. They "walked by faith, not by sight." Those of them who sprang up from among the Cornish mines were distinguished in this respect. One reason may be found in their early introduction to dark, deep, and mysterious scenes of danger, and solemn momently nearness to death. When the miner's habit of companionship with awful uncertainty and unearthly imaginations becomes hallowed by living faith in the presence of Him to whom all worlds are subject, the Christian character

Perhaps in this neglected spot is laid
  Some heart once pregnant with celestial fire ;
Hands that the rod of empire might have swayed,
  Or waked to ecstasy the living lyre.

in that man becomes bold and distinctive in its outline, and full and rich in its energy and tone. Many such were, by Divine impressment, put into the ranks of Methodist " Rounders," as they were called. They were all the better prepared to brave the difficulties and dangers of their Christian calling for having been brought into their position through fearful perils and " deaths oft." Now and then it was proved that their discipline had been as favourable to poetic genius as to preaching power; while in some cases the genius and the speaking gift found their genial and proper scene of action only by some wonderfully fine turn of things.

Some time during the year 1759 a young western miner in his teens had risen from a violent fever, and, allured by the refreshing air of Penzance Bay, had wandered out to enjoy the balmy influences of beautiful nature.

He had not gone far before he fell into the hands of a press-gang, which, under the sanction of the chief magistrate, was on the look-out for prey. The lad pleaded his youth and present weakness. But press-gangs in those days had no tenderness; nor was the mayor disposed to be soft. At the nick of time an honest, peaceful, but fearless Quaker came up.

"What art thou going to do with that lad?" said he to the mayor.

"What? I am going to send him to serve his Majesty."

"There are others more fit for the service," was the response. "Yea, a hundred in this town ; send them ; send idle, disorderly persons, not honest men's sons who live by their diligence and frugality."

"The king must have men," said the official; "if we cannot get seamen we must take others."

"Look upon that lad," answered the tender-hearted Friend; "thou mayest read innocence in his countenance."

"He will look much better after he has been six months at sea; and in time he will be a captain."

"Let him go home," it was still pleaded, "there are men enough to be got without him."

A few more words, and the point was turned. "Make haste home," said the mayor to the lad. And as he moved off he thought of the goodness of God, who by means of that old Friend made a way for his escape; while many of his neighbours were torn from their homes, perhaps never to return. This was not the last nice turn and narrow escape of the young miner. Not very long after, he had to tell a tale of marvellous deliverances in rapid succession. He tells of a wonderful escape from death from the fall of a large stone while he was standing in the tin-pit beneath; and of his being carried down with the earth when it suddenly sunk into an old pit, and being saved from suffocation by being landed in an open space beneath, where another miner was working. "But," says he, "the greatest deliverance happened soon after this. One day as I was working in the bottom of a pit, about ten yards deep, I laid aside my tool, and fell on my knees, and found uncommon enlargement in prayer. In less than two minutes the ground fell in. A very large stone fell before me, which rose higher than my head. Two others fell, one on my right side, and the other on my left; these likewise rose above my head. A fourth fell like a cover, and rested on the top of the others, about four inches above my head. Some scores of small ones fell behind on my legs and feet; while others fell on the cover that was over me. Here I was shut up as in a prison. When my father came to the brink of the pit and found me buried, he fell a weeping. But when he found I was alive, he told me the whole pit would fill to the top. I desired him to go out of the reach of danger. I was a little surprised at first; but it was soon gone, as the stones were large and hollow, and I had sufficient room to breathe. When he perceived that no more stones fell, he got help, and by degrees removed some of the large stones; and after cutting my shoes from my feet, I was got out without receiving the least injury. I cannot help admiring the providence of God in the following particulars:—

"1. I was praying at the time when this happened.

"2. I was kneeling. Had I been standing, I should have been crushed to pieces; had I been sitting, my legs would have been broken with the large stone which fell before me.

"3. They fell in an instant. Had I heard them coming, probably I should have risen from my knees; and then the stones which fell like a cover would have dashed out my brains.

"4. Three large stones fell, one before me, and one on each side; and only small ones behind on my legs. Had a large one fallen there, my legs would have been broken into shivers.

"5. The three large ones that fell were a few inches higher than my head, and were instantly covered with another large one. Had they been a few inches lower, the last would certainly have killed me in a moment. Surely this preservation was the Lord's doing, and it is marvellous in our eyes."

The young man thus brought up alive from the dead was Richard Rodda; born in 1743, in the parish of Sancreed, on the heights between Penzance and the Atlantic; a few miles from the romantic mining district of St. Just, among whose metallic hills it was that he had been so frequently sheltered from death. His earliest recollections were of vision-like insights into revealed truth, of Methodist preachers coming to preach in his father's house, of conflicts in his boyish mind between good and evil, and of Divine lessons coming to his heart through a preserving Providence. "One day," he says, "I was riding at full gallop in company with several others, my horse threw me over his head, and then quite leaped over me; and, although another horse coming close behind did the same, yet I received no hurt." Reflection on all these evident interferences on his behalf from above led him to conclude that God intended to show how soon He could take him away from the scene of action; and that his only way of securing a safe as well as happy life was to obey the conviction that he was called to preach the Gospel of Christ. "One Lord's day," he writes, "we expected a travelling preacher. The people were gathered together from various parts, when word was brought that he could not come. On hearing this, I was desired to stand up and speak to the people. The conflict in my breast was very strong, but I refused to open my mouth." A darkness fell on his soul, and a kind of horror seized him, under which he at length vowed to obey his conviction. "Accordingly," he says, "I exhorted that night, for the first time, which was in my father's house. Soon after, I was desired to exhort in the society; and then, by their advice, I did it in public."

He had taken his proper course, and, from that moment, he was the happy and successful Methodist preacher; sound in judgment, strict in his rule of life, diligent in his work, and exercising his well-balanced powers for the good of saints and sinners. Among his talents was that of poetry; and, like many others, he found his poetic genius called into play by the grace and the joys of his new birth. He had been from early life feeling after God; and in boyhood would fain have found himself an acknowledged member of the Methodist Society. At length, when Mr. Wesley "called over the Society at Newlyn," near Penzance, he was received into membership. For two years, at least, he sought rest for his soul. How he found it, he tells Mr. Wesley in a letter.

"About the beginning of June, 1758, while I was praying in my father's house, and earnestly entreating God to write forgiveness on my heart, the following words darted into my soul, 'Son, be of good cheer, thy sins are forgiven thee.' In that instant my burden was removed, and my soul was filled with peace and joy. But I soon doubted whether this was what many termed 'justification;' and as I had always a fear of deceiving myself, the enemy soon reasoned me out of my happiness, and my soul seemed as far from the blessing as ever. On the 11th of that month, while Benjamin Trembath was praying by me, God gave me a clear sense of His forgiving love. There was not the least doubt remaining of my acceptance through the Beloved. For many days and weeks I was enabled to rejoice in God, my Saviour. Every duty was profitable, as it conveyed fresh tokens of the Divine favour. My understanding was opened to behold the power, wisdom, and goodness of God, in creating, preserving, and governing the world. I saw that the whole earth was full of His majesty and glory. But what most astonished me was the wondrous greatness of redeeming love. To behold the Ancient of days become an infant! The filler of immensity, contracted to a span! The Lord of heaven and earth taking upon Him the form of a servant; and, after fulfilling all righteousness, bowing His blessed head on the cross, to save His avowed enemies! These considerations filled me with love and gratitude, which I expressed in the following lines—

> "Praise God, my soul, whose wondrous love
> Hath drawn my thoughts to things above,
>   Where Jesus ever reigns;
> Let every sinful wand'ring thought
> Be into full subjection brought,
>   Till freed from sin's remains.
>
> "When pure, and perfected in love,
> O, may I never, never rove
>   From Christ, my living Head;
> But steadfast and unshaken stand,
> Obedient to my Lord's command,
>   While by His Spirit led.
>
> "Among the little happy flock,
> Who sit beneath their guardian rock,
>   Will I take up my rest;
> My Shepherd's voice my soul shall hear,
> And, freed from doubts and slavish fear,
>   Shall lean upon His breast.
>
> "His loving arms extended wide,
> Shall press me to His wounded side,
>   Nor let me thence depart;
> But fill my soul with joy and peace,
> And all the fruits of righteousness
>   Shall flourish in my heart.

> "The heavenly spices of His grace
>   Do sweetly now perfume the place
>   Where Satan had his seat;
>   Jesus hath spoil'd the powers of hell,
>   And lo! I now for ever dwell
>   Triumphant at His feet!
>
> "Here will I lie, nor ever move,
>   Till Christ, my Lord, shall say, 'My love,
>   Come up, and dwell with me':
>   Then I on wings of love shall rise,
>   And reign with Him above the skies,
>   To all eternity."

This was his first hymn. Whether his after-course was brightened with other songs is not known; but the one he has left as an expression of his "first love" is happy enough in diction, tender enough in feeling, and sufficiently harmonious in measure and rhythm, to prove that he had "music in himself"; and that he may be classed with Methodist itinerant minstrels. His pilgrimage as an itinerant minstrel and preacher ran through thirty-three years. He lingered in hope, after becoming unequal to farther wanderings, for twelve or thirteen years; and then, with the light of Canaan touching his soul, he looked back tenderly, for a moment, to the time when his first hymn broke from his renewed heart, saying: "It is now about fifty-eight years since the Lord set my soul at glorious liberty, and I have found Him to be a gracious God all the way, faithful to His promise. Not one word has failed. Glory be to His name! I could go to Smithfield and die for His dear cause. I know I could. But now let me enter into the joy of my Lord! Come, Lord Jesus, come quickly!" The Master came, and the old itinerant minstrel verified his own early stanza—

> Here will I lie, nor ever move,
> Till Christ my Lord shall say, "My love,
>   Come up and dwell with Me."
> Then I on wings of faith shall rise,
> And reign with Him above the skies,
>   To all eternity.

In the valley which crosses the lower part of the ancient Cornish town of Redruth, there is a curious architectural relic, called the "Round House." The part of the building from which the name is taken was literally a round house; whether originally a dwelling, or a mill of some sort, does not appear. It stands by the side of a stream which runs down the valley, and, with its heavy chimney-stack and its thickly-thatched conical roof, is a quaint memorial of things as they were two hundred years ago. A kind of wing was attached to it in 1726—a strongly-built dwelling, and very respectable as an ordinary house of that period. A peculiar religious interest belongs to the Round House, the term now applied to the entire building. In the more modern part there is a large room, in which Methodist prayer-meetings used to be held a century ago. In that room, what is called in the county "the great revival" of 1814 began. Eight persons were converted there in a prayer-meeting; and from that meeting there went out the feeling and power which spread through the whole western part of Cornwall, until scarcely a house could be passed in which there was not the voice of prayer and praise. Among the converts in that revival was a young woman of eighteen, the granddaughter of the old Methodist to whom the Round House belonged. "She is still alive to tell the story," says a visitor of the sick, "and is patiently waiting for her Lord's coming in a bed-room over the apartment in which the great work of God began. She remembered her grandfather; was in the house when he died; and would never forget his funeral sermon being preached before the door, where the ash-tree stands, the preacher taking his place on the steps which lead to the upper room at the end of the house. I have often talked with the good old woman about her young days, and have sometimes caught from her lips interesting scraps of information about early Methodism in Redruth. She could call up, now and then, things which her grandfather had said in her hearing about the itinerant preachers in his time. In the year 1781, it seems, there were two preachers who left vivid impressions on the old man's mind. They both visited the Round House as pastors, and occasionally took the lead of meetings in "the large room." They were distinguished as the "Singer" and the "Man of Prayer." The man of prayer was one whose clothes showed the first sign of wear and tear at the knees, and as one who, though he lisped a little, had a voice of prayer which was mighty with God and with man. An illustration of his character was distinctly remembered :—

The chapel at that time was a long building with square windows, a gallery at one end and the pulpit at the other, somewhat after the fashion of what is now called a rostrum, extending for some length against the wall. The preacher stood about the middle of it, and behind him there was a long seat, occupied, as it was said, by "the leaders and principals." Some of these magnates, it would appear, were of sufficient importance, judging from a note of John Wesley's to the itinerant known as the "Singer." "Observe the rules of the Conference," the note ran : "whoever is pleased or displeased, the trustees and leaders will soon trample them under foot if you will let them. But I think you can be mild and yet firm." Now it happened that one of these wilful-footed lay occupants of the formidable seat behind the preacher, asked the man of prayer to dine with him after a Sunday morning service. As soon as they were fairly in the house, the host turned critic, and said to his guest, "You have preached us a very poor sermon this morning, sir."

"What, my dear brother!" was the answer, "kneel down, my dear brother, and let us pray." His critical doctorship could not refuse. So they were on their knees; and the preacher began by saying, "O Lord! have mercy upon this dear brother; enlighten his understanding, and give him to know the truth, that the truth may make him free." The prayer was continued until the critic's heart was subdued, and his critical tongue for ever silenced in the presence of the saintly preacher. This man of prayer was Samuel Bardsley.

The other itinerant was a man of prayer, too, but he had the additional distinction of musical and poetic gifts. He was the "Sweet Singer." It was Benjamin Rhodes.

"Yes," said the old pilgrim of the Round House, "I lie here on my bed, and think it over sometimes: how my grandfather used to talk about his singing, and how the young people used to learn the tunes that he would pitch, and sing the hymns he liked to sing."

"Do you remember any of the hymns or tunes?" it was inquired.

"Well, no; I was but young, and things are getting misty to me now. I do seem to catch a little of what I used to hear. It was something sung in parts, and the voices used to come one after another in some places, and then melt altogether into such sweet music. It used to ring so, something like bells."

"Do you remember the words?"

"One line or so comes to me, but that is all. It is—

"My heart and voice I raise,
To spread Messiah's praise."

"Why, that was Mr. Rhodes's own hymn. I can say it to you all, if you like to hear it. I can't sing it now, as I used to sing it with my father and aunt, who remembered Mr. Rhodes. This is the hymn:—

"My heart and voice I raise,
To spread Messiah's praise;
Messiah's praise let all repeat;
The universal Lord,
By whose Almighty word
Creation rose in form complete.

"A servant's form He wore,
And in His body bore
Our dreadful curse on Calvary;
He like a victim stood,
And poured His sacred blood,
To set the guilty captives free.

"But soon the Victor rose
Triumphant o'er His foes,
And led the vanquish'd host in chains;
He threw their empire down,
His foes compell'd to own
O'er all the great Messiah reigns.

> "With mercy's mildest grace,
>   He governs all our race
> In wisdom, righteousness, and love;
>   Who to Messiah fly
>   Shall find redemption nigh,
> And all His great salvation prove.
>
> "Hail, Saviour, Prince of Peace!
>   Thy kingdom shall increase,
> Till all the world Thy glory see;
>   And righteousness abound,
>   As the great deep profound,
> And fill the earth with purity."

"Ah!" said the old saint, as the hymn was finished, "that makes me feel as if young life was springing up again. Well, I shall be young again soon, and sing with those who are gone up before me to be young for ever."

Mr. Rhodes was a Yorkshireman. He was born in the year 1743, at Kexborough, in the south-west of the county. He had the advantage of being the son of a schoolmaster, and of being the child of a home in which private and family devotion were kept up. The old and happy style of home training was a blessing to him. The household were regularly catechised. While a boy, he was taken to Bristol by his father to hear Mr. Whitfield preach; and under that hallowed voice his young heart received impressions that never ceased to influence his character and life. How charmingly the early minglings of his poetic feeling and his religious sympathies become traceable!

"At about twelve years of age," he writes, "I took a walk one evening into a large thick wood, not far from the town. I left the path, and wandered in the thickest part of it, till I was entirely lost. Night began to close in upon me, and I did not know which way to turn my face towards home. It soon became quite dark. I then gave over rambling, and intended to remain there till the next morning, when I hoped to find my way out. In this situation I found my former impressions begin to return with much sweetness. My soul was drawn out in prayer; I was deeply sensible of the presence of God; my heart overflowed with penitential tenderness, and, under a deep sense of my own unworthiness, and of His goodness, mercy, and love, I sang and prayed with much fervour; yea, I was so thankful that the Lord had found me in a wood that I would not for all the world have missed such an opportunity."

This devout and spiritual tendency of his youthful soul was broken, by-and-by, under the influence of evil example and the unfolding fascinations of surrounding life. Still, his love of the beautiful and the true again claimed the mastery; and though the harmony of his religious notions, as well as his pious feeling, once or twice suffered violence from those who unhappily identified Christianity with doctrinal strife, yet his poetic taste, and pure, simple love, came out of the trial in beautiful and happy companionship.

"My fears were gone," says he, "and the truth of Christianity appeared to me in the clearest light. Not only my understanding saw, but all my powers felt, the truth thereof. I had a deep sense of a present God, whom I approached in the name of Jesus with reverential awe, confidence, gratitude, and love, and could call Him 'my God and my all.' In this happy season my joy frequently prevented my sleep, while my soul was taken up with Him who is altogether lovely; and in ecstacies of joy, in the stillness of the night, I often sang my great Deliverer's praise. All things earthly appeared so empty that I thought nothing here below worth a thought, only as it tended to promote my eternal interest; I only desired grace and glory."

He found himself, with all this, tenderly susceptible of appeals to his affections, and, like many others of his temperament, charms from without drew closely around his young, palpitating heart. But the word of God proved the more powerful charm; and every entanglement of which he was, for a time, in danger, melted from around his heaven-bound soul. In his twenty-first year he began to devote his gifts and acquirements to the service of his Redeemer, and in the year 1776 became a Methodist travelling preacher. He wandered, scattering blessings as he went, through Norfolk and Oxfordshire, Kent and Lincolnshire, Scotland and

Sussex. At length, returning into Kent, he writes, "Since I came into these parts I have lost a sister and mother, who, I believe, are both gone after my father into Abraham's bosom; but I am left behind, almost the only person out of a large family. But how long or how short my day may be, I leave to unerring Wisdom; one only concern ought to possess me—to employ it as I ought; then, at the close of it, I also shall sleep in peace, and, after a short absence, be with my dear departed friends.

> "Thrice happy meeting!
> Nor time, nor death, shall ever part us more."

Thus bereft of all whose smiles had kept him circling as nearly as might be around the scenes of his younger life, he came to Redruth to sing to the Cornish Methodists, and to find consolation amidst the warm sympathies of those whose jubilant piety reflected upon his musical soul the harmonies which his own spiritual songs inspired.

For several years at the opening of the present century, the lofty brow, peaceful face, and thoughtful eye, that had been, during fifty years of itinerant life, turned upon gathering crowds, with brightening expressions of simplicity, truthfulness, loving zeal, and heavenliness, were to be seen occasionally on the sands of old Margate, looking out on the sea, or watching the advancing work of the new pier, or turned heavenward from the top of the bright chalk cliffs, or opened again, now and then, upon the people from the pulpit, or marking with growing interest the rise of the new chapel in Hawley Square; or, like an angel's face, bending looks of kindness by the bed-side of some seeking sinner or departing saint: everywhere and at all times, until the worn-out form sank to its own rest, looking like an embodiment of the spiritual longings, cheerful hopes, and reverent assurance which live and breathe in the second part of his glorious hymn—

> Jerusalem divine,
> When shall I call thee mine?
> And to thy holy hill attain,
> Where weary pilgrims rest,
> And in thy glories blest,
> With God Messiah ever reign?

There saints and angels join
In fellowship divine,
And rapture swells the solemn lay;
While all with one accord
Adore their glorious Lord,
And shout His praise through endless day.

May I but find the grace
To fill an humble place
In that inheritance above;
My tuneful voice I'll raise
In songs of loudest praise,
To spread Thy fame, Redeeming Love.

Reign, true Messiah, reign!
Thy kingdom shall remain
When stars and sun no more shall shine.
Mysterious Deity,
Who ne'er began to be,
To sound Thy endless praise be mine!

Up among the hills of south-west Yorkshire, amidst its glorious border moorlands, stands Old Haworth; notorious, in these times, as the land of romance, where the Brontès lived and wrote, but formerly loved as a place of holier memories. There, one day, in the year 1745, stood up a big, burly, powerful Scotchman, more to be feared than fearing. He was an itinerant preacher. And in his congregation was the parish parson, at that time ignorant of saving grace, but confident that he had college logic enough to confute the preacher. The preacher, however, was so well versed in the Scriptures and the parson's own liturgy, as to be more than a match for his antagonist. The preacher came again; and then Grimshaw, for he it was, stood by the itinerant and gave out the hymn for him. The people shouted, "Mad Grimshaw is turned Scotch Will's clerk! and Scotch Will leads and guides Mad Grimshaw!" The parson now became the inquirer, "How shall I preach salvation by faith," said he, "and the necessity of a clean heart, while I myself do not possess these blessings?" "How?" said Scotch Will, "you must preach them till you experience them; and then because you enjoy them."

The advice was taken; and Grimshaw, writing afterwards to Dr. Gillies, says: "Darney preached at Haworth; the

Lord was with him, indeed; I have cause to bless God for it." Scotch Will was William Darney, who joined Mr. Wesley's society in 1742. He became an itinerant preacher; was very successful in forming societies in various places not before visited; and was a great sufferer from violent persecutions. All his sufferings, however, did not stop his preaching or singing. He was the first man of his order who published hymns of his own making; issuing a volume of two hundred and fourteen hymns, printed in Leeds in 1751. He never claimed to be a poet; and if he had, his claim would never, perhaps, be allowed,—not by Charles Wesley, at least; for under his influence, Darney's verses gave way to better songs. Nevertheless, the rough people whom he taught to sing could appreciate his genius, and loved to sing his hymns, doggrel as many of them were. All honour to the man who did his best for his Lord's sake. One of his spiritual songs was headed, "God is the salvation of His people":—

> Come, O my God and King,
>   Thy will to me make known;
> Salvation do Thou bring,
>   Salvation through Thy Son;
> Seal this salvation on my heart,
> Then I from Thee shall never part.
>
> O let me never doubt
>   What Thou hast done for me,
> Since Thou hast thus wrought out
>   Salvation that is free;
> Seal this salvation on my heart,
> Then I from Thee shall never part.
>
> Salvation from the guilt
>   And from the power of sin;
> For this Thy blood was spilt,
>   The same do Thou bring in:
> All whom the Son doth thus make free,
> They walk in glorious liberty.
>
> O may I daily prove
>   This liberty within,
> And feel my Saviour's love,
>   Which saves me from my sin;
> Then shall I walk in liberty,
> Because the Son hath set me free.

About ten years before he died, Darney retired from his active itinerancy, but continued to work, within a limited circle, on the border-land of Lancashire; and finished his labours, sufferings, and mortal songs in 1779. He passed away in deep peace.

Charles Wesley records a visit to Haworth on October 17th, 1756, and says: "A young preacher of Mr. Ingham's came to spend the evening with me at Mr. Grimshaw's. I found love for him, and wished all *our* sons in the Gospel were equally modest and discreet." On the next day—" He accompanied us to Heptonstal, where I preached. We went on our way rejoicing to Ewood. There the hard rain cut short my discourse. Mr. Allen could not leave us yet, but rode with us as far as Gawksholm." James Allen was a native of Wensleydale, Yorkshire, where he was born, June 24th, 1734. He joined Mr. Ingham as an itinerant evangelist in 1752, and was useful as a hymnist as well as preacher. He left the Inghamite branch of early Methodism in 1761, having changed his views of doctrine and discipline. "My eyes," he says, "were never fully opened till the latter end of October, 1762. How am I now ashamed of my preaching, and the hymn-book I was concerned in printing! Almost every page put me to the blush." Some of his spiritual songs, nevertheless, in their revised condition, have been sung by numberless warm-hearted Christians.

Generations have gone since his peaceful end in 1804; but his voice of psalmody is still heard in such hymns as his on "Worthy the Lamb."

> Glory to God on high,
> Let praises fill the sky;
>   Praise ye His name!
> Angels His name adore,
> Who all our sorrows bore,
> And saints cry evermore,
>   Worthy the Lamb!
>
> All they around the throne
> Cheerfully join in one,
>   Praising His name!

We who have felt His blood
Sealing our peace with God,
Spread His dear fame abroad,
   Worthy the Lamb!

To Him our hearts we raise,
None else shall have our praise;
   Praise ye His name!
Him our exalted Lord,
By us below adored,
We praise with one accord,
   Worthy the Lamb!

If we should hold our peace,
Stones would cry out apace,
   Praise ye His name!
Love does our souls inspire
With heavenly, pure desire,
And sets us all on fire,
   Worthy the Lamb!

Join all the human race,
Our Lord and God to bless;
   Praise ye His name!
In Him we will rejoice,
Making a cheerful noise,
And say with heart and voice,
   Worthy the Lamb!

Though we must change our place,
Our souls shall never cease
   Praising His name.
To Him we'll tribute bring,
Laud Him our gracious King,
And without ceasing sing,
   Worthy the Lamb!

Laurence Batty was the youngest son of Mr. Giles Batty, a respectable yeoman of Newby Cote, near Settle, in Craven, Yorkshire. He completed his education at St. Catherine's Hall, Cambridge, where he formed an acquaintance with Mr. Delamotte, the friend of Ingham and the Wesleys. He adopted the principles, and drank in the spirit of the early Methodists. On his return to Yorkshire he joined Mr. Ingham, and began to preach in the district of Craven. He was the means of converting his parents and his two brothers, William and Christopher, both of whom were somewhat gifted hymnists in connection with James Allen. William, who was born in 1714, was at first an active opposer of Divine truth, but was subsequently a diligent, popular, and devoted preacher of the Cross. He united himself with Mr. Ingham in 1745, and suffered much persecution. His end was sudden, on the 12th of December, 1788. A long poem on "Messiah's Conquest" came from his pen, and he solaced himself amidst his trials with spiritual songs; while he taught many a heart to sing after him on "Salvation to Christ":—

> O dear Redeemer, who alone
>   Can'st give me ease in pain,
> Whose blood did once for me atone,
>   And pardon for me gain.
>
> I once was wholly dead in sin,
>   And ignorant of Thee,
> And walked contentedly therein,
>   Nor knew Thy love to me.
>
> But Thine all-seeing eye then view'd,
>   And mark'd my every way;
> And still in tender love pursued
>   Me, who from Thee did stray.
>
> Thy Name is now through grace become
>   More precious to my soul
> Than sweetest smell of rich perfume,
>   Or Aaron's precious oil.
>
> Without Thy favour, though I live,
>   Life but a burden is;
> Naught else can satisfaction give!
>   Experience shows me this.
>
> My faithless heart, O Saviour dear,
>   Correct with gentle hand;
> In every danger be Thou near,
>   Alone I cannot stand.

Christopher Batty, one year younger than his brother William, was an associate in holy song. Two or three short poems were added to his hymns. His wife, Alice, emulated him in psalmody; and his brother William's colleague, John Green, had the tuneful gift too. As Inghamite Methodist itinerants, indeed, they were banded in the work of supplying their converts with spiritual songs, and many of their hymns live still to testify to the entire consecration of their utmost power and genius to the service of Christ. About thirty years before his course was finished, Christopher Batty became elder and minister of the church at Kendal, from which charge he passed, in his eighty-second year, into immortal union with the glorified choir of early Methodist itinerant minstrels.

CHAPTER XI.

A CONTROVERSIAL SONGSTER.

*Rugged strength and radiant beauty—
These were one in nature's plan ;
Humble toil and heavenward duty—·
This will form the perfect man.*

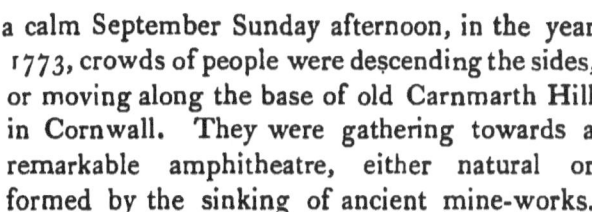N a calm September Sunday afternoon, in the year 1773, crowds of people were descending the sides, or moving along the base of old Carnmarth Hill in Cornwall. They were gathering towards a remarkable amphitheatre, either natural or formed by the sinking of ancient mine-works. It was then a "green hollow, gently shelving down, about fifty feet deep, about two hundred feet across one way, and nearly three hundred the other." At five o'clock it was filled with people, and the ground around for some distance was covered by the crowd; "so that," as an eye-witness said, "supposing the space to be four score yards square, and to contain five persons in a square yard, there must have been about two-and-thirty thousand people." Two persons now appeared standing a little way down on the side of the hollow.

They were clerical in appearance. One was rather a small man, of fair and agreeable countenance, keen of vision, and of strong purpose—evidently a man of power, though now nearing the allotted period of human life. This was John Wesley. He had preached in St. Agnes' "Church Town," at eight o'clock that morning; at one, he was found lifting up his voice to the people in Redruth; and now, at five, he is standing to proclaim salvation to the thousands around him in the celebrated "Gwennap Pit." "It was," he says, "the largest assembly I ever preached to. Yet I found, upon inquiry, all could hear, even to the skirts of the congregation. Perhaps the first time that a man of seventy had been heard by thirty thousand persons at once." That was a grand and awfully impressive scene; " I think," says one who was there, " the most magnificent spectacle which is to be seen on this side of Heaven. And no music is to be heard upon earth comparable to the sound of many thousand voices, when they are all harmoniously joined together, singing praises to God and the Lamb."

The other figure standing by Wesley was that of a man rather taller and less neatly made; a man in the prime of life, with a face that could not be looked at without interest; open, well formed, and manly. The eye that kindled and flashed as the mighty music of the hymn rose from the enthusiastic multitude, was the eye of a thinker, keen, telling of logical wariness and ready skill, and giving out, in harmony with its kindred features, expressions of genius, humour, boldness, ardent temper, and vivid imagination. It was Thomas Oliver's, one of Mr. Wesley's itinerant preachers, his friend and assistant polemic. He now came, in company with Mr. Wesley, to visit his friends in Cornwall. He had been on the ground before, and it was while on this Cornish round, or circuit, that he had the first of those impressive dreams which seemed to have called his poetic powers into action.

" While I was in this circuit," he says, " I dreamed one night that Christ was come in the clouds to judge the world, and also that he looked exceedingly black at me. When I awoke I was much alarmed. I therefore humbled myself exceedingly, with fastings and prayer; and was determined never to give over till my evidence of the love of Christ was made quite clear. One day as I was in prayer in my room, with my eyes shut, the Lord, as it were, appeared to the eye of my mind, as standing just before me, when ten thousand small streams of blood seemed to issue from every part of his body. This sight was so unexpected, and at the same time so seasonable, that for once I wept aloud—yea, and almost fainted away. I now more fully believed His love to me, and that, if He was then to come to judgment, He would not frown, but rather smile on me; therefore, I loved and praised Him with all my heart. Some years after, I had a dream of a quite different sort. I dreamed that I was talking with two women concerning the Day of Judgment. Among other things, I thought I told them I was certain it was very near. On hearing this, I thought they burst into laughter and rejected all I said. Being much grieved at this, I told them, 'I will go and see if it is not as I have said.' Accordingly I went to the door, and looking up southward, I thought I saw the heavens open, and a stream of fire, as large as a small river, issuing forth. On seeing this, I thought I ran back to the women, and said, 'You would not believe me, but come to the door and see with your own eyes that the day is come.' On hearing this, I thought they were much alarmed, and ran with me to the door. By the time we were got thither, I thought the whole concave, southward, was filled with an exceeding thick fiery mist, which swiftly moved northward, in a huge body, filling the whole space between the heavens and the earth as it came along. As it drew near, I thought, 'The day is come, of which I have so often told the world. And now, in a few moments, I shall see how it will be with me to all eternity?' And for a moment I seemed to feel myself in a state of awful suspense. When the fire was come close to me, I was going to shrink back; but thought, 'this is all in vain, as there is now no place of shelter left.' I then pushed myself forward into it, and found that the fire had no power to hurt me; for I stood as easy in the midst of it as ever I did in the open air. The joy I felt on being able to stand unhurt and undismayed amidst this awful burning cannot be described. Even so shall it be with all who are careful to enter in at the strait gate, and to walk closely and steadily in the narrow way all the days of their life; all these shall

> "Stand secure and smile,
> Amidst the jarring elements,
> The wreck of matter, and the crush of worlds."

And now, the dreamer was again in the land of dreams and visions; standing by Wesley's side, looking out upon the awful multitude in the hollow valley which might remind him of "multitudes, multitudes in the valley of decision;" recall his old dreams about "the day of the Lord in the valley of decision;" and, perhaps, awaken a joy at the thought that during the course of his twenty years' pilgrimage since the night of his dream, he had so exercised his hallowed genius as to supply the Methodists with music as well as words to sing in jubilant anticipation of the Judgment. While he was standing on Cornish ground once more, people were everywhere, through the kingdom, singing his tune to his grand Judgment Hymn—

> Come, immortal King of Glory,
> Now in Majesty appear;
> Bid the nations stand before Thee,
> Each his final doom to hear;
>   Come to judgment,
> Come Lord Jesus, quickly come.
>
> Speak the word, and lo! all nature,
> Flies before Thy glorious face,
> Angels sing your great Creator,
> Saints proclaim His sovereign grace,
>   While ye praise Him,
> Lift your heads and see Him come.
>
> See His beauty all resplendent,
> View Him in His glory shine,
> See His majesty transcendent,
> Seated on His throne sublime:
>   Angels praise Him,
> Saints and angels praise the Lamb.
>
> Shout aloud ye heavenly choirs.
> Trumpet forth Jehovah's praise:
> Trumpets, voices, hearts, and lyres!
> Speak the wonders of His grace!
>   Sound before Him
> Endless praises to His name.
>
> Ransom'd sinners, see His ensign,
> Waving thro' the purpled air!
> 'Midst ten thousand lightnings shining,
> Jesus' praises to declare;
>   How tremendous
> Is this dreadful, joyful day.

Crowns and sceptres fall before Him,
Kings and conquerors own His sway,
Fearless potentates are trembling,
While they see His lightnings play:
    How triumphant
Is the world's Redeemer now.

Noon-day beauty in its lustre
Doth in Jesu's aspect shine,
Blazing comets are not fiercer
Than the flaming eyes Divine:
    O how dreadful
Doth the Crucified appear.

Hear His voice as mighty thunder,
Sounding in eternal roar!
Far surpassing many waters
Echoing wide from shore to shore:
    Hear His accents
Through th' unfathom'd deep resound.

"Come," He saith, "ye heirs of glory,
Come, the purchase of my blood:
Bless'd ye are, and bless'd ye shall be,
Now ascend the mount of God;
    Angels guard them
To the realms of endless day."

See ten thousand flaming seraphs,
From their thrones as lightnings fly;
"Take," they cry, "your seats above us,
Nearest Him who rules the sky:
    Favourite sinners,
How rewarded are you now!"

Haste and taste celestial pleasure;
Haste and reap immortal joys;
Haste and drink the crystal river;
Lift on high your choral voice,
    While Archangels
Shout aloud the great Amen."

But the angry Lamb's determin'd
Every evil to descry;
They who have His love rejected
Shall before His vengeance fly,
    When He drives them
To their everlasting doom.

Now, in awful expectation,
See the countless millions stand;
Dread, dismay, and sore vexation,
Seize the helpless, hopeless band;
    Baleful thunders,
Stop and hear Jehovah's voice!

"Go from me," He saith, " ye cursed—
Ye for whom I bled in vain—
Ye who have my grace refused—
Hasten to eternal pain!"
    How victorious
Is the conquering *Son of Man!*

See, in solemn pomp ascending,
Jesus and His glorious train;
Countless myriads now attend Him,
Rising to th' imperial plain;
    Hallelujah!
To the bless'd Immanuel's name!

In full triumph see them marching,
Through the gates of massy light;
While the city walls are sparkling
With meridian glory bright;
    How stupendous
Are the glories of the Lamb!

On His throne of radiant azure,
High above all heights He reigns—
Reigns amidst immortal pleasure,
While refulgent glory flames;
    How diffusive
Shines the golden blaze around!

All the heavenly powers adore Him,
Circling round His orient seat;
Ransom'd saints with angels vying,
Loudest praises to repeat;
    How exalted
Is His praise, and how profound!

Every throne and every mansion,
All ye heavenly arches ring;
Echo to the Lord, salvation,
Glory to our glorious King!
    Boundless praises
All ye heavenly orbs resound!

Praise be to the Father given,
Praise to the Incarnate Son,
Praise the Spirit, One, and Seven,
Praise the mystic Three in One;
    Hallelujah!
Everlasting praise be Thine!

This was the original hymn, first issued from Leeds, about four years after the hymnist's Lord had, as he says, "appeared to the eye of his mind;" and a few years after Charles Wesley had published his hymn—

    Lo! He comes with clouds descending.

Another edition of Olivers' hymn appeared, "altered from the original," and with an addition of fifteen stanzas. In this the author has, here and there, evidently adopted Charles Wesley's expression. His first hymn remains in its own native grandeur.

There is an air of romance about the story of Olivers' life, a mystery about the life's discipline, which prepared him for the work to which he was called, when his varied powers were sanctified by the saving grace of God. In this he was like most of his contemporaries, the early Methodist preachers. Their training as preachers was very distinct from that of more modern and artificial times. It was most evidently superintended by Him who had unmistakably called them, and "thrust them forth as labourers into His harvest."

The poet was a native of Montgomeryshire. He was born in 1725. He was fatherless at the age of four years; a few months, and his sorrow-stricken mother was gone, and then he was cast on the care of one relation after another until he was eighteen. Defective training and bad example in his neighbours made him, at fifteen, a young blasphemer. As an apprentice to a shoemaker, he wasted his days and nights in vice and folly. Nevertheless, he was susceptible of love, though vicious enough to be murderously cruel to the one who loved him.

"For four or five years," says he, "I was greatly entangled with a farmer's daughter, whose sister was married to Sir J. P—— of N——n in that county. What

"Strange reverse of human fates!

For one sister was wooed by, and married to, a baronet, esteemed as one of the finest men in the county. When she died, Sir J—— was almost distracted. Presently, after her funeral, he published an elegy on her of a thousand verses! For her sake he said,

"O that the fleecy care had been my lot,
Some lonely cottage on some verdant spot!

"For some time he daily visited her in her vault, and at last took her up, and kept her in his bed-chamber for several years.

"On the other hand, her sister, who was but little inferior in person, fell into the hands of a most insignificant young man, who was a means of drawing her almost to an untimely end. I cannot omit giving some intimation of this particular, seeing all who are acquainted with my former life know this to be one great aggregate of my folly and wickedness; and seeing it is that which lay heaviest on my mind, both before and after my conversion; and which to this day I remember with peculiar shame and sorrow. However, God, who often brings good out of evil, made it a means (though a remote one) of my conversion. For such was the clamour of the people, and the uneasiness of my own mind, that I determined to leave the country."

Now he entered upon his wanderings as a profane-tongued, miserable vagabond. He went from town to town, interrupting Methodist worship with indecency, or uttering blasphemies in church, or writhing under the lash of conscience, or trying to quiet himself by reading a borrowed copy of a "Week's Preparation for the Holy Sacrament," or contriving and committing new villanies. At one time, he would horrify the profane with his profanities; and at another, secretly acknowledge the good influence of a Methodist innkeeper; not uncommonly met with in those days, when Methodism understood temperance to be a Christian virtue essentially accordant with pure charity. He finds his way at length to Bristol, where, after being robbed of his last penny by a sharper, he one evening met a multitude of people. "I asked one of them," he tells us, "where they had been. She answered, 'to hear Mr. Whitfield.' She also told me he was to preach the next night. I thought, 'I have often heard of Mr. Whitfield, and have sung songs about him; I will go and hear what he has to say." Accordingly I went the next evening, but was too late. The following evening I was determined to be in time. I went near three hours before the time. When the service began, I did little but look about me; but on seeing the tears trickle down the cheeks of some who stood near me, I became more attentive. The text was, 'Is not this a brand plucked out of the fire?' When this sermon began, I was certainly a dreadful enemy to God, and to all that is good, and one of the most profligate and abandoned young men living; but by the time it was ended, I was become a new creature. For, in the first place, I was deeply convinced of the great goodness of God towards me all my life; particularly in that he had given His Son to die for me. I had also a far clearer view of all my sins; particularly my base ingratitude towards Him. These discoveries quite broke my heart, and caused showers of tears to trickle down my cheeks. I was likewise filled with an utter abhorrence of my evil ways, and was much ashamed that ever I had walked in them. And as my heart was thus turned from all evil, so it was powerfully inclined to all that is good. It is not easy to express what strong desires I had for God and His service; and what resolutions I had to seek and serve Him in future : in consequence of which I broke off all my evil practices, and forsook all my wicked and foolish companions without delay; and gave myself up to God and His service with my whole heart. O what reason have I say, 'Is not this a brand plucked out of the fire?'"

"The love I had for Mr. Whitfield was inexpressible. I used to follow him as he walked the streets, and could scarce refrain from kissing the very prints of his feet. And as to the people of God, I dearly loved to be with them, and wished to be a member of their society; but knew not how to accomplish it. At last I ventured to mention it to one of Mr. Whitfield's preachers; but he discouraged me, and therefore I was obliged to give it up."

Shortly after this he left Bristol, and found his way to Bradford in Wiltshire. Here he went at once to the Methodist services. He longed to be one with the society, but could not venture to offer himself. At last, he was noticed, and asked whether he wished to join them. "My heart," he says, "leaped for joy. They took me to the preacher, who gave me a note of admittance. As I returned home, just as I came to the bottom of the hill, at the entrance of the town, a ray of light, resembling the shining of a star, descended through a small opening in the heavens, and instantaneously shone upon me. In that instant my burden fell off, and I was so elevated that I felt as if I could literally fly away to heaven. This was the more surprising to me, as I had always been (what I still am) so prejudiced in favour of rational religion as not to regard visions or revelations, perhaps, so much as I ought to do. But this light was so clear, and the sweetness and other effects attending it were so great, that though it happened about twenty-seven years ago, the several circumstances thereof are as fresh in my remembrance as if they had happened but yesterday."

The renewal of his heart resulted in the rapid development of his mental powers, and their full consecration to his Redeemer's service. He lived now simply to get and to do good. His trials, however, were not over. His discipline was not complete. He was seized with small-pox, and was so afflicted as to become loathsome; was blind for five weeks; and, indeed, was looked on as already in the corruption of the grave. The physician declared that though he had been fifty years in practice he never saw a case so bad as this. One good Samaritan there was who came to him in his extremity, the venerable and beloved Richard Pearce, the landlord of the "Cross Keys" inn. This man had a "church in his house," inn as it was; a church that was often met in the room behind the bar by Wesley, Romaine, and their apostolic companions. Richard Pearce was one of the most saintly men of his time. He befriended the sick man. "Among other things," says Olivers, "he asked me what money I had. I said, 'But little.' He then encouraged me not to fear, telling me that as I was far from my own country, he would take care I had all things necessary. Accordingly he sent me one of the best nurses in the town.

He next sent the chief apothecary the place afforded; and lastly Dr. Clarke, the most experienced physician in all that country."

After six months of suffering in quiet patience, the recovered man rose from his bed, and left Bradford to visit his native place. His first object was to receive a small amount of property which his father's uncle had left him, and his next to pay all the debts which he had left unpaid in the various places of his sojourn during his life of sinful wandering. He accomplished this; having sold his horse, bridle, and saddle, to complete the settlement. Wherever he went, he preached the Gospel which had set him free. Laughed at, threatened with imprisonment, led to the parish stocks, he still pursued what he believed was his calling, until he worked his way back to Bradford. He went at once to the "Cross Keys" to ask Mr. Pearce for his account. Pearce declared he had no account against him. He then, with what means he had, set up in business. But before he had well begun, Mr. Wesley, whose discernment of character and fitness for Methodist work never failed, desired the zealous shoemaker to give up his secular calling and go at once, as an evangelist, into Cornwall. This was to him the call of God. "I was not able," he tells us, "to buy another horse, and therefore, with my boots on my legs, my great-coat on my back, and my saddle-bags with my books and linen across my shoulder, I set out on foot, October 24th, 1753." He footed it as far as Tiverton, in Devon, where a friend asked why he had no horse. The reason was easily given. "Go and buy one," it was said, "and it shall be paid for." Olivers hesitated; but was at last persuaded to accept the offer. "A few days after," he writes, "I went with a farmer into his field. In a few minutes a colt, about two years and a half old, came to me and put his nose upon my shoulder. I stroked him and asked the farmer what he would take for him. He said, 'Five pounds.' We struck a bargain at once, and in a few days I mounted my horse, and have kept him to this day; which is about twenty-five years.

On him I have travelled comfortably not less than a hundred thousand miles, in preaching the Gospel. In this, also, I see the hand of God; for I parted with one horse rather than bring a reproach on the Gospel; and as a reward, He provided me with such another as, in many respects, none of my brethren could ever boast of."

He had now farly entered on his life-work. For forty-six years he bore "the burden and heat of the day." With a clear and strong understanding, a ready utterance, and courage that never flinched, he travelled in various parts of England, Scotland, and Ireland; and amidst all the exposures and inconveniences of Methodist itinerancy, he managed to become well-read in English theology, to learn enough of the original languages of the sacred volume to make him a successful student of God's word, a powerful defender of the doctrines which he had received, and an energetic, convincing, and fruitful preacher of saving truth. Nor was his poetic genius allowed to lie dormant. It was cultured and brought into exercise for his Divine Master's sake. He had gone from Cornwall to Norfolk, from Norfolk to London, from London to Ireland, where his labours were chiefly about Limerick, Waterford, and Cork. While thus engaged in Ireland his tuneful soul put forth his "Hymn of Praise to Christ."

> Our hearts and hands to Christ we raise,
> In honour, blessing, thanks, and praise;
> To Christ the sinner's only Friend,
> Whose love, whose praise, shall never end.
> To Christ the sinner's only Friend,
> Whose love, whose praise, shall never end.
>   Hallelujah, praise the Lord.

> To Christ who bought us with His blood,
> And made us kings and priests to God,
> Be everlasting praises given,
> By all on earth, and all in heaven;
> Be everlasting praises given,
> By all on earth, and all in heaven.
>   Hallelujah, praise the Lord.

> Hail! Jesus, all-atoning Lamb!
> We magnify Thy wondrous Name;
> Thy wondrous Name our tongues employ,
> In hymns of everlasting joy.
> Thy wondrous Name our tongues employ,
> In hymns of everlasting joy.
>   Hallelujah, praise the Lord.
>
> To Thee our grateful songs arise,
> In sounds of praise, through earth and skies;
> Let all the ransom'd race adore,
> And love and praise Thee evermore.
> Let all the ransom'd race adore,
> And love and praise Thee evermore.
>   Hallelujah, praise the Lord.
>
> Let all Thy flaming hosts above,
> Record the wonders of Thy love;
> In ceaseless Hallelujahs sing
> The praise of our eternal King.
> In ceaseless Hallelujahs sing,
> The praise of our eternal King.
>   Hallelujah, praise the Lord.
>
> Let earth and heaven with one accord,
> Resound, Salvation to the Lord!
> And every creature join to bless
> The Lord, the Lord, our Righteousness.
> And every creature join to bless
> The Lord, the Lord, our Righteousness.
>   Hallelujah, praise the Lord.

This spirited outburst of his loving heart and warm genius seems to have struck an answering chord in the Irish soul; for it is said that the verses were set to music by an Irish gentleman, and were sung in anthem style before the Bishop of Waterford in his cathedral on Christmas Day. The poet preacher, on his return from Ireland, was again in London and then at Leeds. A man of his temperament was not likely to remain in celibacy. The questions now pressed themselves upon him, "Am I called to marry?" If so, "What sort of a person would be suitable?—what sort of a person would Christ choose for me?" These questions were calmly and seriously weighed. The necessary qualities in a help-meet for him were considered, and as the result, "I immediately turned my eyes to Miss Green," he says, "a person of a good family, and noted through all the North of England for her extraordinary piety. I therefore opened my mind to her; and after consulting Mr. Wesley, we were married." The marriage was a happy one. But wedlock is not free from trials. The effects of his severe illness at Bradford still lingered about him, and sometimes threatened to finish his career. But he kept in the saddle through several northern counties; and, at last, in improved health, he came again to Bristol; and here he seems to have issued his grandest and most popular hymn, from amidst the sorrows of bereavement. He had seen one child depart from Bristol to its rest; and now the other went. Perhaps these painful proofs of his pilgrim state served to brighten his genius as well as tune his heart for the lofty and thrilling strain of his "Hymn to the God of Abraham."—

> The God of Abraham praise,
>   Who reigns enthron'd above;
> Ancient of everlasting days,
>   And God of love:
> Jehovah—great I Am—
>   By earth and Heaven confest;
> I bow and bless the sacred Name,
>   For ever bless'd.
>
> The God of Abraham praise,
>   At whose supreme command,
> From earth I rise, and seek the joys
>   At His right hand:
> I all on earth forsake,
>   Its wisdom, fame and power;
> And Him my only portion make
>   My Shield and Tower.
>
> The God of Abraham praise,
>   Whose all-sufficient grace
> Shall guide me all my happy days,
>   In all my ways:
> He calls a worm His friend!
>   He calls Himself my God!
> And He shall save me to the end,
>   Thro' Jesu's blood.
>
> He by Himself hath sworn!
>   I on His oath depend,
> I shall on eagle's wings up-borne,
>   To Heaven ascend;

I shall behold His face,
  I shall His power adore,
And sing the wonders of His grace
  For evermore.

Tho' nature's strength decay,
  And earth and hell withstand,
To Canaan's bounds I urge my way
  At His command:
The wat'ry deep I pass,
  With Jesus in my view;
And thro' the howling wilderness
  My way pursue.

The goodly land I see,
  With peace and plenty bless'd;
A land of sacred liberty
  And endless rest.
There milk and honey flow,
  And oil and wine abound,
And trees of life for ever grow,
  With mercy crown'd.

There dwells the Lord our King,
  The Lord our Righteousness,
Triumphant o'er the world and sin,
  The Prince of Peace:
On Sion's sacred heights
  His kingdom still maintains;
And glorious, with His saints in light
  For ever reigns.

He keeps His own secure,
  He guards them by His side,
Arrays in garments white and pure
  His spotless bride.
With streams of sacred bliss,
  With groves of living joys,
With all the fruits of Paradise
  He still supplies.

Before the great Three-One
  They all exulting stand;
And tell the wonders He hath done,
  Thro' all their land:
The list'ning spheres attend,
  And swell the growing fame;
And sing, in songs which never end,
  The wondrous Name.

> The God who reigns on high,
> The great Archangels sing,
> And "Holy, Holy, Holy," cry,
> "Almighty King!
> Who was, and is, the same!
> And evermore shall be;
> Jehovah—Father—Great I Am!
> We worship Thee."
>
> Before the Saviour's face
> The ransom'd nations bow;
> O'erwhelm'd at His Almighty grace,
> For ever new:
> He shows His prints of love—
> They kindle—to a flame!
> And sound through all the worlds above,
> The slaughter'd Lamb.
>
> The whole triumphant host
> Give thanks to God on high;
> "Hail, Father, Son, and Holy Ghost!"
> They ever cry:
> Hail, Abraham's God—and *mine!*
> I join the heavenly lays
> All might and majesty are Thine,
> And endless praise.

It is said that while Olivers was visiting his friend John Bakewell, the hymnist, he went to a Jewish synagogue, and was so deeply impressed with an old Hebrew melody sung by Dr. Leoni, that on his return he produced the stanzas which are metrically adapted to the admired tune. A distinguished hymn writer may be taken as a critic of authority. "There is not in our language," says James Montgomery, "a lyric of more majestic style, more elevated thought, or more glorious imagery: its structure, indeed, is unattractive; and, on account of the short lines, occasionally uncouth; but, like a stately pile of architecture, severe and simple in design, it strikes less on the first view, than after deliberate examination, when its proportions become more graceful, its dimensions expand, and the mind itself grows greater in contemplating it. The man who wrote this hymn must have had the finest ear imaginable; for on account of the peculiarity of the measure, none but a person of equal musical and poetic taste could have produced the harmony perceptible in the verse."

Olivers lived to see the issue of at least thirty editions of his hymn. But he did not live to hear all the soul-music which his hymn has awakened among the spiritual children of faithful Abraham, on their way from every scene of mortal life to their home beyond the flood. Holy women and consecrated men have made it their song in the land of their pilgrimage; and portions of it have formed their final utterances of triumph in crossing the border of their inheritance.

The saintly wife of that saintly man who, in his simple faith, came so near to Abraham himself, William Carvosso, of Ponsanooth, in Cornwall, was called for the last eighteen months of her life to extreme suffering. But her consolations abounded; so that her sweet singing was not silenced even by strong pain. Often were parts of her favourite hymn heard ringing through the house. Now, it would be,—

> The God of Abraham praise,
> At whose supreme command,
> From earth I rise, and seek the joys
> At His right hand:
> I all on earth forsake,
> Its wisdom, fame, and power;
> And Him my only portion make,
> My Shield and Tower.

and then, frequently—

> He by Himself hath sworn,
> I on His oath depend,
> I shall, on eagle's wings up-borne,
> To Heaven ascend.

Depending on that Divine oath, she herself passed into her heaven.

In a little snug retreat under a hill-side, near Callington, in the West of England, the Methodist preachers used to be entertained, with motherly affection, by the aged wife of Mr. Geake, a veteran Methodist leader and local preacher. When the good woman was young, she was always ready, in the warmth of her zeal, to go from place to place assisting the preachers by the use of her fine voice in singing. And now, when beyond eighty, she would say, "My voice is weak, but I can sing still, my heart sings; and often of an evening I lift up my song."—"Can't you give me a morning song?" said a friend one day. "Yes, I think I can." And then, in a thin, tremulous tone, she sang her favourite hymn, which she said Dr. Adam Clarke had taught her, while she was a girl, when he used to preach in her father's parlour. It was—

> The God of Abraham praise.

The Rev. William Worth, when about to finish his Methodist itinerancy, had been lying for some time in silence, as though he were listening attentively. At length he said, "Hark! Do you hear that sweet music?"—"Yes," he added, speaking to the unseen, "precious Saviour, Thou art mine!" Then, breaking forth into praise, he exclaimed—

> "I shall behold His face,
> I shall His power adore,
> And sing the wonders of His grace
> For evermore!"

"Hark!" he cried again; "Hallelujah! glory! glory for ever and ever!"

It was his last shout as he passed up to "behold *His* face."

The great Methodist theologian, too, Richard Watson, after a life of holy familiarity with "the cherubims of glory overshadowing the Mercy Seat," came to the end, frequently giving out his elect song—

> I shall behold His face!

"When," said he, "shall I leave this tenement of clay for the wide expanse? When shall the nobler joys open, and I see my God?" And then the song broke forth afresh—

> "I *shall* behold His face!
> I *shall His* power adore!
> And sing the wonders of *His* grace,
> For evermore!"

A few years after the publication of this hymn, the poet was stationed at Chester. While in that neighbourhood, he visited the place in which he was brought up; and his pluck and shrewd logic were amusingly brought out in an interview with the parish parson.

"I hear you intend to preach in the parish," said he to Olivers.

"I do; yea, and think it my duty to do so."

"You will be punished if you do!"

"I am licensed, and therefore will not be hindered by any man in the parish; no, nor by the Primate of all England!

"But the divine right to preach is found only in the established clergy of this land!"

"Sir," was the closing answer, "the world is large, of which England is but a very small part—an island only, stuck up, as it were, in one corner of it! And as to its established clergy, you know, sir, that many of them are worldly-minded to a proverb; yea, that multitudes of them are drunkards, swearers, pleasure-takers, &c.; and yet you tell me that such a clergy of so inconsiderable a corner of the world are the only ministers of God; and that all others are intruders and deceivers!"

Well done, Olivers! The figment of apostolical succession is too filmy to bear the touch of thy common sense!

While the keen-witted hymn-writer was at Chester, he seems to have composed the only other hymn of his that has been preserved. At the end of a short account of the death of Mary Langson, who died January 29, 1769, at Foxall, in Cheshire, there were the following verses:—

> O Thou God of my salvation,
>   My Redeemer from all sin;
> Mov'd by Thy divine compassion,
>   Who hast died my heart to win,
>   I will praise Thee;
>   Where shall I Thy praise begin
>
> Tho' unseen, I love the Saviour,
>   He hath brought salvation near,
> Manifests His pard'ning favour;
>   And when Jesus doth appear,
>   Soul and body
>   Shall His glorious image bear.

> While the angel choirs are crying,
>   Glory to the great I Am,
> I with them will still be vieing,
>   Glory, glory, to the Lamb!
>   O how precious
>   Is the sound of Jesus' name.
>
> Angels' now are hovering round us;
>   Unperceived they mix the throng,
> Wondering at the love that crowned us,
>   Glad to join the holy song—
>   Hallelujah!
>   Love and praise to Christ belong!
>
> Now I see with joy and wonder
>   Whence the gracious spring arose;
> Angels' minds are lost to ponder
>   Dying love's mysterious cause;
>   But the blessing,
>   Down to all, to me it flows.
>
> This has set me all on fire,
>   Strongly glows the flame of love;
> Higher mounts my soul and higher,
>   Struggles for its swift remove;
>   Then I'll praise Thee
>   In a nobler strain above.

This hymn has on it the impress of Olivers' distinctive talent, and, probably, was attached by himself to the memorial pamphlet which he had written.

When our poet had become unequal to the toils of itinerancy, he settled in London, and "undertook," as he says, "the care of Mr. Wesley's printing." But he could make fine hymns better than he could correct for the press, for under the date of August 8, 1789, Mr. Wesley says in his journal:—"I settled all my temporal business, and, in particular, chose a new person to prepare the *Arminian Magazine*, being obliged, however unwillingly, to drop Mr. O—— for only these two reasons: 1. The errata are insufferable. I have borne them for these twelve years, but can bear them no longer. 2. Several pieces are inserted without my knowledge, both in prose and verse. I must try whether these things cannot be amended for the short residue of my life."

Mr. Wesley, nevertheless, loved Olivers, and highly esteemed his powers as a defender of true Methodist doctrines. Some of the young and pert opponents of these doctrines affected to laugh at the Arminian champion; and even Toplady stooped to the vulgarism of controversy, by representing the venerable Wesley as saying—

> I've Thomas Olivers, the cobler,
> No stall in England owns a nobler;
> A wight of talents universal,
> Whereof I'll give a brief rehearsal:
> He with one brandish of his quill
> Will knock down Toplady and Hill.

This was, perhaps, intended as a parody on Wesley's calm remark at one point of the controversy: "I have not leisure to consider the matter at large; I can only make a few strictures, and leave the young man to be further corrected by one that is full his match, Mr. Thomas Olivers." Sir Richard Hill, too, must needs throw contempt on the logical cobbler, sneering at him, as "one Thomas Oliver, alias Olivers"; but this brought from the saintly Fletcher a fine testimony to the varied powers and consistent character of the divinely-called preacher and gifted writer and hymnist. "This author was, twenty-five years ago, a mechanic, and, like 'one' Peter, 'alias' Simon, a fisherman, and, like 'one' Saul, 'alias' Paul, a tent-maker, has had the honour of being promoted to the dignity of a preacher of the Gospel; and his talents as a writer, a logician, a poet, and a composer of sacred music, are known to those who have looked into his publications."

Olivers outlived his friend Wesley. He died in London, somewhat suddenly, in March, 1799, and his mortal remains found rest in Wesley's own tomb.

The old songster's last effusion was "A Descriptive and Plaintive Elegy on the Death of the late Reverend John Wesley." These numerous verses are valuable as a record by an eye-witness of many interesting facts illustrative of the life, character, and influence of John Wesley. Some of them are given with beauty and effect. The affections of the poet dwell, however, on so many particulars, that the poem, in some parts, fails in dignity, and becomes defective in poetic spirit and musical expression. The closing stanzas will be sufficient to show the author's feeling and manner, as well as the thought and sympathy generally awakened by the departure of an apostolic man.

> The pensive dove, whene'er his mate is fled,
> Coos round and round, then droops his languid head;
> And shall not *we* complain, who feel a heavier load?
> We must—we can't refrain, whilst in this dark abode.
>
> As Israel mourned of old, his fav'rite gone;
> As Rachel mourned her fertile plains along;
> As Mary mourned and wept beneath her Saviour's cross;
> So we, with moans and tears, will now lament our loss.
>
> But though we now lament, the day is nigh,
> When we shall meet again, above the sky;
> And there our songs unite, and join the radiant throng,
> And bow before the throne, and bless the Great Three-One.
>
> Then let us still maintain the truth he taught,
> And faithful prove in deed, and word, and thought;
> The path he trod before, let us through life pursue,
> And help each other on, and keep the prize in view.
>
> But chiefly *we*, who bear his sacred shame,
> Who feed his flock, and still revere his name,
> Let us unite in one, and strive with mutual care
> To help his children on, and all their burdens bear.
>
> For this let us, like him, the world disdain;
> For this, like him, rejoice in toil and pain;
> Like him, be bold for God; like him, our time redeem,
> And strive, and watch, and pray, and live, and die like him.

CHAPTER XII.

THREE LAY SINGERS.

> Moses, the minister of God,
> Rebukes our partial love,
> Who envy at the gifts bestow'd
> On those we disapprove :
> Shall we the Spirit's course restrain,
> Or quench the heavenly fire?
> Let God His messengers ordain,
> And whom He will inspire.

THE wonderful varieties of character, opinion, and talent, which were more or less closely associated with the rise of Methodism, form a study at once curious, interesting, and instructive. The Wesleys and Whitfield, as the leaders of the great religious movement, came into contact with human nature in nearly all its shapes and conditions, all its colourings of accomplishment and manners, and all its degrees of native power. The distinctive doctrines of Methodism proper seemed to rise in clear and sharply developed form from amidst the chaotic heaving and whirls of theological ages; and so, as an experimental and practical system, it appeared to come up shaped and toned by means of contributed force and virtue from all sources of hallowed and even unhallowed intellect, endowment, genius, and learning. The graceless controversialist, Bishop Warburton, in his "Doctrine of Grace," says that "Mr. William Law begat Methodism, and Count Zinzendorf rocked the cradle, while the Devil acted as midwife to Mr. Wesley's new-born babes." This is a lampoon in the naturally coarse style of an unscrupulous scribbler, and a would-be wit; but it indicates the relations of early Methodism to a grotesque variety of things, and touches the fact, that some of the worst manifestations of error and ill-will—Bishop Warburton's temper among the rest—served to promote the good which the first Methodists had so much at heart. It is curious to watch the Wesleys, as, by turns, they have to do with English bishops and mystic dreamers, Moravian dignitaries and converts from among the aristocracy of England, Presbyterian saints, comic authors and mimics, sceptical philosophers, masters in science, and literary giants; with legislators and philanthropists, saintly women in high life and hallowed geniuses in servitude and obscurity; orthodox royalists and northern Jacobites. It is deeply instructive, however, to see how all these varieties were made, willingly or unwillingly, to subserve the great object at which the holy men steadily aimed, and from which no heterogeneous claims of outside character, opinion, or influence, could ever withdraw their simple and earnest bent. Among the varieties of genius, learning, and friendly sympathy which gathered around the Wesleys, one character was remarkable in many respects.

In the early part of 1739, a group which would fix attention at first sight, was seen one day walking out from Little Britain in the direction of Islington, then a north suburb of London. There were three persons. One was a small, neat, clerical figure, with cravat and ruffles the very patterns of neatness; another was similar in size and appearance; but the third was uncommonly tall; and served, by the side of the others, to form a somewhat amusing contrast. He carried a crook-topped stick, and wore a curious low-polled slouched hat, from under the long-peaked front brim of which his benignant face bent forward a cautiously inquisitive kind of look, as if he were in the habit of prying into everything, without caring to let everything enter deeply into him. The comparatively short clergyman was John Wesley. His towering companion was John Byrom, of Manchester, who, among the jottings in his journal for February 7th, 1739, says, " Walked with John Wesley and another young fellow from Mr. Bray's to Islington."

Byrom was at this time about forty-eight years of age, and was therefore much John Wesley's senior, and old enough to think of his other clerical companion as a "young fellow." The tall genius had been trained at Cambridge, and had been introduced to the Wesleys and their godly companions at Oxford, when they were becoming marked as the leaders of the Methodist Club. He had taken an early turn in favour of spiritual religion, and his religious views and feelings had become so different to those of most of the clergy in his day that he shrank from identifying himself with them by taking orders, and at last resigned his fellowship and sacrificed the prospect of Church honours and emoluments. Familiarity with the writings of the German, French, and English mystics deepened his attachment to spiritual pursuits, and prepared him for warm sympathy with the views and experiences of the first Methodists. He sought their society, and was happy to be known as their friend. Though never so far identified with them as to be, in the strict sense, a member of the Methodist Society, yet he was bound to them by ties so close and inseparable that it is impossible to lose sight of him among the early poets of Methodism. Really affectionate as was the friendship between Byrom and John Wesley, their views were so irreconcilable on some of the mystic doctrines, and their characters were so differently shaped, that unity in Methodist action was, perhaps, impracticable. The differences between them are given in graphic style in Byrom's jottings of an interview in Manchester between Mr. Wesley, Mr. Phillips, and himself. The characteristic firmness, clear sense, strong will in the pursuit of his object, unflinching devotion to genuine truthfulness, and pure practical piety on the part of Wesley, are placed side by side with that sprightly, somewhat whimsical, but good-natured genius, that kind of learned indifference, cultured ease, and pious quietude of spirit, which are drawn so finely, and with such finish, in Byrom's own poem on "Careless Content."

I am content, I do not care,
   Wag as it will the world for me;
When fuss and fret was all my fare,
   It got no ground, as I could see:
So when away my caring went,
I counted cost, and was content.

With more of thanks and less of thought,
   I strive to make my matters meet;
To seek what ancient sages sought,
   Physic and food, in sour and sweet:
To take what passes in good part,
And keep the hiccups from the heart.

With good and gentle-humoured hearts,
   I choose to chat where'er I come;
Whate'er the subject be that starts;
   But if I get among the glum,
I hold my tongue to tell the troth,
And keep my breath to cool my broth.

For chance or change, of peace or pain;
   For Fortune's favour or her frown;
For lack or glut, for loss or gain,
   I never dodge, nor up nor down:
But swing what way the ship shall swim,
Or tack about with equal trim.

I suit not where I shall not speed,
   Nor trace the turn of ev'ry tide;
If simple sense will not succeed,
   I make no bustling, but abide:
For shining wealth, or scaring woe,
I force no friend, I fear no foe.

Of *ups* and *downs*, of *ins* and *outs*,
   Of *they're i' th' wrong*, and *we're i' th' right*,
I shun the rancours, and the routs,
   And wishing well to every wight,
Whatever turn the matter takes,
I deem it all but ducks and drakes.

With whom I feast, I do not fawn,
   Nor if the folks should flout me, faint;
If wonted welcome be withdrawn,
   I cook no kind of a complaint:
With none dispos'd to disagree,
But like them best who best like me.

Not that I rate myself the rule
   How all my betters should behave;
But fame shall find me no man's fool,
   Nor to a set of men a slave:
I love a friendship, free and frank,
And hate to hang upon a hank.

Fond of a true and trusty tie,
     I never loose where'er I link;
   Though if a bus'ness budges by,
     I talk thereon just as I think:
   My word, my work, my heart, my hand,
   Still on a side together stand.

   If names or notions make a noise,
     Whatever hap the question hath,
   The point impartially I poise,
     And read, or write, but without wrath;
   For should I burn or break my brains,
   Pray, who will pay me for my pains?

   I love my neighbour as myself,
     Myself like him too, by his leave;
   Nor to his pleasure, pow'r, or pelf,
     Came I to crouch, as I conceive:
   Dame Nature doubtless has design'd
   A man the monarch of his mind.

   Now taste and try this temper, sirs,
     Mood it, and brood it in your breast;
   Or if ye ween, for worldly stirs,
     That man does right to mar his rest,
   Let me be deft, and debonair,
   I am content, I do not care.

The Mr. Bray from whose house the poet says he walked with John Wesley to Islington was a brazier in Little Britain, a Moravian, "a poor, ignorant mechanic, who knows nothing but Christ," says Charles Wesley, "yet, by knowing Him, knows and discerns all things." The doctor very highly esteemed this man, and tells Mrs. Byrom that he found the Bishop of Ely "very civil, affable, and conversable; but," he adds, "I confess myself full as well pleased with the sentiments of the poor brazier. He talks more like a bishop, in one sense."

The name of Byrom will ever live as a "grand master" of shorthand writing. In this character his relation to the Wesleys is deeply interesting. Their journals and their poetry were committed to paper in the shorthand style, which they had learnt to use with freedom under his mastership.

The doctor, who threw most of his learned lessons into verse, recommended shorthand to poets:—

> Consider how the shorthand scheme, in part,
> May be applied to the poetic art.
>
> . . . .
>
> Form to yourself, directly, the design
> Of so constructing a poetic line;
> That it may cost, in writing it *our* way,
> The least expense of ink, as one may say.

Charles Wesley acted on his advice, and jotted most of his hymns in shorthand, just as they arose in his mind. But Byrom was associated with early Methodism more closely as a poet than as a teacher of shorthand. His hand was in the earliest issue of religious poetry by the Wesleys. To the first volume of that long succession of spiritual song-books by which the private and public Methodist hymn service was sustained, the mystic and scholarly Manchester man contributed. His friends, the Wesleys, had asked for some hymns from his pen. He sent his translation of two hymns from the French of Madame Bourignon, and wrote like a kind-hearted, discriminating, tasteful, and judicious friend. The brothers evidently profited by the doctor's advice. However mystical the Frenchwoman might be who wrote the original hymns which Byrom had rendered into English, she had a spirituality and heavenliness of soul which did not cease to find an echo from the kindred minds of Methodism for many generations. Nor has Byrom failed, as a translator, to kindle a delicate warmth of devotion, like that of the mystic hymnist, in the hearts of all who sing his verses " with the spirit, and with the understanding also."

On July 12, 1773, John Wesley was trotting on his way from Liverpool to Birmingham. " In my journey," he tells us, " I read Dr. Byrom's poems. He has all the wit and humour of Dr. Swift, together with much more learning, a deep and strong understanding, and, above all, a serious vein of piety. . . We have some of the finest sentiments that ever appeared in the English tongue; some of the noblest truths expressed with the utmost energy of language, and the strongest colours of poetry." To John Wesley's high esteem and affection for the Manchester poet, the Methodists owe the insertion, in their authorised hymn-book, of the now well-known hymn, which has helped so many winged souls in their upward pursuit of entire holiness. The hymn as now sung has, by alteration, been made to accord with the Wesleys' taste and judgment. Whether their taste and judgment were really superior to the translator's, might have been a question with him, and may be to some others a question still. One likes to catch the feeling, and to breathe the music, as it flowed from the hallowed genius who had such sympathy with the French singer.

> Come, Saviour *Jesus!* from above
>   Assist me with Thy heavenly grace;
> Withdraw my heart from worldly love,
>   And for Thyself prepare the place.
>
> Lord! let Thy sacred presence fill,
>   And set my longing spirit free,
> That pants to have no other will,
>   But night and day to think on Thee.
>
> Where'er Thou leadest, I'll pursue,
>   Through all retirements or employs;
> But to the world I'll bid adieu,
>   And all its vain delusive joys.
>
> That way with humble speed I'll walk
>   Wherein my *Saviour's* footsteps shine;
> Nor will I hear, nor will I talk,
>   Of any other love but Thine.
>
> To Thee my longing soul aspires;
>   To Thee I offer all my vows:
> Keep me from false and vain desires,
>   My God, my Saviour, and my Spouse!
>
> Henceforth let no profane delight,
>   Divide this consecrated soul!
> Possess it Thou, who hast the right
>   As Lord and Master of the whole.
>
> Wealth, honours, pleasures, or what else
>   This short-enduring world can give,
> Tempt as they will, my heart repels
>   To Thee alone resolved to live.

> Thee one may love, and Thee alone,
>   With inward peace and holy bliss;
> And when Thou tak'st us for Thy own,
>   Oh! what a happiness is this!
>
> Nor heaven, nor earth, do I desire,
>   Nor mysteries to be revealed;
> 'Tis love that sets my heart on fire:
>   Speak Thou the word, and I am heal'd.
>
> All other graces I resign;
>   Pleas'd to receive, pleas'd to restore:
> Grace is Thy *gift*, it shall be mine
>   The Giver only to adore.

The poetical doctor was very much in London during 1739, and continually came into agreeable intercourse with the leaders of Methodism. Now he is in some coffee-house, mingling with literary and scientific men, legislators, and wits; now he finds his way to Bray's, the brazier in Little Britain, meeting Charles Wesley there, and taking tea with him; and now working hard as a shorthand teacher, to get bread and butter for his Manchester household. Amidst all his varied action, however, the spiritual with him was ever above the temporal. As he moved about, he longed for retirement with God, and filled up the time of street travel with prayer and hymns of desire. One of the outpourings of his soul, during his hurry to and fro, is found among his hasty jottings—and beautiful it is—as silently breathed before God, amidst the stirring multitudes of the great city. He calls it "A Penitential Soliloquy."

> What! tho' no objects strike upon the sight!
> Thy sacred presence is an *inward* light!
> What! tho' no sounds should penetrate the ear!
> To list'ning thought, the voice of truth is clear!
> Sincere devotion needs no outward shrine;
> The centre of an *humble* soul is Thine!
>
> There may I worship! and there may'st Thou place
> Thy seat of mercy, and Thy throne of grace!
> Yea, fix, if Christ, my Advocate, appear,
> The dread tribunal of Thy justice there:
> Let each vain thought, let each impure desire,
> Meet in Thy wrath with a *consuming* fire.

Whilst the kind rigours of a righteous doom
All deadly filth of *selfish pride* consume,
Thou, Lord, canst raise, tho' punishing for sin,
The joys of peaceful penitence within:
Thy justice and Thy mercy both are sweet,
That make our *suff'rings* and *salvation* meet.

Befall me, then, whatever God shall please!
His wounds are healing, and His griefs give ease:
He, like a true physician of the soul,
Applies the med'cine that may make it whole:
I'll do, I'll *suffer* whatsoe'er He wills;
I see His aim thro' all these transient ills.

'Tis to infuse a *salutary* grief,
To fit the mind for *absolute* relief:
That, purged from every *false* and finite love,
Dead to the world, alive to things above,
The soul may rise, as in its *first* form'd youth,
And worship God in *spirit* and in *truth*.

The bonds of love which held their poetic friend so close to the Wesleys were tested, not merely by different theological leanings, but by dissimilar political attachments. The doctor was well known to be warmly in favour of the House of Stuart. He had gone into France in earlier life, for the sake of avoiding any unpleasant experiences which his principles might entail. And when, in 1745, the Pretender marched into Manchester, he was among those who gave him welcome. His friend, John Wesley, had, a few weeks before, declared to public authority: "All I can do for his Majesty, whom I honour and love, is to cry unto God day by day, in public and in private, to put all his enemies to confusion." And about the time that Byrom was walking out in Manchester with his family, and Wesley's old friend, Clayton, to hear the Pretender proclaimed, John Wesley was quietly engaged in London, finishing his "Farther Appeal to Men of Reason and Religion"; and his brother Charles was "praying with Bridget Armstead, full of desire to be dissolved!"

At this time Byrom had come into family property, and was living in the pleasant country retreat of Kersal-Cell, a little way out from the old busy town. His decided exhibition of good will to the Stuarts necessarily involved him in awkward circumstances at times ; and it is said that on one occasion, when a toast to the king was called for, and to withhold it might be somewhat dangerous; or when the introduction of the Pretender's claims had threatened to result in serious strife, he escaped the difficulty, or hushed the rising storm, by flinging out a clever stanza, impromptu:

> God bless the king—I mean the Faith's defender;
> God bless—no harm in blessing—the Pretender;
> But who Pretender is, or who is king—
> God bless us all—that's quite another thing!

But Byrom never ceased to be distinguished as a Christian, and therefore never lost the comfort of pleasant intercourse with the Wesleys. In May, 1748, "I dined," he says, "with Col. Gumby and Charles Wesley, and went with them to the Methodist Church—English Common Prayers—he preached." The Methodist Church to which he went would be the celebrated "Foundry," in Moorfields.

Ten years later, a gentleman who had accompanied John Wesley to Ireland, writes to Byrom : " I found Mr. Wesley just ready to take horse. I gave your love to him, as you desired, and he was glad I had been to see you, for, notwithstanding any little differences in opinion, I find he loves you sincerely, which I was glad to see." Thus associated with Methodism, the venerable and saintly old genius reached the age of seventy-two. He was cheerful and calm, and still a joy to young people. In affliction he was resigned; and the piety which hallowed his youth now filled him with holy delight. His character, at the last, was a beautiful example of what, many years before, he had expressed a desire for, in one of his translations from the German ; and his last utterances were anticipated in that hymn.

> Jesu, teach this heart of mine
>   True *simplicity* to find;
> Childlike, innocent, divine,
>   Free from *guile* of every kind.
> And since, when amongst us, vouchsafing to live,
> So pure an example it pleased Thee to give ;
> O, let me keep still the bright pattern in view,
> And be, after Thy likeness, right simple and true.

When I read, or when I hear,
    Truths that kindle good desires,
How to act, and how to bear,
    What heaven-instructed faith requires,
Let no subtle fancies e'er lead me astray,
Or teach me to comment Thy doctrines away;
No reas'nings of selfish corruption within,
Nor slights by which Satan deludes us to sin.

Whilst I pray before Thy face,
    Thou, who art my highest good,
O, confirm to me the grace
    Purchas'd by Thy precious blood;
That, with a true filial affection of heart,
I may feel what a real Redeemer Thou art;
And, thro' Thy atonement to justice above,
Be receiv'd as a child by the Father of love.

Give me, with a child-like mind,
    Simply to believe Thy word;
And to do whate'er I find
    Pleases best my dearest Lord;
Resolving to practice Thy gracious commands;
To resign myself wholly up into Thy hands;
That, regarding Thee simply in all my employ,
I may cry, *Abba! Father!* with dutiful joy.

Nor within me, nor without,
    Let *hypocrisy* reside;
But whate'er I go about,
    Mere *simplicity* be guide.
Simplicity guide me in word, and in will,
Let me live—let me die—in simplicity still;
Of an epitaph made me, let this be the whole—
Here lies a true child that was simple of soul.

Jesu! now I fix my heart,
    Prince of Life, and Source of Bliss;
Never from Thee to depart
    Till Thy love shall grant me this.
Then, then, shall my heart all its faculties raise,
Both *here*, and *hereafter*, to sing to Thy praise.
Oh, joyful! my Saviour says, *so let it be;*
Amen, *to my soul*—Hallelujah! to *Thee.*

The lay singers of Methodism, as well as its tuneful "pastors and teachers," have been marked by variety of character, ability, accomplishment, and position. Among them, as in all other classes of human life, the law of compensation has ever shown itself in action, so that when there have not been all the versatile genius and various learning of a Byrom, the balance has been kept by a more intense and unreserved devotion of the fewer talents to one supreme and sacred purpose. If the poetic power has been less sparkling, or less flexible, it has been exercised to the uttermost in fulfilling its own task, and has had its more accumulative fruit from the purity, simplicity, and oneness of its aim.

 The note book of one who used, some years ago, to be often on the roads, has various jottings about parts of Lincolnshire; among the rest, this: "I was dropped at Spilsby. While waiting for a carriage to take me on to Old Bolingbroke, where I waited to see whether anything remained of the old castle in which Henry III. was born, and from which the St. Johns took their title, I walked about the little town. There was a memorial of poor Franklin, the explorer of the north seas; and there was the house in which they said he was born. I stood thinking whether there could be anything in this flat fenny Lincolnshire favourable to the production of men of power such as he—men such as Hereward and his fellow-heroes, the mighty Cromwell and his companion 'committee-men,' and ironside captains, the sturdy theologues such as John Horn of Old Bolingbroke, and that family of still growing power for good to the church and the world, the Wesleys. My ruminations were disturbed by a message, 'The carriage is waiting, sir!' I mounted and was off; soon found myself getting up out of the levels, and, rising gently, was soon on the chalk formations. When about two miles or more out of Spilsby, my eye caught a patch of foliage on the right. There was a village; but there seemed to be a gentleman's country-house, with its woods and copsy surroundings.—'What place is that?'

 "'That's Raithby Hall, sir.'

 "Raithby Hall! What crowds of associated thoughts came up at that sound! Then, I was on the road over which John Wesley had so often passed on his way to and from the hospitable home of Methodist preachers, Raithby Hall, the seat of Robert Carr Brackenbury, Esq. Mr. Wesley's first notice of the place occurred to my mind, and seemed to come with its first freshness, as my eye rested on the scene. 'We went to Raithby,' are the words, 'It is a small village on the top of a hill. The shell of Mr. Brackenbury's house was just finished, near which he has built a chapel. It was quickly filled with deeply serious hearers. I was much comforted among them, and could not but observe, while the landlord and his tenants were standing together, how

> 'Love, like death, makes all distinctions void.'

"There, then, said I to myself, is the very house, the mere shell of which Wesley saw on July 5th, 1779. In that house how often did the warm-hearted, pious 'landlord' show 'much kindness' to the Methodist itinerants! There, too, he learnt to sing hymns from his own soul. And there it was, probably, that his feeling towards those whose ministry had so blessed him prompted his verses on the second chapter of Joshua.

> "Lord, I Thy messengers receive,
> And gladly their report believe,
> Who by Thy order testify
> Of judgment and salvation nigh.
> Hunted by all the faithless race,
> Here they shall find a resting-place;
> And, till the storm is turn'd aside,
> Secure beneath my roof abide.
>
> My love they amply will repay,
> If I their warning voice obey,
> Hang out the covenanted sign,
> The sacred red, the blood divine;
> Then, though thy plagues our land o'erflow,
> And lay our lofty cities low,
> No evil shall I feel or dread;
> Protected by the *scarlet thread*.

"I was glad that I knew something about Raithby Hall, and that I could remember a little about Brackenbury, and a few lines out of his hymn-book. I came back from Old Bolingbroke that way to have another peep at the place where such holy men had walked and talked, and prayed and sung;

and where a visitor had found on a seat in the grove one of the pious esquire's tuneful prayers written with a pencil, thus—

> "Beneath this solitary shade,
>   Impervious to the solar ray,
> Dear Guardian Power my musings aid,
>   Oft as my footsteps hither stray.
>
> Let this delightful gloom suggest,
>   Lessons of import deep and high;
> While conscious awe steals o'er my breast,
>   That God, the All-seeing God, is nigh.
>
> Soon must I quit this lov'd retreat,
>   And waft my flight to distant spheres;
> O might I gain that fairest seat,
>   Where unveil'd excellence appears!
>
> Meantime, my spirit thither borne
>   On wings of hope and warm desire,
> Earth's gayest scenes shall nobly scorn,
>   And ever to its Source aspire!"

Robert Carr Brackenbury was one of John Wesley's favourite companions; a friend deeply loved and deeply loving. He often accompanied the great Methodist itinerant on his evangelizing and pastoral journeys, in several parts of the kingdom, in the Norman Isles, and into Holland. His delicate constitution, however, prevented him from taking that share of labour as a preacher which his heart would fain have enjoyed. His zeal would have carried him to the ends of the earth; but he was held in continuous check by bodily weakness. Nevertheless, in the failure of bodily strength to preach, he appears to have solaced himself by pouring out his desires to publish God's grace, in hymns to the great Source of his own spiritual joy. Thus he sings about his Lord's command to the man delivered from an unclean spirit (Mark v. 19, 20).

> Jesus, at Thy command I go,
> And to my friends the wonders show,
>   Which Thou to me hast shown;
> Thou hast Thy pard'ning love reveal'd,
> The fiend out of my heart expell'd
>   And claim'd it for Thine own.

While thus I testify of Thee,
With genuine, meek humility,
   Thy witness, Lord, inspire;
That all my friends may wake, and fear,
And listen till Thyself they hear,
   And catch the heavenly fire.

Didst Thou in me Thyself reveal,
That I Thy goodness might conceal,
   Or boastingly proclaim?
No, but Thou wilt my wisdom be,
And give me true simplicity,
   To glorify Thy name.

Wherefore, in confidence of grace,
I tell to all the ransom'd race
   What Thou for me hast done;
That all the ransom'd race may find
The present Saviour of mankind,
   And praise my God alone.

The loving invalid of Raithby Hall seems to have clung to his friend Wesley as his father in the Gospel, and his dearest adviser and guide. His feelings towards his venerable friend, and indeed to all who ministered truth to him, may have found expression in a hymn given in his "Sacred Poetry; or Hymns on the Principal Histories of the Old and New Testament." It is from the hallowed story of Naomi and Ruth, and is applied to a minister and his spiritual children :—

Turn again, my children, turn;
   Wherefore would you go with me?
O forbear, forbear to mourn,
   Jesus wills it so to be;
Why, when God would have us part,
Weep ye thus, and break my heart?

Go in peace, my children, go,
   Only Jesus' steps pursue;
He shall pay the debt I owe,
   He shall kindly pay for you;
He your sure reward shall be,
Bless you for your love to me.

Surely you have kindly dealt
   With the living and the dead;
You have oft my burden felt,
   When my tears were all my bread;
Jesus lull you on His breast!
Jesus give you endless rest!

> See! thy sister is gone back
>   To her gods and people dear;
> Weeping soul! a wretch forsake,
>   Why should'st thou my sorrows bear?
> Turn and let thy troubles cease,
> Go, my child, and go in peace.
>
> O entreat me not to leave
>   Thee, my faithful guide and friend;
> Let me to my father cleave,
>   Let me hold thee to the end;
> Thy own child in Christ I am,
> Follow thee, as thou the Lamb.
>
> Never will I cease to mourn,
>   Till my Lord thy tears shall dry;
> Never back from thee return,
>   Never from my father fly;
> Do not ask me to depart,
> Do not break my bleeding heart.
>
> Where thou go'st I still will go,
>   Thine shall be my soul's abode;
> Thine shall be my weal or woe,
>   Thine my people and my God;
> Where thou diest, with joy will I
> Lay my weary head and die.
>
> There will I my burial have
>   (If it be the Master's will),
> Sleeping in a common grave,
>   Till the quick'ning trump I feel;
> Call'd with thee to leave the tomb,
> Summon'd to our happy doom.
>
> God do so to me, and more,
>   If from thee, my guide, I part;
> Till the mortal pang is o'er
>   Will I hold thee in my heart;
> And when I from earth remove,
> Meet thee in the realms above.

Some of the last words from his "faithful guide and friend" must have been precious to him. "I congratulate you upon sitting loose to all below. . . My body seems nearly to have done its work, and to be almost worn out. . . . It gave me pleasure to see your letter, dated Portsmouth, and to hear that your health is better. I hope you will be able to spend a little time with us here; and if you choose to lodge in my house, I have a room at your service and we have a family which I can recommend to all England as adorning the doctrine of God our Saviour."

In three months from the date of this note Brackenbury was in the house to which he had been so affectionately invited, and saw the aged prophet, whom he so loved, take his upward flight. He himself followed erewhile, and realized the fulfilment of his own resolve :—

> God do so to me, and more,
>   If from thee my guide I part;
> Till the mortal pang is o'er
>   Will I hold thee in my heart;
> And when I from earth remove,
> Meet thee in the realms above.

The saintly John Fletcher of Madely was ordained deacon and priest in the year 1757. John Wesley says, " He was ordained at Whitehall; and the same day, being informed that I had no one to assist me at West Street Chapel, he came away as soon as ever the ordination was over, and assisted me in the administration of the Lord's Supper." The newly-ordained man did not come alone that day. There had been a dignified and even reverend-looking lay gentleman at the Whitehall ordination service, interested in the reception of Fletcher into the ministry. He walked with the young clergyman to West Street Chapel, and as they walked and talked, it would be difficult, perhaps, to say which person bore the more engaging marks of reverent meekness, modesty, and child-likeness. The layman was rather the senior. He was a Derbyshire man, born at Brailsford. There, in early life, he had read Boston's " Fourfold State." His heart was arrested by its lessons of truth, and was led, at length, into "newness of life." Under the constraint of his " first love," he began publicly to call his neighbours to repentance ; and among his first spiritual children were the ringleaders of those whose persecutions had threatened him with great peril. On coming to London, his association with the Wesleys and their companions began ; and, like many of those first Methodist believers, he devoted his powers to Christ, both as a preacher and a hymnist. This was John Bakewell, at whose house in

Westminster Thomas Olivers wrote his sublime hymn to "The God of Abraham," and who rivalled his friend Olivers by producing, if not so grand a hymn, yet one as widely known, and as graciously hallowed to Christian singers by the Spirit's unction—a hymn full of solemn pathos—an adoring salutation to Christ—

> Hail! Thou once despised Jesus!
>   Hail! Thou Galilean King!
> Thou didst suffer to release us;
>   Thou didst free salvation bring.
> Hail! Thou universal Saviour!
>   Bearer of our sin and shame;
> By Thy merits we find favour:
>   Life is given through Thy Name.
>
> Paschal Lamb, by God appointed,
>   All our sins on Thee were laid;
> By Almighty love anointed,
>   Thou hast full atonement made.
> Every sin may be forgiven,
>   Through the virtue of Thy blood;
> Opened is the gate of Heaven:
>   Peace is made 'twixt man and God
>
> Jesus, hail! enthron'd in glory,
>   There for ever to abide;
> All the heavenly hosts adore Thee,
>   Seated at Thy Father's side.
> There for sinners Thou art pleading;
>   There Thou dost our place prepare;
> Ever for us interceding,
>   Till in glory we appear.
>
> Worship, honour, power, and blessing,
>   Thou art worthy to receive;
> Loudest praises, without ceasing,
>   Meet it is for us to give.
> Help, ye bright angelic spirits,
>   Bring your sweetest, noblest lays;
> Help to sing our Saviour's merits,
>   Help to chant Immanuel's praise.
>
> Soon we shall with those in glory
>   His transcendent grace relate;
> Gladly sing th' amazing story
>   Of His dying love so great.
> In that blessed contemplation,
>   We for evermore shall dwell,
> Crown'd with bliss and consolation,
>   Such as none below can tell.

Little did Boston think, when he was writing his "Fourfold State," that, under God, he was giving life to a Methodist lay preacher and leader who for eighty years would gather spiritual fruit of his labour, and by whom all the evangelical churches in England and America would be set a-singing to the "Galilean King" through all generations. Unlike some of his contemporary hymnists, he proved faithful to the Christian people of his first choice; and there was evidently something about his home influence which saved the descending line of his family from such deviations as have sometimes dimmed the honour of Methodists in the third generation. His precious hymn, the only one left to us, as far as we know, was numbered the hundred and third in the Methodist collection of 1797; but the appointed committee of revision omitted it from the edition of 1808. The reasons for that omission are not known, as committees seldom give reasons. Bakewell's family circle wondered, doubtless, and queried among themselves in familiar chat; but the venerable hymnist's quietude was not broken. "Well, well," said he, "perhaps they thought it not worth while inserting." Rather, perhaps, his modesty outweighed his sense of slighted merit. The hymn, part of it at least, as altered by Toplady, has now again found admission to a Methodist place.

Methodism must, in many ways, have owed much to Bakewell. "When I came to Greenwich," says Mr Jeremiah Lacy, writing in 1802, "I had no knowledge of any person who feared God. I was like a fish out of water. I opened my room, and invited my neighbours to go with me to the throne of grace. It pleased the Lord to open the eyes of some, and break the hearts of others; and having the comfort, through good Providence, to find Mr. Bakewell in the town, I recommended them to his fatherly care. He took upon him the kind office, and met us once a week in his own house till the chapel was opened; and his labours have not been in vain in the Lord." Mr. Bakewell was a beautiful example of that true catholicity which Primitive Methodism was remarkable for. In whomsoever he saw any marks of

Christ's mind, he saw a brother; and this principle of brotherhood was practically shown forth in his life. The spirit of the man is in his hymn. It is truly a catholic hymn; and therefore is an elect song among all classes of Christians.

An old lover of this hymn had been sitting listening to a devoted Christian woman, who, amidst great infirmity, was reclining on her couch, chanting in sweet undertones—

> Jesus hail! enthron'd in glory,
> There for ever to abide.

Breaking off her song for a moment, she turned and said, "Whose hymn is that? It is a precious one to me. It keeps me the whole day sometimes, and through wakeful hours at night, too, in communion with my glorified Saviour. Who wrote it?"

"It was written," was the reply, "in 1760, by John Bakewell, one of Wesley's early members at the Foundery."

"Bakewell—Bakewell! Surely it may be the same as wrote a letter which I have read in one of the old Methodist magazines—dear old volumes! they were real *Methodist* magazines. I think the letter is in the volume for 1816. Just take it down from the shelf yonder, and read it. It is about Christian brotherly love."

The letter was read. The afflicted one fixed upon some paragraphs as the more impressive to her mind; this among the rest: "I took the liberty of giving you my thoughts on brotherly love, and the unity which ought to subsist between the children of God. I have been confirmed in my opinions on these subjects by reading the fourth chapter of the Epistle to the Ephesians. . . . This one point, the unity of the Spirit, he presses with seven arguments. . . . It is as if the apostle should reason thus: If the Church, your mother, be but one; God, your Father, one; Christ, your Lord, one; the Holy Ghost, your Comforter, one; if there be but one hope, one faith, and one baptism, it is certainly your bounden duty to live together in love as one, endeavouring to keep the unity of the spirit in the bond of peace."

"Now, I like that," said the good woman; "I like the

spirit of it as well as the argument. Is the writer the same as he who wrote the hymn?"

"Yes."

"I am glad to know that. It is so like the man who taught me to sing—

> "Soon we shall with those in glory
> His transcendent grace relate;
> Gladly sing th' amazing story
> Of His dying love so great;
> In that blessed contemplation
> We for evermore shall dwell,
> Crown'd with bliss and consolation
> Such as none below can tell.

Now read the finishing prayer of his letter."

"May God of His infinite goodness grant that we, and all serious Christians, of every denomination, may labour for a perfect union of love, and to have our hearts knit together with the bond of peace; that following after those essential truths in which we all agree, we may all have the same scriptural experience, and hereafter attain one and the same kingdom of glory."

"Oh, how that seems to agree with the feeling which his hymn gives me!" said the invalid. "I long to meet all lovers of Jesus, and

> Gladly sing th' amazing story
> Of His dying love so great."

The mortal part of John Bakewell rests not far from the tomb of his friend John Wesley; and there is the inscription:—

Sacred to the Memory
OF
JOHN BAKEWELL,
LATE OF GREENWICH,
WHO DEPARTED THIS LIFE MARCH 18TH, 1819,
AGED NINETY-EIGHT.
HE ADORNED THE DOCTRINE OF GOD OUR SAVIOUR
EIGHTY YEARS,
AND PREACHED HIS GLORIOUS GOSPEL
ABOUT SEVENTY YEARS.
"The memory of the just is blessed."

CHAPTER XIII.

A CHOIR OF HOLY WOMEN.

To thy friend, O woman! be
As thy tender lute to thee;
To thy tones so pure and fond,
How that lute's soft notes respond!
Voice and lute as one are felt:
How they mingle! how they melt!
Thus doth heaven-born friendship make
Holy harmonies awake.

MANY a good, clever woman has failed to leave an impression on the world simply for lack of money, place, and title. A mystery this may appear, but it is a fact. Lady Huntingdon, known among her friends as "the elect lady," would scarcely have made such a mark, and left such a name, were it not that Providence sometimes carries out the purposes of Divine goodness by turning wealth, rank, and influence to gracious purpose. Lady Huntingdon was faithful to her position, and could command for her own name even more than, under other circumstances, would be awarded to a woman of her mental degree. Her goodness gave influence to her rank, and her rank secured command for her goodness. She was closely connected with the early spread of Methodism. It is said by some that "at one time she held a bridle in the mouth of John Wesley"; but this is saying too much. The Wesleys honoured her as an eminent saint in high life; but when, in her familiarity with the claims of lofty position, she went beyond the province of a lady, affected the spiritual dictator, and called upon all the clergy under her influence to invade John Wesley's own conference "in a body," and "insist upon a formal recantation" of their published creed, as "Popery unmasked," or "another gospel set up to exclude that of Jesus Christ," she found something in the Wesleys against which she was powerless. John Wesley, especially, had so much truth and logic on his side, so strong a will, so skilful an ecclesiastical policy, and a heart so conscious of its own integrity, that she and her friends found themselves constrained to retreat, under apology, from their somewhat ridiculous position. She was no match for the Arminian leader in the arena of doctrine and church discipline. Nor could she rival the Methodist leader of song as a hymn maker. Like many of her evangelizing contemporaries, she issued a hymn-book for the use of her followers, and, like them, associated hymns of her own with selections from the spiritual songs of others. Her hymn-book was sent out under a title which seems to be somewhat characteristic: "A Select Collection of Hymns, universally Sung in all the Countess of Huntingdon's Chapels ; Collected by her Ladyship. 'What meanest thou, O sleeper? Arise, call upon thy God!' Bath : Printed and Sold by S. Hazard." The first hymn in the book, said to be her own, is perhaps a reflection of her own character, in its simplicity, devout warmth, and entire Christian spirituality :—

> Companions of Thy little flock,
>   Dear Lord, we fain would be ;
> Our helpless hearts to Thee look up,
>   To Thee, our Shepherd, flee.
>
> Oh! might we lean upon that breast,
>   Which love and pity fill,
> And now become those lambs caress'd,
>   That in Thy bosom dwell.
>
> How sweet that voice, how sweet that hand,
>   Which leads to pastures fair ;
> Shows Canaan's milk and honey land,
>   Provided by Thy care.
>
> As one in heart we all rejoice
>   The sinner's Friend to praise ;
> The Shepherd died—oh! 'tis His voice!
>   He'll us to glory raise.

Whatever may be thought of its measure of poetic vigour, the lady who lived and breathed the spirit of this hymn, while moving in the "high places" of the land, could scarcely be a favourite with ordinary frequenters at court.

"Pray, madam, are you acquainted with Lady Huntingdon?" said good old George III. to a noble lady who had spoken of her offensively.

"I am not," was the response.

"Have you ever been in her company?"

"Never," replied the marchioness, somewhat astonished.

"Never form your opinion of any one," said the king, "from the ill-natured remarks and censures of others. Judge for yourself, and you have my leave to tell everybody how highly I think of Lady Huntingdon."

The royal estimate of the distinguished and pious countess was given on another occasion, at court, to Lord Dartmouth. "I was much taken with her appearance and manner," said George; "there is something so noble, so commanding, and withal so engaging about her, that I am quite captivated with her ladyship. She appears to possess talents of a very superior order, is clever, well informed, and has all the ease and politeness of a woman of rank. With all the enthusiasm ascribed to her, she is an honour to her sex and her nation."

The "enthusiasm ascribed to her" was really of that pure and intense nature which must distinguish a soul like hers when born into "newness of life" and unreservedly consecrated to the service of Christ. Her husband, Earl Huntingdon, was an exemplary Christian. Of a serious cast, even in childhood, she was at length arrested by a remark from Lady Margaret Hastings, who had been converted by the instrumentality of the Wesleys' companion, Benjamin Ingham. The converted lady said that ever since she had believed in the Lord Jesus for life and salvation she had been "as happy as an angel." This happy religion the countess sought and found, and her newly-found spiritual life found expression in one of her hymns. The hymn, in its poetry, shows occasional weakness, lacks harmony here and there, while there are defects of rhyme and rhythm; but withal, it was, doubtless, sung by herself and her spiritual kindred as the truthful utterance of their newly-tuned hearts—

> The blessed Jesus is my Lord, my love,
> He is my choice—from Him I would not move.
>
> Away, then, all ye objects that divert,
> And seek to draw from my dear Lord, my heart!
>
> That uncreated beauty which hath gained
> My ravish'd heart, has all your glory stain'd.
>
> His loveliness my soul hath prepossest,
> And left no room for any other guest.
>
> Above 's my home, my country is above,
> That blessed land of life, of light, and love.
>
> There my dear friends, fled home, with God are blest,
> Thither are swiftly hasting all the rest.
>
> There lives my Lord, and there I long to live:
> He gave these longings, and Himself will give.
>
> In the meantime, Lord, show Thyself to me,
> Till Thou shalt please to take me up to Thee.
>
> In Thee now let me find so much of rest
> As may with more desire inflame my breast.
>
> So seize on me that we no more may part;
> Till Thou shalt take my soul, Lord, keep my heart;
>
> And dwell in me, till I with Thee shall dwell;
> This earth with Thee is Heaven, without Thee, hell.

Some people may look for more of dignity in songs from a countess; but childlike zeal was now her supreme feeling. Nor can it be wondered at that a lady who put so many unworldly congregations a-singing such psalms, and who sent so many preachers of spiritual godliness through the land, would create uneasiness in high ecclesiastical quarters. A Lord Bishop poured into the ear of majesty some complaints against the zealous preachers employed by Lady Huntingdon. They disturbed his diocese.

"Make bishops of them—make bishops of them," was the smart reply.

"That might be done," said the prelate; "but please, your majesty, we cannot make a bishop of Lady Huntingdon!"

"Well, well," said the king, "see if you cannot imitate the zeal of these men."

To this good advice, the queen added—

"As for her ladyship, you cannot make a bishop of her, 'tis true; it would be a lucky circumstance if you could, for she puts you all to shame."

In the case of one so appreciated and honoured by majesty, and so graciously taking a lead in the work of evangelical religion, it is quite natural that some should be forward to claim for her rather more than her due. She was useful, though not of high genius as a hymnist; yet the honour has been claimed for her of being the author of Robinson's fine hymn—

> Come, thou Fount of every blessing.

This effort on her behalf, however, has been made with more zeal than success. The evidence given is not weighty enough to turn the current of tradition. The hymn, as given in her collection, has been botched, apparently, and there have been queer attempts to put patches on it; but one thing is clear enough, that Robinson's hymn, and the best specimens from her ladyship's pen, are not of the same family; at all events, are not creations of the same mind. Lady Huntingdon's "Judgment Hymn" is, perhaps, her best; but there is the same occasional want of power, as in all the effusions ascribed to her; the same want of masterly ease, and the same proneness to limping movement; nothing of the full-toned, but plaintive, sweetness of harmony and pathos so evidently native to the genius which breathes in Robinson's verses. This is her ladyship's Judgment Hymn:—

> We soon shall hear the midnight cry,
> And Gabriel's trump shall shake the sky,
>   And cleave the starry plain;
> The angel-herald shall proclaim
> Redemption, through the slaughter'd Lamb,
>   And break death's pow'rful chain.
>
> Then shall the Judge descend in clouds,
> Circled around with countless crowds
>   Of the celestial choir;

Before whose rapid, glorious ray,
The frighted heavens shall flee away,
    And hide themselves in fire.

How, how shall sinners venture nigh,
Before the Lamb in yonder sky?
    Yet, oh! they must draw near,
To hear the dreadful word—depart!
Which, like some deadly-pointed dart,
    Their hearts will wound and tear.

While vengeful, fiery tempests hurl'd,
Shall chase them downward to the world
    Of everlasting pain;
Then they their helpless grief shall mourn,
Who to the Lamb would never turn—
    The Lamb for sinners slain.

Dear Lord, I sink at Thy pierc'd feet;
Oh! let me, by experience sweet,
    Taste Thy forgiving love.
And when Thou dost to judgment come,
Take me with Thee to Thy blest home,
    In Salem's land above!

Oh! when my righteous Judge shall come,
To fetch His ransom'd people home,
    Shall I among them stand?
Shall such a worthless worm as I;
So sinful, and unfit to die,
    Be found at Thy right hand?

I love to meet among them now,
Before Jehovah's feet to bow,
    Though viler than them all;
But who can bear the piercing thought—
What if my name, should be left out—
    When He for them shall call?

Dear Lord, prevent it by Thy grace;
Oh! let me see Thy smiling face
    In this my gracious day;
Thy pard'ning voice, oh! let me hear,
To still my unbelieving fear,
    Nor let me fall away.

Among Thy saints let me be found,
Whene'er th' archangel's trump shall sound,
    To see Thy smiling face;
Then, loudest of the crowd, I'll sing,
Till Heaven's resounding mansions ring,
    The riches of Thy grace.

This early Methodist lady outlived her friend Whitfield, and lingered on this side Jordan a few months after John Wesley passed. She lived long enough to see John Wesley's character in clearer light. A little before her own departure she said: "This night I shall go to my Father. . . . Can He forget to be gracious? Is there an end of His loving kindness? . . . My work is done; I have nothing to do but to go to my Father!" She went on the 17th of June, 1791, having spent just eighty-four years in her pilgrimage.

At the time of Lady Huntingdon's departure there was a young Methodist girl of sixteen living in Lombard Street, London, who, though born in what some would think an unfavourable spot for the spring and culture of poetic genius, was a poet of a much higher and richer class than the hymnist of Donington Park. This was Agnes Collinson—afterwards known as Mrs. Agnes Bulmer—who, on her departure into light, August 29th, 1836, was spoken of by another poet of Methodism, W. M. Bunting, as "one of the most intellectual and holy women, probably, whose presence ever adorned the world." Her school-days were scarcely over when she made her first venture, as a poet, by sending some lines to John Wesley on the death of his brother Charles. The venerable hymnist expressed his pleasure, and became her first faithful but gentle critic. Almost immediately after this, she received from him, as her pastor, her first ticket of membership in the Methodist Society; and her refined genius was now fully consecrated to Him to whom she had given her heart. Like the poet to whose memory she devoted some of her first lines, she warbled several of her sweetest songs amidst the sharpest trials of domestic life. She, too, proved that the daily experiences in the family home most blessedly simplify and brighten the poet's consecrated genius. Through half the year 1822 she might have said, " I am made to possess months of calamity, and wearisome nights are appointed to me." Her husband, Mr. Joseph Bulmer, was passing under affliction to his heavenly rest. He had long been a faithful, humble, warm-hearted, and unselfish member and officer of the Methodist Society; but bereavement was now coming on his earthly home. The clouds were gathering, and in the present dimness, and with a darkening prospect, the devoted wife, just before the hour of widowhood came, fled with her burden to Him who "giveth songs in the night"; and then her heart gave forth its hymn of sweetly harmonized sadness, spiritual longing, reliance, and reverent hope :—

> High on Thy heavenly seat,
>   Jesus, to Thee I pray!
> O see the sinner at Thy feet,
>   Nor turn Thine ear away.
> Embolden'd by Thy word,
>   By want and weakness prest,
> To Thy Divine compassions, Lord,
>   I pour my full request.
>
> I ask the joy unknown
>   That from Thy presence springs
> When, prostrate at Thy awful throne,
>   Thy mercy's shadowing wings
> Temper the light which breaks
>   Resplendent from Thine eye;
> When soft the whisp'ring Spirit speaks,
>   "The Lord is passing by!"
>
> I ask that sight of faith
>   To humblest mourners given,
> That view of Thy mysterious death,
>   Thy pleading pow'r in heaven,
> Which calms the troubled breast
>   When guilty fears invade,
> And bids the trembling spirit rest
>   In Thy perpetual aid.
>
> I ask that hallowing fear,
>   That heaven of humble love,
> Which joins a saint in worship here
>   To saints redeem'd above.
> E'en now the veil withdrawn,
>   In fellowship with Thee,
> Oh, might the day of glory dawn
>   The twilight shadows flee!
>
> On me, Thy suppliant child,
>   Be all Thy form imprest,
> Thy nature pure, Thy spirit mild;
>   That, meet for heavenly rest,
> I may that call attend
>   Which shall my soul remove,
> And from Thy footstool here ascend
>   To share Thy throne above.

This hymn first appeared in the "Methodist Magazine," to the poetic department of which Mrs. Bulmer contributed for several years. Her widowhood was made still more disconsolate in 1825, when her venerable mother, after two years of close companionship with her widowed daughter, left this world for her scene of repose nearer to her Divine Lord. The lonely poet now bent her mind to the composition of her great work, "Messiah's Kingdom." "The longest poem by a lady in any language," says James Montgomery, "that I am acquainted with. It seems to embrace the sum of the lessons which an immortal spirit has learned of itself, of its fellow-creatures, and of God, on its progress to glory and felicity, through a world fallen and miserable. The versification is distinguished by remarkable freedom and fluency. It is a volume from which hundreds of happy quotations might be made."

Montgomery is just. How often the reader of her tuneful pages is arrested by some majestic, beautiful, or touching utterance—as when he hears the poet's voice to fallen man, overtaken by the flood:—

> Then, hapless man, the soil that gave thee birth
> Groan'd with thy weight of crime! Dissolving earth
> Felt the incumbent curse; and thou, in vain,
> With trembling steps, along the liquid plain,
> Urgedst thy tardy, unavailing flight!
> Lo! the tall cedars on the mountain's height
> Bow to the raging storm! Thy last resource
> Beneath the whirlwind's dire convulsive force
> Falls, crashing, thundering down; the forest shakes,
> The rifted adamant asunder breaks.
> Loud bellowing waters fill the chasm beneath;
> Above is vengeance! all around is death!
> Nature's wild dissonance returns thy groan,
> Till all is silence! Ruin reigns alone!
> Above the measureless, the formless waste,
> She sits, exulting o'er a world defaced!
> Around her throne the spoils of vengeance sweep,
> And Judgment heaves the billows of the deep!

And again, when she gives her fine paraphrase on the Saviour's words, "The wind bloweth where it listeth, and thou hearest the sound thereof, but canst not tell whence it cometh, and whither it goeth ; so is every one that is born of the Spirit ":—

> As through mid-air the sweeping current blows,
> Or, gently gliding, sinks to soft repose,
> All uncontroll'd by man, who knows not where
> Fierce hyperborean storms their shafts prepare,
> Or whence, descending mild, on balmy wing,
> Soft zephyr comes to fan the flowers of spring ;
> So works, by human counsels undefined,
> The teaching Spirit on the pliant mind;
> Nor to the world His secret course declares,
> But unperceived His instrument prepares ;
> Then in the finish'd work unfolds His skill,
> And bends His agent to His perfect will.

And again, her awe-inspiring sketch of the weird scene of unhappy Saul's appeal to witchcraft :—

> It was a fearful night when fell Despair
> Drew from Gilboa, and his captains there,
> The guilty, gloomy king to tempt the path
> From mortal step debarr'd ; Heaven frown'd in wrath,
> Nor moon nor twinkling star its radiance lent,
> To guide the silent travellers as they went
> Down the deep glen by Endor's mountain wood,
> To seek the demon's haunt, 'midst rocks that stood
> Frowning precipitous beneath the ground,
> Where cavern'd vaults repeat unearthly sound ;
> Where wizard spells, and incantations dread,
> And howling murmurs o'er the buried dead
> Break not on mortal ears ; nor mortal sight
> Scans the dire deeds of those who hate the light.

What lover of the Bible does not hold the blessed Book nearer to his heart while he catches the poet's spirit, and cries :—

> Hail, Holy Record of supernal love !
> Thy living lines even seraphs search above,
> And saints below with holy wonder trace,
> Intent to learn thy mysteries of grace.
> Stupendous register of truth sublime,
> 'Tis thine to chase the darkling mists of time ;
> To cheer the mariner with friendly light,
> Through shelving rocks to guide his course aright :
> To show beyond the deep, that peaceful shore,
> Where waves subside, and tempests rage no more ;
> But heaven's unsetting splendours radiant glow,
> Nor seasons change, nor night of sorrow know.

> Eternal Oracle of Truth, thy voice
> Bids misery hope, and holy Faith rejoice;
> The wayward step of thoughtless youth restrains;
> Soothes hoary age, amidst its cares and pains;
> Pours heavenly music on the raptur'd ear,
> When Death's dread angel draws in stillness near;
> Proclaims beside the grave, that destin'd hour,
> When strangely quicken'd by all-conquering power,
> Each captive, from its dark recesses brought,
> Shall share the victory by Messiah wrought,
> Emerge from Hades' deep sepulchral gloom,
> And wave his palm of triumph o'er the tomb.

And who does not rejoice with trembling over the doom of a blood-stained empire, as he reads:—

> Long, long his flight th' avenging angel stay'd,
> Forbearing Love the stern behest delay'd;
> Long rose the prayer of mediatorial grace,
> As fuming incense in the holy place;
> It came at length—the word of wrathful ire;
> That seraph flame unfurl'd his wings of fire;
> Forth from the sacred shrine as lightning past,
> And down to earth his burning censer cast.
> Soon darkling clouds eclips'd the cheerful sky,
> Hoarse tempests howl'd with loud and dissonant cry,
> While throes convulsive heaved the solid ground,
> And, sullen echoing through the gloom profound,
> Unearthly voices fill'd the startled ear
> With wail portentous of destruction near.
> Then fell thy throne, proud mistress of the world!
> Then from its mountain height impetuous hurl'd,
> A wreck it floated on the ruthless tide
> Of fierce barbarian anarchy, whose wide
> And rushing waters, with tempestuous sweep,
> Bore diadem and sceptre to the deep,
> Roll'd dark and dreadful o'er thy proud domain,
> And left thee withering 'midst thy heaps of slain.

This fine poem is remarkable for the variations of its grandeur and beauty. The poet has skilfully introduced lyrical pieces here and there, not breaking the unity of the poem, but rather making its harmony more rich. Some of these lyrics are of great beauty, and some have a grandeur about them. They are ingeniously set, and sparkle like gems in the finely wrought texture of the pages. Wordsworth has an allusion to the rainbow, its effect on him in youth, the effect it still has, and the effect he hopes it will have in his old age :—

> My heart leaps up when I behold
> A rainbow in the sky;
>> So was it when my life began,
>> So is it now I am a man,
> So be it when I shall grow old,
>> Or let me die!

This is simple; but how cold and void of those richer and deeper lessons which the Christian thinker finds in the rainbow; and how inane its music seems when followed by Agnes Bulmer's lofty, yet quietly instructive, touching, and inspiring hymn on the token of the covenant between God and the world after the flood :—

> Gloomy cloud, that, low'ring low,
>> Shadowest nature's lovely light,
> Wide thy deepening darkness throw,
>> Catch the sunbeam bursting bright;
> Gently on thy humid breast,
> Bid its soften'd splendours rest.
>
> Wild the wind, and fierce the flood,
>> Foaming, roaring, raved and rush'd;
> Thunders roll'd—the voice of God:
>> Now the angry storm is hush'd,
> Now the eddying whirlwind sleeps,
>> Ocean seeks its barrier deeps.
>
> Beauteous bow! thy arch sublime,
>> Resting on the distant hills,
> Leads me back to earliest time;
>> Hope my pensive spirit fills,
> In thy softest hues I trace
> Gentler, lovelier beams of grace.
>
> Lo! the tempest's rage is o'er,
>> Flashing fires no longer gleam;
> Solemn thunders cease to roar,
>> Silvery clouds resplendent stream;
> Bright the bursting sun appears,
> Ararat its summit rears.
>
> From his floating home released,
>> Noah on the mountain stands,
> Spreads the sacrificial feast,
>> Lifts to Heaven his praying hands,
> Listens to the Voice Divine,
> Looks on thee, peace-speaking sign.

Hush! the word of promise breaks,
  Not in thunders hoarse and loud;
Lo! the covenant-Saviour speaks
  Softly from the symboll'd cloud:
Rise! the storm of wrath is pass'd;
Judgment shall not always last.

So upon the anxious heart,
  Chafed with sorrow's wild alarm,
When the troubled clouds dispart,
  When the rough wind sinks to calm,
Breaks the light from distant spheres,
Falling on a mist of tears.

Sun of Righteousness! from thee
  Soft those lucid rays descend,
Mildest mercy beams on me;
  Whispers every storm shall end,
Now the covenant-sign is given,
Bright appears the bow in heaven.

Resting on th' eternal hills,
  Arching high the emerald throne,
Heaven with hallow'd light it fills,
  Sends its soft effulgence down.
Holy light! I hail thee now,
Circling, mild, Emmanuel's brow.

Yes, that meek, resplendent sign
  Presages a cloudless sky;
Heaven's eternal light shall shine,
  Truth and mercy meet on high,
Righteousness and Peace unite,
Mingling beams divinely bright.

Hush, my sorrow! from a storm,
  Fierce, and terrible, and wild,
Sprang that bow whose splendrous form,
  Radiant, round the Reconciled;
Glory's fountain set in shade,
Earthly lights retired dismay'd.

From the Cross, where darkness shrouds
  Him who suffered there for me,
In the fearful tempest clouds,
  Resting dread on Calvary,
Mercy's beaming sign appears,
See, believe, and dry thy tears!

There used to be a part of Manchester, in going through the smutty brick-ways and murky air of which one might have found it a pleasant relief to exercise the mind in banishing all that was disagreeable from present view, and to set the imagination to work in restoring the natural scenery as it used to be. To look down from Pin Mill Brow on the winding valley beneath old Ancoat's Hall, and to purify the river until it was again a trout stream; to reclothe the banks with hazel and alder, and the upland slopes with oaken copse; and to surround the old hall with its primitive wood and glades once more, would be a mental joy that might serve to beguile one's way up the hilly street into the midst of the grim, gigantic, brick-built, cotton mills. On the top of the swell, however, other joys would come to those who were alive to sacred associations. There was the Ancoats' Methodist Chapel, which, with all its latter-day grime, had been clean once; and dingy as it necessarily became inside and out, it was the birth-place of so many souls, and the gathering-place of so many holy people, that the sight of it always brought up devout thoughts and balmy memories. The putting down of the first stone of that building is now associated with the life and music of a hymn that was first sung when that foundation was laid. Mr. James Wood, of Grange House, requested Mrs. Bulmer to write a hymn for the occasion; but as she was just entering on a journey to Preston, no other opportunity presented itself than that which was offered in the coach. There she composed the beautiful verses. They were sent to Manchester the next day; and those who gathered round the ground-work of the New Chapel, sang,—

> Thou who hast in Sion laid
>   The true Foundation stone,
> And with those a covenant made,
>   Who build on that alone:
> Hear us, Architect divine!
>   Great builder of Thy Church below;
> Now upon Thy servants shine,
>   Who seek Thy praise to show.
>
> Earth is Thine; her thousand hills
>   Thy mighty hand sustains;
> Heaven Thy awful presence fills,
>   O'er all Thy glory reigns:

> Yet the place of old prepared
>   By royal David's favour'd son,
> Thy peculiar blessing shared,
>   And stood Thy chosen throne.
>
> We, like Jesse's son, would raise
>   A temple to the Lord;
> Sound throughout its courts His praise,
>   His saving name record;
> Dedicate a house to Him
>   Who once, in mortal weakness shrined,
> Sorrow'd, suffer'd, to redeem,
>   To rescue all mankind.
>
> Father, Son, and Spirit send
>   The consecrating flame;
> Now in majesty descend,
>   Inscribe the living Name—
> That great Name, by which we live,
>   Now write on this accepted stone;
> Us into Thy hands receive,
>   Our temple make Thy throne.

Since then, from how many a devout assembly gathered in town and city streets, on village greens, on country roadsides, on moorland plains, on wooded heights, and by valley streams, has the music of that hymn risen to Heaven like morning incense or evening sacrifice!

Mrs. Bulmer, in her "Messiah's Kingdom," rejoicing over Christian England as the

> Gem of the ocean, whose pellucid light
> Shines like the sun's in every region bright,

sings to her native country—

> Heaven, to thy hands the lamp of truth consign'd:
> 'Tis Thine, with grateful heart, to all mankind.
> Its quick'ning, gliding, cheering beams to show,
> O'er earth's dark bounds to bid its glories flow.

Methodism has taken a large share in fulfilling this missionary calling of England. Nor have holy women been lacking in readiness to brave "perils in the deep," and "perils in the wilderness" of heathendom, in order to diffuse the truth which has hallowed their own character and gifts. Some of these have names among the poets of Methodism; and their genius has been called into happy exercise in unfolding the scenes of missionary labour, and in recording the results of Christian sacrifice.

One of these has said: "Life is full of poetry. The stream of every day has its sparkle and its shade. The natural and the moral world have each their myriad touches of beauty, the more deeply affecting because it but gleams from the wreck that sin has occasioned." Some of such gleams come to us reflected from the poetic pages of "Adeline," the scenes of whose missionary wanderings and life still live in the light of her genius. Few who have crossed the seas, on their missionary way to heathendom, have so pleasantly helped us to realize ocean scenery as this gifted and pious wife has done. Listen to her on the broad deep—

> Sparkling and silent, save where finny life
>   Sported in gladness, was the ocean floor;
> Gemm'd with the thronging stars that, far from strife,
>   Gazed lovingly, as they would fain adore
> Their own bright images; while evermore
>   Phosphoric gleamings, as a thousand fires,
> Flicker'd and flash'd the deepening azure o'er,
>   Like shiver'd lightnings, or the shattered lyres
> Of seraphs fallen, flung from the celestial choirs.
>
> I was alone—in thought, in soul, alone—
>   On that wild world of waters; and I gazed
> On its calm glories silently, as one
>   By lonely grandeur 'wilder'd and amazed;
> Yet ever and anon, as splendour blazed
>   From some fair planet, or bright silver star,
> My spirit woke from reverie, and praised
>   The fount of beauty, who, with nought to mar,
> Strew'd thousand gems of light in the blue heaven afar.
>
> The azure paled, for morn's clear, rosy light,
>   Glow'd in the far east; one light arch of gold
> Glow'd in the horizon faintly, as the night,
>   Departing, bade the gates of day unfold;
> Star after star from the blue concave roll'd,
>   And the dark ocean—not a wandering cloud
> Dimm'd the pure zenith, as in calm untold
>   It hail'd Aurora, radiant as she bowed
> When first adoringly she own'd her Maker, God.
>
> A thousand hues of glory, rich and rare,
>   Burst on my vision; rainbow hues of light;
> Tints woven of the sunshine, gaily fair;
>   Gold, emerald, rose-hued, amber richly bright,

And regal purple, fading to the light
  Of softest sapphire:—Oh, the gorgeous blaze
That flash'd around me, as in kingly might
  The day's proud monarch flung his royal rays
O'er the wide main that shone and sparkled 'neath his gaze!
Joy was it on the bounding waves to ride,
  Foaming and flashing with the rising breeze;
To watch the spray-wreaths floating on the tide,
  Like sunbeams glancing on the billowy seas!
To list the roar, the eternal melodies,
  The noise of waters, ocean's ceaseless well,
From the deep sea-halls, echoing as the trees
  Of myriad forests, roused by hidden spell,
To pour their murmur forth in wild, continuous swell.

Nor does "Adeline" less happily make us feel as if we were with her at noontide and evening amidst the tropical plain and palmy oasis:—

The desert spread around me, silent, vast,
  And shadowless as ocean, 'neath the glare
Of noontide splendour; one wild, arid waste
  Of fearful solitude, that the hot air
Swept over scorchingly; stern, parch'd, and bare,
  As scathed for ever with a with'ring blight,
Away, away, in weary gloom afar,
  Pathless it stretch'd, and the broad, sultry light
Pour'd down in dazzling floods on the dim, aching sight.

I wander'd on o'er that wide, trackless plain,
  No guide save tropic sunlight, till the day
In glory faded, and the starry train
  From the deep azure flung a silvery ray
Of quivering lustre on my weary way;
  Sweet was the change! the dewy radiance fell
Cool, soft as spring-time, when its zephyrs play
  On founts and blossoms, and bright things that dwell
'Mid wak'ning leaves that flush wood, grove, and hidden dell.

Dimly afar, in morn's enkindling blaze,
  A verdant isle I mark'd amid the waste;
And thither sped in gladness and amaze,
  As its green palms in golden light I traced;
Clustering and tall, that lonely spot they graced,
  While 'neath their shadows fragrant cup and bell
Gleam'd out 'mid verdure beauteous, and cast
  Sweet odours round them, as a perfumed spell,
From desert gloom to lure to their bright citadel.

. . . . .

I linger'd there! the leafy dimness shed
  O'er its still beauty fell upon my soul
As evening twilight, when the sunset red
  Hath left cool shadows in the clouds that roll

O'er heaven's blue concave. Wild'ringly there stole
    Athwart my spirit the rich, deep repose
Of its hush'd quiet, that, without control,
    O'erwhelmed my being, while its glad thought rose
To Him who 'mid the waste bright gems of beauty throws.

Happy is the woman who may be classed with those of whom St. Paul said they " labour with me in the gospel ; " and who in their missionary labour have been, like him, " in journeyings often, in perils of waters, in perils by the heathen, in perils in the wilderness, in perils in the sea ; " and yet, like him, amidst all and after all, " in everything give thanks." Such blessedness seems to have been " Adeline's " attainment ; and one of the best efforts of her devout poetical genius is found in the hymn which, with so much simple beauty of thought, tuneful cheerfulness of feeling, and grateful harmony of language, engages us in blessing God for His " Blessings."

For thousand, thousand mercies new,
    At dawn and vesper hour;
The early and the later dew,
    The sunshine and the shower;
For founts of ever-springing bliss,
    For hope's unclouded ray ;
For life's thrice blessed sympathies,
    We bless Thee day by day.

For fond affection's richest love,
    For household tones of mirth,
For melodies that hourly pour
    From hearts of kindred birth ;
For many a fireside thrill of love,
    For many a joyous lay ;
For peace that emblems peace above,
    We bless Thee day by day.

For untold sympathy that dwells
    Enshrined in love's fond breast ;
For springs that sorrow most reveals,
    Thrice hallow'd and thrice blest !
For waves of blessedness that steep
    Our lot in radiant day ;
For happiness unknown and deep,
    We bless Thee day by day.

> For hope of better things above,
>   Through Him who died for all;
> For love divine—eternal love,
>   That raised us from our fall;
> For all the Christian's holy dower,
>   His anchor, hope, and stay;
> For all, our God of love and power,
>   We bless Thee day by day.

One of the brightest blessings that God ever gave to "Adeline," or Mrs. Sergeant, was her own poetical child, E. F. A. Sergeant, whose mental inheritance from her mother unfolded its life and beauty in very childhood. Some of the gifted young songster's verses gave pleasure to lovers of tuneful thought and expression when she was only eleven years old, or between that and her fourteenth year. "For some two or three years," says her mother, "every device was resorted to—by recreation, employment, and school duties—to divert the mind. Those efforts, however, were unsuccessful; and what was evidently the gift of nature has been allowed—with less interruption—to develop itself. . . . Mind—untrained and undisciplined—the sport of every vagrant thought and wild imagination—overrun by the rank weeds of sloth and indecision—is a curse and not a blessing. But, cultured by the hand of love, enriched and brightened by rays from the Sun of Righteousness, kept and tended 'with all diligence,' and ever fragrant with the dews of a holy consecration to Heaven—then, how radiant become its flowers of truth and purity!—how sweet the influence of its odorous grace!—how bright the beauty of its upspringing plants of celestial wisdom!"

The glad mother of this young musical soul is right. And among the child's poems there are "flowers of truth and purity." Such as the young poet's utterance to her own lyre; which has all the charm of fresh, youthful simplicity and sweet naturalness of music:—

> Within my hand is a little lyre,
>   And anon I strike its chords,
> Though I cannot sing in words of fire
>   The poet's thrilling words;

But I raise my fingers willingly,
    And what I think I sing,
And words that are felt come thrillingly
    And an echo often bring.

My lyre may not be rich and sweet,
    But yet one thing I know—
It is not tunèd to repeat
    Alone these things below.
For though so oft an earthly strain
    May mingle with my song,
My voice shall not be spent in vain,
    It does to God belong.

The strings are feeble, poor, and weak,
    But they are loved by me,
Some time, perchance, they too shall break;
    But in eternity
I know my lyre will speak again,
    And ne'er will break its strings—
It shall speak in the land where is no pain,
    Where angelic music rings.

My lyre is not an idle thing,
    It does not idly lie
That the wind alone may make it sing,
    Or on its breezes die.
My lyre—I cannot lay it down,
    So ask us not to part;
'Tis my solace from the world's cold frown,
    To warm and cheer my heart.

And in my hand I hold this lyre,
    If music from it come,
Pray that I soon may hold it higher,
    In my eternal home.
My lyre—it is a precious boon;
    And, midst the world's cold art,
There needs some precious boon to cheer
    And sanctify the heart.

So tell me not that I must lay
    From me this precious thing;
But what I fancy, think, and say,
    Oh, give me leave to sing!
For, when within my hand I hold
    This lyre, though low and faint,
It will reach that city pure of gold,
    And the ears of God and saint.

How gentle, and yet how deeply powerful for good, are some of the reflections of youthful experience, when thrown from one young soul upon another, brightened by true poetic expression! "I was born," says a young disciple, "in a home of sorrow. I was brought up amidst family disjointments, jarring cares, straits, difficulties, discomforts, and all but hopeless toil. Sprightly as I was, gay by nature, of warm and sanguine temper, I found it very hard, at times, to keep my heart from bitterness, and to hold up my spirits against the weight of things. Even when, by the grace of God, the joy of early piety came to strengthen my soul, the trials from without were, now and then, sore enough to make me weep. I was in danger of thinking my lot worse than anybody's else. But I met the other day with some lines, written by a young girl, that made me blush at first, but afterwards they put spirit into me, and balanced me, somehow, so that I feel easy and content. They have taught me one thing—that my early trials may be intended to prepare me for being, in some humble way, like my Lord, a sympathizer with those who are tried, and a helper of the poor and sorrowful, and in that way brighter comforts may come to weigh against my early troubles. Thank God for E. F. A. Sergeant's little poem. She called it, "My Life"; and her song shall be the song of '*my* life!'"

> Far be it from me I should choose
> A life of constant light,
> For where the shadows are not deep,
> The sunshine is not bright.
>
> To speak, to touch another's heart,
> We must have felt the woe;
> And words that heal another's smart,
> Proceed from those who *know*.
>
> Experience teacheth us alone
> What joy can never do;
> We cannot comfort ere we feel
> The loss and sorrow too.
>
> To have no grief were but to fill
> Our lives with dreary joy;
> Lone we should stand if naught we met
> Our comfort to destroy.

Each one has met with woe; and I
  Shun not the general fate;
I would not fear to meet the storm,
  But calmly turn and wait.

I would not have *all* joy—*all* woe,
  I ask for dark and light;
For where the shadows are not deep,
  The sunshine is not bright.

In more senses than one the Divine promise is often fulfilled, "Your sons and your daughters shall prophecy." Hallowed poetic genius, whether youthful or mature, is never fruitless. "Adeline" did not sing in vain; nor has her gifted child been left without a witness to the power of her early song.

CHAPTER XIV.

POETICAL DIVINES—FATHER AND SON.

> What is our duty here ? to tend
> From good to better—thence to best;
> Grateful to drink life's cup,—then bend,
> Unmurmuring, to our bed of rest;
> To pluck the flowers that around us blow,
> Scattering their fragrance as we go.

N the north-west Cornish coast there are several remarkable deposits of sand, driven in seemingly by the sea, at some time in the remote past. They are thrown up into undulating wave-like ridges, or are left like chains and clusters of small hills, covered here and there with slight sea-side vegetation. One of these deposits is near the entrance to Hayle Harbour, and stretches along the coast for some distance as a kind of sea barrier, behind which the dwellings of the little town line the valley road or gather on the upland slope. Into this sandy wilderness, one evening in May, forty years ago, six young men wandered for the purpose of quiet talk. They found at last a deep hollow, in which they were entirely secluded from all human eyes and ears. And there they knelt on the sand, and earnestly prayed for one another that God would be their guide, instructor, and comforter on the morrow; for on the morrow they were to stand on their examination as candidates for the Christian ministry. They prayed until they felt that all their interests would be managed by the same wisdom, rectitude, and power as had "placed the sand for the bound of the sea by a perpetual decree, that it cannot

pass it, and though the waves thereof toss themselves, yet can they not prevail; though they roar, yet can they not pass over it." The morrow came. In the morning, at five o'clock, they were at service in the chapel, and not long after six o'clock they were standing in the presence of their examiners. One of the six was tall, thin, and pale. He looked as if he had come up from the gates of the grave. He had been "sick of a fever;" and had been raised from the bed just time enough to stand where he now was. Almost immediately on his taking his place, his eye met the eye of one of the ministers before whom he stood; and, in a moment, those two souls seemed to touch, and to feel that they were in some way akin. The eye which had met his was one of those whose look, if once caught, appears for ever to follow the soul on whom its light has fallen. The minister was comparatively young, but his face was thin and pallid, having indeed rather a death-like pallor. His countenance seemed to belong to a sphere of more ethereal thought and feeling than this world. It gave evidence of a penetrating and discriminating power, finely balancing a buoyant imagination. At first sight he would be thought to have the genius of a poet in unison with the qualities of a grave divine. Great deference was paid to him, and in the course of the examination he was requested to put any questions which he thought proper to the candidates. He turned to the pale young man, as if his sympathy ran in that direction, and with a fixed look of keen scrutiny, softened by kindness, he asked whether any inspired passage occurred to him just then showing that the name Son, as applied to the Second Person of the Holy Trinity, properly belonged to the Redeemer's Divine nature. The reply was—

"Yes; if eternity of existence and unchangeableness belonged exclusively to the Divine nature, the name Son of God, as applied to Christ, properly belonged to his Divine nature; as the apostle in the seventh chapter of the Epistle to the Hebrews, speaks of Melchisedek, as a type, being "without father, without mother, without descent, having neither beginning of days nor end of life, but made," in these respects, "like unto the Son of God."

"I thank you," said the questioner; but as he leant back in his seat, a peculiar light passed over his intellectual features, and seemed to settle in his beaming eyes, as if some happy thought had sunk into the depth of his being. It was so. He had been mentally laying the foundation of a great argument on the Divine Sonship of Christ; and the allusion to Melchisedek had opened a new current of thought, and a fresh line of scriptural argument; and when his masterly volume appeared, it contained a chapter which was the fruit of what passed in that little vestry at Hayle.

The one who had put the question was Richard Treffry, junior, whose name, among theologians, will ever be associated with the doctrine of Christ's Divine Sonship. Treffry was a divine, but he was a poet too, though the living memorials of his poetic genius are neither so widely known, nor of such permanent influence, as the fruits of his theological ability and culture. His poems, with the exception of a few verses, are in what may be called melancholy or plaintive keeping with his own early rapidity of movement towards the tomb. He was never robust; but the labours and exposures of his first Methodist circuit, Sevenoaks, in Kent, had a fatal effect on his constitution—an effect which was, perhaps, rendered more certain and painful by what may be termed youthful inattention to proper precautionary modes of obviating the mischiefs of frequent exposure. The whole secret of his future sufferings is given by himself in an account of his toil and rough travel. It is a doleful picture, and affords a clue to much of the mournful tinging of his poetic thought and expression. The first effort of his poetic genius with which we are acquainted was put forth amidst labours and sufferings which must have deeply weighed down his native capacity for enjoying the picturesque and beautiful landscapes of Kent. Friendship seems to have given the first inspiration, and from his circuit in " the hill country," he congratulated his friend, Mr. Nye, of Tunbridge Wells, on the birth of a daughter. Bright as the occasion was, the sombre tendency of his imagination is traceable throughout the poem, gentle as its music is, and delicate as are the turns of thought; while he makes the father's joy brighter by contrast, or chastens that joy by showing how it may melt into the more lasting joys of an immortal home.

> Awake, my muse, and swell the votive lay,
>   Nor let dull indolence thy powers enthrall;
> O'er all thy harp-strings let thy fingers stray,
>   And pour thy festive strain at friendship's call.
> All hail, my friend! The cup which Heaven decrees
>   To many a human fellow-being here,
> Is dark and bitter with the noxious lees
>   Of sorrow's vintage, and the draught of fear.
>
> Full many a wretch on life's uncertain wave,
>   In hope's bright sunshine spreads his ample sail,
> Hangs his gay streamers o'er the glassy grave,
>   And lightly glides before the perfumed gale.
> But disappointment clouds the radiant sky,
>   And tempests rise, of care, disease, and woe;
> The curling foam-bleach'd billows roar on high,
>   Or beat upon the shrinking bark below.
>
> And rude, and ruder still the tempests dash,
>   And wild, and wilder still the winds resound,
> And thunders roll, and lurid lightnings flash,
>   Till all is lost, beneath the wild waves drown'd.
> Thy lot is cast beneath a milder sky,
>   Far from the dangers of a swelling sea;
> Glows a sweet home before thy glist'ning eye,
>   And joys connubial pour their smiles on thee.
>
> Swift fleet the hours which fill thy happy year;
>   Days, weeks, and months, with peace and hope replete
> Heaven smiles upon th' hallow'd dwelling here,
>   And tells of future bliss at Jesu's feet.
> Already has thy first-born lovely boy
>   Fled from this world of toil, and woe, and strife,
> Secur'd the bowers of everlasting joy,
>   And grasp'd the amaranth of eternal life.
>
> Wreathed one more tie to bind thy heart to Heaven,
>   Yet linger still about thy hallow'd soul,
> Till back it spring to God, by whom 'twas given,
>   Mingling in heavenly love without control.

Another babe to thy paternal sight
  Heaven grants, to train in wisdom's lovely ways,
When o'er her mind fair reason's glowing light
  Shall rise and shed its intellectual rays.

Conducted then by revelation's hand,
  Sin to renounce, and faith in Christ to know;
Walking and living by Divine command,
  Her path with heavenly blessedness shall glow.
But, oh! too fast these future visions rise,
  Life is uncertain at its best estate;
Thy babe, perchance, is born to walk the skies
  Before youth's beauteous, gay, and hopeful date.

When, then, thou fold'st her in thy fond embrace,
  And all the father rises in thy heart;
Or when thou bend'st in rapture o'er her face,
  With thoughts too big for utt'rance to impart,
Then, then, oh, think, this gem is but Heaven's loan!
  A loan—not gift; but lent awhile—not given.
Much as I love thee, child, thou'rt not my own,
  Thou art th' entrusted, hallow'd child of Heaven.

When age and slow decay, with stealing pace,
  Shall bleach the man-like honours of thy head,
Upon thy brow its wrinkling fingers trace,
  And all of youthfulness is past and dead,
Then, should she live, in thy domestic sphere,
  May she a star of virtuous radiance shine,
Gilding the sunset of thine age while here,
  And pouring beauty o'er thy life's decline!

Richard Treffry was the contemporary of another Methodist poet, William M. Bunting. They were ordained side by side. They might be called representative sons of the older Methodist prophets. They were distinctive types of a transition age in Methodism—an age which, while they lived, they and men of their standing and school held back from rushing to its close. When they passed, that age began rapidly to yield to what follows. They were men of more general culture, it may be, than their fathers, but, like their fathers, they were eminently preachers, after the old rich intellectual types, both puritan and episcopal; men who drank deeply themselves into evangelical truth, and solemnly realized both the joys and terrors of an unseen and eternal world. Both were polished men; both were men more in the spiritual than in the temporal world; both were poets;

and both were sacrifices to their own work of love—frequent, long, thoughtful, and earnest preaching.

Both Bunting and Treffry were sons of remarkable men. Treffry was the son of Richard Treffry, who became a Methodist preacher in 1792. The father's memory is balmy in his native county. He was a manly, noble-hearted Cornishman. The early Methodist preachers have many, many a time jogged along in the saddle over the old turnpike-road from St. Austell, westward. It ran along on the summit of a ridge, which sent out its spurs on either hand to shelter the more cultured valleys, whose tributary streamlets fed the river Fal, on the one side, and, on the other, the little rivers which finish their wanderings in romantic Veryan Bay. There, by the road-side, on the high ground not far from the ancient town of Tregony, is the village of Newton, the elder Treffry's birth-place. There he came, under the truth from the lips of Methodist itinerants; there, at the age of sixteen, he became savingly acquainted with his Saviour; and there he was constrained by the love of Christ to call his neighbours to repentance. The name and influence of the untrained young evangelist still live on the scenes which witnessed the first outflow of his zeal.

"I recollect him," says one to whom the surroundings of his early life were familiar; "the awe with which his appearance as a preacher used to inspire me when I was a boy seems to creep over me still when I think of him. A dark-looking man, of strongly-marked, manly features, with eyes that searched your very soul from under their dark, shaggy brows. He was the same in appearance, allowing for wear and tear, when I saw him, years afterwards, sitting among public men at a public meeting, unmoved, calm, and grave. I had learnt by that time to know the warm, generous feeling of the great heart that beat under that unpolished outside. A faint image of his first wife follows me, too. She was a Methodist woman of the old style, in spirit, manner, and dress. She esteemed no calling more honourable than that of her husband, and had zeal, intelligence, and hallowed gifts equal to the work of a 'helpmeet,' even in the more public part of his sacred duties. It is said that she would not shrink from a journey into the country to conduct a religious service among the rural folk, if affliction or other unforeseen hinderance fell in his way. A story goes of his requesting her to aid him in this way in a small village chapel that I know very well, and that when she had fairly entered on her address to the people, he, having followed her from home, stepped in, and heard one of his wife's public utterances for the first time. It is said that after that she was not so easily persuaded to act the 'helpmeet' in that particular way. I used to hear my father say that Mr. Treffry was a sound, solid preacher, always clear as daylight, full of strong sense, never talking above the people's understanding, and driving home everything to their heart and conscience. He could write, too, and sometimes did a little in the way of poetry. My mother, who knew what it was to see a darling infant pass quickly away to the skies, used to quote some of his lines 'On the Death of an Infant Son' with a tear in her eye—

> " O'er thy much-lov'd infant's urn,
> Wipe thine eyes, and cease to mourn;
> Cease to drop the grief-stain'd tear,
> Dare not think thy lot severe;
> Dare not ask, why Heaven, so soon,
> Tore from thee thy bounteous boon?
> Why disease's blasting power
> Nipped so soon the lovely flower;
> Why those cheeks, as lilies fair,
> Must for worms a feast prepare.
> God's decrees are just and right,
> All His paths are paths of light;
> All created nature lies
> Open to His piercing eyes.
> He hath called thy babe away
> From the dungeon of its clay;
> Hous'd the plant, to bloom above,
> In the sunshine of His love.
>
> . . . . .
>
> Didst thou once, with raptures high,
> On thy offspring feast thine eye,
> And behold the new-born boy
> With a mother's dear-bought joy?

> Greater joys and raptures higher
> Now thy feeling breast should fire;
> Thou hast nurs'd beneath thy care
> A child for God, a heavenly heir!
> May this thought, like healing balm,
> Smooth the tempest to a calm.

"There was one thing about Mr. Treffry which I never could well make out. I used to think that a man who could write poetry—real poetry—must have it in his soul; and if he had it in himself, it seemed to me that he would catch life from other poets, and read their verses so as to make people feel the beauty and meaning which he felt himself. But from the way in which he gave out the hymns, it really was no difference whether one had more beauty or meaning than another. They might as well have had neither beauty nor meaning. He would run along the lines in a kind of drone, as if he were a drone-bee humming in the bell of a foxglove; and every word, no matter what it meant, or how important it was, had the same tone, and time, and accent, and emphasis, as its smallest neighbour. Now, for my part, I would rather hear some men read the hymn than I would listen to the preaching of others: the hymn from some lips has more life than many a sermon. And yet they say Mr. Treffry enjoyed other people's poetry, and had tune enough in him to make poetry himself. I suppose it was with him in that, as it was in some other things. You could not tell at first what the man was within from what appeared without. From his looks, and his way of speaking and behaving sometimes, you would think that he was a sour, rude, rough, unmannerly man. It appeared as if he had never learnt manners; as if he never cared to learn them; and as if not even the grace of God had given him any polish. But stop a little. Find him out fairly, and you would soon be charmed into love for him, as a right-hearted, gentle, tender-spirited, benign, and loving man. He had the soul, at least, of a Christian gentleman. The diamond was pure, though the coating, for a time, was rough. So it might be as to his real taste and talent for poetry. One of his first pieces, at any rate the first that I ever read, was in one of the old magazines, and it was, like very many of the poems in the Methodist magazines of those days, all 'to the memory' of somebody or other. This was 'On Miss Hannah Treffry, who died of fever, November 22, 1802, in the 20th year of her age.' She was his sister.

> "In what soft numbers shall my muse rehearse,
> The mournful subject of my humble verse;
> With pensive mind deplore th' untimely doom,
> And trace a sister's passage to the tomb?
> What, though thy parents boast no honoured name,
> No worthless grandeur, no exploits of fame;
> What, though no splendid epithets of praise
> Announced thy birth, or mark'd thy early days;
> What, though no passion prompted thee to roam
> Far from the limits of thy humble home;
> What, though thy early hours were ne'er applied
> To high ambition and excessive pride,
> To waste thy strength with dissipated throngs,
> In midnight revels, or by impious songs;
> What, though to thee no bold, adventurous swains,
> In amorous ditties and poetic strains,
> Paid grateful homage—faithless vows express'd,
> To raise a tumult in thy peaceful breast;—
>
> Yet shall the muse for thee the tribute bring,
> In pensive numbers touch the tuneful string—
> For thee in melancholy strains declare,
> The soft endearments of thy tender care;
> For thee this memory faithful shall retrace
> The open features that adorn'd thy face;
> Review thy actions, innocently kind,
> The fairest index of an artless mind;
> For thee this breast shall heave the labouring sigh,
> While the tears stagnate in my mournful eye;
> Nor shall thy lovely image e'er depart,
> While life invigorates this hallowed heart.
>
> See the pale wretch, absorb'd in anxious care,
> And stung with deepest anguish and despair,
> Who inly groans beneath the load of life,
> And longs to end the dark and doubtful strife,
> Is left unnoticed—such the high decree—
> While the fierce archer shoots his darts at thee!
> So when the flowers of the spring display
> Their silken leaves to catch the solar ray,
> The blasting tempest checks the beauteous bloom,
> And wastes the pleasing prospects ere 'tis noon.

"With keenest grief I see thy labouring breast
By torturing pain and anxious care oppress'd;
The fierce disease increasing strength obtains,
And the pale current stagnates in the veins;
Around thy bed thy weeping parents view
(While ceaseless tears their aged cheeks bedew)
Their tender offspring panting hard for breath,
And the heart struggling in the pangs of death!
What now avail the well-proportion'd frame,
The vigorous body, or the youthful flame;
The potent charms which mark the healing art,
Or the big sigh that rends the parent's heart!
All ineffectual!—prayers and tears are vain
To extract the arrow, or assuage the pain;
For ere this globe, which pendent hangs in space,
Had twice perform'd its swift, diurnal race,
The foe relentless spoil'd thy tender form,
And took the enfeebl'd citadel by storm:
While the blest spirit upward bent its way,
And left the putrid mass of lifeless clay!

Oh, could the muse on sacred pinions rise,
And trace thy rapid passage through the skies,
With steadfast eye thy blest escape survey,
From midnight darkness to immortal day!
See, from the source of uncreated light,
Celestial glories burst upon thy sight;
The joyful view would bring the kind relief,
And chase this sad satiety of grief,
Dispel the gloom that hovers in my breast,
Absorb my tears, and put my doubts to rest.

But sullen clouds of thickest darkness spread
Their sable curtains o'er the silent dead;
The silent dead their final fate conceal,
Nor can the boldest fancy pierce the veil;
But though the veil obstructs the human sight,
The ways of God are equal, just, and right;
This cheering truth inspires my humble breast,
With calm submission to the high behest."

According to the "old magazine" alluded to in these recollections, this utterance of Mr. Treffry's muse was issued in Truro, just before he left that town for his appointment at Camelford. Camelford! What and where is Camelford? The question may not be unfairly put even in these days, for as yet the geography of their own country has not a very important part in the schooling of English scholars. It may still be possible for a cockney to know just as much as the old London watchman, who, while chatting with a traveller at night, as he was directing him to his inn, inquired from whence his companion came, and when told from Cornwall, cried: "Cornwall! Ah!—yes! Cornwall—that's outside Britain, I think!" Camelford is a queer old town in Cornwall, and yet, according to landmarks, it is neither "outside" nor inside Britain. It is in a valley, among the mountain moorlands of the ancient border-line between north-western Saxondom and the land of the Cornish Britons. It is on the river Camel, or "winding Alan," which, after many a twist and turn, finds its way into the Bristol Channel. It is under the shadows of Roughtor and Brownwilly on the one side, and on the other it is sheltered by the heights which run out to the wild cliff, on which are the weather-beaten ruins of Tintagel, or King Arthur's Castle. It marks, as tradition says, the scene of the battle, fatal both to Arthur and his nephew, Modred, in 542; and of a later contest in 823, between the Saxon Egbert and the Western Britons. The little town is in the parish of Lanteglos; and the difficulty of finding out its whereabouts was once felt even by a parson in search of it as his ecclesiastical "living." Dr. Daniel Lombard, who was the son of a French Protestant, and had, until his presentation to Lanteglos, spent most of his days abroad, came, in the early part of the last century, to take possession of his parish before his pronunciation of English names was quite complete. He travelled on and on, passed through the place he was seeking, found his way down to the Land's End and back again, vainly inquiring, in an accent which nobody understood, for *Lan-te-glos-juxta Camail Ford*. He found it at last, and died there.

In 1803, Mr. Treffry came to it with less difficulty, and was the first local Methodist bishop who took up his abode in Camelford as the centre of his evangelizing action. Here his poetic faculty was cherished. And here, soon after his verses on his sister's death were published in the "old magazine," his son Richard was born. That son grew up with an instinctive liking for the peculiar scenery of his native province. Years afterwards, when it had been proved that he inherited poetic power from his less cultured but naturally tasteful father, and when he had shown that his poetic genius was in harmony with his noble gifts as a divine and a preacher, in a letter to his father he gave beautiful expression to the feelings with which he visited his birth-place and the scenes of his boyhood. "Off in a car to Camelford—dined at Mr. Ivey's, with Mr. Truscott—went to see the house in which I was born. . . . Well, you know all the rest, or may guess it. . . . How the smell of burning turf, and the smiling faces, and the broad, western dialect of the peasantry, and the blossoming primroses, and the rude, rugged, precipitous rocks, all were right pleasant to my sense; how I felt that I had something of a Cornish heart still, in spite of the vicissitudes of the world ; how I longed for some rational company to admire with me certain beautiful edifices exhibiting the elementary principles of architecture ; how I ejaculated wishes to the throne of grace for you and mother ; how I sung—

> "Could I but climb where Moses stood,
> And view the landscape o'er,
> Not Jordan's stream nor death's cold flood
> Should fright me from the shore!

All this, and a thousand other things, you must fancy."

Like his father, he had become a Methodist preacher. He entered on this work from the same principle and with like feelings and motives as did his venerable parent; who records his heart's joy in his son's course :—"To have a son engaged in the work of the ministry, was to me a source of unspeak- able pleasure ; and especially the Methodist ministry, which in early life won the warmest affections of my heart, and which, after a lapse of more than thirty years' engagement in it, then possessed the most cordial approbation of my judg- ment, and held the highest place in my esteem."

As the poetical evangelist moved about in his itinerant work, in Surrey, Yorkshire, Nottingham, and London, he always evidenced his love for the beautiful in nature. His correspondence often showed his gift of poetic expression; and he learnt to enjoy sympathy and intercourse with souls akin to his own. Among those to whom he became the more closely knit by the bonds of taste and affection, was an old colleague of his father's. The intimacy must have begun while he was yet a boy; but when his old friend passed away from his itinerancy, just as the young poet had closed his first year's labour as a pilgrim preacher, the feelings of his heart were poured forth in " Stanzas inscribed to the Memory of the Rev. John Bryant, by one who Loved him while he Lived, and who still venerates his Character, and laments his Loss :"—

> Peace, all is peace!" th' expiring warrior said,
>   While o'er him friendship hung in speechless woe,
> And mission'd envoys watch'd his dying bed,
>   To bear his spirit from these scenes below.
> On his pale cheek there came the heavenly glow,
> Immortal hope glanced brightly from his eye,
>   Telling of victory o'er every foe;
> Calm as the lake untouch'd by zephyr's sigh
> The messengers of glory saw the Christian die.
>
> The strife is closed!—from her incumbering clod,
>   Upborne on angels' wings, the spirit flies
> Swift towards the dwelling of her Father—God,
>   And swells with new and untold ecstacies;
>   In the vast regions of her native skies
> Beholds what human tongue can ne'er unfold—
>   Floods of unfading glory; to her eyes
> The secrets of eternity unroll'd;
> And on her ear came pouring strains from harps of gold.
>
> Farewell, dear saint! our loves to thee shall cling,
>   And if, while basking in th' eternal bourn,
> Our grief could earthward bend thy angel wing,
>   Oh! would not tears embalm thy humble urn,
>   Till to thy kindred dust thou should'st return?
> Forgive the frenzy of the thought! Ah, no!
>   No; while the pastor, husband, friend, we mourn,
> We would not bind thee to this world of woe:
> Go, then, to thy bright mansion, loved and honoured, go!
>
> Tell me, ye guardians of th' immortal spheres,
>   Who watch the springs of human sympathy,
> Do happy spirits cherish human tears?
>   And when the breast is cold, and dim the eye,
>   In the dark frost of reckless agony,

> Do they the kindly influence distil—
> The welcome, melting, sorrow-soft'ning sigh?
> Do they the heart with balmy unction fill,
> Like dew descending on the earthquake-riven hill?
>
> O Thou, that hearest prayer! we look to Thee;
> To Thee, thy people's Helper in distress,
> Save us from murmuring at Thy dread decree!
> We drain the cup, the cup of bitterness.
> Our worldly, selfish yearning we confess.
> Our friend is gone, but Thou art still our Friend,
> Unknowing lapse of time, or change of place:
> Our bud, our hopes, from earth-born dreams ascend
> To heaven, to Thee, to rest and joy that ne'er shall end.
>
> Farewell, dear saint! no more shall sorrow's frown
> O'er life's enjoyments cast its baleful hue;
> Nor dark affliction weigh thy spirit down!
> No more shall pain thy wearied form subdue,
> Or fierce temptation dim thy mental view.
> Long, long the mortal fight thou hast maintain'd;
> At thy broad shield full oft hell's arrows flew;
> But now, O joy! the victory is gain'd,
> And endless life and heavenly blessedness obtain'd.
>
> The grave thy body hath received in trust,
> Awhile in silence and in peace to sleep;
> And Christ stands sentinel upon the dust,
> Safe to redemption's destin'd day to keep.
> Oh! then, no more o'er thee shall sorrow weep;
> For wearied nature shall at length expire;
> And angel harvesters the world shall reap;
> Then, in the wreathing of the final fire,
> Sun, moon, and stars to dark oblivion shall retire!
>
> Then the deep groan of dust-clad souls shall cease;
> Then, then, mortality itself shall die;
> O'er the expanse shall reign perennial peace,
> And Death be swallow'd up in victory.
> The phœnix body from the earth shall fly,
> Clad, for the glory of its new abode,
> In the bright vestments of eternity.
> Fleet quickly, Time! away, earth's wearying load!|
> The bride of heaven descends, the spouse of Christ our God.

In this we have deep sympathies with suffering human nature, and close fellowship of feeling with the spiritual and unseen world around us; calm confidence in Him who lives to hold the keys of hades and of death, and jubilant anticipations of an immortal future, all truly set to music by one who had no mean gift of uttering happy thought and feeling in tender and graceful measure,

The early formation of friendships has, in some cases, a mystery about it. In looking at the linked characters, as they have been subsequently developed, one is at a loss to know how the hard and the gentle, the selfish and the unselfish, the pretentious and the modest, the humbug and the real, ever get linked as they sometimes are. Yet so it has been. This can be accounted for, perhaps, only on the principle that those who have thus early associated under the overmastering influence of Christian first love, have ever afterwards felt themselves, on the one side at least, bound by the law of charity to hold the bond sacred through all the subsequent variations of taste, temper, and pursuit. Some such associations were probably formed by the younger Treffry in the warmth of early Christian affection. And to these, doubtless, he was faithful, though some people might find it difficult to know how or why. At all events, the Church and the world have not unfrequently been the better for things which they have failed to understand. Were it not for some of his earlier associations, our young poet-preacher might never have left us even a few good proofs of his poetic talent. There might not, at least, have been so much in the elegiac form among his remains. The only other available specimen of his elegiac stanzas appears to have been written while he was in Nottingham, in the height of his popularity as a preacher and public speaker; and in the midst of the travail and toil with which men endowed as he was are liable to be taxed, even to the death. But his work was one of love; and if the more public work was sometimes made to yield to the claim for a moment's private indulgence of his cultured taste, even that semblance of relaxation was a work of love, as will be seen in his verses to the memory of a young lady who had been taken to a brighter world from the home of her childhood. The poem is brightened with some gems of thought richly set. It shows fine discrimination, and exquisite tenderness. There is a tasteful variety and delicate beauty of illustration. The poet's conception sometimes rises above the beautiful, and he sustains throughout appropriate force and music of diction. The elegy does honour to the writer's imagination, taste, and feeling:—

> As some bright cloud, by evening's sunlight painted,
>   Glows in the purple of celestial dye;
> And, ere its beauty by earth's mists is tainted,
>   Fades to the calmness of the spotless sky;
> Such was she to us in her purity.
>   Her rainbow life has melted into light,
> And like a strain of magic melody,
>   That pauses on the bosom of the night,
> She was on earth an hour—then heavenward wing'd her flight.
>
> Yet as the echo of such music swells
>   The pensive heart through every coming year,
> E'en so thine image, my fair sister, dwells,
>   To tender thought and hallow'd memory dear.
> Sister!—ay, so I called thee; and when here
>   Thou would'st have smiled approval of the name;
> Still thus I hail thee, by this votive tear,
>   Since he, thy brother, is to me the same,
> And must be, while life beats within this mortal frame.
>
> She sleepeth—where? not in the tearless tomb,
>   Where tired misanthropy demands repose;
> Nor went her sun down in the fearful gloom
>   Which sleeps upon the parting day of those
> Who laugh through life, to tremble at its close;
>   Yet she had smiles!—smiles we may ne'er forget;
> Yes, she had smiles and tears; as the young rose
>   Most fragrant seems, with evening dew-drops wet,
> So beautiful her face, where smiles and tears were met.
>
> Oh! there are tears for thee—big, bursting tears,
>   (Not those in heartless mockery which flow),
> And yet our sorrow is not that which tears
>   The heart like lightning; not the speechless woe,
> The frenzied, paralyzing grief, which ne'er may know
>   Aught but despair; hope beams upon thy grave,
> Not as a meteor in its wand'ring—no;
>   For He whose arm almighty is to save,
> Walk'd o'er death's tide, and shone to thee across the wave.
>
> She sleepeth—where? not in the warrior's grave;
>   Her winding-sheet is pure; nor rests her head
> Deep in the darkness of some ocean cave,
>   Like a lost pearl; nor in the marriage bed;

And yet, my virgin sister, thou art wed;
    Swells on our ear thy nuptials' festal strain,
And thine espousals chaste are heralded
    Through heaven's high arches; angels swell thy train,
And hail thee as a bride—a bride without a stain.

But who is He, the Bridegroom of thy soul?
    He with the crimson vest and flaming eye;
Beneath whose feet clouds, fires, and tempest's roll;
    Whose smile is bliss, whose frown is misery;
From out whose glances countless lightnings fly;
    Who speaks, and speaking, cleaves the spheres asunder;
Who sways His sceptre o'er earth, sea, and sky,
    To whom ten thousand angels praises thunder,
While startled demons flee, o'erwhelmed with fear and wonder?

'Tis He who quaff'd the mantling cup of pain;
    Writhed in fierce anguish in the noon-day night;
That man might be deliver'd from the chain—
    The fearful yoke of sin: that heavenly light
Might illustrate eternity to sight,
    And hope of blind and reckless souls; 'tis He
Who vanquish'd in the fell and mortal fight
    The powers of hell, and rose to Heaven to be
For ever King of Kings! the Christ! unconquer'd Deity!

Beautiful spirit; when the Bridegroom's word
    Thrill'd on thine ear to summon thee away;
When gently parted was the silver cord
    Which bound thee in thy sisterhood of clay,
And angels rapt thee to thy native day;
    Didst thou quiver in some sudden fears,
As swift thou flittedst through th' empyrean way,
    To where Heaven's gate its lofty arch uprears?
And hadst thou aught of sympathy with human tears?

Dost thou yet mark the red and swollen eye,
    The pallid cheek, the corrugated brow,
The heart dilated in strong agony?
    Know'st thou the grief which wrings our spirits now?
And, oh! if angels pity, wilt not thou?
    And when that solemn pensiveness distils
O'er our sad souls, we know not whence or how,
    Is it not thou that hold'st the urn whence trills
The stream of heavenly peace, which all our sorrow stills?

Yes! thou wilt come, in stillness of the even,
    When light is fading from the dark blue sky,
When no cloud sleeps upon the face of Heaven,
    When floats the night-wind's softest minstrelsy,—
Wilt come from out thy dwelling-place on high.
    Yes! thou wilt breathe upon our secret soul,
Inspire high thinkings of eternity;
    The mists of earth from off our spirits roll,
And wing our ardent hopes to Heaven's illustrate goal.

> As through the night of heaven some mellow'd beam
>   Upon the soul of sleeping faith is shed,
> So thou on earth wert like a holy dream,
>   Bright and distinct, but, oh! too quickly fled;
> And now reality is perfected;
>   Thou art an angel of the upper skies;
> And when the final trump shall rouse the dead,
>   Thy spotless beauty from the earth shall rise,
> And endlessly expand in quenchless ecstacies!

Alas, for the fair promises of life to ripening talent and conscious power for good! Our young poet broke down with his bright prospects before him; and was called from the joys of action to retire and to languish in weakness and decline.

> Spirits are not finely touch'd
> But to fine issues.

But, as in Treffry's case, these issues are sometimes brought out through the fires of affliction. In the month of November, 1830, he is on his way to Penzance, in his native county, seeking that equable climate which is unsurpassed in its adaptations to sufferers such as he. It was in that quiet retreat, in the bosom of that beautiful bay, that he matured and sent forth those theological, moral, and biographical pages which must ever distinguish his memory. It was beautiful to see him, in his retirement, so peaceful, so hopeful, so full of gratitude,' and, at times, so cheerfully resigned, amidst so much that would keep frail human nature in the dust. Even when one with whom he corresponded had possibly winged a temptation to the tremulous invalid by telling him about the health and competence which he himself enjoyed, the meek answer is, "the general aspect of my affairs is comfortable. Health and competence are blessings which we may not estimate, except at a very high price; but disease and poverty may consist with true enjoyment, as my present state abundantly testifies." Notwithstanding disease and poverty, however, he was sometimes in his poetic vein. One effusion of his muse, in his Penzance cottage, remains to us, and this was, as far as we know, his last. It serves to indicate the bent of his mind as he moved towards the end.

"I have made a bit of poetry," says he to his father; "I wrote it one evening this week, in consequence of the subject coming into my head in some of the sleepless hours of the night." The verses are on "Saul of Tarsus":—

> No trumpet was blown, as the gate they pass'd,
>   Nor banner flung over their fierce array;
> But they rode like the breath of the desert blast,
>   Fleetly and silently passing away;
> Yet many look'd on that haughty man,
> Whose eye was the star of the fiery van.
>
> With frequent fasts his cheek was paled,
>   And there sat a frown on his brow of pride;
> And scorn on his quiv'ring lip prevail'd
>   As he thought on the Name of the Crucified;
> And his heart was as hard as the steel of his spear,
> To the whispers of pity, or the murmurs of fear.
>
> On—on!—the towers of Damascus are nigh,
>   The accurs'd Nazarenes are giv'n to our hand;
> When, lo! an ineffable blaze from on high
>   Burst, sudden as thought, on the hurrying band;
> And the glowing flood of that flashing light
> Dims the cloudless sun in his noonday height.
>
> Vain is the speed of the startled horse,
>   And vain is the force of the glittering spear;
> The scorner hath ended his ruthless course;
>   The victor of Galilee triumpheth here,
> And His words of mystic spirit appal
> The awe-stricken heart of the prostrate Saul.
>
> There is night on his eye, and remorse on his brow,
>   As he sits in his chamber, helpless, alone;
> For the deeds woke up in his memory now,
>   Can riches, or blood, or sorrow atone?
> Yet hope in fair promise the future arrays,
> For the Crucified pleads, and the Pharisee prays.

This thrilling bit is the more precious from the circumstances under which it came from his soul. He was soon to be in the immortal home of poetry, and music, and truth. In one of his last letters to his father he says, "You will receive this sheet, if all be well, on my birthday, which as it is likely to prove the last, will also, I do not doubt, be the best birthday of my life. My kind love to Mr. William Bunting. Tell him I am going down towards the grave tranquil *within,* and surrounded *without* by all the mercies I can desire."

He lived to see the beginning of 1838. " On the morning of the new year," says Mrs. Treffry, " about three o'clock, he awoke from a refreshing sleep, and, calling me to him, said, 'Well, I am spared, contrary to the opinion of my dear friends, to see the beginning of the year 1838. And what shall be my salutation to my dear wife this morning? Shall I wish her a happy new year? Yes; I believe she will find it to be such in the highest sense; the most happy in the abundant overflowings of Divine grace and consolation.' 'And what shall I wish you?' I asked. 'That I may spend it in Heaven?' was his reply." The wish was fulfilled.

A little before his death he expressed a desire to see his wife. The interview was deeply affecting, and the parting scene inexpressibly solemn. "We had often," said she, " conversed of that dreaded hour ; " and it was now come. With a look of ineffable tenderness, he bade her adieu ; and she, with a tremulous voice, and in an agony of grief, said, " We shall soon meet in glory." " O yes, yes ! " he replied, with marked emphasis, but with difficult utterance. She expressed her willingness to remain with him, if she could minister to him any consolation; but he said, " No; go and pray." " This was the last sound," says Mrs. Treffry, "I ever heard from those lips, whose melody of tone had so often fallen on my ear and heart with a power of subduing and melting influence."

He departed in the presence of his father, leaving the noble old man to await his summons into the world to which his sons and their mother had gone before him. In four years from his son's departure he too had fled. He finished his mortal life in quiet old Maidenhead. "Thank God," said he, a few months before the end, "I just creep about the house; that is all. I have little acute pain; my sufferings are very tolerable; but the restlessness and weariness I feel are not so easily borne. I begin to languish and sigh after that better country, 'the house of my Father and God,' whither the forerunner is already entered, and entered for me, to plead my cause, and intercede on my behalf. Oh, what deep and unfeigned gratitude animates my breast for a good hope, through grace, that I shall live for ever! I have no merit; I mention none of my own righteousness. The labours of my life are all laid aside; I value them not. I am a sinner, but Christ is my Saviour, and no other do I need." Brave old pilgrim! He is among Methodist songsters for ever!

CHAPTER XV.

TWO POETICAL METAPHYSICIANS.

Methought I heard a reverend old man speak ;
  Grey were his locks, his eyes were calmly bright;
The rosiness of youth was on his cheek,
  And as he spoke, a heaven of truth and light
  Open'd itself upon my inner sight.

A MODERN writer, whose aristocratic volumes contain very many pages of rich and rare English, becomes popular, for one at least, when he describes a character figured by some great painter as "small-headed, not being specially given to thinking," as if he really believed that none but big-headed people can think. "Whether this be Ruskin's adopted creed or not," says an old observer, "one cannot be blind to the fact, that small, compact, harmonious heads sometimes grace the shoulders of some of the calmest, clearest, happiest, most far-sighted, and useful thinkers among us. Nor can I forget that one, whose venerable form was familiar to me in early life, distinguished himself by habits of profound thought, remarkably small-headed as he really was. This was Samuel Drew, "the self-taught Cornishman," whose history and character his eldest son, in a pleasant style, has given to the world as "A Life Lesson." My first sight of Mr. Drew left an impression which retains its freshness to this day. No one whose eye was in any way used to observe manifestations of mind could see him and forget him. I had gone to the morning service in the Falmouth Methodist Chapel one Sunday, and was seated in a front pew of the side gallery when my attention was caught by a tall slender figure moving up the aisle below, somewhat quickly, but with an action very expressive of strong decision. There was a looseness in the style of his hair and a lankness about his dress which, at first sight, gave his person an air of carelessness; but a full glance at his face was enough to prove that the seeming carelessness really betokened a habit of frequent retirement into the more distant regions of thought; while it indicated the tendency of his unselfish nature to neglect itself in its thoughtfulness and care about others. The lines of thought in his face were remarkable for their depth and significance; but there seemed to be beneath them a calm and cheerful expression of ever living kindness, tender sympathy, and true good nature; although it was very evident that his smile might, under some circumstances, become sufficiently sarcastic to inflict hidden torture on those whose folly or vice provoked him to give satirical sharpness to his arguments. His eye, however, would strike one, as revealing most of his inner man. It was dark, but never fierce. When in repose, it was beautifully expressive of inward quietness and ease; and yet no one could meet its gaze without feeling as if it looked into the secret places of his soul. I distinctly remember my uncomfortable feeling, on the preacher's account, for my own father, supposing that, like myself, he felt an instinctive inclination to shrink from the searching power of its peculiar light; and yet, who could fear it when he had once seen it kindle at the voice of truth, and brighten with devotional thought and feeling? Ah! to many, that eye has long been dim, but not to me. The soul that spoke through it when I first met its glance seems to speak to me still; and often have I felt as if I had caught its meaning again while I have been enjoying a review of his history.

How frequently have I wandered and mused over the scenes of Samuel Drew's birth and training and early mental efforts! He was born in a lone cottage about a mile from the town of St. Austell, in Cornwall—dear old St. Austell! Who that has seen thee throned on thy verdant hill-side, can forget thy quiet sway over the laughing valley? Drew's birth-place, I say, was a lone cottage—it was not a silent one, though, for its one ground-floor room and two sleeping nests were always regaled with the click and thump of what is known in that neighbourhood as a "stampses," a rude mill for pounding tin ore. Our metaphysician's father was a "tin-streamer." And by-and-by the son Samuel began his career at the "stampses," as a "buddle-boy." Three halfpence a day were his wages at first; and he thought himself of great importance when able to earn a shilling a week. Alas, for the lad! he soon lost the pious Methodist mother to whom he owed his earliest moral and religious lessons; and then his fearless character entered on its remarkable course of discipline. It is an interesting fact in his mental history, that the death of his mother touched to the quick his then rude and reckless nature; and so deeply moved his heart as in some way to make his intellect spring, and give promise of the wonderful unfoldings of its later life. The feeling never entirely lost its quickening power over his mind. "When we were following my mother to the grave," said he, years afterwards, "I well recollect a woman observing, as we passed, 'Poor little things, they little know the loss they have sustained!'" That touch upon his heart was mysteriously associated with the first literary shaping of his thought. His earliest attempts at composition took the metrical form; and under the promptings of a heart still melting at the loss of a mother, he wrote:—

> These eyes have seen a tender mother torn
> From three small babes she left behind to mourn.
> One infant son retired from life before;
> Next followed she whose loss I now deplore.
> This throbbing breast has heaved the heartfelt sigh,
> And breathed afflictions where her ashes lie.
> Relentless death! to rob my younger years
> Of soft indulgence and a mother's cares;
> Just brought to life, then left without a guide,
> To wade through time, and grapple with the tide!

In the midst of his literary success in after life, he said to a literary gentleman, who had taken great interest in him, and wished to know something of his early history: "On visiting my mother's grave, with one of my children, I wrote the following. The first couplet is supposed to be spoken by the child.

> "'Why looks my father on that lettered stone,
> And seems to sigh with sorrows not his own?'
> 'That stone, my dear, conceals from human eyes
> The peaceful mansion where my mother lies.
> Beneath the stone (my infant, do not weep!)
> The shrivelled muscles of my mother sleep;
> And soon, my babe, the awful hour must be
> When thy sad soul will heave a sigh for me,
> And say, with grief, amidst thy sister's cries—
> "*Beneath this stone our lifeless parent lies.*"
> Shouldst thou, my dear, survive thy father's doom,
> And wander pensive near his silent tomb,
> Think *thy* survivors will perform for *thee*
> What *I* do *now*, and *thou* wilt *then*, for *me.*'"

"*Stone*, in these lines," continued Mr. Drew, "is a mere poetical figure. My mother's grave has no such ornament. My father's circumstances would not allow it, if he had been inclined to erect one. I am unacquainted with the rules of art, and the orderly methods of composition. I wrote these lines from the impulse of my own feelings, and the dictates of nature." As such, who that knew him, in the full development of his genius, and philosophic and literary power, does not view them with interest, as marking the budding time of his distinguished mental powers? They serve to show that his soul had original tunefulness, as well as the logical and metaphysical faculties which self-culture afterwards brought up to such noble proportions.

In his eleventh year, the young genius appears as an apprentice to a parishioner of St. Blazey—half cobler, half farmer. The history of his mental struggles, bodily hardships, queer adventures, hazards, deliverances, and achievements, now forms a curious chapter, verily a "Life Lesson." "Long-legged Sam," as his companions termed him, promised then to be anything rather than the deep, logical thinker, the literary man, and the preacher.

"How often," says the old observer again, "have I

followed him in thought through his early perils on the road, perils on the cliffs, perils on the sea, life among smugglers, poaching expeditions, day-dreams, night goblins, truant flights, hunger-bitten times, miscellaneous readings, first exercises in native logic, and prize cudgel-fights: all these rise before me in turn, and take their place in the moving life-picture of the lad whose mind, as his amiable sister said, "always seemed above control." Then comes his first interview with Adam Clarke, the young Methodist preacher, whose ministry at once surprised him, and fixed his attention, and then set him, as he says, " a thinking and reasoning." His conversion follows, under very touching circumstances. He was brought to religious decision as the result of his last interview with a dying brother, whose death-bed was a scene of holy triumph. From the moment of his conversion his mental faculties, awakened into life before, sprang rapidly into higher proportions, took a decided course, and happily unfolded their native power. Their first modes of expression showed poetic tendency and taste. A copy of his earliest composition under Christian influences gives indication of defective culture, as might be supposed; but there is enough of poetry in it to establish a claim to genius. And it is valuable as a relic, illustrative of the struggles which a true genius had with difficulties resulting from a lack of early instruction. The choice of his theme, "Christmas," marks the now religious turn of the young man's character; and the spirit of the lines shows the depth and warmth of his devotion:—

> Farewell, ye scenes where desolation reigns,
> Pride domineers, and wraps the world in chains!
> Ye rayless shades of intellectual night,
> Empires in blood that pall the human sight;
> Ye scenes, in which life's varied forms appear,
> Where heathen gods their magic standards rear,
> And folly, leagued with vice, dance round the passing year;
> Ye lamps, that life's nocturnal portrait drew—
> Heroes and arms—I bid you all adieu!
> A nobler form, descending from the skies,
> Claims my attention, and detains my eyes,
> Directs the mind in its uncertain flight,
> And breaks upon me in a flood of light.

Through night's dim shades a heavenly form descends;
Grace lights his paths, and peace his steps attends.
Where careful shepherds watched their fleecy care,
In all the rigours of December's air,
A herald voice proclaimed an angel near,
And with new glories raised th' expiring year.
When thus the form in heavenly strains began—
"Hail! favoured earth!—hail! highly-favoured man!
I come, designed by that Almighty Lord,
Who formed yon worlds with His prolific word,
When formless chaos and the realms of night
Produced creation to my ravished sight—
I come, designed by that Almighty King:
Rejoice, O earth! ye barren mountains, sing!
Through thy domains glad tidings shall abound;
Thy sons enslaved shall hear the joyful sound;
Through frozen climes, where seas forget to roll,
Truth shall prevail, and spread from pole to pole;
Where burning zones receive the solar rays,
Joy, breaking forth, the illumin'd word shall seize;
No tribes shall mourn a partial favour given,
No soul exempt, reproach neglectful Heaven.
For on this day—on this auspicious morn,
In Bethlehem town the incarnate Godhead's born;
The promised seed prophetic seers foretold—
Foresaw—predicted—did by faith behold—
The mighty God! mankind's eternal Friend!
Great Prince of Peace! whose kingdom knows no end
On hay reclined, in swathes He now appears;
A simple manger now the Godhead bears!"
He paused—when, lo! a multitude was heard,
Whose heavenly songs the astonish'd shepherds scared—
"Glory to God in highest strains be raised;
Feel it, O earth—and be thy Maker praised;
O'er earth's long shores peace shall extend her sway;
Her sons shall hear hostilities decay;
Good will to man shall smile on every plain,
And peace and plenty greet the world again."
Here ceased their song; then, from the dusky shade,
Through realms of light, their radiant wings displayed.
Say then, my muse, what theme will charm the ear,
Warm the cold soul, and draw the pious tear?
Say how the Godhead, wrapped in human clay,
Threw by the glories of unclouded day,
The Gospel standard through the skies unfurled,
And held out mercy to a ruined world?
Hail! blessed time! auspicious era, hail!
Hail! conquering love, and truth that must prevail!
O'er earth's wide face unveil the sacred road
That leads from darkness to the throne of God!
The swarthy sons of Afric's torrid soil

And Lybia's wastes shall feel thy genial smile;
India shall rise, forgetful of her stores,
To meet salvation on her native shores.
No more shall warriors spread their dire alarms,
Form new allies, and call the world to arms;
War's fatal trumpet sound her blast no more;
No reeking slaughter bathe her steps in gore.
Earth's fertile vales the quickening voice shall hear,
Rise into plains, and mountains disappear;
Rough places smoothed shall richest pasture yield,
And crooked paths produce a fertile field;
Thy savage tribes shall be at length subdued,
And, conquered, rise, in righteousness renewed.
Those swarms that pressed where splendid greatness shone
Shall quit her interest to promote their own;
Despotic power—that human scourge—shall cease,
And captive slaves from servile chains release;
Types shall no more to anti-types extend,
Rites disappear, and priestly orders end.
Refulgent scenes shall these dark days succeed,
And Gospel truths in radiant circles spread;
Men's present aims with future interest blend;
To distant worlds the rising soul shall tend;
Messiah's power shall renovate the whole,
And truth, combined with love, pervade the human soul!

The young unlettered genius who could write such lines as these would be sufficiently conscious of his power, and have a feeling of success strong enough to dispose him to further efforts. His next achievement was the production of twelve hundred lines of "Reflections on St. Austell Churchyard," a somewhat sombre theme, and worked out with not very bright results, as far as accurate English and correct verse are concerned, but wearing the impress of a mind capable of profound thought, and of emulating the first masters of tuneful measure. Some parts of it might remind the reader of Pope; and Pope was rather a favourite with the self-taught student. In his later life, he one day quoted Pope in conversation.

"You don't seem to be so bitter an enemy to Pope as some of our zealous ministers are," said one.

"I think, sir," was his reply, "it has become the pulpit fashion to decry Pope, but it is easier to reprobate than disprove his positions. When this is done, it will be time enough to censure them."

One who was acquainted with Mr. Drew, says: "A few years ago I was one of a select party that went up the Thames in a small steamer to Twickenham. When we came opposite to Pope's villa, Mr. Drew, who was with us, directed our attention to it, and making some observation which I now forget, took off his hat, 'in honour,' as he said, 'of departed greatness.'"

A large part of his poetical "Reflections" is argumentative, not unlike Pope's "Essay on Man," which, perhaps, in his fondness for Pope, he had in his mind as a model. The interest deepens around this part of the poem when it affords us what seems to be a kind of poetic embryo of his great work on "The Immateriality and Immortality of the Human Soul." To read his preface to that immortal book, is to have a charm thrown about everything associated with his first conceptions of the argument. There is a kind of poetry breathing through the sentences. "Advancing in years," he says, "the author's probationary period is drawing to a close; and the crisis cannot be remote that will dismiss his spirit from its earthly abode to the regions of immortality. Associating then with the disembodied, detached from all material organisation, there can be no doubt that he will see much reason to alter many of his views respecting the momentous subject on which he has written. He, however, concludes this preface under a full conviction that, although unable to communicate any corrections of what he may then discover to be erroneous in his essay, he shall have new evidence, bursting upon him like a tide of glory, to establish beyond the possibility of a doubt 'The Immateriality and Immortality of the Human Soul.'"

Yes, all things on that subject are clear to him now. All his arguments are seen in true light; and answers have been given to the questions which, as they first arose, found an utterance in measured lines:—

> What is the soul? and where does it reside?
> What gives it life—or makes that life subside?
> Are souls extinct when bodies first expire?

> Can Death's cold hand extinguish heavenly fire?
> First, what is life?—define the human soul—
> That vital spark that animates the whole.
>
> . . . .
>
> To form the soul do subtle parts conspire?
> Does action live through every part entire?
> Consists the soul of elemental flame?
> Can high-wrought matter its existence claim?
>
> . . . .
>
> Now, if the soul be matter thus refin'd,
> If it has parts connected or disjoin'd,
> Then follows—what these propositions teach—
> That some corporeal instrument may reach,
> And reaching there, its ruin may portend,
> Its death accomplish, and its being end.
>
> . . . .
>
> This is no soul—for matter cannot think;
> And thought destroy'd would make the soul extinct;
> Since what has parts must be dissolved again,
> And in its pristine elements remain.

The poet seems to have intended the publication of his poem, as the manuscript has a preface attached. And whatever poetry or metaphysics he had, the preface shows that he had strong common sense. "When I consider myself," he says, "my subject, my circumstances, my situation, and my neighbours, I cannot think this apology unnecessary. When this appears in a public manner, I expect some will despise—some ridicule—some pity—and some, perhaps, applaud me for my undertaking. To please every one is impossible. One objection will be (I expect) continually raised—which is—*you had better mind your work*. It may not be unnecessary, in reply, to observe—it had but little interference with my labour; nothing to its detriment; but has been chiefly the produce of those evening and leisure hours which too many of my age dedicate to profligacy, wicked company, and vice."

On second thought, Mr. Drew shut up his poem, and eventually put his thoughts in such a prose form as secured for him a place in the history of thoughtful literature that he will never lose. It may be that, in withdrawing his poetic pages, he was influenced by reasons such as he, long afterwards, expressed in friendly talk.

"Poetry," he remarked, "is about the worst article that can be carried into the market of literature. Merit is no criterion by which circulation may be calculated. A happy concurrence of wind and tide may sometimes accomplish, in a lucky moment, what no talents or efforts can effect. This will throw a halo round an author's name, and then all his productions will sell. Even when uttering the most consummate nonsense, he will be thought to 'snatch a grace beyond the reach of art.' Nine-tenths of the booksellers in London know that nine-tenths of mankind are fools, and must be treated accordingly."

It is a joy to watch Samuel Drew in happy companionship with the few authors who shared in the work of training and nurturing the future master of thought. Bunyan's "Pilgrim" took a leading part, and Franklin's "Way to Wealth;" and above all, the knotty pages of John Locke. The story of his upward tug for knowledge, and his steady perseverance under accumulative difficulties, is most instructive. One is kept under a stimulating charm while watching the first manifestation of his power in the lists against Tom Paine; or witnessing the generous patronage of the venerable antiquary John Whitaker; or marking the resistless plunges of the logical shoemaker's awl into the vulnerable sides of Parson Polwhele, the anti-Methodist anecdote-maker; or following his thoughts in his first great essay on "The Human Soul;" or in his adventurous passage into the mysteries of the "Resurrection;" or in his efforts towards a prize essay on "The Being and Attributes of the Deity;" or in his literary connection with Dr. Coke, his contributions to the history of his native county; or his long and honourable relation to the Caxton Press as editor of the "Imperial Magazine." He was a preacher, too; not popular, nor fond of popular preachers, it would seem.

"What do you think of that sermon?" somebody asked after listening to a very popular man.

"I think, sir, that, deprived of their long 'O—'s' and great 'O—'s,' many such discourses could be contained in a nut-shell."

It required brains much larger than the contents of a nutshell to take in a sermon of his. His sermons were enjoyable to calm thinkers only. As a Methodist, he was more remarkable for his keen philosophical insight into the tendencies of Methodist organisation than for his contributions to its poetical literature. His poetic faculty was mostly indulged within the circle of his own household. There, reproof was sometimes given in playful rhyme, as when he wrote on a piece of waste paper, and left the lines for the servants to read—

> Amidst the wonders Islington can boast,
> That which must puzzle and surprise us most,
> And give to bold credulity a shock,
> Is Drew at breakfast before eight o'clock!

But the more delicate and tender employment of his muse would be in expressing his warm paternal affections. So his gentle heart makes its meaning felt, with amiable inattention to the claims of critical taste, in one of his usual addresses to his youngest daughter on her birthday.

> Accept, dear Mary, on thy natal day,
>   This kind expression of a father's love;
> Warm from his heart it flows without decay,
>   To thee in deeds—in prayer to God above.
>
> Thy childhood past, but not matured in years,
>   Thy parents view thee in a path of strife,
> And watch those steps with anxious hopes and fears
>   That soon will stamp thy destiny for life.
>
> The dangerous ocean which thy barque must sail
>   Has rocks and shoals unseen, or found too late;
> And those who venture under passion's gale
>   Will suffer shipwreck on the shores of fate.
>
> Taught from thy youth those tempting scenes to shun,
>   Where serpents lurk beneath delusive flowers,
> Where folly's minions dance, and are undone,
>   By fashion lead to dissipation's bowers.
>
> Revere the precepts which instruction gives;
>   Experience, reason, urge thee to be wise.
> A father's voice may warn while yet he lives;
>   O may Heaven's counsel lead thee when he dies!
>
> A Power unseen o'er thy steps presides,
>   To guard thy feet in virtue's sacred road;
> The Cross atones—the Saviour's spirit guides
>   From vice and sorrow to the throne of God.
>
>   . . . .

> An aged widow should thy mother prove,
>   Who nursed and cherished thee with tender care,
> Repay that kindness with a daughter's love,
>   And in thy comforts let her claim a share.
> Should he who writes prove destitute, forlorn,
>   Wrinkled and gray, his lingering hours beguile;
> Age and decrepitude, oh, do not scorn,
>   But cheer his evening with a filial smile.
> Then, when thy parents, summoned to the skies,
>   No more admonish, or thy actions see,
> A generation yet unborn may rise,
>   To pay those duties rendered now by thee.

Some of these closing lines are touching, especially when read with the knowledge of his subsequent experience of being left "forlorn," bereft of his wife. But he realised the full answer to his prayer for the final comfort of a " filial smile."

Though most of his writings were of the severe and more profound order, there was a kind of tender poetry in his home life; and his eldest son has given us a delicately touched picture of his "calm decay," and the solemn beauties of "the closing scene;" while the inhabitants of his native town have given expression to their affection for him, and have recorded their estimate of his character on a tablet, which they placed in the church of his native parish, St. Austell, Cornwall.

To the Memory of
SAMUEL DREW,
A NATIVE OF THIS PARISH,
WHOSE TALENTS AS A METAPHYSICAL WRITER,
UNAIDED BY EDUCATION,
RAISED HIM FROM OBSCURITY
INTO HONOURABLE NOTICE,
AND WHOSE VIRTUES AS A CHRISTIAN
WON THE ESTEEM AND AFFECTION
OF ALL WHO KNEW HIM.
HE WAS BORN MARCH 3RD, 1765,
LIVED IN ST. AUSTELL UNTIL JANUARY, 1819,
AND, AFTER AN ABSENCE OF FOURTEEN YEARS,
DURING WHICH HE CONDUCTED A LITERARY JOURNAL,
HE RETURNED TO END HIS DAYS IN HIS NATIVE COUNTY,
AS HE HAD LONG DESIRED,
AND DIED AT HELSTON, MARCH 29TH, 1833.

To record their sense of his literary merit and moral worth, his fellow-countrymen and parishioners have erected this tablet.

Human character is an interesting study as to the numberless varieties in its degrees of power; but the interest greatly deepens when all the differences in the balance of personal qualities are considered. In one case, as with Samuel Drew, the metaphysical power, the logical force, and the technical severity, are of such weight as to leave but little to the account of poetical genius, and less to musical taste. In another instance, of which the Rev. David McNicoll was an example, the metaphysical faculty, though of equal calibre, appears to be less, because of its combination with richer fancy, nobler imagination, and a finer musical sense. But while it is interesting to observe the nice differences in the balance of character, it is curious to see how, in the course of our observation, at an unforeseen and unaccountable turn, long scattered, fragmentary recollections of character are brought together, so as to answer to each other, and to combine in giving a kind of re-embodiment and new life to almost forgotten excellencies. An illustration of this is associated with the memory of David McNicoll. Two or three years ago, an old traveller and his wife found their way down to a romantic little harbour on the English Coast, looking out between its bold, sheltering headlands, upon the mighty Atlantic. They were kindly received in a Methodist home, where, on entering the dining-room, they were simultaneously drawn towards a painting on the wall, and both cried, as with one voice—

" Why, there is David McNicoll!"

" It looks like Jackson's painting," said the traveller.'

" No," the master of the house replied; " it is a copy—one of my attempts, by way of exercise."

" Well, it is good, isn't it?" said the traveller to his wife. " He looks there just as I remember him in my youth. I saw him in the pulpit; he was praying, and lounging on the cushion and Bible, some would say, lazily; but it was rather, as it seems to me now, illustrative of his peculiar entireness of reliance on the providence of God, to whom he was speaking. He seemed to be ' rolling himself on the Lord,' as an old Scotch divine would say : and Mr. McNicoll was a Scotchman. I shall never forget that prayer; or rather shall never lose the impression then left on my mind. I was but a boy; but I had a feeling of awe, while I listened to him. It appeared to me as if his soul were swimming out into some great depth; as if he were at home among the great waters, and had delight in finding himself out of sight of land. That old familiar verse has often come to me when his figure and action in the pulpit have been imaged to my mind :—

> " There shall I bathe my weary soul
> In seas of heavenly rest,
> And not a wave of trouble roll
> Across my peaceful breast.

"It is strange that years afterwards, when he had really passed out into the great expanse of another life, I met with his ' Poetic Remains,' and there was the fragment of a poem, on 'The Pleasures of Devotion,' the opening passages of which renewed my early impressions of that prayer, and gave greater clearness and power to my conviction that he must have found pleasure in passing from prayer into communion with that God who fills immensity, and brightens all worlds with the light of redeeming love. Let me try to give the lines :—

> " Devotion! holiest offspring of the skies,
> Friend of the contrite, of the good, and wise !
> Teach me a song unknown to fancy's dream,
> Thyself my inspiration and my theme.
> Come, prophets, martyrs, and ye banded few,
> Sent by your Lord, rise to my raptured view;
> Lend your pure fires, and pour the unclouded ray,
> To light the muse on her celestial way.
> But, chiefly, Spirit of the Eternal One,
> Gift of the Father's love, sent by the Son,
> The Guide, the Comforter, the pleading Friend,
> By whom, with groans, our inwrought prayers ascend—
> O might Thy hallow'd energy Divine
> Feed every spring of thought, trace every line ;
> Stamp the just precepts of the suppliant art,
> And bid the song transmit them to the heart.
>
> Primeval Power ! when first the sons of light,
> Bright morning stars, burn'd on the brow of night,
> By Thee inspired, their symphony they sung,
> And God's high Throne with adorations rang.

Full vision'd with intelligence, they gazed
Each on the glittering host, rapt and amazed,
To know the Almighty One, whom none could trace,
To hear some secrets of His purposed grace;
To view the Source of Being in their own,
God in His image, God supreme, alone;
The God without a cause, or bound, or end,
Whom none may judge, whom none can comprehend;
Essential life, around, beneath, above;
The infinite sublime of power and love;
Wholly in every place—diffused, immense;
Unseen, untouch'd—yet felt; serene, intense;
All truth, all justice, and all holiness.
Unfading centre of true loveliness.
Immutable, unmoved; sole, ceaseless spring
Of force that moves in each created thing;
Veil'd in His own insufferable light,
That shrouds the blazing sun with tenfold night;
Yet manifest, by dazzling proofs, amid
His matchless works, that never can be hid;
Whose wisdom runs through nature's wondrous frame,
And always seeks and finds some glorious aim;
All whose perfections infinite are shown,
And summ'd in one—the grandeur of His throne—
Goodness—that ceaseless calls them into play,
And lights the glory of their boundless way;
Goodness, still flowering into love, and this
Bursting with fruits of never-fading bliss;
Goodness, the measure of the deep-struck plan,
That saved the world before the world began.

Farewell the forum, and farewell the strife
That gives to senates all their charm and life.
Farewell the gay parterre, and gorgeous court,
Where beauty beams, and princely peers resort.
I turn me to this lone, ungarnish'd cell,
Where God, and truth, and peace, and rapture dwell:
This is my strong fortress in temptation's wars;
My school where truth shines from beyond the stars.
The sainted soul here banquets with her Lord,
From all her guilt to all His love restored."

"Your impression of McNicoll and mine," said the traveller's wife, "must have been received about the same time, during that visit of his to this neighbourhood. We knew nothing of each other then, nor of each other's impressions. Strange, isn't it, that we should come together here, as man and wife, to have our impressions renewed and compared before this portrait, taken by one who never saw him? You were impressed with his prayer; I was struck with his singing. It was in my father's house, where music was our life. How he charmed us! There, in that likeness, is that same canny sort of look of his which I remember so well, as he sang a Covenanter's song—

> "Our solemn league and covenant
> Is al a braken throo.

"That singing almost made Covenanters of us all."

Recollections of this "sweet-singer," as he was when a boy, have been happily preserved. One of that primitive race of Methodist evangelists, who brought their strong natural endowments into the field immediately after Mr. Wesley's departure, the Rev. John Stephens, says, "In the year 1800, I was appointed to Dundee. I had not been long there before my attention was fixed on "Little David," as he was familiarly called by our friends in his native town. He was young, small, short, round-faced, with a ruddy complexion, eyes beaming with benignity, softened by the shade of his dark, shaggy eyebrows, and a forehead indicating more than ordinary intelligence. His voice was singularly melodious, and as his pious father was the leader of the singing in our chapel, assisted by several members of his family and other friends, David had full scope for the exercise of his musical talents in the worship and praise of Almighty God. This, I have often thought, was a great mercy; for such was his passionate fondness for singing, in addition to his fine voice, that, had it not been for the influence of religion, it is probable he might have been engaged, in after life, as too many similarly gifted persons are, in strewing flowers and diffusing fragrance on the path which leads multitudes to eternal ruin. From this snare he was saved by the blessing of God on the instructions, prayers, and example of his worthy parents, connected with the ministration of the Gospel in our chapel."

"Little David" grew up under these home and church influences, until, soon after his sound though early conversion, he was persuaded to exercise his gifts as an exhorter. Those who heard his first utterance said, "This modest, humble lad has preaching in him, if we can only get it out." It was got out; and the "humble lad," in mature life, became remarkable as a thinker, as a writer, both in prose and verse, and as a profound yet attractive preacher. There proved to be in him a rare association of fine intellectual faculties, moral powers, and spiritual gifts. This is to be seen in the deep and subtle metaphysics, the unbroken closeness of logic, and the illustrative skill of his obstruse "Argument for the Truth of the Bible;" the elegance, taste, and delicacy of his "Essay on the Stage," the discrimination and judgment of his essays on "Taste" and "Poetry," and the clear, copious, elevating thought, brightly winged imagination, balanced judgment, rich fulness of expression, and reverent and lofty tone of his sermons. The finest of these qualities show themselves in beautiful combination in some of the best passages in his poems. As a poet, he finds in nature "more than meets the eye," and tells us, with much beauty :—

> I love the dawnings of the beautiful,
>   The budding rose, the earliest green of spring,
> The sun just entering heaven's rich vestibule,
>   The soonest lark when first she mounts her wing,
> And the young moon at eve, whose virgin face,
> Side-long reveal'd, shines with a modest grace.
>
> Shall these give pleasure to the glowing sense,
>   But to the soul yield nothing more refined?
> Nothing of purer touch to recompense
>   The busy wonderings of the searching mind?
> Yes; hues and forms are but the mystic wand
> That starts the visions of her fairy-land!
>
> For "more than meets the view" lies in the bloom;
>   The fruitage of a distant day shines there.
> Twice charm'd we see the pent flower burst its tomb;
>   Twice, as when from the harp, swept by the air,
> A soft, sweet note seems sounding from on high,
> That with a deeper note chimes harmony.

. . . .

> Then look, my soul, not on the narrow field
>   Of this low, weedy world; lift up thine eye;
> Pursue the ever-lengthening vale; and yield
>   Thy homage to the mountains; there descry,
> At every new ascent, still nobler heights,
> Feasting thy hopes with infinite delights.
>
> These give celestial temper to the soul,
>   To meanest things of earth a sweet sublime;
> Urge us to rush upon th' eternal goal,
>   Till Death himself shall die, and hoary Time
> Take youth's bright form, his night turn into day,
> Dwell in new worlds and cast his wings away.

Mr. McNicoll had been in the Methodist ministry for nearly thirty-four years, when he was to be seen, of an evening, occasionally walking in friendly chat, with one of his own order, up and down on the broad path by the side of the cemetery in Liverpool. His talk was mostly on the shortness and vanity of mortal life, and its close relation to the realities of the life to come. He spoke as a man on the verge of another world, and the thoughts expresssed during one of those conversations seem to have been embodied in his verses on "Life."

> "What is our life?" ofttimes we ask,
>   But look for no reply;
> Still turning to some busy task,
>   And know not, care not, why.
>
> Thankless, we deem our life but spray
>   Dash'd on a barren shore,
> That glitters in the sunny ray,
>   Then falls, and is no more.
>
> Yet time is true eternity,
>   Just shaded by the grave;
> The first bold billow of a sea
>   That knows no refluent wave.
>
> 'Tis more—it speaks with God-like power
>   Our ceaseless weal or woe;
> From some small fount, in life's brief hour,
>   These deep extremes shall flow.
>
> Source of all blessedness and strength!
>   O help our weakness, Lord!
> And guide us through life's little length,
>   That we may keep Thy word.

> Then on the sure foundation laid
> In Zion we shall build;
> And soon our final home, array'd
> In light, shall stand reveal'd.
>
> But those who shun the Rock, and think
> Smooth sand the corner-stone,
> Whelm'd in the tempest-crash shall sink
> Eternally undone.

"Our friend, McNicoll, will not live long," said the one who had walked with him, on returning one evening from the cemetery path to his home.

"Why do you think so?" it was inquired.

"Why! His soul is mellowing for Heaven; God is preparing him for Himself."

And so it was. Mr. McNicoll's family appears to have been gathered around him by the arrangement of the Great Father. All were there. The evening was happy. He smiled on the full group around the table; spoke cheerfully to them; knelt down, and pleaded for each, and commended all to God; gave his fatherly blessing; and, retiring to his room, he was, in a few minutes, gone into the immortal life for which his life on earth had been a preparation.

His companion in the evening chats by the cemetery, the venerable Dr. Dixon, has now joined him, leaving the record of the impression which the rich-toned preacher and poetical metaphysician had left on his soul—"Of all the men I ever saw, Mr. McNicoll always appeared to me as the happiest."

CHAPTER XVI.

LATER-DAY CLERICAL HYMNISTS.

> He gave the Shepherd to His flock; His hand
> Convey'd the rod of power; the minstrel band
> Waked at His word the trumpet or the lyre;
> He gave the herald's voice, the poet's fire;
>
> . . . .
>
> All flowed from Him, His wisdom all inspired,
> He formed the instruments His hands required,
> His Church in perfect symmetry to raise,
> And fill His temple with His glorious blaze.

ONE day in the course of 1847 a knot of young lawyers were standing at a stationer's window in Chancery Lane, and were expressing admiration to one another as they gazed at a newly published portrait of a chief in their profession. A venerable-looking man, in passing, stopped a moment to look; his face was most benignant, serene, and yet happily radiant. He was between eighty and ninety years of age; but his clear eye, in a moment, detected in the portrait a cloudy tinge and gloomy expression. "That man was not happy," said he. "Why do you think so?" asked the young lawyers, in a tone of displeasure. "A happy man shows it in his countenance," was the quick response; and the old man passed on, with a joyful light on his face, leaving the silenced group to their own reflections. This was Father Sutcliffe, as he was called, the Rev. Joseph Sutcliffe, a lingering relic of Wesley's race of preachers, a last surviving link between Wesley's generation and the next. This Methodist patriarch, born at Beildon, in Yorkshire, February 13,

1762, had in his youth attended meetings in which Grimshaw, of Haworth, John Nelson, Crosse, of Bradford, and John Wesley, himself had taken part. He has happily fixed for us some reflections of his early experience while he lived a young Churchman. He calls his verses " Litanies and Confessions."

>When in the round of giddy life,
>I little knew the inward strife
>   That now invades my breast;
>But when the light on me had shone,
>I saw myself a wretch undone,
>   Devoid of peace and rest.
>
>I saw the good—the good approved,
>But still my heart its evils loved,
>   And strove to shun the day;
>I shunned myself, a hateful sight,
>And in my folly took delight,
>   And went the more astray.
>
>Happy I seemed before men's eyes,
>And wore a mask of gay disguise,
>   To hide my secret pain.
>Ah! what is such a life but death,
>Which stifles all the heavenly breath,
>   And leaves me with the slain.
>
>My mind, enlightened, spoke for God,
>Preferred the good, the heavenly road,
>   But said—'Tis yet too soon ;
>I strove to make a compromise,
>Before His face to temporise,
>   Who sees at night as noon.
>
>I knew that earth was not my good,
>But yet the phantom still pursued,
>   Pursued it with delight;
>'Twas then I felt the war within,
>Which marshalled all the powers of sin,
>   Against my God to fight.

The young inquirer one day heard a Methodist describe his conversion in terms which awakened earnest thought. "That man," thought he, "has something to make him happy that I know nothing about." He sought this "something" for himself; and, while occupied in his ordinary work, he received such a joyful answer to his prayer, that he cried out, "This is what the Methodist spoke of in the class-meeting." Seventy years afterwards he would hold listeners in happy suspense while, with feelings still fresh, he told over again the story of his joys, his doings, and his companionships, in the time of his "first love." He began his ministry as a Methodist preacher, by Mr. Wesley's appointment, in 1786. The whole of Oxfordshire was his circuit, in the year of Mr. Wesley's death. He completed his fifty years of active service in Rochester; and then took up his residence in London, where, for twenty years more, he bore his testimony for Christ, sometimes in public, but always by a bright and lovely example of pure, tranquil, and joyful Christianity. His Biblical, literary, and theological attainments were remarkable. Besides the heavy ordinary work of a travelling preacher, he instructed the world and the Church by his pen. His literary life was marked by many curious incidents which he used to relate with interesting freshness when he was an old man of ninety. Among his works were "A Gentleman's Guide to the English Language;" an "Essay on the Godhead of Christ;" "Sermons on Regeneration;" "Geological Essays;" a "Catechism of the Christian Religion;" a "Translation of Saurin's Sermons;" a "Defence of the Immortality of the Soul;" and his original, spiritual, edifying "Commentary on the Bible," remarkable for its devout evidence of his heavenliness, as much as for its proofs of his well-digested learning. With all this, he had "music in himself." He was one of the Poets of Methodism. His verses, like his prose pages, abound with thought characteristic of a saintly genius, who had grace and power to give a Scriptural tone and spirit to his effusions, and to make his learning serve in attuning the soul for spiritual song. Many of his stanzas are transcripts of his hallowed mind, full of meaning, and beautiful for transparent simplicity. A volume of "Psalms and Hymns," and his "Union Version of the Psalms, in Various Metres," contain much that generations to come will like to chant in their most spiritual moods; and many a psalm that will help to preserve the memory of a commentator who was devoutly familiar with the idioms of the sacred languages, in which he loved daily to read his Lord's revealed will. His version of the second Psalm fairly shows the faithfulness and skill with which he could make both the meaning and music of the Hebrew pass pleasantly into English tunefulness and sense. He calls it "A Psalm of Prophecy"—

> Why do the Gentile nations rage,
> And Israel's hosts with them engage,
> As though to them the power were given
> To overthrow the work of Heaven?
>
> The rulers join the tumult's throng,
> And kings are led to do the wrong;
> Jehovah laughs their pride to scorn,
> Exalting high Messiah's horn.
>
> This day the Sire declares the Son
> Associate of the Father's throne;
> He bids the angry earth be still,
> And foes o'errules to do His will.
>
> He publishes the high decree
> Of grace to all that bow the knee;
> But those who do His anger dare
> Shall perish in the hopeless war.
>
> Thou art my Son, I hear Him say,
> Ask what thou wilt on this glad day;
> I give the heathen world to Thee,
> To set the sons of Adam free.
>
> Then hear, O earth! both judge and king,
> And haste your early vows to bring;
> And kiss the Son while wrath delays,
> Nor longer dare despise His grace.

Among sundry jottings found in an old note-book is this:—
"It was about two years before his death that I was first introduced to the venerable Joseph Sutcliffe, at an evening party of missionary friends, at the Centenary Hall and Mission House, in Bishopsgate Street, London. He was seated; and his daughter was standing by his chair, like a guardian and ministering angel. He looked the picture of a saintly Methodist patriarch, a beautiful embodiment of

mature benignity, kindness, simplicity, and love. One felt as if to speak to him, and to listen to his holy utterances was to have a sort of preparation for first introductions to "just men made perfect." Strange associations of thought began to run through my mind when my eye passed from his happy countenance to his neck dress; for the question arose within me, 'Does he owe anything to the influence of his first superintendent?' The image of that superintendent came up before me as I have seen him pictured, and as I have heard him described by my father. Mr. Wesley sent Joseph Sutcliffe to Redruth, in Cornwall, as his first circuit; and there his superintendent was Francis Wrigley, a little man whose face betokened a disposition to pry into all personal appearances. At that time there were signs of change in the fashion of Methodist preachers' neck dress. Wrigley was orthodox. He wore a neckerchief—verily, a neckerchief, not like that sign of later times, that white dog-collar, like something now worn by Popish priests, and young, modern Methodist parsons. Wrigley's neckerchief was real and substantial cambric, folded so as to show no end. Some preachers were venturing on a visible bow in front. This new fashion Wrigley did his best to check. My father told me that, at any great gathering of preachers, it was Wrigley's way to creep about, quietly looking into the thing; and wherever a little knot was discoverable, he would manage to get near enough to take the little ends between his finger and thumb, and looking somewhat quizzically into the wearer's face, would say, 'What's this, my brother? What's this, my brother?' All this passed within while, for a few minutes, I had the gentle old primitive saint before me. And again and again the old chapel at Redruth, and the figures of the neck-bow hunting superintendent and his 'young man' would rise, and the question would press itself once more—'Had Wrigley anything to do in the formation of Sutcliffe's neck-style?' Then came graver thoughts. I saw in the one before me an old veteran, now nearing the finish of his more than ninety years' life-battle; an aged Christian champion; a Methodist missionary spirit, come to this centre of Methodist missionary action, this annual gathering of those who still claimed the 'world as their parish;' and come as if he would have his full share of joy in the results of a century's toil, before he said to his approaching Lord, ' Now lettest Thou Thy servant depart in peace, according to Thy word; for mine eyes have seen Thy salvation.' Nor could I help thinking of the old poet's own missionary hymn, a favourite with me, and, as I afterwards found, a favourite with his family:—

> "Zion, arise and shine;
>   Thy light, thy God, is come;
> His glory beams with rays divine,
>   He calls thy children home.
>
> On thy anointed race
>   He sheds the Spirit down,
> To sound afar His righteousness,
>   And make His mercy known.
>
> Like gentle showers of spring,
>   It falls on distant lands;
> The little hills rejoice and sing,
>   The valleys clap their hands.
>
> Many through all the earth
>   Are running to and fro,
> To give the expected ages birth,
>   And vanquish every foe.
>
> Support them in the fight,
>   Where ancient vices reign;
> And may they, in the Spirit's might,
>   The rights of God maintain.
>
> Let valleys for them rise,
>   And rocks and hills give way;
> Applain their path to win the prize,
>   And haste the latter day.
>
> Let truth her beauties show,
>   And grace her charms disclose;
> And lay the daring idols low,
>   And triumph o'er Thy foes.
>
> May every pagan knee
>   Bow down beneath their word;
> And every tongue confess to thee
>   That Jesus is the Lord.

> May all the heathen lands
>   Be sprinkled with His blood;
> And Ethiopia stretch her hands,
>   To embrace the Saviour God.
>
> May all the nations know
>   The Lord's redeeming love;
> Unite them to thy Church below,
>   And then thy Church above.
>
> From Zion shine abroad,
>   With beams of truth and grace;
> And let the earth be filled with God,
>   And healed with righteousness.
>
> O haste the happy day,
>   The prophet's cheering theme;
> And wipe thy people's tears away,
>   And reign the Lord supreme."

Dear old man! The weight of ninety years could not keep his songs from breaking forth. He would sing in "the house of his pilgrimage" to the joy of his family, with all the liveliness of a child, and the reverent tone of an "old man in Christ." If there were any tears, they were those of overflowing gratitude; as when Thomas Jackson's notice of him in his "Life of Robert Newton" was read, he wept for some time, asked to hear it again, and then mingled prayers with his tears for those who thus remembered him. His conversation was full of sacred joy, heavenliness, and consecrated knowledge, even to the last. On the 14th of May, 1856, aged ninety-four, a short illness checked his voice; but his face grew brighter and brighter, till his sanctified spirit passed into pure immortal brightness.

"I never pass along here," said a friend to his companion, as the train was nearing Sherborne, in Dorset, "without thinking of John Bustard, the active life of whose body and mind, tongue and pen, drew to a close in Sherborne, yonder."

"Who, and what was he?"

"He was a Methodist preacher, whose memory I respect as the author of some 'Memoirs' of young people which did me good, and have, I believe, been blessings both to the

Church and the world. He was one of the older stamp of travelling preachers. He was a Sheffield man by birth, born in 1783. But, like the greater part of his brethren of that class, he was a wandering light—now here, now there; but everywhere, having 'a psalm, a doctrine, a tongue, a revelation, an interpretation' for his neighbours; and having them always 'to edification.' I say, he always had 'a psalm,' for he was a psalmist in his way, and had some genius for giving wholesome lessons, to young people especially, by putting them to sing truth expressed tunefully in his simple and thoughtful hymns."

"Did he publish any of them?"

"Yes, while he was fulfilling his ministry at Deal, in Kent, after labouring in various places for ten years, he sent out his first little volume of forty-eight pages, entitled 'Kent Sunday School Hymns.' The whole edition was sold in the neighbourhood; and more than forty years elasped before a new issue appeared. When he retired, in his sixtieth year, from his more active life as a preacher, his leisure here near Sherborne was improved and beguiled by the preparation of a larger book, including his former hymns, with additional pieces, chiefly on Scriptural themes. It was published as 'Scripture Themes, in Rills and Streams; being Effusions in Verse, on Scripture Characters, Facts, Morals, &c.' Some of his hymns are suited to adults, and might tempt many to lift up their voices."

"Does your memory serve you with one as a specimen?"

"I'll try. The first in the book is, perhaps, one of his best; and it is not unwisely placed in the front. A quaint old man, whom I knew, used to act on the principle of putting the worst side of himself foremost in his first interview with anybody. 'It is best,' he said, 'for then one grows upon people.', I am not sure, however, that the principle is a wise one; for I often think of an oracular saying from the lips of a great and good man. 'The first and last things are always impressive.' And I think that in a book, as well as in the opening of a public address, a good impression made, to begin with, goes far to secure the object of the author or speaker. Well, John Bustard begins with a hymn of 'Praise to God,' and helps us to sing thus:—

"Hail, Lord of angel hosts above!
Of all earth's sons below!
By whom we are, and live, and move,
Whose greatness we would show.

Thyself—eternal! naught beside
Can justly vie with Thee:—
Not those Thy bounty has supplied
With immortality.

Whate'er we see, or hear, or know,
Imprinted with Thy Name,
Fails not Thy excellence to show,
Thy greatness to proclaim.

What beauty—order, harmony,
In all Thy works we find:
But we, in Revelation, see
The glories of Thy mind.

The sun on smaller orbs doth shine,
And needeth not their rays;
So as the praise we give is Thine,
Thou needest not our praise.

We do not with our praise presume
To pay the debt we owe;
But bring it as a sweet perfume,
Our gratitude to show.

Yes—we would gratefully receive
The blessings Thou hast given;
And sing hosannahs while we live
On earth, and then in heaven.

Though feeble is the voice we raise
Before Thy sacred throne,
We emulate the seraphs' praise,
To make Thy glory known.

While nature, providence, and grace,
Thy attributes proclaim,
We e'er shall have a theme for praise,
And will extol Thy Name."

"Thank you," said the companion, as the train pulled up, "John Bustard's first hymn, at all events, is worthy of a place in a 'Book of Praise.' I detected no feebleness in the rhyming, nothing offensive in the rhythm; while there are some happy turns of thought; and the spirit of the hymn lifts the mind into devotion, and does the heart good."

There are some things which, when looked at singly and separately from their proper associations and surroundings, appear to be ill-proportioned and tuneless; but when viewed in their fitness to other things, and in their natural adaptation to circumstances, inspire us with a sense of beauty and harmony. So, were many of our popular songs to be judged irrespective of origin, allusion, the power of adapted music, and passing times and circumstances, they would scarcely find a place among the productions of poetic genius. It might be so even with our own national anthem. Such a thought occurred to one who was passing a Primitive Methodist meeting-room as the closely packed congregation was singing. The earnestness, the harmony, the spirit, and the influence of the singing would arrest any soul that was alive to the pleasure of hearing a large number of good human voices in unison, under the inspiration of warm devotional feeling. The known character of the singers, the memory of the one who furnished the words that were sung, and the thought that the same song had been sung by millions of happy Christians, to whom high-class poetry would be comparatively powerless—all served to deepen the feeling that verses which could call up harmonies of soul and voice from such multitudes, and with such effect, had a poetry in them of their own which, if not evident to a severe reading critic, is felt by those who find themselves the better for singing:—

> Christ, He sits on Zion's hill,
> He receives poor sinners still.
> Will you serve this Blessed King?
> Come, enlist, and with me sing :
>   I His soldier sure shall be,
> Happy in eternity.

Surely, if the spirit of Hugh Bourne, the author of this hymn, could have heard that assembly of his followers, as with joyful swing and swell they repeated the chorus again and again,

> I His soldier sure shall be,
> Happy in eternity,

he would have found his heaven brightened by the thought that the hymn had been the utterance of his soul, poet or no poet, in the estimation of critics.

That Hugh Bourne should ever have been a hymnist may be considered a marvel. It is a fact, however, that he set all the Methodist camp-meetings a-singing in all places, and through all times. He was born in a romantic part of Staffordshire, Fordhays, near Stoke-upon-Trent, April 7, 1772; and after living for four score years a life of continuously intense devotion to Christ and His kingdom among men, he fell asleep amidst visions of old companions in glory. His hymn on "Walking with God" might be the record of his own life's walk:—

> Enoch, the seventh, walked with God
>   Through a long course of years;
> He rested in the Saviour's blood,
>   While in this vale of tears.
>
> While here on earth he lived by faith,
>   And grew in perfect love;
> By faith he triumph'd over death,
>   And rose to Heaven above.
>
> May we, like Enoch, walk with God,
>   And in His image grow;
> Still live by faith in Jesus' blood,
>   And speak His praise below.
>
> At last triumphant, may we rise,
>   Through His almighty love,
> To shout His praise beyond the skies,
>   And reign with Him above.

A peculiar interest gathers around Hugh Bourne, both as a preacher and a hymnist. Timid as he naturally was, his zeal was such that, under the pressure of circumstances, he became the originator of that large branch of Methodism known as the "Primitive Methodist Church." He became a Methodist on his conversion in 1799. In the course of

1800 his business called him to travel over the district of Dales-green, Hornseahead, Mow Cop, Kidsgrove, and Congleton. In these journeys he met with a few spiritually minded people, and on the day before Christmas, 1800, a meeting was held for devotion. The spirit of prayer was on them. They met again and again, and always parted with regret that they could not prolong their seasons of pleasure. One day it was suggested that they "should have a meeting upon Mow Cop some Sunday, and have a whole day's praying." That meeting was held, and was the germ of the "camp-meetings," afterwards to become so remarkable. In 1801 Bourne began to preach. A time of spiritual revival followed, throwing its influence far and wide. William Clowes became Bourne's associate; and soon they had assemblies after the style of American camp-meetings, their first being held on the Cheshire side of the rugged hill known as Mow Cop. The Methodist authorities by-and-by interfered and opposed the movement. This was unhappy. It was another of the ecclesiastical mistakes for which the Church has so often suffered; but out of which, sometimes, as in this case, Divine wisdom has brought many blessings. There was a separation. Bourne and Clowes took the lead in a new organisation; and in 1811, the distinct society was formed at Tunstal. Then came the necessity for "A Collection of Hymns for Camp-meetings, Revivals, &c., for the use of the Primitive Methodists." In this work, Bourne was assisted by an eccentric preacher and rhymer, William Sanders, who could hold a conversation in rhyme; and was now prepared to suggest ideas to his chief, who had the more scholarship and judgment. The hymns, as might be expected, breathed deep piety, burning love for souls, and intense zeal for Christ. Defects in music there might be. Bourne's purpose, however, was to keep the revival spirit alive, and to fan the flame of zeal among a people to be affected most by hymns, simple in thought, homely in language, and expressive of the wants of generally poor and unlettered folk. The history of his followers is the proof of his success. Thousands upon thousands have arisen to obey the call of their departed hymnist, and have pursued the objects which he placed before them, singing, as they toil, of "Salvation for All."

> Ye sons and daughters of the Lord,
> Arise, and preach His sacred Word;
> Go forth, endued with power and grace,
> And preach the Word in every place.
>
> In streets and lanes declare His name,
> And in highways His truth proclaim;
> In open fields His standard raise,
> And sound the great Jehovah's praise.
>
> To wretched outcasts straight make known
> What Christ, the Lord, for them hath done;
> Go, lead them to the Saviour's blood,
> That they may praise a pard'ning God,
>
> Unlock the treasures of His grace
> To every child of Adam's race;
> Teach them in righteousness to grow,
> And perfect holiness below.

Up among the storied places of the old northern border; amidst the floating memories of "Chevy Chase" and the "Hermit of Warkworth," where the shades of monkery used to haunt the ruins of Hulne and Alnwick Abbeys; by Malcolm's Cross, the witness of the Scotch William the Lion's capture, and within the walls of Alnwick Castle; about the close of the eighteenth century, there was a boy who used to prowl with that enthusiastic, lively, but harmless curiosity with which none but boys of genius prowl. His boy-like prowling may be called harmless, though it might have been sufficiently free to be in keeping with the battle-ground of old "moss-troopers," and sufficiently wild to accord with the ballad poetry of the region. The boy may have caught some of the spirit of that wild minstrelsy, and that spirit may have had something to do in the shaping of his character, and with the bent of his tastes. He was born at Alnwick, on May 16, 1784. His grandfather was a Methodist, who built the first Methodist chapel in the old border town. His grandmother was a Scotch Keith, and had acted as an associate in the management of the Methodist Orphan House, in Newcastle, with the woman who heartlessly jilted John Wesley. His mother, too, was a Methodist "character" in the town, a worthy woman. His own conversion resulted in his admission to the Methodist ministry in 1806. He became literary, and popular, though sterling, as a preacher. His genius and tastes were too free, and his mental pursuits too varied, to allow of desire on his part for official distinction, or of readiness in officials to distinguish him. In the year 1817 he resided in Sheffield, and formed a close friendship with two poetic spirits, James Montgomery and J. Holland. Here his tuneful genius was revived; and, moved possibly by the old spirit of the borderland, as well as influenced by his poetic companionship, he issued a poem, entitled, "Edwin; or, Northumbria's Royal Captive Restored," with other small poetic pieces. The versifying trio in Sheffield gave their genius to the aid of Sunday Schools; and young voices were often heard singing the songs furnished under the well-known initials—"J. M.," "J. H.," and "J. E." Some of these appeared afterwards as a collection of nineteen "Hymns for Children, for Sabbath School Unions, and School Anniversaries, by J. E.;" that is, by James Everett, for he it was. The preface of the second edition was dated Manchester, 1831. And some may be living with a lively recollection of a hymn that was sung there as "A Hymn of Thanksgiving for Preservation from Cholera." Those who, at that time, in other parts of the kingdom, became painfully familiar with scenes of pestilence, will all the more revere the memory of a Methodist hymnist who had taste, and feeling, and music enough in himself to teach his neighbours and their children to sing.

> Within our isle, along our shores,
> The angel of destruction pours
>   The vials of his wrath:
> The rich, the poor, the young, the old,
> The strong, the timid, and the bold,
>   Have met him in their path.

But vainly do they interpose!
O'er isles and continents he goes,
 Nor aught can bar his way:
In Russia and the glowing East,
In seasons, climes—expected least,
 He marks his route with prey.

He dips like sea-fowl on the tide,
And reappearing far and wide,
 Surprise and terror spread;
He breathes, and sickness in his breath
Induces agony and death:
 The living fear the dead.

While moving his mysterious round,
In life and health we still are found,
 Before our Master's face.
Let now, O Lord, Thine arm be bared,
And whom Thy providence hath spared,
 Save fully by Thy grace.

In awe of Thee we still would stand,
In prayer to Thee we bear our land,
 And still on Thee rely:
Remove the scourge, upon us smile,
And bless Thy church, our King, our Isle,
 Then bear us up on high.

The man who could hymn it in this manner was worthy of the task which afterwards devolved upon him. He, with others of equal freedom of spirit, though of less genius, had, in 1849, to pay the penalty of restlessness under ecclesiastical rule, tightly held by those between whose style of constitution and his own all sympathy had been lost. His pen, it had been alleged, had been too free, and not willing to drop it, he was dropped from his old connections. The United Free Methodist Churches were formed; and at their annual assembly in Sheffield, in 1859, he, with another minister, was appointed to prepare a hymn-book for the use of the numerous separated societies and congregations. Were there no other good flowing out from amidst the unhappy ecclesiastical displacements of that period, one spiritual song of James Everett's, found in the hymn-book of the new churches, would charm the lover of bright psalmody into forgetfulness of all the unaccountable infatuations of contentious men, by leading him up to sing on "Mount Tabor":—

> How glorious the mount to behold,
>   With Jesus transfigur'd in light,
> When seen by the prophets of old,
>   Who triumph'd and glow'd at the sight!
> When seen by apostles—amaz'd—
>   The story of death on their ear,
> Who shrank from the glory that blaz'd,
>   Yet said "It is good to be here."
>
> What emblem more bright to the eye?
>   What union below so complete?
> Two delegates sent from the sky,
>   The Christian disciples to meet!
> Where each for his church may attend,
>   And honour the old and the new,
> Acknowledge the Lord as a Friend,
>   The Head of the whole to the view.
>
> That Head we confess and adore,
>   Adore, as united we stand,
> Confess Him, like those gone before,
>   Who lov'd to obey His command;
> And fully transform'd by His grace,
>   May we, as transfigur'd He shone,
> Behold the bright smiles of his face,
>   And, "like Him," be claim'd for His own.

Samuel Dunn was James Everett's companion in tribulation when they found themselves pressed by the tight discipline of the Church whose ministry they had adorned. Dunn, whom Dr. Adam Clarke, his friend, had called "the Apostle of the Shetland Isles," had shown himself in early life equal to his mission, or any mission for Christ. He was strong in will, of unconquerable courage, of vigorous intellect, and untiring zeal. He came of a hardy stock. His birthplace was a quaint little fishing port on the southern coast of Cornwall, the zig-zag, up-and-down streets and alleys of which seemed to be made for the advantage of smugglers in their runs from officers of the revenue. The Dunns went far to people the homes of Mevagissey, and among the progeny was Samuel, born in May, 1798. He was brought to enjoy "peace with God" during what was called in Cornwall "the great revival of 1814." He became a remarkable Methodist preacher.

"I should never have thought, when I first knew you," said he to an old friend whose pages at times were thought to be somewhat florid, "that you would have shown yourself so imaginative. Look at my writings—my style is otherwise."

Yes, verily, so it is. And who that knew Samuel Dunn in his mid career could have suspected that he would turn poet at sixty? Poet? No, he never turned poet; nor was he born one. Yet at sixty he began to write hymns; and some of them are good helps to devotion. He intended them to be nothing else. On his separation from the Church of his fathers, he became the pastor of a congregation which he gathered in Camborne, in Cornwall, a town and neighbourhood in which his labours as a Wesleyan minister had been largely and richly fruitful. Then, for the first time, he conceived the notion of writing hymns for his people, as well as preaching to them. He did it, and a large number of hymns were published in a volume entitled, "Hymns for Pastors and People." They are all on portions of Scripture, and are intended to express, in measured words, the substance of sermons which he has delivered to his congregation. He aimed at providing spiritual songs embodying the full scope of the texts on which they are founded; and to examine them is to find soundness of doctrine, evangelical experience, and warm encouragements to devotion. Fine poetic beauty must not be looked for; though here and there the reader may be filled with "a sweet surprise" at meeting with touches of beautiful thought, finely expressed; as when he sings about the prophet's vision of the holy waters from the temple—

> Oh, the river! oh, the river!
>   Now we feel its influence come;
> Deeper, broader, fresher, sweeter,
>   Onward, onward, give it room.
> Lo, the river! lo, the river!
>   Is become a mighty sea;
> Sinking deeper, we rise higher,
>   Cleans'd from all impurity.

The hymnist sometimes fails in his imitations; and when, also, he attempts to decry a particular vice in rhyme and measure, he has not enough of poetic genius and skill to do it well. But while he sings on the themes which, as a Methodist preacher of the old cast, he keeps distinctly before his own soul, and puts distinctly before his hearers, he succeeds in fulfilling his purpose as a hymn writer. Thus, in his way, he is happy in the simple tunefulness of his song on " The Perfect Man " :—

> The perfect man has faith in God,
>   A hope within the vail;
> A joy that swells like Jordan's flood,
>   A peace unspeakable.
>
> He loves the Lord with his whole heart,
>   And serves Him with his might;
> In all things acts a humble part,
>   And ever walks upright.
>
> When the last messenger shall come,
>   His spirit to release,
> And waft him to his heavenly home,
>   He will depart in peace.
>
> O Jesus, wash me in Thy blood,
>   And perfect me in love;
> Uprightly may I walk with God,
>   And reign with Thee above.

"There was once a curious and rather exciting scene at Camborne," says an eye-witness. "I was invited by Mr. Dunn to join him in an out-door religious service. I went. On entering the town, I found myself marched with a large number of praying and singing men to a position closely in front of a booth, occupied, during the fair, by a company of wandering players. I soon discovered that it would require all the power I had to preserve my gravity. The first thing I saw, on stepping upon the chair placed for me, was the ' clown ' of the company standing grinning by the side of a huge black dog, which stood supported on his hind legs, with clerical bands on his neck, and one of Mr. Dunn's tracts hanging from his paw. No muscle of Mr. Dunn's face moved. With a clear voice he gave out a hymn. His men sang mightily. And they had need to; for the player's band struck up, and the clown cut capers. Then man after man on our side lifted up his voice in prayer. I was called upon to speak, but failed to master the din from the stage. Then my stern companion tried; and when his voice failed, he would hold up large placards with scriptural sentences on them, such as 'The wages of sin is death!' and continue to point to the words until a lull afforded another opportunity for prayer or exhortation. The players at length tried squibs; but Dunn defied them; and a crowd of miners, who could be still, and sometimes, perhaps, enjoy the fun,—some of them at least,—while the Methodist preacher was untouched, considered a shower of fireworks by no means fair play, and rushing upon the booth, they made it shake and quiver beneath their charge. The fifers and drummer fled. The poor clown shrieked with pain and terror in the grip of iron hands, and at length the field was cleared. Dunn then lifted up his voice to the people, and besought them, for Christ's sake, and their own, to 'flee from the wrath to come.' The singing at the close was thrilling, and a Quaker, who had been quietly watching the whole proceeding from a window, said afterwards, 'I tell thee, there was a deep moral effect.' There was more than that, I believe, as the fruit of those four hours' 'battling with the devil on his own ground,' as Dunn called it. Often since then have I thought of that scene as illustrative of a burning desire to save men; 'by all means to save some—pulling them out of the fire.' This, I am persuaded, was the overmastering desire of Samuel Dunn, and to this constraining zeal, he gave characteristic expression in a hymn which he issued from that same Camborne under the heading, 'Save Some':—

"Unsaved, O Lord, the people are,
  Guilty and know not Thee;
Without Thy love, without Thy fear,
  In sin and misery.

By unbelief they have denied
  And mocked Thee to Thy face;
And in their prejudice and pride,
  Despised Thy richest grace.

> Oh! that I could some sinners win,
>   Thy love who have not known!
> And raise them from the death of sin,
>   To live for Thee alone.
>
> Gladly would I take up my cross,
>   Despise, like Thee, the shame;
> And count all worldly gain but loss,
>   To glorify Thy name.
>
> Cheerful to snatch the brands from hell,
>   I would myself deny;
> Pray, and exhort, invite, compel,
>   Suffer, and toil, and die."

Perhaps no better sketch of this zealous preacher and hymnist was ever given than one from the pen of his friend Everett. "Samuel Dunn, an intelligent face, middle size, active, industrious; one of the first Wesleyan missionaries to the Zetland Islands; author of some single sermons, and has also published excellent selections from the voluminous writings of Dr. Adam Clarke, J. Goodwin, Calvin, &c.; great care, judgment, and somewhat concise, as well as precise; clear, good style, though not rich or elegant; substantial matter; sometimes rousing; vehement in his delivery, but not impassioned; devout in his manner; all studied; faithful, conscientious; clear, good voice; rapid, when loudest; inflexible; not wrapped up in the chrysalis of pomp, like an insect in the pupa state, which some showy preachers too much resemble; but a real workman, whom some writers would classify among the principal organs of human greatness."

CHAPTER XVII.

A POETICAL [SATIRIST.

> Sow thy seed, and reap in gladness!
> Man himself is all a seed;
> Hope and hardship, joy and sadness,
> Slow the plant to ripeness lead.

AT six o'clock on a May morning, some forty years ago, the Methodist Synod of a south-western province met for the transaction of Church business. From five to six o'clock the presbytery had sat with the congregation to hear a sermon from a young man now attending the Synod for the first time. The Methodists then seemed to act on the faith that

> The breath of morn is sweeter far
> Than all the livelong day beside.

They had not as yet ceased to observe John Wesley's mode of taking time by the forelock. Other estimates of the comparative value of day and night were, perhaps, coming into fashion even then; but these itinerants were not given to change. At all events, they were simple enough to lag behind in the march of Methodist civilization. What could be expected at their great distance from central intelligence and culture? At six o'clock, then, they were at business, and almost the first act for the morning was to pronounce judgment on the twelve months' reading of the young man whose sermon they had just listened to. His list was handed in. Alas! for him, he felt in conscience bound to report on the entire course of his year's study. He had been disposed to "sow beside all waters." Greek, Latin, French, and English classics were wrought up in his system with ecclesiastical history, biblical criticism, and Methodist theology. To some minds it appeared as if the student had been spending too much of the year in questionable company. So the presiding elder thought. Now, it happened that the chair was held by a divine who thought himself a poet. Everybody did not think so. It was known that the young man now before his elders did not think so. Perhaps he had learnt, in communion with true poets, how to estimate false ones, who have the knack of making dull prose go in limping rhyme. At all events, he had not put the chairman's poem into his list. The chairman became severe. "There was," it was pronounced, "too much poetry in this young man's list of books. It would have been better for him had he spent more time in solid reading, such as would have been more in keeping with pulpit work." The young student was dumb. But at this crisis up rose a presbyter as advocate. There was nothing imposing in the figure of the advocate. He was not above middle height, was rather thin, and somewhat of a stooping form, with the bearing of one who would be more at ease among books than in ordinary genteel society; or who, having his choice between the drawing-room and a cell, would say—

> Let my lamp at midnight hour
> Be seen in some high, lonely tower,
> Where I may oft out-watch the Bear,
> With thrice-great Hermes, or unsphere
> The spirit of Plato, to unfold
> What worlds or what vast regions hold
> The immortal mind that hath forsook
> Her mansion in this fleshly nook.

His face, however, would at once fix attention; and, as he leant bending over the table, and throwing a momentary glance around before he turned his eye on the chairman, it was clear that his decision would be heard with interest. There was something in his countenance that might indicate possible hardness: high cheek-bones, with other severely-outlined features; a mouth somewhat prominent, but with lips compressed in such a way that they seemed to be wanting moisture; eyes that could come out with a flash, or retire under the powerful-looking brow as if to gather fresh light. Every feature could evidently take part in expressing keen wit and biting sarcasm; and yet, in combination, they were capable of giving out the language of gentleness, kindness, and generosity.

"Mr. Chairman," said he, while satire and waggery seemed to play on his upper lip and under his eyebrows, "I speak with submission. It surprises me to hear *you* complain of too much poetry. On looking over this list, there is surely logic, biblical criticism, and sound theology enough to balance all the poetry, and poetry enough to keep the beam steady. It might have been a doubtful matter had the poetry been flimsy or false; but all the poetry here is *true* poetry, and, in relation to the other readings, nothing other than a lump of pure sugar in a good cup of tea." This was said with a smack of the lips, which might be expressive of longing for such a cup. "But I suspect, sir," he continued, "that this young brother has given us his course of study rather than his ordinary reading. These classical authors, I dare say, he has studied in the originals, more for the sake of securing closer acquaintance with the original languages of the Sacred Volume than for anything else. Am right?"

"Yes," was the response from the young preacher.

"I thought so. And now, if I am in order, I should like to ask how he has managed to do all this in the course of the year, amidst his circuit wanderings and so much pulpit work? Where has he been able to go through these studies?"

"In the saddle," was the answer, "in the fields, along the seashore, and, when weather admitted, in orchards, sitting up in some high forked tree, so as to be at rest and have my book at command."

"Well, then, Mr. Chairman," concluded the advocate, "I

think our young brother is to be commended for his 'pursuit of knowledge under difficulties.' Like some others of us, he had no college retreat; but he has made one for himself, as I believe every man will who is really called of God to such work as his. 'Too much poetry!' Why, what he has read is just enough to show him what *good* poetry is; and you may be sure that, having learnt to enjoy and use the good, he will never waste his time and thought on what is *poor*."

There was a moment's waggish glance at the chair, and the advocate sat down, throwing a look of kindness and complacency on the one for whom he had pleaded.

That advocate was our poetical satirist, John Wesley Thomas. And never did human face more curiously show good-humoured contention between satirical intellect and generous heart than did his, while addressing the "poet" who complained of "too much poetry." Yet it might strike one, while looking at the satirical poet as he settled into repose, and sat in silence at the Synod, that there was something in his thoughtful countenance at times which betokened the lingering effects of some experience in his life which answered to his poetic "Dream":—

> I had a dream, which was not *all* a dream—
> Methought I stood upon a rising ground,
> And at a little distance I observed
> A peaceful lake, that lay outspread before me;
> The chilling breath of winter had swept o'er it,
> Had stilled the gentle motion of its waves,
> And changed its waters to a rocky floor.
> Not long I paused, but ventured down upon it;
> Strong it appeared and beautiful as marble;
> And, pleased, I wander'd on its polish'd surface;
> But, ah! when least I fear'd or thought of danger,
> It suddenly gave way, and I sunk down
> Into the dark abyss that lurk'd beneath!
> The rushing waters stopp'd my feeble breath,
> And vainly struggling to emerge—I woke.
>
> Was not that lake an emblem of the breast
> That covers o'er with Friendship's sacred name
> Its own dark schemes of selfish cruelty?
> Such I have met with in my pilgrimage;

> And oft, alas! the trusting heart will find
> That those on whom its fond affections fix
> Are likest to the deep and frozen lake—
> Slippery, and dark, and cold, and treacherous.

The poetic powers of our dreamer appear to be chastened at times. His gifts were sterling, and some of them were carefully cultured. But his imagination now and then seems to be timid, or to lack vigour and freshness, or to be, in some way, held in check. As a translator he can wing his way by the side of his author, and is manifestly capable of appreciating and giving equal expression to what even a Dante conceives. But his own poetry sometimes lacks imaginative life. This applies more especially to the pieces which take his favourite form of composition, that of the sonnet. This is his elect form, because, as he says, "being of moderate length so as to admit of condensation and terseness, it affords an opportunity of presenting a vivid and striking representation of some interesting scene or event." The fact seems to be, however, that in many of his sonnets he has studied condensation at the expense of poetic charm, and has cultivated terseness until he has become prosy. In such cases, he has failed to be either vivid or striking; and the failure has been rendered the more certain in his sonnets from sacred history by his evident effort to keep reverently to the inspired record, or to give a literal rendering of the sacred text in the form of English verse. Such cases of partial failure, however, do not prove that our poet has no real merit. If Milton wrote some prosy sonnets, so might he. His sonnets from the Pentateuch are not all failures. His first is, perhaps, his best. It is a powerful concentration of sublime thought, and in spirit and manner is accordant with the passage on which it is founded. There is dim grandeur, with awe-inspiring prospects into the infinite; and a noble, anthem-like swell of devout homage and praise. It is "The Beginning":—

> "In the beginning!"—yea, this wondrous All
> Had its *commencement!*—Oh! the dark profound
> Which Thought surveys, when on that earliest bound
> Of time she pauses—like some cherub tall;

> Nor can the abyss that lies beyond appal:
>   On daring wing she soars! Eternity—
>   The illimitable realm of mystery—
> Receives her; yet she apprehends no fall.
> It is her home; for He inhabits there
>   Who is her Sire; and in His outspread wings
> She finds her safety. Lo! this fabric fair
>   He raised, created—heaven and earth; all things.
> And they are His. All nature claims His care,
> And with His Name in one grand chorus rings.

In his sonnet on "Sinai," also, he is equal to his theme. We have a vivid and striking view of the awful and mysterious solemnities attendant on the revelation of God's law to Israel; and by a graceful turn we are led to begin our adorations at Sinai, and to close them with peaceful reliance on the Cross:—

> On Sinai's lofty steep, where Moses stood,
>   The majesty of Israel's God he saw,
>   From whom, while he received the fiery law,
> The sapphire pavement at His feet he view'd;
> Far off remain'd the trembling multitude;
>   For from the midst of darkness and thick cloud
> Flash'd the fork'd lightnings, peal'd the thunders loud,
> And the deep trumpet-blast each heart subdued.
> Well might they fear Thee, O Eternal King!
>   For in Thy justice terrible art Thou!
> To Thee our sacrifice of praise we bring;
>   Before Thee we present our homage now
> From Sinai, where Thy fires terrific burn,
> To Sion's calm, and Calvary's Cross we turn.

One of his sonnets founded on New Testament truth has associations of its own. An old friend of the poet's once came upon him in a quiet little country parsonage at Helmsley, in North-east Yorkshire. The sight of one with whom, for a little while, he could exchange sympathies, and in whose company he could indulge in talk on his favourite themes, made his face bright with one of those smiles which, over whatsoever face they pass, always appear to be the temporal likeness of smiles with which kindred spirits will first greet one another in the ethereal state. Nothing would do now but a drive through some of the choicest and most suggestive bits of the surrounding scenery. The gig was soon turned out—and such a turn out! It looked at first sight as if it must inevitably afford everybody who trusted it a "turn out," or a "turn over." The Helmsley Methodist parsonage was furnished with kind hearts, and with hallowed genius; but it certainly could not boast of either groom, or gig-mop, or harness-brush, or oil-bottle, or water to waste in improving outside surfaces to-day, which were sure to be spattered again to-morrow. Whether the gig had springs or not cannot be certified; but, doubtless, the horse had none.

At length the travellers started with a motion which, as one of them said, was in tune and time with the motion of the horse—poor thing, it was, as the term is, "pin-bound," and, indeed, was rather rickety on all fours. On going down hill, especially, one rider, at least, saw that they were every moment in danger of a swift passage over the low splash-board—verily a *board*—either from the beast finding his nose too near the ground, or from its failure to keep itself from sliding back on its tail. The poet was the driver. But reins to him were scarcely worth care, and his whip served chiefly as a kind of little pennon to be waved to the music of his travelling talk. Themes for talk were abundantly suggested by the road, and Helmsley Castle with its surroundings. The boundaries and inner scenes of Duncomb Park silently gave names from the history of English high-life and literature. Then came reviews of earlier manners, criticisms on character, stories of distinguished life, and illustrative passages of poetry and prose. Then, comparisons of English classics with more ancient standards, and again, unfoldings of thought about the holy beauties and grandeurs of divinely-inspired books. It was during that drive that the one who was driven learnt for ever to think of the driver as a man of wonderfully deep and various resources. He seemed to be at home in every circle of English poets, essayists, and wits; to have caught all that was worth catching of the thought and spirit of earlier representative men. His reverent familiarity with God's Word was endlessly instructive. Select passages of all lengths, from all his favourite authors, seemed to be kept for appropriate use, ranged in his memory, like books in the well-arranged library of a man who could at any time, even in the dark, put his finger on the volume he wants.

It was not always easy to enjoy the full advantage of this wayfaring companionship. The driver appeared to be entirely oblivious of everything which served to keep the nervous sensibilities of his companion in tremulous motion. Now and then a caution would suddenly seem called for; perhaps on some stony steep—

"Hold up your reins!"

"All right!—as I was saying, Dryden smartly hits the character of Villiers of Buckingham, who used to make our old Helmsley Castle ring with his revelries—

> "Stiff in opinions, always in the wrong,
> Was everything by starts, and nothing long:
> But in the course of one revealing moon,
> Was chymist, fiddler, statesman, and buffoon;
> Then all for women, painting, rhyming, drinking,
> Besides ten thousand freaks that died in thinking."

"Oh! Take care! That was a close shave!"

"Yes!—and Pope was a close shaver, wasn't he? With what a disclosing sweep his razor went over some pates! You ought to go over to Kirby-Moorside, and see the scene which he has immortalized as that of the gay duke's miserable death—

> "In the worst inn's worst room, with mat half hung,
> The floors of plaster, and the walls of dung;
> . .   . . . .
> No wit to flatter, left of all his store;
> No fool to laugh at, which he valued more;
> There, victor of his health, of fortune, friends,
> And fame, this lord of useless thousands ends.

By-the-by, did it ever strike you that Samuel Wesley's 'Epistle Concerning Poetry' may have given Pope the idea of his 'Dunciad?' Some have thought that Byron caught his notion from the same 'epistle,' and worked it out in 'English Bards and Scotch Reviewers.' But whatever may have been the case between Wesley and Pope, I don't think Byron ever cared to read Wesley, or to know anything about him."

"He could use a Wesley, however," it was replied, "when he wanted him to point a lance against poor Southey. You remember when, in his 'Vision of Judgment,' Southey is brought up to [the gate of Heaven as a witness on the question whether the spirit of the late king should be admitted; and instead of witnessing for his king he begins to trumpet his own works:—

> "He had written much blank verse, and blanker prose,
> And more of both than anybody knows.
>
> . . . . . .
>
> He had written Wesley's life ;—here, turning round
> To Satan, 'Sir, I am ready to write yours,
> In two octavo volumes, nicely bound,
> With notes and preface, all that most allures
> The pious purchaser ; and there's no ground
> For fear, for I can choose my own reviewers ;
> So let me have the proper documents,
> That I may add you to my other saints.'"

"Yes, Byron was a dark-spirited satirist; but now let us get on to Rievaulx Abbey."

So they went on, until the old Abbey was in sight; and leaving the horse to be the quiet keeper of the gig, they entered on their researches. It was evident that the old brotherhood of Rievaulx, however false their principle of saintship was, had very properly kept an eye to the beautiful in situation, to good surface soil, and perhaps to subsoil also, as well as pleasant waters to beautify, refresh, and supply table delicacies. The quietness of the lovely valley that morning was delicious. Nature seemed to feel and rejoice in showing that, while false human modes of doing homage to the Divine One might melt into ruin and pass away, all her sense of dependence remained fresh, and all her pure modes of glorifying her Maker and Redeemer were still in harmonious action. Her Father's smile was still on her. As the two companions passed around the outer parts of the ruin, one called the other's attention to what looked like evidence of fire-action on the foundational masonry; and this, in connection with the observed fact that a curious conglomerate, like deposits of blackish matter, cropped up here and there, gave rise to interesting speculations as to whether there were not workable iron in the neighbourhood, and whether the monks had been ironmasters in their time, and whether this strange deposit which ran for some distance at variable depths were not the remaining refuse of their fires and furnaces. Amidst these speculations, however, they turned to enter the interior of the ruin. On coming to the entrance of the choir, for the nave was gone, they were advancing on what was now the grassy pavement of the church, and were beginning to speculate on the old architect's reasons for placing the building north and south instead of east and west, when their steps were arrested. There, under fine old lancet-lights, on what seemed to be a sunken stone of the once "high altar," in a beautiful posture of repose, was a living full-grown lamb! The sight was sufficiently striking, and associations of suggestive thought became very impressive. There stood the poet and his friend in silence, surrounded by the quiet beauties of that nature whose loveliness they had been rejoicing in, and about whose stores of riches they had been raising questions. They were standing, too, amidst the crumbling memorials of a system whose principle was false both to nature and to grace; and there, on the fallen altar of that system, was a gentle, peaceful, unblemished lamb, unmoved at human footsteps, as if it were intended to be the innocent symbol of a "Lamb in the midst of the throne," keeping His place, till universal nature shall pay Him homage, and everything that is not in harmony with His works and will shall cease for ever to mar His pure designs. Whether the thought which the poet afterwards expressed in the form of a sonnet was at that moment first kindled may not appear till the two friends meet again; but one thing is certain, that when, after some years, the poet's sonnets were read by his friend for the first time, one of them was instantly associated in the reader's mind with the remarkable coincidence in Rievaulx Abbey. Nor, as he thinks, will that association ever be dissolved while he lives to enjoy the poet's finely turned thought, and well attuned expression, in "The Cross Anticipated."

> He who foresaw the ruin of mankind
>   Through Adam's fault, and thence redemption plann'd,
>   Adapted Nature to this purpose grand,
> From the first dawn when light on *chaos* shined,
> Till in the *cosmos* life and beauty join'd.
> He from the world's foundation did ordain
>   That sacrifice, the Lamb for sinners slain,
>   That Mercy might with Justice be combined.
> Hence through the mighty cycles of the past,
>   While worlds for lost but ransom'd man He built,
> He laid up treasures on a scale so vast,
>   To bless, chastise, avenge—and pardon guilt!
> Thus, while Creation testifies our loss,
> Nature herself does homage to the Cross!

The companion in travel to Rievaulx Abbey expresses his wonderment at the poet's richfulness of memory, especially as to classic English literature. But the readiness, as well as fulness, of that memory, became, some time afterwards, the source of intense amusement and pleasurable surprise in a scene very different to that of an old quiet abbey. It was a scene in which the leading figure should be a Methodist district chairman. Not a poetaster this time—rather a proser. For Methodism supposes every man to have his own order, if not his own place. Let it be said again, this chairman was not one by any means given to fancy or feeling, but was

> Full of wise saws and modern instances.

He was not a man for pictures, but was edifying on safe settlements of ecclesiastical property. He was one of those who could feed on the skin of anybody's "Trust Act," "Peto's Act," or any other Act. So that, as a matter of taste, he would know no difference between a roast beef dinner and one of dry bread. He was great, therefore, in routine; and, like a clock himself, he always required every other body to go like a pendulum also. It will be seen at once that he acted quite in character during a session of his provincial presbytery when, just before dinner, he seriously reflected upon the unpunctual ways of some of his young clergy, and told them that if, after dinner, there were any delinquents, he should call them to an explanation before the meeting. Dinner-time came; dinner-time passed; and now the clock called the session to be re-opened. But, lo! the chair was vacant! There was not even a ghost to take the seat of honour in the absence of flesh and blood. The clock ticked, and the first quarter chimed, but the punctual chairman was not in his place. An hour passed; and then there was an appearance, a candid confession, and an apology. His after-dinner nap had unhappily settled too heavily on his wiry brain, and when he awoke, he awoke to a deep sense of something like retribution for his intended severity on late comers. It was a new scene in "Measure for Measure."

> Haste still pays haste, and leisure answers leisure;
> Like doth quit like, and *measure* still for *measure*.

The subdued chairman never thought it needful to ask what scenes had been acted during his recess. Had he inquired, how could he have borne the rehearsal? It had been, indeed, a new performance, illustrative of "As You Like It." In the presence of the empty chair, for a little while, the younger clergy, who had been threatened with castigation, were disposed to enjoy a session of their own devising; but at the nick of time John Wesley Thomas—always as ready to defend young men from themselves as from those who manage to outlive the genuine naturalness of their life—rose to address the chairless meeting; and, to show himself one with the youngest, and to invite them to take their share in the interlude, he called on them to choose one out of ten or twelve poets whom he named, and he would undertake to rehearse from that one as long as the chairman happened to be missing, or to take any other poet when they wished for a change. He had been fulfilling his promise, amidst occasional thunders of applause, for the greater part of an hour, when the opening of a door at the back part of the room gave token of the chairman's arrival. It was a triumph of memory on the poet's part, but a triumph, too, of tact, taste, and brotherly kindness. Yes, our poet could be a boy among boys, though the outbreaks of his boyishness might sometimes be awkward, like that of Johnson when he turned out to please the young wits by joining in their morning frolic; yet it was genuine good-natured sprightliness.

Our poet could be tender, too, tender as a woman. Otherwise we should never have felt the gentle plaintiveness, the delicate pathos, and the tremulous lingering of sorrowful fondness which find utterance in his "Lament of Mary Queen of Scots on leaving France":—

She sate upon the vessel's deck, her tears were falling fast,
While tow'rds the fading coast of France her lingering looks were cast,
But beauty shone through her distress, like sunbeams thro' a cloud,
And musical her accents were, while thus she 'plain'd aloud:

" Farewell, my France, a long farewell!—I ne'er shall see thee more!
My hopes of earthly happiness have perished on thy shore!
I lov'd thee, and I love thee still—yea, more than I can tell—
And now my bursting heart exclaims, ' Farewell, my France, farewell!'

" I see thy shores receding fast—they fade upon my sight,
And soon above them will be spread the closing shades of night.
To-morrow, when the morning dawns, I shall be far away;
But I will ever think on thee, and for thy welfare pray.

" My husband's ashes rest with thee—a sad but precious trust—
And there my sainted mother lies—oh, sacred is thy dust!—
Though Scotland calls me to her crown, yet, by a mightier spell,
My thoughts, my hopes, my all, are *thine*—Farewell, my France, farewell!

Whatever he may have thought of Mary's cause or character as queen, he understood her feelings as a woman, and realised them so as to breathe them into verses which make the reader's feelings vibrate at their touch. His tenderness was not that of mere sentiment; it belonged to a sound heart of love. His poetic English rendering of Solomon's Song is evidently a work of love, and the form into which he throws the sacred Canticles recommends itself by the light which it sheds on the character and design of the Divine effusion. He gives it as "The Bridal Week: a Hebrew Eclogue." "The action occupies the six days of the week. The first five are preparatory, and on the morning of the sixth (Friday morning) the marriage ceremony and procession take place." The actors and speakers throughout are the bride, the bridegroom, and chorus of virgins. On the whole, the poet is successful in the music of his English metrical version; sometimes happily so, as when the tenderness and purity of conjugal affection find expression in the intercourse of the married pair during the wedding procession. The chorus of virgins meet them and sing:—

> *Chorus.* What fair one from the desert do we meet,
> With her belovèd in communion sweet?
> *Bridegroom.* Beneath the citron-tree I wooed thee; there
> I from thy mother's hand received my fair:
> And she that bare her did that hour preside
> O'er nuptial rites, and plighted thee my bride.
> *Bride.* Oh! place me as a seal upon thy heart,
> And on thy arm, that we no more may part:
> For love is strong as death, and jealous fear
> More unrelenting than the sepulchre:
> Like blazing fires, its shafts consume the frame,
> Or like the all-dreaded lightning's vengeful flame.
> *Bridegroom.* To quench our love not torrents can avail;
> To o'erwhelm it deluges would fail:
> Lands, houses, gold, all, all would worthless prove;
> No match, no substitute for priceless love.

This is effectively rendered by one whose estimate of married love was pure and high. But the translator in his "Vale of Siddim" puts his own heart's conceptor of pure love, conjugal love in particular, into the lips of an angel. The utterance is worthy of an angel's lips, but most beautiful as the outflow of a truly loving human heart:—

> True love is light from heaven,
> Stainless and pure; a spark immortal given;
> A ray from the eternal sun, its source,
> Thither to raise the soul. *In* Heaven its force
> Unites the blessèd in communion sweet,
> And perfect joy, and harmony complete.

> On earth, where'er it takes its hallowed stand,
> It joins two hearts in an eternal band;
> Waves its bright wings, and lights its golden lamp,
> With flame which neither age nor death can damp.
> To mortal and immortal beings, this
> Is life's best life: without it even bliss
> Could never satisfy; it is a dower
> Fit for the sons of God.

When the poet's warm heart kindles into devotion, and his reverent spirit hymns it with saints before the Flood, or patriarchal worshippers, or mediæval choirs, his genius is evidently happy in its consecration. His hymns are better than most of his sonnets. In the "Hymn of Paradise" there is a sprightly, buoyant simplicity which is finely suited to primitive innocence, intelligence, and rectitude:—

> Unbounded source of joy!
> To Thee our grateful Sabbath hymn we raise;
> To Thee for all Thy gifts, let songs of praise
> Our lips employ.
>
> We see Thee not, but know
> Thy voice of love, that stirs the morning air;
> To us Thy messages the angels bear
> Who come and go.
>
> Thy works declare Thy might:
> The glorious sun, that climbs the steep of heaven,
> Shines in Thy praise, with beams which Thou hast given,
> Intensely bright.
>
> Yon azure sky serene,
> Lofty and vast, was by Thy hand outspread:
> Thine are the trees which wave above our head
> Their branches green.
>
> For these delightful bowers,
> For life and all its blessings, we this day
> On Thy turf altar our thank-offerings lay,—
> These fruits and flowers.
>
> With one restraint—but one—
> All Paradise is ours, with what the tree
> Of life portends, an immortality,
> On earth begun!
>
> Hail, universal Lord!
> Whom all Thy works in earth and heaven proclaim,
> By us for evermore Thy glorious name
> Shall be adored!

But with all Wesley Thomas's tenderness and kindheartedness, and genial warmth of love for all beauty and truth, he could be as hard as steel against the advances of error and mischief, and as unsparing as lightning against the pretensions of falsehood and vice. He had great logical ability and ready aptitude of expression. He was keen and skilful; knew when to pierce and when to crush. He could wing his arguments with satire, and, when it was deserved, he could stand aloof to watch his victim under the effects of a castigation, with a sarcasm sitting on his lip that might be called grim. There was no malice; and if there were bitterness, it was against folly or hypocrisy or pretentious error. His birthplace seems to have afforded the circumstances which first called his satirical powers into play. Indeed, he owed a great deal to his native city and its surroundings.

He began his life in old Exeter, on August 4th, 1798. He came of a good stock—that is, of a family distinguished by all who knew them best, for good sense, fixed principle, and steady habits, industry, order, mental vigour, kind dispositions, strong attachment to evangelical truth, and devout cultivation of spiritual piety. Their love for Methodism is indicated in the name given to their son, John Wesley. There were very few educational advantages for John. But the few were made the best of; so that, in the end, the mind of our poet became so self-disciplined, and so largely stored with certain and various knowledge, that he found an eminent place among those who have learnt to know much and to be truly wise in making the best of their learning. But John's genius and taste found a school among the natural grandeurs and beauties which met his earliest steps, as he wandered among the hills, or on the lovely banks of the Exe. And nearer at home would be the wonders of the old storied city. But there were also things not beautiful, not true, not in harmony; and these, perhaps, gave the first exciting touches to the poet's keen sense of ridiculous inconsistency; and awakened the satiric power which lived in close association with the music of his soul. In his "War of the Surplice," issued under the name of "Anti-Empiricus," he lashes the late Bishop of Exon and his young clerical devotees for their pertinacious efforts to restore Romish doctrines and ceremonials in the Church, in opposition to the better clergy and people of the city and diocese. The poem is happily in Hudibrastic vein. Butler's old anti-Puritan battery is smartly taken, and cleverly turned, with sweeping effect, upon the Laudites themselves. The poet's sketch of the young priest whose doings opened the "War of the Surplice" is characteristic:—

> It was at Oxford, as I said,
> That our young pastor had been bred;
> And therefore much, of course, must know,
> Although thrice "pluck'd" at "little go."
> In Greek and Latin so proficient,
>   His mother tongue he valued not;
> In mathematics not deficient,
>   He o'er the "bridge of asses" got.
> Profound in antiquarian lore,
> And in the fathers—quite a bore.
> The dullest things they ever wrote,
> The most was he inclined to quote;
> And gave them credence unrestricted,
> Even when themselves they contradicted.
> In metaphysics an adept,
>   His thoughts he ranged and stored away;
> Like moonbeams in a phial kept,
>   To be produced some other day.
> A body, he'd convince each dunce,
> Might be in heaven and earth at once;
> And rotten wood and dead bones still
> Be multiplied by miracle.
> But his theology was held
> At that in which he most excell'd.

Then comes the young Oxonian's first appearance, affording a mark for keen satirical play :— .

> Now, through the aisle with solemn pace,
> Preceded by a silver mace,
> He moves; and now the pulpit reaches,
> Where, in *white surplice* clad, he preaches.
> These symbols speak to people's eyes,
> And in them much of meaning lies.
> The silver mace, the church's dower
> Betokens, both of wealth and power—

The rod of rule!—the season gone
When gold and silver she had none!
And the white surplice, flowing free,
May hide a world of mystery.
The stains of sin it doth not wipe,
Yet covers: this "convenient" type
Of freedom and of holiness
Our clergy owe to good "Queen Bess";
Who also was, as history notes,
The inventress of hoop'd petticoats.

The sermon follows—a parody, and yet to the life :—

The reverend gentleman his text
And sermon thus pronounces next:
"In chapter second, fifteenth verse,
First Thessalonians—short and terse—
These words we have : ' Hold the traditions.'
My brethren, there are two positions
With which I preface my discourse,
And hope you will perceive their force.
The first of these shall be a caution
Against that most erroneous notion,
Which gives the right to all the nation
Of scriptural interpretation,
And thus makes every man a Pope;
Which you don't wish to be, I hope.
The right to interpret and to judge,
By individuals, is a fudge.
Much evil is occasioned by it ;
And I as strenuously deny it—
As Frenchmen do the 'right of search';
It is the province of 'The Church.'

. . . .

What I've to offer on ' Traditions,'
Will be arranged in three divisions.
In other words, I claim attention
To three things which I have to mention :

The first is *Clerical Authority*.

. . . .

The next in order of progression
Is *Apostolical Succession*.
The churches by the apostles planted,
To bishops, as their heirs, were granted;
The authority the former wielded
   Has to the latter been convey'd ;
The obedience which to them was yielded
   Must be to priests and bishops paid.
By spiritual descent they gain
This right, through an unbroken chain ;

And they can trace it, one and all,
Up to St. Peter and St. Paul.
However wicked or impure,
They can incur no forfeiture,
The channel of this gift is stain'd—
　　Yea, in some places foul and squalid;
But were the devil himself ordain'd,
　　His ministrations would be valid.
And some, I own, have worn the mitre,
Whose conduct has not been much brighter.
'Tis only from the bishop's hands
The priest who by the altar stands
Could gain the right to his high function,
Or have the apostolic unction.
However holy they may be
Who exercise the ministry,
If not in this succession, they
Can only lead mankind astray;
They're sacrilegious thieves, or worse,
Whom Christian rulers should coerce;
And them hereafter doth await
Abiram's, Dathan's, Korah's fate.

Thirdly, the *Sacraments*.

．　．　．　．　．　．　．

These are essential to salvation
For all mankind, in every station.
With these the Christian Church provides
Five ' Sacramental rites ' besides.
First, for the young there's Confirmation ;
Then Penance, for our souls' purgation;
Unction, for people *in extremis*,
　　To consummate all penance past;
Orders, of which the grace we deem is
　　Official. Matrimony's last.

And now, I offer, in conclusion,
A few remarks on Absolution.
Each real penitent should seek,
Not seldomer than once a week,
A private audience with his priest,
To whom his sins should be confess'd.
By whom the absolution wanted
In proper season will be granted.
He stands between your souls and heaven,
And pardons by his hands are given;
As I have heard our bishop say
Sometimes, on Visitation day,
'Whose sins ye shall remit—retain—
They are forgiven or bound again.'
Thus priests of heaven possess the keys,
To shut or open as they please."

This sermon, like all those which it represents, is supposed to be *read* in some ten minutes, on the Church principle, that—
The Sermon's part of the Communion.

Those who have been bracing up their spirits on the waters of the Scotch lakes, and have brought their imaginations into full communion with wild hills, weird glens, and haunted giant oaks of the old Caledonian forest, and would now bring themselves by a pleasant process of transition to be tenderly sensitive to the first soft appeals of beauty from the English lakes, should leave the northern train at Penrith and dream a little under the lone fragment of its old castle till the coach starts for Ulswater and Ambleside. Once fairly seated and off, the exquisite natural interweavings of the soft and the sublime will soon disclose themselves. Not far, however, out of Penrith, before the waters of the Eamont begin to show their filial connection with the deep blue waters of the lake, and before the horses have fairly turned their heads from the green suburbs of Penrith, the coachman, with a significant nod towards the left, will say,— at least, the coachman used to say,—" The grounds of Brougham Castle!" There is no time now to see where the castle is, or what it is like, but there, it must be taken for granted, it is, behind the leafage of the woods, and on the bank of the little river which runs to lose itself in the waters of the Eden. Whatever the castle may be thought of, the grounds are worthy of more leisurely observation, on one account at least.

Somewhere about fifteen years ago (1860) two figures might be seen at times, in favourable weather, pacing quietly up and down on the grounds near the castle. Both were remarkable, each in his own way. One of them could not be seen without the thought arising, "Who is he?" and the other, in passing, might move a smile or excite curiosity. As to one, " I saw him once," said a gentleman, "coming out of the train, and I said to myself, 'That must be he;' nobody could mistake that outline of face, that inquiring and commanding eye, that seemed to be so used to look through all scenes of human life, to range all nature, and to expatiate through all regions of thought." The other, in bearing, was not so much at ease; indeed, there was an indefinable awkwardness and carelessness of appearance which sent the eye to his face and head for information; and then he appeared so intent upon something beyond your sight, and so evidently engaged in solving some problem, or pushing his way somewhere into the unseen, that it might be a question which of these two passing figures was the more noticeable. There was occasionally something so irresistibly comical about the nasal action of the one, and there seemed to be something in the play of the other's lips so powerful, by turns, to tickle or make you cautious, that to watch them was to be kept oscillating amidst unsatisfactory speculations and queries. To see them together, both in the full play of their distinctive peculiarities, was never to forget the pair. One was no other than Lord Brougham himself; the other was the Methodist preacher, John Wesley Thomas.

There was between these two the mutual recognition of mental power, various knowledge, and literary taste; and who shall say that Lord Brougham did not appreciate the association of these in John Wesley Thomas with simple and warm attachment to "the truth as it is in Jesus"? But it was as the translator of Dante that the poet's way was opened to occasional companionship with the literary peer. Both loved Dante; and over his pages both geniuses could commune. The man who had caught so much of the spirit and manner of the great Italian, and who, in the opinion of leading critics, had proved himself equal to the work of giving all English readers the privilege of enjoying the "Divina Comedia," even in its author's own rhythmical style, might be received into friendly chat with an English peer, plain Methodist preacher though he was. According to some peerage laws, the two could have nothing in common; but by right of genius and mental rank, they were peer with peer on Brougham Castle grounds.

A traveller who happened to be in the North of England at the time when people talked about the Methodist preacher's friendly intercourse with the old Chancellor tells how he met with the poet on the platform at a public meeting in Penrith. They sat close to each other, and the stranger describes his own impression as to the translator's impractical, abstracted appearance. In the course of the meeting, just in the middle of a speech from a gentleman who was interested in the question before the audience, the absent-looking poet drew a note-book from his pocket, and, producing a pencil, proceeded to make jottings. The first thought was, that he had not been so withdrawn from the business of the meeting as he had seemed to be; that he had, after all, been taking a personal interest in it, and was now taking notes of what the present speaker was saying by way of preparing to make some remarks himself; though it did appear remarkable that he should find anything worth noting from the lips that just then were in rather wordy exercise. Still, the note-taker scribbled on, until happening to cast a side glance at his paper, without designing improperly to overlook him, the traveller was surprised, amused, and intensely interested to see that the poet was rendering a passage from Dante into English. He was, in fact, relieving his own weariness, and improving the time by pursuing his task of translating the last part of his great work, "Il Paradiso." He had been all his lifetime "sowing beside all waters," and he was at it still. He lived to complete his purpose. "The Trilogy" was before the world; and the now old, but successful, Methodist poet had his crown of honour from those who would willingly ignore his claims as a Methodist preacher, but could not lose the pleasure of doing honour to the translator's genius, learning, and taste.

To render into his native tongue the great Italian's vision of the river " proceeding out of the throne of God and the Lamb " was doubtless one of Mr. Thomas's last works of love, and like all works done from pure love, it has its own living beauty :—

And light I saw like to a river flowing;
  Ruddy with lightnings, 'twixt two banks it roll'd,
  Deck'd by the stream whose wondrous flowers were blowing,
From the stream issued sparkles manifold,
  Which 'midst the flowers on each side radiate,
  Like rubies in a setting form'd of gold.
With odours then as if inebriate,
  They sunk again into the wondrous gurge,
  And as they entered, others issued straight,
"The high desires which now inflame and urge
  To know what thou dost see, please me the more,
  The more they make thy bosom swell and surge;
But of this water thou must drink, before
  In thee can be allayed such thirst intense."
  So spake mine eyes' fair sun; and furthermore
Added, "The stream and topazes which thence
  Emerge re-entering, and the smiling flowers,
  Are shadowy prefaces of their true sense.
Not that these things yet lack the ripening hours;
  But, that thy sight to objects so sublime
  Soars not, is through thy own defective powers."
Not swifter does the infant in life's prime
  Rush to the swelling breast, if its awaking
  Has been delayed beyond its usual time,
Than to the stream I turn'd, in hope of making
  Mine eyes more perfect mirrors, and stoop'd there
  To quaff the wave, thence new perception taking.
And as the fringes of mine eyelids were
  Drinking thereof, the river seem'd to me
  From lengthened shape to have grown circular.
Then, like those persons whom in masks we see,
  Who, if their borrow'd show be laid aside,
  Quite other than at first will seem to be;
Even so that festal joy was amplified;
  The flowers and sparkles glow'd with brighter sheen,
  So that both courts of Heaven I now descried.
Splendour of God! Thou by whose light I've seen
  The lofty triumph of the Kingdom true,
  Give me the virtue to describe that scene.
There is in Heaven a light which brings to view
  Him who creates to that created one
  Who doth in Him alone his peace pursue.

The happy translator of this vision was soon on the banks of that very river. A few hours before he saw and drank for himself, he was told of his nearness to life, and gave, like a true Christian poet, his last mortal utterance—

    Hope springs eternal in the human breast!

CHAPTER XVIII.

A TUNEFUL SON OF A PROPHET.

Should the well-meant-songs I leave behind
With Jesus' lovers an acceptance find,
'Twill heighten even the joys of Heaven, to know
That in my verse the saints hymn God below.

IN a snug old-fashioned parlour, with its walls tastefully hung with portraits, all suggestive of good and happy memories, there sat a few rather bookish folks, pleasantly interchanging thoughts about past times. It was far away from the great world, with nothing to break the agreeable quietness but the chirping of sparrows in a Spanish laurel-tree which partly shaded the windows, leaving space enough for the eye to range over the garden borders, decked with lilies of the valley. A volume of the Wesleys' poetical works on the table gave rise to the question of Methodist poets and poetry. One of the company said—

"I was once in the studio of an eminent artist in London, in full enjoyment of chat, while the painter pursued his work on the canvas. Something in the conversation led him, by-and-by, to drop his pencil and pallet, and turning to a large portfolio, he drew out a proof engraving of a portrait which he had successfully finished.

"'Have you seen this?' said he, resting the sheet on an easel.

"'No, not before now,' I replied. 'How beautiful! One could look on that face for ever! And how like the man!'

"'Well, then, please accept one; you may like to renew the pleasure of looking at it.'

"It was the portrait of the Rev. W. M. Bunting—I need not say, the eldest son of Dr. Jabez Bunting. There the likeness now hangs. It is a favourite companion of mine. Silent it is, in a sense, but it has charming powers of response to my soul while I am sitting here, or pacing the room sometimes, in order to drive off disagreeable thoughts by stirring up pleasant ones. That picture recalls the lovable man's image. He seems often to live before me again. There are not all the tokens of suffering and careful thought which marked his brow in later years. Nevertheless, the artist has given as much of his life and character in that face and figure as could be put into a painting. What a biographical gem is that sketch by his brother, Thomas Percival Bunting! I wish, among the multitude who try their pens at biography, a few, at least, would study this model—its condensation of life, its beautiful polish, its brotherly tenderness, its faithfulness, and its reverent feeling.

"We were talking about the Poets of Methodism; W. M. Bunting was one. He was born a poet—born with music in himself; and, I was going to say, born a preacher. At all events, there seems to have been a Divine chrism on the child, made up of the mingled virtues of poetry, music, and pulpit power. It may have been in answer to his father's prayer, for when the father was told that a son was born unto him, he fell on his knees and prayed that if it were God's will, the boy might become a Methodist preacher. Or it may have been in response to his mother's devout wish; for it might have been said, 'She spake in her heart; only her lips moved, but her voice was not heard.' That boy inherited much from his parents, and owed a great deal to home training. He grew up in a house 'where religion held strict rule, and where the ways of religion were pleasant;' a thoroughly Methodist home—Methodist after the earlier, earnest, and great-hearted type. The mother's character and influence were most sacred. What a beautiful home-scene one of the family allows us to look at: 'Our mother taught her Sunday-school at home. . . . She taught us very seriously; but there was an air of lightsomeness, and a tone of freedom, and almost gaiety, which made us natural and sincere. She sang us into song; and my brother's quick ear and fine taste for music (one great solace of his suffering life) were first wakened by the charm of her voice; whilst his fingers strayed wildly over the keys of the old family piano before they could firmly hold his porridge-spoon—strayed wildly at first, but soon, self-taught, won the wandering sounds into harmony. And so the accustomed hymns, with their accustomed tunes—and there was the sympathy and sanctity of marriage between them—became sermons to us, as the melody ran 'very swiftly,' 'a pure river of water of life,' or lingered, laden with thoughts which would not hurry.'"

Thus tuned for after life, it is beautiful to listen to the young poet in his eighteenth year, paying his earliest poetical tribute to his "Mother on her Birthday":—

> For her, on the morn of her birth,
>   Who fondly exulted at mine,
> For tenderness, wisdom, and worth,
>   A wreath of remembrance I twine:
> She heard me when "Mother" was all
>   These infantile lips could essay;
> And hers is my tribute, though small,
>   And she is the light of my lay.
>
> My mother! ah! say if there be
>   A charm in that exquisite sound,
> Which e'er must be hidden from me,
>   And only a mother hath found?
> A mother's indulgence I crave,
>   If that charm I weaken in aught;
> Forgive me, wherever I have,
>   And smile on me when I have not.
>
> The day that has wakened my praise
>   Be doubly, delightfully blest!
> And bless'd be each of thy days,
>   My earliest guardian confest!
> And if I must witness the last,
>   Oh! oft to thy chamber I'll steal,
> My tears on thy coffin to cast,
>   For those on my cradle that fell.

> There is something, I may not define,
>   That whispers—It never shall be;
> *That* wretchedness shall not be mine,
>   The summons is first unto *me*.
> But if with thyself and the saints,
>   A lot everlasting be given,
> Farewell to the hour of complaints,
>   And we shall be born into Heaven!

The tender beauty of this spring-tide outflow of his heart and genius is like a precursory vision of that tuneful combination of gifts and graces, thought and feeling, which, in his matured character, shed such blessing upon all who came within the range of its light.

As with the primitive assembly of Christ's disciples, all the gifts they possessed, and the lessons they had been taught, could not be effectually exercised until the promise of the Father was fulfilled, and they had received power from on high; so with every individual in the Church, whatever his natural talents may be, and of what value soever his advantages of training, all are powerless for the great purpose of life till the Holy Ghost quickens all by renewing the heart and inspiring the man with the love of Christ. When W. M. Bunting was in his eighteenth year, his whole nature was awaiting this life-giving touch. He was conscious of power, and, perhaps, had an indefinable feeling after work to which alone his power was adapted. He believed, however, that he himself must be consecrated before his powers could be consistently engaged in consecrated work. He must have the "anointing from Him." He felt his need of it now; and was in the posture of the Psalmist when he said, "In the morning will I direct my prayer unto Thee, and will look up;" or rather, "In the morning I will arrange for Thee, and expect." The main current of his boyish feeling had, from the beginning, set in towards a preacher's course; and seemed to run on mysteriously in a line with mental and moral processes of preparation for such a course. There have been other cases illustrative of his. It is said of one of his contemporaries that his first and favourite child's play was to rear empty boxes, in a way to imitate a pulpit, and sometimes he and his brother would fight for the chance of preaching the first sermon in it. The same minister tells how, when advanced in boyhood, his mental and moral condition was in danger of being damaged by evil companions. A sight of one of Sir Walter Scott's volumes begat such a taste or rather rage for books that he shut himself up to reading, until, for lack of other supplies, he had recourse to the Bible, which continued to be his elect study until its pages begun to reflect saving light upon his converted and renewed soul, and he was at once constrained to preach Christ to his former companions. In some cases of remarkable revivals of religion, there have been conversions strikingly sudden, and strikingly followed immediately by the employment of the freed and quickened powers in preaching to sinners or "prophesying" in the church. "There! see!" said a minister once, in such a Pentecostal scene, when a young man, who had been agonizing for mercy, sprang on his feet in an instant, and, with a beaming face, began to exhort those who were around him to come to Christ,—"There! see! The Lord can make a preacher in a minute!" Generally, however, sudden as the call and power to preach appear to be, there has been a foregoing process of preparation. The faculties have been under drill; the mind has been getting into a posture of readiness; the life-giving spark alone is wanted. That comes; and the whole man is in action. Of this, our poet's experience affords a beautiful illustration. His brother says of him, as a boy, "He never played with us. . . He was very sedate and serious. From the time he could frame a sentence his passion was preaching. I cannot say he played at it, for he went as gravely through the exercise when he was three as when he was sixty. Quite as happy as his father was he, as the quiver became fuller of young children; for we were his lawful spoil for a congregation. As in later years, his sermons seemed very long, especially to restless hearers. Like many other young, self-constituted priests, he was a Ritualist; and if no other vestment could be found meet to typify his sacred function, his night-dress, and, under pressure, his bed-sheet, made him feel vastly real and important."

Bunting's school-days were days of growing preparedness for what he was afterwards to be and to do. His turn for quick and lively satire revealed itself, and his taste for music and his poetic power were rapidly developed. Then his soul was secretly awakened to a sense of its sinful helplessness out of Christ. His pursuit of God's reconciling mercy began, and, for a time, was kept up with supreme earnestness; while he continued his unrelaxed bent upon school duties and intellectual culture. To see a young man carrying on an agonizing strife for Divine mercy simultaneously with the full daily stretch of his mental energies in pursuit of knowledge, is to be most profoundly impressed with the grandeur of those powers with which God has endowed human nature. Could any eye have looked into our schoolboy's inner world during some of his last school-days, it might have had an insight into the mystery of this two-fold yet not discordant action. He went to and fro with prepared lessons for his scholarly tutor, while every step was taken in warm and longing expectation to meet with Jesus. The Saviour met him. Where was that meeting?

Nothing more significantly reproves the clinging fondness of some people for that species of Christian Fetishism which confines the Divine presence, for the most part, to consecrated places, or fixes it in and around certain hallowed symbols, than the fact that the Saviour so often chooses to reveal Himself to seeking souls, most graciously, in the most ordinary way-side places of daily life. When He disclosed Himself to a guileless man under the fig-tree, and spoke to an inquiring woman, as He spoke to no other, by the well-side in the public-way, He gave His creatures notice that where a human heart sincerely opens itself to Him, no spot is otherwise than sacredly fit as the scene of reconciliation. A penitent son transacting business behind a counter is called by his pious father to throw a passing glance on a passage in the New Testament, and there and then is filled with peace. A mighty and skilled wrestler, smitten in his conscience, descends to his work in the mine, and is, by and by, heard filling the dark depth with "songs of deliverance." A broken-hearted ploughman spends his meal-time on his knees in the ditch, and hears a Voice which makes him spring into new life, and ever after to plough in hope. Yes; the high road, the open boat, the ship's deck, the stone quarry, the pit on the common, the sentinel's beat, the battle-field, the workshop, and the crowded street, have all been consecrated by converting grace.

Have you ever gone to and fro over London Bridge amidst the ceaseless current of human life? If so, you have had, perhaps, some inward queries about the countless secrecies of thought, and feeling, and motive, and purpose, which have been around you, close to you, touching you, and still defying your keenest scrutiny. When sometimes tempted to think hardly of the multitude, it is good to reflect that, possibly, under the worst appearances, there are blessed transactions going on, by spiritual telegraph, between this one or that one in the moving crowd and the great Author of all life in all worlds. It was so in one instance, at least, somewhere towards the autumn of 1823.

Young Bunting had been for some time a senior scholar in the old Grammar School of St. Saviour's, Southwark. He passed to and fro over London Bridge every day; and one day, having lived for some months in earnest desire for "peace with God," his prayers were answered. As he walked on, the blessed spirit, with a voice which can never be mistaken, repeated to his heart the Saviour's words, "Him that cometh to Me I will in no wise cast out." He felt that the Saviour was close to him. There was the spiritual touch, and the sinner was made "perfectly whole." Who witnessed that miracle on London Bridge? Known to none among the visible crowd, it was witnessed from above, and issued in fruit which has proved accumulative below. The earliest result was the rapid unfolding of hitherto reserved powers. The preacher appeared suddenly to have entered on his mission. But his poetic genius took wing with even more speed than his pulpit power. A poem on "The Ministry of Angels," from his pen, appeared in the *Methodist Magazine* in the year of his conversion; and one portion of it has all the warm passion of a soul in its "first love," with its native music now brightly attuned to the Divine voice, and its imagination purified and strengthened for ranging "the heavenlies":—

>Saviour, to whom my strain I bring,
>My lowly, loyal offering,
>What excellencies cluster not in Thee?
>   The arm to slay, the heart to bless,
>   Omnipotence and tenderness,
>A Sovereign's grandeur—brother's sympathy!
>   For Thou couldst stoop with men to dwell,
>   Incarnate God! Immanuel!
>   And then for men wert crucified:
>Heights, depths, to reach to finite mind denied!
>   O Cherubim, to *you* 'tis mystery!
>   O Seraphim, *ye* cannot love like me,
>For whom the Prince of Love, *despis'd, rejected*, died!

>—And lives again! my suit to plead,
>To guide my steps, and guard my head,
>And help and hope, and peace and power afford,
>   Yea! even as my need shall be
>   With Thy "dear might" encompass me,
>Thou Angel of the Presence of the Lord!
>   Then onward dauntlessly I'll press
>   O'er ocean steep, or wilderness.
>   And, ah! if Thou sustain my faith,
>Haply I would with Thee descend beneath,
>Where chilling airs, and mists funereal fall,
>And midnight heaves her sombre-spreading pall,
>The sepulchre of man, the noiseless vale of death.

>When this poor body droops and dies,
>Its strength in desolation lies,
>And all is pain, and tremor, and decay,
>   When as the gates of Zion ope,
>   These eyes to Thee are lifted up,
>While their last light is languishing away;
>   Then send me from Thy holy hill,
>   Thine angels to befriend me still,
>   And—all the world's endearments fled—

> Curtain, with unfurl'd wings, affliction's bed:
> So be my chamber, 'neath their sweet control,
> The sanctuary of a suffering soul,
> Where rays of Paradise their gradual glory shed.
>
> Then, welcome joys invisible,
> Transcending thought, ineffable!
> Fruition and eternity be mine!
> Welcome th' assembly of the blest,
> Whose myriad voices never rest,
> But in one long triumphant anthem join!
> Yet, when I mingle with the throng
> That to the upper Church belong,
> This, this my first desire shall be,
> Give me the sight of Him who ransom'd me!
> Jesu! of all the good to angels given,
> Of all the beauty and the bliss of heaven—
> Bliss, Beauty, Heaven itself—I ask a sight of Thee!

Throughout the year of his spiritual birth, the young poet seems to be ever lingering before the Crucified, as if, in solemn awe and reverent love, he would fain wait till all the meaning of mysterious Calvary entered for ever his adoring soul. His new-born spirit had caught that subduing view of the great sacrifice, and his own interest in it, which constrains all by whom it is realized to sing—

> Let all Thy love, and all Thy grief,
> Graven on my heart for ever be!

As a preacher, he wants now to be, like Paul, ever ready, from the depths of his hallowed being, to cry, "God forbid that I should glory save in the cross of our Lord Jesus Christ, by whom the world is crucified unto me, and I unto the world." And as a poet, he would have all his powers made holy by exercising them, first of all, amidst the scenes of Calvary. It has been said of him that his "trial sermon" "rang with the true tone of a man divinely called to the ministry;" and it may be said, as to his first devout poetic essays, that they were instinct with the life, and tuneful with the native expression, of true poetry. His "Scenes at Calvary" are now touching in their plaintiveness, now impressive and striking in their prophetic visions, and now tender and exalted in their Christian devotion. There is something finely appropriate in the rhythmical movement of this hymn-like effusion :—

> The clamour of the crowd is spent,
>   Nor aught of sound is stirring,
> But of the women's wild lament,
>   To long-lost joys recurring;
> And *there* the loved disciple sits,
> Watching the latest light that flits
>   Athwart *that* shadow'd visage.
>
> But,—where yon clouds their columns rear,—
>   What strange, terrific vision?—
> The Signet and the Hand appear,
>   Sealing the dread commission;
> And, bearing it through middle skies,
> On downward wing the Herald flies,—
>   He flies to execute it.
>
> . . . . . .
>
> Heaven's myriad host stoop wistful down,
>   From bolder heights of glory;
> Then make in softer music known
>   The wonder-kindling story;
> And cherubim and seraphim
> Repeat, prolong, th' adoring hymn,
>   But louder, loftier swell it.
>
> That Herald whom Jehovah sent,
>   With awful signs investing,
> Returns with speed benevolent,
>   The mystic fact attesting,—
> "'Tis finished! saints and men be glad!
> The debt, the mighty debt, is paid,
>   And God Himself hath paid it!"
>
> . . . . .
>
> No wanderer shall He pace again
>   Thy streets, O holy city!
> Nor, when again He cometh, rain
>   O'er thee the tears of pity;
> But He shall come to do thee harm,
> And crush thee with His strong right arm,—
>   That arm, how dire its vengeance!
>
> No more depress'd by toils and pains,
>   But terrible in wonder,
> On fire-shod steeds, with rushing manes,
>   And necks enwrapped in thunder,
> Calvary! o'er thy heights shall ride
> Th' unconquerable Crucified,
>   And sweep thee into ruin

> I see Him, as of old He came
>   By whelming floods attested,
> And as, in panoply of flame,
>   He shall return invested;
> With meteor-eye, and naked brand,
> Crude desolation in his hand,
>   He comes,—prepare to meet Him!
>
> Hasten, O Christ, Thy victory!
>   Dispread and then complete it;
> And bring Thy royal advent nigh,
>   To such as long to greet it.
> But ne'er from this devoted heart
> The mem'ry of Thy love depart—
>   The mem'ry of Thy passion!
>
> Thy Cross, the standard of my hopes;
>   Those nails, my load sustaining;
> That spear, which richest fountain opes,
>   To heal my soul's complaining;—
> Shall, long as life, my glorying be,
> And lasting as eternity,
>   The burden of my triumph!

The name of W. M. Bunting is more widely known as that of a hymn-writer. One hymn of his now forms a part of the annual "Covenant Service" of the Wesleyan Methodists throughout the world; yet this was one of his first productions, and was written before he was fully eighteen years old. His father was occupied in London from 1821 to 1824 as editor of the *Methodist Magazine* and other literature of Methodism. One morning, in 1824, at the breakfast-table, he introduced a hymn as an anonymous contribution, and introduced it for the purpose of calling attention to its merit. The author was sitting at the table, unsuspected by his father to be the contributor of such verses. How should he have a suspicion that his boy's hand was in this? It was, in most respects, so mature. The lad might write verses on his mother's birthday, or give his imagination wing amidst the scenes of Calvary, or pour forth the devout utterance of his "first love" for Christ; but this hymn was a concentration of a Christian pilgrim's long life experience, and evinced as clear and full an insight into the deeper and more delicate workings of a Christian heart in the presence of its God as ever Charles Wesley himself has shown in his experimental hymns. It may be that some will be tempted to omit the third verse from public use, because of its alliterative quaintness and its somewhat prim antithetic mode; yet, with all this, it guides the soul into Divine communion, so holily familiar, and is so much in the manner and spirit of the old Puritan form of covenant in which the people join, that, after all, the devout singer is loth to lose its music. The service known among Methodists as "The Renewal of the Covenant" is solemnly observed on the first Sunday of every year. The members join in an impressive form of personal dedication to God, and then unite in the celebration of the Lord's Supper. Appropriate hymns were provided for the service by Mr. Wesley; but when the original hymn-book was enlarged, in 1830, Mr. Bunting's hymn was inserted; and since then it has come very largely into use as the leading hymn for the service. It is worthy of this distinction. The old "Covenant Hymn" by Charles Wesley, beginning with

> Come, let us use the grace divine,

is finely adapted for general use by the assembled society; but Bunting's hymn is more suitable, in that, while all can join, it expresses in particular the feelings of each, so as to make the service, to every one, a personal act of confession and sacrifice. Charles Wesley's hymn, beginning with

> O, how shall the sinner perform
> The vows he hath vowed to the Lord?

is rather to be used "after the renewal of the covenant," and even then the alternations between doubtfulness and swelling confidence, fear and jubilant hope, appear to be too frequent and sudden; nor is the metrical form of the hymn fairly consistent with the states of mind which it expresses. Our young poet's metre and rhythm more beautifully become the approach of the tremulous and expectant soul; while it breathes that child-like tenderness which so sweetly accords with its covenant transaction with God. It is, indeed, by its general use, proved to be unsurpassed as the opening hymn of the Covenant Service, while Doddridge's inimitable utterance of jubilant feeling and hopeful rest in covenant blessedness must ever be most appropriate at the completion of the solemn new year's transaction. How many hearts from year to year have been melted while they have uttered the young Methodist poet's verses as their opening hymn to their covenant God! and how many, when the covenant grace has been sealed on their hearts, at the Lord's table, have sung with holy joy—

> O happy day that fixed my choice
> On Thee, my Saviour and my God!

Whose spiritual song perpetuates the wider and richer blessing, that of the saintly Doddridge, or that of the newborn lad of eighteen, whose first hymn, within seven years of its issue, was sung in the most solemn assemblies of Methodism throughout the world? No soul that had learnt to breathe the true spirit of a Covenant Service can ever forget the subdued delight with which it found itself furnished with means of expression when, for the first time, it joined in singing—

> O God! how often hath Thine ear
>   To me in willing mercy bow'd!
> While worshipping Thine altar near,
>   Lowly I wept, and strongly vow'd.
> But ah! the feebleness of man!
> Have I not vow'd and wept in vain?
>
> Return, O Lord of Hosts, return!
>   Behold Thy servant in distress;
> My faithlessness again I mourn;
>   Again forgive my faithlessness;
> And to Thine arms my spirit take,
> And bless me for the Saviour's sake.
>
> In pity of the soul Thou lov'st,
>   Now bid the sin Thou hat'st expire;
> Let me desire what Thou approv'st,—
>   Thou dost approve what I desire;
> And Thou wilt deign to call me Thine,
> And I will dare to call Thee mine.

> This day the covenant I sign,
>   The bond of sure and promised peace,
> Nor can I doubt its power divine,
>   Since seal'd with Jesu's blood it is.
> That blood I take, that blood alone,
> And make the cov'nant peace my own.
>
> But, that my faith no more may know
>   Or change, or interval, or end,
> Help me in all Thy paths to go,
>   And now as e'er my voice attend;
> And gladden me with answers mild,
> And commune, Father, with Thy child!

It is said of Dr. Jabez Bunting that he never, as a preacher, excelled his first sermon. Certainly it may be said of his son that he never, as a hymn-writer, surpassed this, his first hymn.

The young poet now entered the Methodist ministry, and for a quarter of a century, in full active service, he gave the best proofs of a Divine call, as a Christian preacher and pastor. Those who saw him and heard him in his earlier course describe him as "tall, thin, juvenile, and altogether interesting. His manner was collected, grave, and impressive. He spoke with much distinctness, and was a master of emphasis. . . . From the first his sermons abounded in a certain tender poetry of thought and phrase. . . . Now and then a light and colour were thrown upon the composition, which not only beautified the places where they fell, but lit up and harmonized the whole landscape. . . . His later preaching did not altogether lose, though it did not sparkle so brightly with its former passages of beauty. The flowers had ripened into fruit." There was great increase of point and power; and "less of digression into those almost irresistible topics of remark with which impudent heresies, the follies of what are called leaders of thought, and the dogmatisms of modern magazines and newspapers, so seriously annoy sensible Christians. He came to live above that world also, and lifted his people with him; ignoring rather than contradicting it. . . . His sermons and the services he conducted were unusually long." Public worship was with him, as it was with the best of the Puritans, the business of the Lord's day. This was a matter of conscience; and, though it involved opposition and unpopularity, he kept up his testimony against the "world which hates to be preached to, and to churches, increasingly worldly, which prefer any occupation, in the sanctuary or out of it, to the meek hearing of God's word." Throughout his public course, however, whether forsaken by hearers who do not cultivate religious thought, or whether appreciated and beloved by those who do; all who knew him felt that his spirit, and motive, and aim, in his work, were such as he expressed in one of his own hymns, put into the lips of "A Christian seeking to be useful":—

> Oh! for my Master's generous mind,
> That I might live to bless mankind,
> A selfish quietude contemn,
> And serve the Lord by serving them;
> Nor all in secret joy expend
> The gifts which on my soul descend.
>
> Too well I love to glide unseen,
> With twilight, through some lone ravine,—
> Where earth, o'erhanging high, hath bent
> An interposing firmament,
> And flowers along its brink that glow
> Are stars to that still world below.
>
> But 'tis a nobler joy to move
> In open tracks, with life, and love,
> And, scattering blessings in my train,
> Receive them in new bliss again;
> Earth's broider'd robe beneath me spread,
> Heaven fondly brightening o'er my head!
>
> I covet years in duty spent,
> Unspotted, useful, and content;
> The Christian home, the crowded shrine,
> The paths of charity divine,—
> And like the last my Master trod,
> A death-bed witnessing for God.

Confirmed disease, spasmodic asthma, obliged the poet-preacher to retire at length from active life. He had been trained to action; he was now to be disciplined by suffering.

For seventeen years he was by turns the imprisoned sufferer, the occasional preacher, the wise and gentle pastor, and the unselfish "friend in need." It was a holy pleasure to him, when permitted, to hear that Gospel which it had been his joy to preach.

"I shall never forget the first time I saw him in my congregation," says a minister who used to visit the neighbourhood of Mr. Bunting's residence. "It was in a small, thoroughly Methodist Chapel in Kentish Town, not very far from Highgate Rise, where the invalid lived. On rising in the pulpit to begin the service, my first glance fell upon the well-known form. There he was, as a loving pen has so happily sketched him, 'a tall emaciated man, with a high white forehead, very bald—what hair was left, dark brown and silky; his eyes grey, large and luminous; with a nose which indexed, as Coleridge teaches, a right royal will; with delicately-moulded mouth and chin; with hands of exquisite form and colour; with the look, altogether, of a man not of this world; unmistakably a minister of religion. He made you think of the risen Lazarus, walking pensively from his first to his second sepulchre.' Yes, this was the man as I saw him, just inside the door under the little end gallery. Kentish Town could not boast then of its large, Gothic chapel, so-called—one of that modern class, under whose aspiring roofs, in so many places in the land, the Methodists are now faintly trying to keep up the spirit and aim of Methodism. The old chapel was small and snug, and my distinguished hearer was near enough to me to allow an opportunity of marking the expressions of his devout soul while he listened to the Word. He took part in the service as if God's house were his home. His voice was feeble; but, oh! with what feeling and expression he joined in singing that heavenly-toned hymn—

Come, Holy Ghost, all quickening fire.

His soul was intensely moved in giving tuneful utterance to one verse in particular—

> My peace, my life, my comfort Thou,
> My treasure and my all Thou art!
> True witness of my sonship, now
> Engraving pardon on my heart;
> Seal of my sins in Christ forgiven,
> Earnest of love, and pledge of heaven.

The sermon—during which his radiant eye was never turned from the preacher—was an exposition of Ephesians i. 12, 13, 14; and his prayer at the close was a beautifully simple transformation of the leading thoughts in the sermon into a reverent and loving appeal to God on behalf of himself, the congregation, and the preacher. The tremulous warmth with which he afterwards expressed his gratitude to the Author of truth for the light and comfort afforded to the teachable hearers of Christ's word, so touched me that I have been thankful ever since that he had been, once at least, among my hearers."

The poetical genius of this devout hearer in God's house was always alive to the beauty and sublimities of nature, and to the silent teachings of nature as well as grace. In the May of 1839 he was able to travel, and found his way into some of the richest and wildest scenes of Devonshire. "We called at Holnicote," says he in a letter, "a seat of the excellent Sir Thomas Acland, and one of the most Eden-like spots that ever peered on my senses, or my fancy either. As we reached lovely Lynton, it began to rain fast, and this day has been one of stormy wind and cold. We are delightfully quiet, having anticipated 'the season.' Our windows command a magnificent, and now a wild, sea-view, with the accompaniments of bold headland and, more inward, deep ravine, rambling brooks, and the freshest verdure of spring-time. My spirits are alternately exhilarated and soothed by our situation, and my heart rejoices in God."

He could hardly fail to catch inspiration amidst such surroundings. To such inspiration we owe, perhaps, some of his recorded thoughts "Among the Mountains":—

> Yon mountain altars! smoking to the skies,
> As with mute, reverent Nature's sacrifice!

> And, lo! as erst, but now to common sight,
> Propitious splendours gleam from cloud of light!
> Symbols, at least, be these of acts that bind
> Created to the soul-creating *mind.*
> Nor is the lesson lost, dread Lord, on mine;
> Which, resting on Thy word, accepts a sign
> From lesser oracles. "The sea," O God,
> Oft as "the sanctuary," Thy feet have trod;
> And him Thou callest blest, who, pure in heart,
> Sees Thee in all Thy ways—divinest art!
> Paternal, all-pervading Deity,
> Thy voiceless works invite my soul to worship Thee!

Nor could his deep affliction, when at home, shut up in the chamber of suffering, entirely check the music of his consecrated genius. His sufferings were great at times, and yet these failed to prevent him, even at the risk of life, from rising to administer comfort to those who, he thought, were worse afflicted than himself. His afflictions could not even check the playful humour by which he sought, at times, to brighten his friends' spirits and his own. His wit had been proved to be bright and keen. He could skilfully wield a sharp weapon when it was needful; but his hand was always under the command of a reverent and loving heart. He could put forth a pun, but he was too wise to be an habitual punster. A punning Methodist preacher is always a wearisome inconsistency.

> How every fool can play upon the word!

He could be humorous, witty, and playful enough, however, to relieve the gloom of his sick chamber. As an invalid, he had begun to practise quaint modes of filling up moments of depression, as soon as he had taken up his abode in the dwelling where he finished his course: as when he gave "A Christmas welcome to divers sparrows which perched themselves on the branches of a plane-tree in front of my casement":—

> Quoth Christ, No sparrow falleth to the ground
> Without your Heavenly Father's sov'reign will:
> Who guides you hither in your sunny round?
> Quoth Faith, It is my Heavenly Father still.

> God sent His saint good news by carrier-dove;
> God sent His seer by ravens each day's dinner;
> God sends blythe sparrows, in His thoughtful love,
> To sit and sing beside a downcast sinner.
>
> Ye peep into my room, as ye would say,
> How fares our friend, by whom so well we fare?
> Ye chirrup, Cheer up! clouds will clear away!
> Ye spring toward heaven, and bid my heart be there.
>
> No good's too little for great Love to do:
> A bird's an angel when from God it comes;
> And He, who sends my cheer, wing'd mutes, by you,
> Will send you soon by me your Christmas crumbs.

Now, the sufferer could, on occasions, laugh with a lively friend; could play with a white mouse which used to visit him on his dying bed, and share his meals; and, when able to write, could interweave pleasantries with plaintive accounts of himself, and records of pious submission. At a time of great suffering from prevalent high winds, he writes to a friend: "I have been coughing, or panting, or protecting myself by changes of posture, &c., during most of the time; reading restrainedly, thinking hurtfully (to myself) but helplessly, and praying much in fragments and gasps, in solitude, or in the company of sleepers. I suppose we must be some hundred feet higher in the air than you; and I have often felt as if I were a sick and wingless crow, swinging with the wind in a crazy nest, at the top of one of Miss Coutt's elms, on the other side of the lane. Then I have had hours of inevitable and cough-exasperating talk with my womankind—have I not?" One mode of short relief for himself at this time was that of indulging his playful music in a song:—

> A poor old crow, with wounded wing,
> Here in my windy nest I swing,
>   Up in the high elm-tree;
> I can't fly forth; I can't hop down;
> And every lad from London town
>   May have a shot at me.
>
> I'd rather be a barn-door bird
> On some snug roost, by storms unstirred,
>   Down in a lowland farm;
> Nightly with hen and chickens housed,
> Early, by sweet, warm sunshine roused,
>   And all day hid from harm.

But an end must come. The thoughtful preacher, the sympathising, diligent pastor, the helpful friend, the musical companion, the genius, the wit, the Methodist poet, has to pass the limit of mortality. He had seen a lovely daughter depart before him. He had himself, again and again, been led to the brink of the river, within touch of the waters. He had heard the oldest Methodist preacher then living preach the last Methodist sermon he would ever hear. He had, for the last time, conducted family worship on the anniversary evening of his daughter's departure, dwelling on his own unworthiness to enter Heaven except among those whose robes were made white in the blood of the Lamb. "It was with them," he said, "that my dear child found an entrance, and that is the only way for me—the blood of the Lamb." He had kissed his "Blessed Bible," as one of his last actions. His last consolations, in the body, were found in portions of his loved hymn-book; and his last utterances were words of sympathy with some of his suffering neighbours and fellow Christians. And now he was to realise the desire which he had expressed in a hymn, whose sweet solemn music and deep feeling are so attuned to the mysteries of Gethsemane, and the sanctities of "The Christian's Chamber." The hymn is founded on St. Luke xxii. 39—44: "He came out, and went, as He was wont, to the Mount of Olives; . . . and being in an agony, He prayed more earnestly."

> Oh, never could my Master seek
>   The hour of lonely prayer,
> But troubles more than sighs could speak
>   Would haunt His vision there.
> He felt the chill o'ershadowing awe
>   Which warns of storms to be;
> And in the place of prayer foresaw
>   The scene of agony.
>
> But when the dreaded hour drew nigh
>   On that frequented spot,
> Blest answers came to many a sigh
>   By all but God forgot;

> And angel comforters had leave
>   To gather many a tear
> Which e'en the breathless, listening eve
>   Failed, when they fell, to hear.
>
> Thy follower, Jesus, would I be,
>   Where'er Thy feet have trod!
> And dear, like Thine, have been to me
>   My lonelier hours with God;
> Him in my chamber oft I seek,
>   Him on my bed desire;
> And when of death my tremors speak,
>   His words new trust inspire.
>
> Yet, if the foe should find me here,
>   And traitor doubts intrude,
> Angel Jehovah! Thou wilt cheer
>   My soul's dread solitude.
> And while the future beams on me,
>   The past this balm shall bear—
> The scene of mortal agony
>   Was long the place of prayer.

His end was come. There was silence. Wife and daughter were watching. A verse of one of his hymns was now to take the light of a prophetic longing, and to be fulfilled. He had once sung—

> When on death's lone bed I lie,
> Languishing in peace to die,
> May some spirit, hovering near,
> Sing a Saviour in my ear!

That spirit was now present. He lay supported by his daughter, and, angel-like, she repeated softly in his ear the text which, forty years before, had opened to him the door of spiritual life: "Him that cometh unto Me, I will in no wise cast out." The balmy promise wafted him to Paradise.

He was born, on the 23rd of November, 1805, as it proved, to be a preacher. He was born a poet, born with "music in himself;" and was born into the life above on the morning of November 13th, 1866, from the room where his organ stood. To those who judge "according to the appearance," his "harp was turned to mourning, and his organ into the voice of them that weep;" but to those who live by faith, his soul is uttering new melodies, and his poetic genius is for ever breathing fresh harmonies of thought and sound.

CHAPTER XIX.

AN INSPIRED YOUNG MAIDEN.

> Can any mortal mixture of earth's mould
> Breathe such divine, enchanting ravishment?
> Sure something holy lodges in that breast,
> And with these raptures moves the vocal air
> To testify his hidden residence.

AMONG our more refined pleasures, one of the most agreeable is that serene feeling which perfect harmony inspires. A delicate sense of this is sometimes enjoyed while the eye reposes upon the forms and colourings of silently-living nature; but it is realised more frequently, perhaps, and in greater fulness, when we catch through the ear a "concord of sweet sounds." Such a feeling indicates our high relation; for all the deeper researches of science, as well as all the teachings of revelation, show that, whether as the Creator of worlds, or as the Saviour of men, God is the "Lover of concord." There is no harmony among creatures, however, so pleasing to Him, or by which He is so glorified, as the harmony of sanctified human nature. "Whatsoever things are true, whatsoever things are honest, whatsoever things are just, whatsoever things are pure, whatsoever things are lovely, whatsoever things are of good report; if there be any virtue, and if there be any praise," all are combined in the truly hallowed man; and so combined as to form a beautifully consistent whole; a character in which there is nothing unpleasantly prominent, and in which its graces are so agreeably blended, that to see it is to realise a

> A strain divine
> Ariseth softly from each leafy dell,
> And streamlet's gush—
> My soul awaketh! With the gentle heart
> Of Nature it would bear a joyous part.

sense of beautiful symmetry, and of harmonised life. Such a character may inspire a feeling akin to that which is wakened by the music of a perfect choir. An example of this amiable godliness once lived in Devonport, in Devon— a man about whose life there was a tuneful charm. His voice was as pleasant as his example. Those who remember his musical taste and skill might compare his life to the harmony with which he would sometimes regale his friends. He was a master of music. Never were some of Händel's divine solos rendered more thrillingly effective than when he sang, and played the accompaniments to his own voice. On one occasion a friend, who had been deeply moved by the music, remarked, at the close, that nothing had ever brought heaven so near to him.

"Ah!" said the musician, "I once heard music far more heavenly in this very house."

"When, and by whom?" was the inquiry.

"I can tell you when," said he, "but by whom it was I cannot say. It was years ago, when we had a beautiful little one. The child appeared to be happiness itself. Oh, so lovely! It was very dear to us. It was truly enshrined in my heart. God saw fit to touch the darling. The touch seemed to brighten it, and yet to withdraw it from us. It lay on the very brink of life, and I began to feel how hard it was to let it go. Midnight came on, and I paced the adjoining room, just where we are now, and 'besought God for the child.' It was a solemn hour of watching and prayer. At length I heard distant music. It drew near and yet nearer; I was struck with the music even amidst my sorrow. Indeed, even my prayer was suspended. My first thought was that a regiment was on the march out of town, and was led by the full band. I had been used to military band music, and, indeed, to all other classes of music; but music like that I could not remember. What regiment was it? or what could it be? It approached; and so sure was I that it was as I first supposed, not recollecting the hour of the night, and not stopping to reason on the extraordinary character of the harmony, which I seemed to feel as well to hear, I threw up the window to watch the passing of the band. I saw nothing. There was nothing to be seen. The music passed, and was melting off in a way that filled me with peaceful awe, when, at that moment, the nurse opened the door of the room, and whispered, 'The child is gone!' I leave you to think how near that music brought heaven to me. What should I have seen if my eyes had been unveiled while my ears were open to the music? My precious child went off amidst the angelic band!"

"What was heard by that friend," said one who had listened to the story, and rehearsed it, long after, in a quiet evening circle, "was just what a young modern poet realised in poetic vision, and which the music of her vision would help every one to realise who believes that the harmonies of the unseen world are closest to us when this life breathes most of sorrow."

"Can you give us the vision?" said one of the company.

"Yes, the poem is called 'The Mother's Vigil.' The mother is shown as a night-watcher over her dying child. The poet sees what the mother did not:—

> .... "They were angels come
> To carry the young spirit to its God.
> One o'er the babe-brow bent, and gently wav'd
> His graceful hand above it, to allay
> Its burning fever, softly fanning back
> The pale, pale drooping curls, that scarce had form'd
> Their slender satin threads to circles yet.
> The second held the small hand tenderly
> Twin'd in his own cool, fragrant fingers, soft
> As Eden's blossoms, ofttimes bathing it
> With balmy kisses; the third angel touch'd not
> The dying loveliness, but gently fanned
> Th' immortal flame within it, and in tones
> That melted as they gush'd, warbled a song
> Of everlasting love.
>
> SONG.
>
> Sweet eyes, close, close in sleep,
> No longer shall ye weep;
> Death's slumber, damp and deep,
>   Presses your lids so white;

Pale temple of the infant saint,
Thy pillars shake, thy lamp grows faint,
   Dying in heaven's light.

Slumbering soul, arouse;
Fann'd by the waving boughs
   Of life's immortal tree;
Shine forth, thou spark struck from God's fire-harp strings,
Flash to the fannings of our bending wings,
And mingle in the flame of seraph kings,
   In the deep crystal sea.

Ah! thou art waking now!
Eternity's broad shade hath touch'd thy brow;
Awake, beloved, thy angels o'er thee bow;
   Redemption's lamb new born,
Forsake thy trembling shrine. Ah! let it be
To thy sad mother a dear gift from thee;
Why dost thou shudder? Leave it, thou art free;
   This is thy life's first morn.

Start not! our mighty arms are twin'd beneath thee,
Our golden feathers white and warm enwreath thee,
   And death the chain will sever
That links thee to thy cell; his shaft is gold;
Fear not, 'tis wing'd with kisses, though so cold.
'Tis past—the pang across thy breast hath roll'd:
   Now thou art free for ever.

Fall into our arms, and wide above thee
   We will spread a canopy of wings;
We will bear thee home to those that love thee,
   Where the cherub choir for ever sings.

Sparkling spirit! now thou, shouting, leapest
   Out into life's everlasting sea;
Measure with the heart of heaven thou keepest,
   And thy pulse is feverless and free.

Spread your pinions, angels, wave them lightly;
   Ruffle not the sacred, sleeping air;
To the zenith cleave your passage brightly;
   Seek the throne, and drop the jewel there."

"Thank you! thank you!" said many voices, "who is the poet? She seems to have been among angels, and to have brought back some of their tones as well as their spirit of song."

"The poet was Emma Tatham."

Emma Tatham, at the time she wrote "The Mother's

Vigil," was not much more than a child herself. She was but seventeen. She was the daughter of an upholsterer who lived on Holborn Hill. At first sight, she would appear no other than a little small-featured girl, with nothing about her face, or head, or manner, or bearing, but just what English taste likes to see in a pretty, quiet, intelligent, and good-natured English maiden. Perhaps she might pass you again and again, and you would never think that you had caught the eye of a poet. It has become a sort of creed that—

> The poet's eye, in a fine frenzy rolling,
> Doth glance from heaven to earth, from earth to heaven;

But you would never see the "fine frenzy" in the eye of this sweet child; no wide sweeping "glance"; but simple, serious, amiable expression, such as cheers but never startles the ordinary life of homes like hers. Who would look to find a poet where she was found? In boyhood it used to be a joy to wander along the sea beach, as near as might be to the line of waves, as they came either gently curling and unfolding their silver fringes, or thundering on before a heavy ground swell. The joy was to search for little rare and delicate shells or polished gems of coloured quartz. These were looked for along by the ridges of tangled weed, and pebbles, drift wood, and wrecked shell-fish, which the latest tide had thrown up. But now and then the richest treasures would be come upon in some little rock hollow or cranny, or all but hidden behind some glittering heap of sea-waste. Something like this it is, while we wander among the streets of London. Gems are to be found there; but not generally among the more prominent, pretentious, and shiny, though slimy, soaked, and unsound entanglements of social material. Rather, they are lighted on when least looked for—on spots which the rambler might pass and repass all his life long without suspecting his nearness to things so "rich and rare." There is a pleasure in wandering through the street-scenery of London. That scenery is remarkable. Not that the streets are picturesque; most of them have lost that character. Not that they are so grand, except in the vastness of their grouping; nor that they are so pleasantly varied in their style—London houses and London streets have somehow kept to a kind of sameness, which allows any one ordinary street to be taken as a type of all its neighbours; but the deep interest is in the associations which crowd upon the mind, as you foot it in and out through the dull brick-lined avenues of the great artificial wilderness. In one locality alone: who can pass in front of the Foundling Hospital on to Russell Square, by the British Museum, through Bloomsbury, and Theobald's Road, and in and out around Gray's Inn, without walking in company with such men as Johnson and Händel; or in association with the learning and genius and science of ages; or without thinking of Russells and Bedfords, of Shakespeare and his commentators; of Bacon and his law, philosophy, and reverses; or without picturing to himself some of the stirring scenes in the fashionable and public life of old England? And yet, one might, for years, have passed the "boundary house" of the Bedford Estate in Theobald's Road, on his way down through that quiet little path to Holborn which affords a peep into Gray's Inn Garden, without ever supposing that in that unnoticeable, ordinary street dwelling such a hallowed genius was born as the author of the "The Dream of Pythagoras"; yet so it was. In that house Emma Tatham first saw the light of this world on October 31, 1829. The house would become distinguished to the lover of true poetry as soon as it was known to be the first home of so gifted a child. One might stand and look, and ask, were it proper, on what principle, or for what reason, should such an ethereal spirit have its entrance into life in that dingy depth of a dingy city. Read her "Dream of Pythagoras," and the wonder will deepen. The poem takes its rise from a passage in the Abbé Raynal's "Travels of Cyrus"—"The soul was not then imprisoned in a gross mortal body, as it is now: it was united to a luminous, heavenly, ethereal body, which served it as a vehicle to fly through the air, rise to the stars, and wander over all the regions of immensity." The poet casts the philosopher into a dream, and on his awaking he unfolds the teachings of his dream to his disciples:—

> 'Twas but a dream;
> And yet from shadows may we learn the shape
> And substance of undying truth. Methought
> In vision I beheld the first beginning
> And after changes of my soul. Oh joy!
> She is of no mean origin, but sprang
> From loftier source than stars or sunbeams know.
> Yea, like a small and feeble rill that bursts
> From everlasting mountain's coronet,
> And winding through a thousand labyrinths
> Of darkness, deserts, and drear solitudes,
> Yet never dies, but, gaining depth and power,
> Leaps forth at last with uncontrollable might
> Into immortal sunshine and the breast
> Of boundless ocean—so is this my soul.
> I felt myself spring like a sunbeam out
> From the Eternal, and my first abode
> Was a pure particle of light, wherein,
> Shrined like a beam in crystal, I did ride
> Gloriously through the firmament on wings
> Of floating flowers, ethereal gems, and wreaths
> Of vernal rainbows. I did paint a rose
> With blush of day-dawn, and a lily bell
> With mine own essence; every morn I dipt
> My robe in the full sun, then all day long
> Shook out its dew on earth, and was content
> To be unmark'd, unworshipp'd, and unknown,
> And only lov'd of Heaven. Thus did my soul
> Live spotless like her source. 'Twas mine to illume
> The palaces of nature, and explore
> Her hidden cabinets, and, raptur'd, read
> Her joyous secrets. Oh return, thou life
> Of purity! I flew from mountain-top
> To mountain, building rainbow-bridges up—
> From hill to hill, and over boundless seas;
> Ecstasy was such life, and on the verge
> Of ripe perfection. But, alas! I saw
> And envied the bold lightning, who could blind
> And startle nations, and I longed to be
> A conqueror and destroyer, like to him.
> Methought it was a glorious joy, indeed,
> To shut and open heaven as he did,
> And have the thunders for my retinue,

> And tear the clouds, and blacken palaces,
> And in a moment whiten sky, and sea,
> And earth : therefore I murmur'd at my lot,
> Beautiful as it was, and that one murmur
> Despoil'd me of my glory. I became
> A dark and tyrant cloud, driven by the storm,
> Too earthly to be bright, too hard of heart
> To drop in mercy on the thirsty land;
> And so no creature lov'd me.

The dreamer then goes through all his dark experiences as a cloud; melts at last into a desert's heart, and springs in the form of a wild flower. Scorched by the sun, a dew drop falls into his "burning bosom;" his spirit rushes into it, and he becomes a dew drop; then caught into the firmament, he is hung in a rainbow; shook by the wind into the depths of ocean, he sees all the mysteries, beauties, and grandeurs of the great deep. Ocean tosses him among the great mountains, and he witnesses the wild and majestic storms of the elements. He then sprang up winged, and flew as lightning "across the ocean," flashed among the tempests of the hills ;

> Glanced
> Upon the mighty city in her sleep,
> Pierced all her mysteries with one swift look;

then rose to "learn a loftier lesson," and became a star; is called to obey "the spirit of wisdom;" is tempted to aim at being a god unto himself, but resisting the tempter, he sings with the stars. Again he falls, to learn "a lesson more severe;" is cast into "hot fires," to be taught submission, and being victorious, is snatched away :—

> To yet another lesson, I became
> A date tree in the desert, to pour out
> My life in dumb benevolence, and full
> Obedience to each wind of Heaven that blew.
> The traveller came—I gave him all my shade,
> Asking for no reward; the lost bird flew
> For shelter to my branches, and I hid
> Her nest among my leaves; the sunbeams ask'd
> To rest their hot and weary feet awhile
> On me, and I spread out every arm

> To embrace them, fanning them with all my plumes.
> Beneath my shade the dying pilgrim fell
> Praying for water; I cool dewdrops caught
> And shook them on his lip; I gave my fruit
> To strengthen the faint stranger, and I sang
> Soft echoes to the winds, living in nought
> For self; but in all things for others' good.
> The storm arose, and patiently I bore
> And yielded to his tyranny; I bow'd
> My tenderest foliage to his angry blast,
> And suffer'd him to tear it without sigh,
> And scatter on the waste my all of wealth.
> The billowing sands o'erwhelmed me, yet I stood
> Silent beneath them; so they rolled away,
> And rending up my roots, left me a wreck
> Upon the wilderness.
>   'Twas thus, my sons,
> I dream'd my spirit wander'd, till at length,
> As desolate I mourn'd my helpless woe,
> My guardian angel took me to his heart,
> And thus he said: "Spirit, well tried and true!
> Conqueror I have made thee, and prepar'd
> For human life; behold! I wave the palm
> Of immortality before thine eyes;
> 'Tis thine; it shall be thine, if thou aright
> Acquit thee of the part that yet remains,
> And teach what thou hast learn'd."
>   This said, he smiled,
> And gently laid me in my mother's arms.

As the reader is borne along, sometimes breathless, on the pinions of this young enthusiastic genius, he feels that the flight, though adventurous, is vigorously and unerringly maintained. "In heaven and on earth, in the seas, and in all deep places," the poet's imagination sweeps along exulting in its might, but moving with easy freedom, as if there were no region of ideal beauty, grandeur, awfulness, or purity in which her spirit was not at home. Her command of expression, her luxuriance of imagery, her natural mastery of measure, the rich music of her rhythm, the compass as well as clearness of her conceptions, the exquisite spirituality of her taste, her lovely naturalness, and simple purity of aim, all combine to awaken the question, how should it be that all this, combined in one lovely young soul, should spring up to charm us from a dim apartment in the foggy centre of a crowded city? The bright genius and unaffected and pure taste of Emma Tatham seem to have little, or nothing, in common with her native street; but, it may be, she owed something to the native seat of her forefathers. From her ancestors and their surroundings, she might have inherited something of the wild, the free, the expansive, the vigorous, the simple, and the pure. The young poet was never more than a hundred miles out of London in her life. She had never seen nature in her entire inviolate purity and freedom, and yet her imagination was familiar with it; and all she had of the ideal was as much in harmony with the realities which to her outer vision were unseen as if she had been born where nature most strongly and tenderly courts the sympathy of human souls. Her tender allusions to the home of her fathers show that she felt the mysterious reality of her mental and, perhaps, moral inheritance. Her distinctive character may have taken its shaping not only under the influence of her immediate parents, but from influences in harmony with theirs coming from farther back on the family line, and from the natural surroundings and primitive life of the old family home.

There are few scenes in which boldness, massiveness, wildness, and expansion are found in more remarkable combination, with the peaceful and the picturesque, than the dales of northern Yorkshire. There, the soul always has before its eyes some pure impress of Divine power or loveliness; and may realise, by turns, the loftiest pleasures of solitude, and the sweetest joys of rural life. To pass from some dim quarter of a dingy city, by a rapid transition, into those northern dales is to quaff refreshment and inspiration which seem to have life-long virtue. The night can never be forgotten when, having left the city amidst its business stir, two ramblers, in pursuit of geological and antiquarian objects, found themselves, in the quiet evening, lounging amidst the ruins of Bolton Abbey on the banks of the Wharf. The evening's sojourn in that delicious retreat seemed to prepare us for exploring the wilder recesses of the great limestone water-shed above us. We started on our way north, sometimes walking and sometimes wheeling it, as best we could. We breathed the air of Barden Moor, and pressed on, thinking of the "White Roe of Rilston," courting the waters of the Wharf till we left them to their own music in Langstrothdale Chase, and found our way up through the rugged pastorage of Bishop's Dale, paying homage, as we marked them, to the old hills which had for so many ages kept watch and ward over the Yore Valley. The glories of Wensley Dale filled us with song, and we went on our rambling march, often stepping to our own music. Sometimes we lingered to taste choice bits of beauty, such as we found at Aysgarth—a fine old bridge spanning the river, several waterfalls, or "forces," giving a charm to both eye and ear; under or over the hoary arch of the bridge, a richly wooded abrupt steep, coming down to the water's edge; and then by a graceful curve wending round to the right, the river losing itself in deep dark foliage—all combined to form one of those natural pictures which hush the soul into dreams of undying beauty. Then following the course of the river, we met with an invitation to rest in the venerable presence of Penhill. We were in West Witton, Emma Tatham's ancestral home; an old village straggling for a quarter of a mile along the mountain shelving, about halfway up from the bed of the stream, high enough for us to enjoy a long glance up the dale towards the hill-tops of Westmoreland—a glorious scene—and down for miles towards old Middelham, where Richard of York began his crooked life, on to the blue heights of Cleveland, and then the valley beneath, with old Bolton Castle amidst its rich foliage, and old Redmire, where Wesley used to halt on his way to Wensley. Here on this hill side, with these scenes at command, and with opportunities of chit-chat with dales-men, peeps into pleasant homes, and a few entertainments on the simple but delicious luxuries of that healthful dale, we began to feel as if we knew something more about the spring head of Emma Tatham's genius—a genius which at one moment takes a sweep with unflagging wing through the higher regions of poetic creation, and at another, with graceful ease, lights amidst the simple, tender, and unrestrained amenities and endearments of human life. Who could help thinking that she owed much to her Wensley Dale blood, and to the healthy inspiration of that natural scenery with which her ancestors had been familiar. Though born far away from such scenes, her genial, sensitive, and reverent spirit seemed from her childhood to be feeling after them. This is touchingly shown in the fact that the first pluming of the young poet's wings was for a flight to Wensley Dale and West Ditton, the family home of the Tathams. Amidst the murky scenes of Holborn Hill, this genius claimed familiarity with old Penhill of the Dale, and proved itself in its first essay to be as truthful and free as the dales to which it felt itself to be akin, though as yet untrimmed, homely, and child-like. This is one of her first pencil sketches—

> In Wensley Dale there lies a village sweet,
> Where meadow, mountain, tree, and river meet;
> Majestic Penhill there erects his head,
> And Ure sweeps proudly o'er his rocky bed;
> Fair fields, and garth, hollies and poplars there,
> With modest flowers and high-grown hedges share.
> There lived, not long ago, a noble man—
> Surpass him, British Islands, if ye can!
> Head of the Tatham family, which same
> Has ever justly borne a virtuous fame;
> A gentle manly soul, a heavenward brow,
> Such are its true distinctions even now.
> These give a dignity, yet nobler far
> Than is conferred by coronet and star;
> And if, in future years, the Tatham's heir
> Shall cease this high inheritance to share,
> No matter, though he be in name their head,
> The true old Tatham family is dead.

She records, with beautiful simplicity, her family's obligation to Methodism. Her grandfather heard the first Methodist sermon that was preached in his native village under an ash tree; and Emma alludes to the result of that service as seen in her grandfather's simple, pious, and well-ordered household—a household of which one whom she calls "Mark" was a good and happy member. She playfully pictures the evening circle around the old hearth, and then says—

> The mother watched with love's most gracious pride,
> The sire would sometimes chuckle, sometimes chide,
> Meanwhile good Mark looked on and always smiled;
> His heart was young and light as any child.
> Time had passed softly o'er him. Though his face
> Was bright with hoary patriarchal grace,
> His soul was youthful still, brimful of love
> To all on earth below and all above.
> Sunshine was in his look where'er he came;
> Each spirit caught and owned the genial flame.
> O, palaces, such joys ye seldom know,
> Though music in you breathe and nectar flow.

Everybody who has spent the years of early life amidst the freshness of wild granite hills, with their copsey hollows and clear valley streams, orchard slopes, and pure green meadows, learns to feel that everything in nature looks clear and pure where the dear old granite shows itself. And when one has learnt to look from hill-side to sea, and from sea to his own tide-washed birth-place, and everywhere to find freshness, simplicity, transparent life, and trustiness of heart, he is in danger of being painfully surprised, and oppressed with a feeling of contamination, when, for the first time, he enters on the smutty scenes and artificial life of a great city. The unveiling of men and things to him will prove revulsive to his senses, while it shakes, if not shatters, his long-cherished reverence for what he had known only by repute. Many a man of simple faith has become an unbeliever in purity when admitted to a great centre of action, and allowed to have his first peep behind the scenes of sophisticated character and life. Many a young Christian has had his own truthfulness broken at seeing, for the first time, the untruthfulness of those whom, while looked at in the distance, he had been taught to revere.

"I am sorry," said one of this class, "that I ever went to London. There I lost my own pure simplicity, and there I lost my confidence in the pure simplicity of others. Nevertheless, I have been somewhat corrected. I found exceptions, and learnt at last that even there, amidst all the difficulty with which true nature kept herself alive, and with all the difficulty of knowing when humanity has its true face on, and when not, I have met with gems of character as pure and as free from flaw as I ever now expect to find on this side Paradise. One night I had, with a companion, left the House of Commons, and had walked towards the City, till sick, weary, and footsore, I was obliged to stop on Holborn Hill, and rest myself against a lamp-post. Everything in London appeared to me to wear a dirty veil. True, my circle of observation was as yet but small; such, however, as it was, it proved unfavourable to the culture of faith either human or divine. And as to love, I was out of love with everything and everybody, myself included. Had I known what I discovered some time afterwards, I should have been saved from further indulgence of sceptical thought and feeling. How little did I think that night, as I was leaning ready to faint under a sense of depression on my whole man—a depression which seemed like the effect of a gathering furnace heat around one —how little did I think that I was fuming just under the window of a room in which, perhaps at that moment, one of the purest, freshest, most rarely gifted and beautifully simple spirits that ever lived to glorify God by the consecration of its poetic genius was courting the inspiration under whose power she had, not long before, with a voice calm, clear, and musical in its modulations, read to her Christian pastor some of her first poetic essays. Yes, there I was on the pavement under that room over the shop where the tuneful and cultured soul of that minister had drunk in Emma Tatham's rich, thrilling, love-inspiring appeal on behalf of God's Love. O that I could have heard it that night! But I often live that night over again, and feel as if the words came to me in my depression on that old Holborn Hill :—

> "Be thou rich or poor,
> Joyful or sorrowful; in cities loud,
> Or cottage lonely, by the surging shore;
> Amidst the mountains, 'neath the waving palms;

> Among the citron groves, in the dark wilds
> Of pathless forests, or the heaving deep;
> Far in the icy zone, or compass'd round
> With the hot equinoctial—love is there.
> Love omnipresent still surrounds thy paths,
> Meets thee where'er thou goest; He hath thrown
> His arms wide as the shadow of the Cross
> Extends, and from that infinite embrace,
> Only by sin canst thou thy soul exclude.
> Yes, God is love; this priceless truth alone
> Is balm for all thy sickness.

"We had not left Holborn before I knew what was partly the cause of my depression and faintness. A heavy storm of some sort was coming. My sensitiveness to some silent influences of nature had been touched; I had felt precursive tokens. Now, however, the tremulous gaslights indicated the tempest's approach. Nor was it too dark for us to see the sailor's dread, 'weather-dogs,' coursing with growing speed in advance. Now and then, too, there seemed to be shrill voices in the distance, foreboding disaster. As we mounted the hill towards Newgate, there were moanings and howlings around the dark walls, as if the spirits of all the crime, and misery, and conscience-horror, which the old prison had ever witnessed, were coming to wreak vengeance on its present generation of inmates. We quickly got into our shelter in Newgate Street. The storm was now up; and 'the powers of the air' came on in terrible force. Ours was a watchful night, spent in alternations of painful suspense and overpowering awe. Little did we think that, while we were passing the night thus, there had been a young girl in an upper room in Holborn who, under kindling inspiration, was pouring out from her raptured soul a high-toned 'Tempest Hymn,' in harmony with the grand 'accompaniment of the hurricane!' Years passed; Holborn Hill was gone, buried under the feet of a generation having neither strength, taste, nor time, for anything but level roads; and the young Holborn genius herself had fled for ever to a holier and more peaceful hill; before I knew that, that night-storm in 1846 had given birth to harmonies which now serve to brighten and hallow my recollections of it. The lofty hymn which that Christian maiden composed while the anthem-peal of the tempest still rung in her soul, and which she read with such hushing effect to her Methodist pastor in the little Holborn parlour, has given me an ear for storm music, and I often sing with Emma Tatham when the wind rises :—

"Almighty God! whose hand of power the raging winds can tame,
The mighty tempest echoes with the thunder of Thy Name;
I hear him through the city rush, lifting his voice on high;
Dark terror rides his stormy wings, and pallid death is nigh.
'Tis night, deep night! the city sleeps, and listens in her sleep
To thy gigantic voice, O storm! to thy tremendous sweep.
Thou rollest o'er her countless roofs, in glory wild and free;
And I, a trembling watcher, am alone with God and thee.
Who walks upon thy boundless wings, that shake the land and ocean?
Who speaks in thy stupendous voice, and guides thy mighty motion?
O God of night, and storm, and power! O God, all praise above!
Hear me, great God of majesty! hear me, great God of love!
I worship Thee in solitude, I worship Thee in fear;
But the sighing of a lonely heart Thou wilt not scorn to hear.
I listen to Thy awful voice, I feel Thy weight of power;
I bend my soul beneath Thy hand, in this tremendous hour!
Yet art Thou not *my* Father still, though storm and darkness reign?
Who, in all tempests past, hast saved, wilt Thou not save again?
Praise to Thee, high Omnipotent! even now methinks I hear,
Amidst the blast, the angel-song around Thy glory clear;
And countless choirs above the stars, in pealing chant sublime,
Are praising Thee in solemn joy, high o'er this stormy clime.
Hark! the loud hallelujah shout, bursting from throne to throne,
From star to star, from sun to sun, in everlasting tone;
The saints adore th' exalted Lamb, and all the heavens reply:
Could I but hear the blissful strain, and join the glorious cry!
Even the tempest as he roars—the night winds as they roll—
Seem thund'ring forth Thy lofty praise: praise is creation's soul.
Is not a spirit in the storm, and on the blast a voice?
Hark! the giant wind his anthem sings: earth, tremble and rejoice!
And listen; ocean far away has caught the lofty key,
He is thundering through his fathomless depths majestic psalmody;
His seething waves are mad with bliss; they rise in glory crown'd,
Then sink into the grand abyss in reverence profound.
Stand on yon lonely bark and gaze—look round on every hand;
She is rolling out in the raving deep, a thousand miles from land,
Rocking over the mountain heights, cleaving the waves asunder,
She reels along her terrible road in darkness, death, and thunder.
Hark! the surging forests roar aloud, th' eternal mountains shake,
The list'ning stars in solemn strain the boundless chorus take,

And swelling, as they flash and fly, the everlasting song,
Infinite hallelujah soars from every burning throng.
The storm makes man to worship: rise, sleeper, rise! and see
All holy things and spirits belov'd are praising God, but thee.
Jehovah, we adore Thee, thron'd the heaven of heavens above.
Speak to us with Thy solemn storm, but let Thy voice be love.
Come not in anger, Mighty One! receive our lowly prayer,
O God, most high and merciful! O God, Thy people spare!
We are guilty, we are sinful, yet the spotless Lamb hath bled;
The lightnings of Thy justice fell on His most lowly head.
Then spare us, Lord; send forth Thy peace, Thy calm-creating Dove;
Speak to us with Thy solemn storm, but let Thy voice be love.
Earth! rise and join thy sister stars, roll shining on thy way,
And, as thou rollest, beam as bright, and sing as loud as they,
The new creation dawneth, and the Lamb of God shall reign;
The Prince of Peace shall triumph over war, and death, and pain,
All glory to Jehovah! our Father, Saviour, King!
Shout, shout, triumphant hurricane! stars, saints, and angels, sing!
All glory to Jehovah! Let creation swell with song!
Praise, power, and worship infinite to Him alone belong!
Glory to Christ, our Saviour! Jesus, Thy name we bless,
And give our lowly hearts to Thee in faith and thankfulness;
The storms of life—the storms that rage in each unhallow'd soul—
Dissolving in Thy potent breath, to cradled calm shall roll,
As when on old Gennesaret the Tempest heard Thy will,
And wildest winds and waves confess'd Thy mighty 'Peace, be still!'
Oh, when our heart is overwhelmed, when flesh and spirit fail,
When terrors seize the trembling breast, and sin and hell assail,
Compassionate our wretchedness, let mercy be Thy will,
Speak peace unto the trembling soul, and bid the storm be still."

The young poet's scene of life was changed. She had found her way to Margate, old Margate! There is a venerable charm about the name still. Old Margate! Yes, there is still something that properly bears the name. Quaint old streets, no two alike, scarcely two houses alike: why should they be? Why should human dwellings follow the modern fashion of taking rank, like bricks ranged for drying in the brick-field, in violation of both nature and art? No, let old Margate form itself in its more natural way; and so it has. Its homes, of all shapes and sizes, seem to have followed one another, as natural herds do, in irregular line, and, when so disposed, have formed into circles or squares to have a look at one another. Into one of these variously disposed dwellings Emma Tatham was, while yet a girl,

brought by her parents, in hope of securing for her and
themselves more healthy life. This, perhaps, was a mistake.
In the autumn of 1847, however, she was an inmate of
No. 7, Addington Square. It was called a square, but it
was in mode somewhat after one of nature's fantastic
groups. The various homes had taken position as if they
were not quite at home with each other, or as if, in a sudden
fear, they had turned back to back; while their nearest
neighbours, also, standing at accidental distances from each
other, continued to gaze at the curious posture their neighbours had assumed. From the old-fashioned bow windows
of her little abode our young poet could see little but an
apology for a garden on the other side of the half-formed
road. There was a larger railed garden adjoining her house,
but she had no look-out upon that. She had access, of
course, to the pier, or to the tame sands at the foot of the
cliffs, or perpendicular chalk sea-walls, with their natural
capping of shallow soil and green turf. She could pace
the summits of these cliffs, and look out at the stretch of
sea, sometimes blue, sometimes drab, and sometimes both.
Or she could wander on the background of undulating cornfields and pasture, marred by no roadside weeds, nor varie-
gated by turfy common; intersected by ways not very
shady, or streamlets tinged with leafiness, winding their
way towards the little gullies in the chalk cliffs. This was
a relief from the great city, a great change from Holborn
Hill, and afforded some fresh excitement for a young spirit
longing for nearer communion with veritable nature. The
soul of the young songster luxuriated in what there was
of nature, and was "rejoiced," as she said, "to come
and dwell with my beloved ocean, and flowers, and cliffs, and
clouds, and stars, and storms, and sunsets." It was here that
she poured out some effusions sweetly characteristic of her
muse. New objects called forth new manifestations of the
pure naturalness, jubilant freedom, and loving simplicity of
her genius. Here it was that she gave forth her melody
"To the Sea Bird":—

Oh, that thou hadst but a soul, sea-bird!
    As thou swimmest in heaven so high,
A spirit to know how thy white wings glow,
A spirit to feast on the scenes below,
    And the waves of the sparkling sky.

Oh, that thou hadst but a soul to feel
    How the sunbeams have rob'd and crown'd thee;
How the earth to thee doth her beauty reveal,
How the ocean doth spread and the heavens unseal
    Their secrets of glory around thee!

Oh, that there were but a heart to beat
    To the sweep of those graceful pinions!
A soul to ride in a chariot so fleet,
To float in the track of the sunbeams' feet,
    And revel in light's dominions.

Oh, that my soul for a moment might be
    To thy beautiful wings up-caught!
That I might on a midsummer morning flee
Through many bright forms over forest and sea,
    As Pythagoras wildly taught.

I would borrow, king eagle, thy loftiest wing,
    And soar where no eye-beam could follow;
A carol of praise I would joyfully sing
In the breast of the beautiful bird of the spring,
    In a lonely and moonlighted hollow.

Then I would hide in the skylark's throat,
    And descend on the rainbow's arch,
On the clouds of the storm I would fearlessly float
And rock on the winds an invisible boat,
    And follow the thunder's march.

Then would I change to a drop of the spray,
    And dance on the wings of the gale,
Mad as the hurricane whirl on my way,
Over fathomless valleys and mountains at play,
    And over the breakers pale.

Out in the ocean at wild midnight,
    A thousand leagues from shore,
My spirit should dance round the arches of white,
When the steeds of the tempest are raving with fright,
    When the heav'ns and the deep do roar.

I would then be transform'd to the wand'ring gale
    And chisel the broken waves,
Gloriously swelling the mission-bark's sail,
Flushing the cheek of the pining and pale,
    And sighing o'er far-away graves.

> I'd whisper of hope to some sorrowful ear,
>   And say to the slave, "Thou art free!"
> I would catch on my wing every sweet I came near,
>   And then fly away home, O my own mother dear!
>   To bring all my treasures to thee.

There is nothing which more tenderly indicates God's divine sense of the beautiful than his sometimes evident choice of a fitting scene for the close of a mortal life. How happy it seems for God to choose the transition scene of a pilgrim soul's departure in accordance with the pilgrim's genius and taste, and as near and like as possible in beauty and peacefulness to the heavenly inheritance. Happy is it, too, for the pilgrim to feel that the beauty of the river bank, on the one side, serves only to enrich his anticipations of the more lovely retreats on the other.

"What a paradise you have here!" said Lady ——, as she first caught the view which opens in front of a gentleman's cottage residence in the West of England; "we have nothing like this on any of our estates. I envy you," she continued, turning to the venerable owner of the paradise.

"I am glad you like it," was his response.

"Like it! Yes, indeed I would leave all we have to enjoy life in this retreat. I wish—but no—on second thought, I should not wish to live here. I should be afraid of losing it. I fear I should be unwilling to leave it."

"But it may be enjoyed as a type of something better to come, may it not?"

"Ah! There it is. I am not in a condition to think pleasantly of anything beyond it."

At this moment the lady caught sight of tears starting from the eyes of a woman who was in attendance.

"My good woman, what is the matter? Are you in trouble?"

"No, my lady. I beg pardon. I couldn't help my tears!"

"Why do you weep, then?"

"Partly because your ladyship can't think pleasantly of a

better world than this, and partly for joy. God is so good to me as to keep my paradise till I come, and while I am here, to let me look at this place every day, as a sort of picture of what He will give me as my own by-and-by."

"I wish I could weep such tears as yours, my good woman! God bless you!"

The beautiful lesson was not lost.

The good woman's joy was the joy of Emma Tatham. God led her into a retreat which her genius, her taste, and her heart might enjoy for a little while, " as a sort of picture " of the land which she was soon to enter as her own. She began her course in the depth of city life; she was led out to regale her spirit by the sea, and to dwell a little with her "beloved ocean, and cliffs, and clouds, and storms, and sunsets;" and now, having seen her last sunset by the sea, she was guided to one of the most tranquil scenes of English rural life, that she might sing among the leafage, and be hushed into quiet readiness for realising the immortal visions which her inspired soul had longed for. To ride from London to St. Albans, and to ramble along by the quiet stream which gives freshness to the undulating scenery around Redbourn, to ruminate under majestic elms within sight of the old storied abbey; or to go chanting through the leafy avenue which adorns the finely turfed folkland of Redbourn, and to look around upon the simple homes of the enchanting village which nestles in sweet companionship with its neighbour hamlet, amidst gardens, bright meadows, and park-lands, is to think of Emma Tatham coming there as to the land of Beulah. Here our young pilgrim came, in company with her mother, and was ministered to by those who loved her with much affection. Her last days were spent in doing good to the young and to the poor. Her last smiles were blessings. Her kind host heard her voice one morning, and, entering her room, saw her face bright with holy joy. "Tell my dear father," she said, in a loud, clear voice, "that no death-bed could be happier than *mine;* and tell him that it is all glory, glory, glory! Jesus has been with me in the night, and smiled on me." She was now to realise her own conception in that exquisitely tender, yet glowing poem, which she had entitled, "To Die ":—

> The babe dies peacefully in the warm arms
> Of its sweet mother, while the glowing life
> Of the fond heart whereto she presses it
> Half binds the fluttering dove to its white cage,
> And keeps the pulse at play. Oh! she would pour
> Her own life into the cold babe with joy!
> Therefore she binds him so about her heart
> To make him still live on, thinking to blend
> Her being with the babe; but, lo! the bud
> Of immortality, nursed in her breast,
> Hath blossom'd into Heaven. So let ME die
> Where the warm life of Jesus shall inspire
> My fainting spirit, and His heart shall beat
> New pulses into MINE.

Now she felt the full power of the Redeemer's claim on all the gifts with which He had endowed her. "Tell my dear father (for he will not deny my last request) if he loves me, he will not let *one word* of mine be printed which is not as pure, and holy, and true as human frailty could write with the aid of the Holy Spirit." After an interval of suffering, she again greeted the return of her loved Sabbath, and called up her own verses "To Music":—

> Ah, meet *me* at the portal of the grave!
>   Come with the echoes of my sister's lyre,
> And teach *me*, as I pass the parted wave,
>   To wake with Jesus' name my harp of fire.

Calmly passing, she gave out "faint as if far-off sounds of triumph"—"Glory!" The last tremulous whisper was of "Glory!"

Her mortal remains are in the little cemetery attached to the Independent Chapel at Redbourn—placed there at her dying request. The spot is marked by a simple memorial stone. Behind this stone there is a white rose tree, the branches of which sometimes bend and appear to embrace the inscribed name of the one who once sang so lovingly "To the White Rose":—

Art thou created for a sinner's sight,
　　Form'd for these eyes to gaze upon? Oh·say,
Could purity so exquisitely white,
Fragrance so soft, be only to delight
　　Ungrateful man, and strew a rebel's way?

What hand hath moulded thy ethereal grace?
　　Did'st thou from this dark earth indeed arise?
O miracle of beauty! in thy face
Pale holiness and glowing love embrace,
　　And in thy hidden heart perfection dies.

The softest, richest blush thy bosom hides,
　　The very breath of love thy sighs distil,
God's finger-mark on every leaf abides,
His tender touch in thee, how mildly! chides
　　Our harsh distrust and waywardness of will.

I should have deem'd thee form'd for angels' eyes,
　　For angels' foreheads only—Eden's bowers—
How can'st thou live beneath these changing skies,
And breathe this atmosphere of sins and sighs,
　　O perfect loveliness? O flower of flowers!

But I have learn'd from thy mute eloquence
　　That God hath love to man beyond our thought;
For what but love, unspeakable, intense,
Breathes from thy bosom on the ravish'd sense?
　　Oh, with what love to sinners thou art fraught!

It is as if Heaven did our path beset,
　　Besieging us with omnipresent prayers;
To melt these icy hearts so frozen yet,
Ears, eyes, assails, yea, stoops to kiss our feet,
　　Lays for our happiness ten thousand snares;

Thinks nought too beautiful, too soft, too fine
　　To shower on man, the rebel, the unclean!
O lavished goodness! generousness divine!
Written on every flower, in every line,
　　And on each glorious bird of beauty seen.

All springing like a million gushing streams,
　　From Calvary's dear hill—thither we trace
The tireless love, whose many-colour'd beams
Pursue our steps, and hover o'er our dreams,
　　And hold our struggling hearts in strong embrace.

O flower! beloved flower! the Hand which bled,
　　Transfix'd in anguish to the Cross, for me—
That Hand so delicately shaped, thy head,
The ointment of His sweetness on it shed,
　　And taught the language of His love to thee.

Now I will tell thee, O thou perfect flower,
    What thou art like. There was a fair, pale child,
Came, as thou comest, in our lowly bower,
To be my mother's joy for one brief hour,
    And then she died, but on death's bosom smil'd.

Thou art like her—that fading glow of thine
    Resembles the last colour on her cheek;
She was like thee; a heart and hand divine
Made holy beauty o'er her spirit shine,
    And perfected the praise she could not speak.

Yes, sister, gather'd young, a white moss-rose
    Born but to open on thy Saviour's breast,
Purer and fairer than the whitest snows,
While in thy heart love's living colour glows,
    And joy's rich fragrance on thy head doth rest.

Emma Tatham had a deep, mysterious affection for that glorified young sister, though she had never seen her. They are in companionship now for ever.

CHAPTER XX.

A BARD FROM THE MINE.

> No race is more erratic than the bards ;
> This moment low, then towering o'er the hills;
> Sighing in shadow, smiling in the sun,
> And visited with visions pearl-beset.
> Theirs is a wondrous mission, and the world
> Grows brighter for their beauty ; deserts bloom,
> And crime is chased where wildernesses moan.

"BEHOLD, this dreamer cometh!" said a lady, playfully, as she was nearing a somewhat remarkable figure which was coming towards her on the road.

"What do you mean?" inquired the dreamer.

"Mean? Why, I mean that whenever I meet you out of doors, you appear to be in a dreamy state, as if you saw nobody, or nothing; and you look as if you were gazing into a world which other people do not see."

"Well, perhaps there may be some truth in what you say. I may appear absent, as I really am sometimes."

The absent-looking man might have quoted his own lines, and said to the lady : "You know that

> I'm fond of travelling old deserted paths,
> Searched by the winds, and soft with solitude;
> . . . .
> Of musing lonely by old Ocean's shore,
> And roaming widely through the fields of thought."

The poet, for such he was, might well be suspected of dreaming as he walked. The slight, forward bend of the head, the quiet step, the features of harmonious thoughtfulness, the eyes half veiled by their lids, as if they wished to enjoy their own visions without interruption from outside; and the fine bald forehead, revealed by the lifting of his hat, all told the passing observer that the man was in spirit akin to him who, from taste and habit, "went out to meditate in the field at eventide." But join him as a friend, and talk with him freely about nature and grace, the beautiful and the true, home life and immortal peace, and at once every feature would have its charm of utterance, and the veiling eyelids would be lifted so as to reveal the soft, blue, loving, poetic eyes, mildly radiant, and gently reminding you that you were in communion with a sweetly toned soul.

He had been for some years pacing to and fro, at times, on that road where the lady met him as the "dreamer." And no wonder that he seemed to be looking at what other people did not see; for his walks were often beguiled by the inwardly rising music of some new sonnet, sometimes, perhaps, "To the Passing Month," or, "To the Hawthorn," or, "To the Thrush," or, "To the Skylark;" thus—

> Hail, sweet musician! At the earliest dawn
> Shaking the dew-drops from thy fluttering wing;
> And, oh! how sweet it is to hear thee sing,
> And drink thy music, floating o'er the lawn!
> Hail, harper of the cloud! I bend me low
> In humble adoration at thy shrine,
> Rapt with those spirit-notes that round me flow,
> Gushing upon my soul in airs divine!
> Hail, harper of the cloud! When new-born day
> Peers o'er the mountain-tops I'll haste away
> To drink thy mellow music. Power is thine,
> Beloved minstrel, with thy melting hymn,
> Stole from the chimings of the cherubim,
> To raise my thoughts above earth's dusty line!

The poet was John Harris; for twenty years of his life a working Cornish miner. He solaced himself, during that time, and charmed his neighbours by the issue of "Lays from the Mine, the Moor, and the Mountain," "nearly all written under very unkindly outward circumstances, at times when he has been oppressed by domestic cares, and when his health and spirits have been crushed by the drudgery of toiling in one of the oldest and deepest mines in Cornwall." He himself in later life gives, in a letter to a literary friend, an interesting and instructive sketch of his early course. "The muses found me," he says, "at a very early age, even when I plodded, satchel in hand, to the thatched school-house on the edge of the common, to get my daily lessons from a one-legged country schoolmaster. This, and the Sabbath-school in the neighbourhood, were the only sources I had for an early education. But I was fond of books from a child, and often stole away from my play-fellows into some solitary place to read and meditate. The tales of my mother, as we sat around the evening fire, sometimes filled my young imagination with wondrous dreams. Born on the crest of the hill, amid the crags and storms, I grew up in love with Nature, and she became my chief teacher. When I was a boy, I used to write rhymes for my play-fellows on the clean side of cast-off labelled tea-papers which my mother had brought from the shop; then listen while they read them with rapt delight. At the age of nine I was taken off from school and put to work in the fields. At the age of twelve I was put in the mine to work on the surface; and, one year later, I descended into its dark depths to labour hard for my bread; and in the same mine I have been digging day and night to this day. Many of the pieces published in my first volume were originally written on the crown of my hat, as I sat in the twilight amid the heath-brakes of our Cornish hills. I always feel a pure inspiration in the open-air, and generally compose out of doors."

The poet claims for his verses merely "the humble merit of originality and simplicity." They are remarkable for original power and simple beauty. But they have what some would deem higher characteristics of true poetry. His imagination is fruitful in happy combinations and rare similes. His epithets, here and there, are richly suggestive, transparent treasuries of distinctive beauty, poetic microcosms. The poems show considerable native wealth of diction, and refined taste is not unfrequently manifest in the choice of words. When his descriptive powers venture on foreign ground, he may, at times, fall into inconsistency. Defective knowledge betrays him into descriptions not quite true to nature. In this, however, his genius may not be more at fault than that of the great master painters, who give us Scripture scenes so unlike the reality that a Biblical critic once spoke the truth severely when he said, "such painters are liars." Poets as well as painters should know those features of nature which they undertake to pourtray. But Harris on his native soil is true to life. His pictures of nature have a freshness about them almost as inspiring as that of the scenes themselves which first courted and called forth his native genius. "I am not a native of Cornwall," said a gentleman of taste to the poet, " but you have given the distinctive scenery of the county such a charm for me that I could wish myself a Cornishman." The poet always has a holy purpose. His lessons are often touching, and always pure. His home sympathies are very tender. The joys and sorrows of human life are sacred things to him; and he touches them with a feeling that gently draws responses from every heart which comes within the range of his influence. How charmingly his descriptive powers and the warm affections of his soul intermingle and brighten each other's beauty in the opening of his poem on "The Love of Home":—

> The earth is fair with fields of happiness,
> With bowers that blossom everlastingly,
> With gems that sparkle on and never fade,
> With streams that murmur sweeter and more sweet,
> With flowers that wither not from moon to moon,
> With gardens where the roses fill the year,
> Affections cling around them ivy-like,
> Entwining them for ever, till the hills
> And silent valleys dimly fade in death.
> Such is our birth-place garlanded with green,
> Fragrant with love-shoots of our early time,
> Gemmed with pure thoughts that glow through after-life,
> Songful amid the sunshine of the past
> And clinging to the memory evermore.

See yonder pilgrim with his hoary locks,
Sitting beside the streamlet in the vale,
Which glides from rock to rock exultingly.
Before him, in that altered arbour's shade,
Lie the rough ruins of his father's cot,
Prostrate among the climbing ivy leaves,
And the rank grass which withers where it grows.
Oh! how those granite blocks, untouched by art,
Are murmuring to him on this April morn;
There's not a scattered fragment in that pile
But has a tongue, a most enchanting tongue,
Which captivates him with its eloquence,
And binds him to the mossy primrose bank.
They tell him of his mother and his sire,
His sunny sisters, lovely as the light,
The dear companions of his childhood hours,
And all the painted landscapes of his life.

Why does the tear-drop, gushing from his eye,
Steal over his sad face so silently,
Until it drops into the silver brook,
Startling the timid trout that watches there?
Why does he ever and anon start up,
Snatching his staff, then sits him down again,
And gazing still is still unsatisfied?
Why does he come among the early flowers,
As now he comes and lingers here alone
Among the ruins of that rended nest,
As if he saw a white robed angel there?
This was that old man's birth-place. Four-score years
Have swiftly hurried o'er the pilgrim's head,
Leaving sad traces of decay behind.
But that pure principle which Nature gives,
And fosters in the breast of every one,
Burns on and on from youth to manhood's prime,
And smoulders not amid the snows of age.

His lyric vein, too, is sometimes, for beauty, like the serpentine adornments of his own "Kynance Cove," whose hollow caves

Are dashed with images of flowery hues;
And on the rocks, like beautiful psalm-leaves,
Are odes of music lovely as the light
Trilled by the sea-nymphs in their watery robes.

This might have been anticipated from his early expression of love for his lyre:—

Little music-breathing lyre!
Once again I touch thy wire;
Once again a song I raise,
Pensive warbler, in thy praise.

> On my father's broomy height,
> In life's morning clear and bright,
> 'Neath the craggy rocks, which lie
> With white faces to the sky,
> Lichened o'er with many a lay
> Of the old times passed away,
> Stony chroniclers outspread
> On my mountain's heathy head,—
> In their mystic shadows lone,
> First I heard thy plaintive tone;
> First my hands essayed to bring
> Music from thy trembling string,
> And my soul's mysterious fire
> Warmed to hear thee, little lyre!

One of his first lyrics was "To the First Violet," and it is one of his best. When presenting it to his friend the late Dr. George Smith, of Camborne, the doctor, who was more of an antiquary than a poet, said, "Try something else, John; everybody writes about violets." "That may be true," was the reply, "but everybody who has any power of his own will have his own violet, and his own way of making love to it." John took the doctor's advice, however, and tried something else, and never succeeded with more sweet effect than when he gives his lyrical recollections of home in "The Mother's Teaching":—

> Without, the angry elements
>   Were raging in their ire;
> Within, the mother spoke of Christ,
>   Beside the cheerful fire.
> Her little ones were sitting round,
>   To whom the world was new,
> Drawing the honey from her lips,
>   Like flow'rets drinking dew.
>
> She told how Christ a baby was
>   In Bethlehem of old;
> He came from heaven in human form;
>   So holy men have told.
> He came from heaven in human form,
>   His frame a human clod,
> He suffered, wept, and died below,
>   And then went back a God.
>
> The seed thus sown in early life
>   Was like the precious grain,
> When warmed by vernal suns, and cheered
>   By spring's refreshing rain.

> Dark days of weariness and cloud
> May often intervene;
> But then the little blade smiles forth,
> And then the ear is seen.
>
> The parting blast of years hath blown
> Upon this little band,
> And scattered them, like forest leaves,
> Around their fatherland.
> And that loved mother sleeps below,
> Beside the village fane;
> But, written on the earth and sky,
> Her loving words remain.
>
> Those lessons by the holy hearth
> Are travelling on and on,
> Although the voice which uttered them—
> That mother's voice—is gone.
> From age to age their course will be
> For evermore the same,
> Till children's children joy to bless
> That mother's sainted name.

"How solemn was the grandeur of old Carnbrae the last time I stood on her brow! It can never be forgotten," says a mountain rambler; "that wild, romantic scramble up among the scattered masses of granite which lay in heaps among the furze and heath; the venerable old fragment of a castle on the top; the curious piles of weather-beaten rocks, looking as if they had been familiar with the lights and shadows of the world's childhood; and the glorious prospect of hills, and plain, and sea which opened around one;—all contributed to give me a sense of enlargement and exhilaration, strangely associated with feelings of awe, which, I believe, I shall never entirely lose. I had a volume of Harris's poems with me, and, while sitting in one of the rock-basins on the summit of what has been called the Druid altar-stone, I enjoyed a most pleasant kind of inspiration under the charm of the poet's voice. I heard a step on the green turf, and, looking up from my book, there was an unmistakable type of the Keltish family, evidently a miner, with an intelligence and a shrewdness in his sallow face which quite disposed me to court his company a little. This was soon secured, for, with the natural inquisitiveness of the race in that province, there was a native polite readiness to communicate information to one who proved willing to receive it. He might be called a cultured man—in his own line of pursuit at least. As a matter of course I spoke about that which, at the first glance, seemed to be the most ancient thing about the hill, the old fragment of a castle perched on its eastern brow, looking down upon the parish church of Redruth in the deep valley.

"That castle is old enough," said I, "some parts of it, at all events, to defy the most deep-sighted inquirer into its origin. An old writer in King Edward the Fourth's time saw it, they tell me, and jotted in his note-book '*Turris Castelli Karnbree*.' But coins have been found to witness that Roman soldiers have entered it; and that long before Cæsar formed his plan for a visit to Britain, Keltish chieftains had commanded within the walls which their ancestors' workmen had reared. The foundations are primitive, beyond the earliest records of British art. And yet that castle is a thing of the present compared with the mysterious piles of rock that were venerable long ere the first British Islander made a foot-print on the hill. Perhaps no human eye ever saw any other prospect from Carnbrae than the miles of undulating landscape which we now see, stretching towards the sea. I have a notion, however, that at some period in the past this hill, and the others in a line with it, must have been granite island-peaks or headlands of the coast line."

"Well, I don't know about that," said my companion, "but I know something about the antiquity of the hill. You must look into its foundations to judge of its age. You see it is one of a line of granite hills running towards Camborne in a south-westerly direction. At the base of the line there are mines of sufficient depth and range to afford curious and interesting means of knowing something about the under-ground relations of the uplifted hills of granite to the more level deposits of "*Killas*," as we call it, or clay-slate, which lie northward between Carnbrae and the sea. If we may take the state of things beneath the more western valley, as indicating the relative position of the granite and the slate along the whole line of primitive hills, then it is found that the granite continues to dip below the surface at the same angle as the hill; that at the depth of several hundred fathoms it rises again so as to form smaller hills; and that then, from the summits of this lower range it sweeps down a second time into a much deeper valley; the clay-slate overlying all these undulations. The stratification of the slate as it appears upon the granite is horizontal, or nearly so. At the junction of the granite and the slate, the granite is sometimes jaggy, with the slate curiously fitting into it, and at other points the union is that of two hard and smooth surfaces pressed tightly together. Here and there the slate is somewhat softer at and near the line of contact; but in no case showing any indications of igneous action, either by the disturbance of the strata, or by difference of composition or colour. There is an apparent variation in the character of the granite as it is near or more distant from the point of junction. The nearer kind, which has been called transition granite, is comparatively loose, fragmentary, and affording no solid masses of any useful magnitude; the deeper rock upon which this is superimposed is compact, and capable of being worked for purposes of art. The metals are found either in the slate, in the neighbourhood of its junction with the granite, or in the transition granite; never, it would appear, in the lower and more compact beds of the primitive rock. Large, separate portions of granite are sometimes found in the midst of the clay-slate, without any dike connecting them with their kindred mass below; or any kind of fault which might account for their position. Appearances might dispose one to think that by some means they had been tumbled or rolled into the deposit of clay while it was submarine, and before it had taken its present indurated character and form. But who can tell? Perhaps, as you say, sir, Carnbrae and its neighbour hills might have been headlands once looking out upon the waters beneath which the strata of clay-slate were quietly settling into position. There may have been ages of deposition, and ages of settlement and induration; ages for the accumulation of metallic treasures, and periods of great upheaving; times of drainage, and seasons of vegetable spring and growth; until, where the waters had been, there was grass, wood, open field, copse, and slopes of heath and furze, covering a hidden world of mineral wealth. I wonder how long that wilderness rejoiced before a mortal foot invaded it! and how long had the old upraised ocean-bed covered its glittering stores before any primitive 'tinner' found a clue to its veins? You talk of antiquity, sir; here it is indeed? If you want real ancient grandeur, you must wander down about the foundations of Carnbrae. Those who talk about the antiquities up here on the hill may be silent before the man who can say, 'I went down to the bottoms of the mountains; the earth with her bars was about me for ever!'"

"Thank you, very much," said I to my intelligent miner, "but you remind me of what I was just now reading. Here are lines written by one who has gone down into the old depths you speak of. Let me read them to you:—

> "Hast ever seen a mine? Hast ever been
> Down in its fabled grottoes, wall'd with gems,
> And canopied with torrid mineral-belts,
> That blaze within the fiery orifice?
> Hast ever, by the glimmer of the lamp,
> Or the fast-waning taper, gone down, down,
> Towards the earth's dread centre, where wise men
> Have told us that the earthquake is conceived,
> And great Vesuvius hath his lava-house,
> Which burns and burns for ever, shooting forth
> As from a fountain of eternal fire?
> Hast ever heard within this prison-house
> The startling hoof of fear? the eternal flow
> Of some dread meaning whispering to thy soul?
> Hast ever seen the miner at his toil,
> Following his obscure work below, below,
> Where not a single sun-ray visits him,
> But all is darkness and perpetual night?
> Here the dull god of gloom, unrivall'd, reigns,
> And wraps himself in palls of pitchy dark!
> Hast ever breathed its sickening atmosphere?
> Heard its dread throbbings, when the rock has burst?
> Leaped at its heavings in the powder blast?

> And trembled when the groaning, splitting earth,
> Mass after mass, fell down with deadliest crash?
> What sayest thou?—thou hast not?—come with me;
> Or if thou hast, no matter, come again.
> Don't fear to trust me; for I have been there
> From morn till night, from night till dewy morn,
> Gasping within its burning sulphur-cloud,
> Straining mine eyes along its ragged walls,
> And wondering at the uncouth passages
> Dash'd in the sparry cells by Fancy's wand;
> And oft have paused, and paused again, to hear
> Th' eternal echo of its emptiness."

"I remember the lines," said the stranger, "they are from John Harris's poem on 'Christian Heroism.'"

"Do you know Harris?" I inquired.

"Oh, yes; I was in the same mine with him—Dolcoath; it is one of that cluster that you see yonder towards Camborne. John worked in that mine for twenty years; making poetry all the while. Times were bad with him now and then; but I suppose, like some others, even when things were at the worst, he could thank God, as he says, for

> "The springs of hope
> Which bubble up among the mounds of care

"I was glad, and I believe 'one and all' were, when we heard that our old comrade, a brave 'Cornish boy,' had carried off the prize for his poem on the Anniversary of Shakespeare's Birthday; though there were so many competitors from England and America. I sent up a hurrah for our Cornish poet, who once sang—

> "Bathed in the ruddy light,
> Flooding his native height,
> A youthful bard is stretched upon the moss;
> He heedeth not the eve,
> Whose locks the elfins weave,
> Entranced with Shakespeare near a Cornish cross."

"I left the stranger on the top of Carnbrae; but have not lost the tones of his voice, nor the charm of the lessons which he impressed upon my mind and heart."

In a sequestered valley among our poet's native hills, shadowed by the leafage of a romantic churchyard at the base of a rugged carn, there is an old thatched cottage with its thick mud walls carefully whitened on the outside, and kept beautifully fresh within. It is a miner's home. There husband, wife, and nine children, healthy, cheerful, and devout, have spent days of labour and enjoyed their evening repose. The good man came down the valley towards his home with a friend one winter's night. They had been joining their valley and hill-side neighbours at evening service in the little sanctuary at the vale-head. And as they walked, they talked about Providence, how finely it keeps in tune with saving grace.

"What are the average gettings at the mine now?" it was inquired.

"Well, on an average about three pound, or three pound ten, a month."

"That is small, compared with the wages of coal-miners, and spinners, and weavers, in the North. Some of them get as much in a week as you do in a month, yet they and their families are, many of them, scarcely fit to be seen, Sundays or Mondays, indoors or out, and are never contented; while you appear to be happy, to live decently at home, and to dress well—on Sundays, at least. How is it?"

"I suppose it is because we are thrifty, content with wholesome food, and decent clothes. But I believe the great secret is that we have learnt to love God, and to let Him manage for us, while we try to serve Him. A few years ago, some of our men were tempted to go to South America, for the sake of getting a little fortune, as they said. They wanted me to go with them; but I began to think whether it was right to risk my life, to leave my wife, and, above all, to risk my soul, by leaving my native land, with all its religious advantages, to go to a country full of temptations, and with no helps to piety, all for gold. I prayed often about it, and reasoned the matter before God. And I believe I was helped to make up my mind by a blessed little hymn that was made by John Harris, who used to work at Dolcoath, a miner like myself, and knowing by experience the trials of a miner.

"Do you know the hymn?"

"I think I can recollect some of it, if not all, now":—

> "I ask Thy heavenly guidance
> In all things here below;
> Do Thou direct my footsteps
> The way that I should go.
> Oh, teach my heart submission,
> Whate'er my lot may be,
> Contented that my Father
> Should ever choose for me!
>
> With Thee I do not falter,
> To walk the dim unknown:
> The yet untrodden future
> Is in Thy hands alone;
> And be it sun or shadow,
> Rough waves or smiling sea,
> A garden or a desert,
> The Lord shall choose for me.
>
> If up the stony mountain
> My painful pathway lie,
> Or through the darksome valley,
> I dare not question why.
> The fields may lose their verdure,
> And leafless rise the tree;
> All things are ordered wisely—
> The Lord shall choose for me.
>
> If in deep shades I wander,
> Where clouds obscure the sun,
> And flow no streams of comfort,
> Thy perfect will be done.
> What now appeareth dimly,
> I soon shall fully see,
> When God's own glory shineth—
> The Lord shall choose for me.
>
> And when the cord of silver
> At last shall loose its hold,
> And in the strife is broken
> The mystic bowl of gold;
> When loving friends are watching,
> And earthly shadows flee,
> As heaven's first beams are breaking,
> The Lord shall choose for me.

"I used to go about humming to myself, now one verse and then another, till at last I made up my mind to abide in the house of the Lord at home, and trust Him who had always so far provided for me and mine. My comrades went; and it happened to them as I feared it might to me, if I had gone. They made their fortunes, as people say, but they lost their souls. I went on very well for a time, till things seemed to take a bad turn with me. I was on 'tribute'—you know what that is—it is taking certain ground to break, on speculation. If ore is found, our percentage may be a little fortune; but if no ore, no pay. As I say, everything failed with me; and then I was tempted to reflect upon myself for stopping home. But the Lord knew my motive, and I cried to Him in my distress. I had a rising family, and nothing for them. I cried for help; and one day, it seemed as if a voice said, 'you know such and such a ground at the mine, go and offer to take it.' Well, I went, and took it; and soon cut into a rich bit, and got enough in a month to put me into comfortable circumstances. Not that I was rich, except in Christ; but I have brought up my nine children, gave them decent schooling, and taught them to get an honest living. To this day, I have never wanted bread on my table, a fire on my hearth, or the blessing of a happy, contented home. Thank God!"

"Thank God!" responded the miner's companion, who also remembered some of John Harris's lines, and repeated them, to illustrate his happy friend's condition and experience:—

> "Who hastes to heap up gold shall find
> A heavier burden on his mind;
> But happy he who is content
> With what the hand of Heaven has sent.
>
> Contentment is the loveliest lot;
> She dwelleth oft in lowly cot
> With him who is of humble mind,
> And leaves the palace far behind.
>
> Of all the nymphs in virtue's train
> That haunt the wood, or hill, or plain,
> However low my lot may be,
> Oh, may contentment dwell with me!

"I should like to see thy birth-place, John Harris," said a lady to the poet; "wilt thou be my guide to it?"

The lady, as her mode of address tells, belonged to the "Society of Friends." And there was a cheerful, comfortable something about her face, form, and manner, which served much to adorn and recommend her style of religious life. John was too delicately sensitive to the charms of such companionship to hesitate for one moment. The journey was arranged, and away they went over the hills. But, alas, for the lady! the last half mile was unapproachable by wheels, and not to be touched by horse's feet. The lady and the poet, who now took the lead, had to foot it up the side of the cairn, on the wild brow of which the poet began his life. They followed one the other up "Stoney Lane," over granite splinters, pebbles, and small boulders, between hedges rich, to the poet's eyes, with golden furze, and violets, and young unfolding ferns, until, coming to the open downs, their turfy path led through the furze to what appeared to be the last human dwelling in creation. It was an interesting picture, that of the peaceful Quaker woman and the author of "Peace Poems," keeping one another in peaceful countenance as they toiled up the hill in the fretting heat, by speculations on the effect of John Harris's peace lyrics on the disposition of a pugnatious world. Even a Quaker might feel his blood stirring as the poet would give vivid reality to the passage of the "War Fiend":—

> On sweeps the War-fiend, on his car of flame,
> By hungry coursers drawn, whose iron teeth,
> Gnash in their fury for a human meal.
> On sweeps the War-fiend, shaking his hot brand,
> With red hair streaming in the sulphur blast,
> And visage dark with blood! On sweeps the fiend,
> Pushing o'er vineyards trampled in the dust,
> O'er palaces and peasant homes in tears;
> O'er widows, wailing for their husband's slain ·
> O'er children, weeping for their murder'd sires;
> O'er friend, left friendless in a world of foes;
> O'er sobbing households, ruined, rent, and riven;
> O'er lover, prostrate on the field of death;
> O'er maiden weeping for that lover there;
> O'er hamlets drenched in blood, o'er towns destroyed,
> O'er cities soaked and burnt to wretchedness;
> O'er plains with corses strewn, or white with bones;

O'er countries saturate with human gore,
Where shrieked the cormorant his doleful note;
O'er kingdoms shaken with the thunder-blast,
Ploughed up with ruthless bullets, where the sky
Was hung in clouds of darkest drapery.
On sweeps the War-fiend on his maddening march,
With his stern train of smiting followers,
That stab, and shoot, and chop, and rip, and pierce,
And murder in broad day.   Earth groaned and writhed
Beneath the huge calamity it bore!

The only house on the brow of the hill was a modern one, bare and cold—the house of a miner, with a family of seven children, living, or trying to live, upon forty shillings a month. The old straw-thatched, boulder-built cottage, with bare rafters and clay floor, locally known as the "Six Chimneys," was gone, all excepting the foundations, and here and there a few feet of wall. The view from the old court was wide and wild. There were furzy and moorland valleys, and some of the most bare and bleak hills of the granite district: Carnbrae on the one side, and on the other the breezy mountain undulations, over which lay the high road to Helston. The scene was inspiriting, with all its weird loneliness. Nature, however, seemed to do honour to the poet, who had so honoured her. The primroses clustered by joyful crowds in the old deserted garden, as if they would adorn and perfume the memory of him who had so lovingly sung to the first, for the season, that had smiled on him:—

Joy to thine opening eye,
  Thou little lonely flower!
The first that cometh blossoming
  Within my English bower.
A thousand griefs are past,
  A thousand tears are shed,
Since on this bank I saw thee last
  Lift up thy yellow head.

Hail to thy timid glance!
  And to thy perfume, hail
And, though the north storm may advance,
  Oh! do not look so pale;
But bloom and blossom on
  Within thy mossy bower,
Till Winter and his storms are gone,
  Thou little trembling flower!

Thou bringest songs of birds,
    And many a pleasing spell—
The violet-haunts among the elms—
    We know them passing well.
A thousand other tales
    In thee the poet reads,
Thy sisters clustering in our vales,
    And sparkling in our meads!

Then bloom and blossom on,
    And gem our wither'd isle,
Till Winter and his storms are gone,
    And tender sunbeams smile;
When flowers of every hue
    Shall thy companions be,
And millions in my fatherland
    Look up and smile like thee!

And under one of the rude boulders which had guarded that cottage hearth there was a bright clump of violets in purest bloom, looking as if they were proud of decorating the nook once enjoyed by him who gave tuneful welcome to "The First Violet":—

    Hail to thee, little flower,
    Within thy own dear bower,
Smiling among the wiry broom,
Like Hope's bright star and clouds of gloom!
I bend me o'er thy sweet blue eye,
Dropping salt tears, I know not why,
Feeling a warm inspiring fire,
Sweeping my fingers o'er my lyre,
Singing within my heathy bower—
Hail, hail to thee, Spring's early flower!

    Yes, thou art come to dwell
    With Memory in her cell—
To call her from her still retreat,
And place Remembrance at her feet.
Though thou art gilt with vernal bloom,
Thou tellest of the dark, deep tomb;
Thou tellest of the wide blue sea,
Where waves and storms are wont to be,
And where, upon its boundless tide,
Far, far away, my kindred ride.
Because they hasten from my bower,
Hail, hail to thee, Spring's early flower!

    Oh! could they hear the lark,
    Singing till it is dark,
Fluttering his wings those meads above,
And warbling forth his notes of love

And could they, in our meadows bound,
Gaze on those cowslips scatter'd round,
See all those daisies on the plain,
They surely would come back again,
To feast their eyes within my bower
Upon my little violet flower!

What were the words I said?
Thou speakest of the dead?
Ah, yes! thou tellest of decay,
How earthly splendours pass away!
An hour or two—come smile on me,
And I shall bid farewell to thee.
Here birds will sing, and flowers will bloom,
When I am hidden in the tomb.
But I would sleep with thee, sweet flower,
Companions in my mountain bower.

And oft my ghost shall roam
Around my native home,
And here, beneath the wan moon's light,
Weave garlands for the brow of Night.
Blue herald of a numerous line,
Stamp'd with the mighty Maker's sign,
The impress of the Hand Divine;
Blending, thou seem'st to kiss the sod—
Who sees thee sees a ray of God!
Because He shines within my bower,
Hail, hail to thee, Spring's early flower!

It was pleasant to sit on the brow of that hill, amid the ruins of the old cottage home, and awaken in the soul the music of the verse which was inspired there:—

Hail to thee, mountain birth-place! Not a rock,
O'er-written with the stanzas of the storm;
And many rocks are shooting from thy crown,
And hanging from thy girdle—not a rock
On which my sire and grandsire oft have stood,
And where I've climbed in childhood's cheerful spring,
Gazing into the deep blue summer sky,
And smiled to see the earth so beautiful—
No, not a rock around my native place,
But what I love, as if akin to me!
There's not a hedge-row, gemmed with ivy-leaves,
There's not a floweret in my father's lea,
There's not a sofa, with its seat of sod,
Where the tired pilgrim sits in Nature's hall,
And gazes on the portraits of the past;
There's not a moss-bower in the dear old *croft*,

> Where the young muses wooed the singing boy,
> To list at evening to the harping breeze;
> There's not a wild cave where the tempests roar,
> Rolling their bass blasts round the fire-scathed rocks;
> There's not a flaw upon its furrow'd front,
> But seems even now a portion of my life!

To look around, however, upon that scene, as it first enters the eye of a rambler, and then to look at it in the light which the poet's genius casts upon it, is to be strongly disposed to the doctrine that the beauty and the grandeur, the interest and the lovableness of nature are rather in the soul of the beholder; or that a poet's imagination is creative, and has power for ever to invest with charms that for which common observers have little or no natural taste.

"If this scenery is so delightfully inspiring to thee," said Harris's Quaker companion, "what will the lovely neighbourhood of Falmouth be?"

Ah! good lady; Falmouth, with all its beauty of surroundings, though now to be his abode, can never have an inspiring power for our bard equal to that of his own native, dear old Bolennowe Hill, and its kindred cairns!

"One of the most touching episodes in the life of John Harris was his first reading Campbell's *Gertrude of Wyoming*. He had selected it from the library in the village school, and, pocketing the prize, hastened to a secluded place, where he might peruse it in quiet. "Here," he says, "I threw myself down, and drew the book from my pocket. At my feet a clear stream went wandering on its way; birds sang on the branches of the trees over my head; sweet flowers shed a delicious fragrance around; bees hummed, and butterflies floated among the honeyed cups; while before me, as through a silver vista, rose the sun-lighted hills of the Land's End, and the blue waters of the Atlantic Ocean."

Among his noblest effusions, is the poem on the "Land's End;" and in that characteristic utterance, he has finely associated the wild grandeurs of the old headland with the cherished legendary lore of the old Cornish folk:—

Haunt of the sea-bird, city of the crag,
Kingdom of granite, gallery of the muse,
Poem of wonders, page for poet's eye;
Storm-brewing chamber, whence the winds are loosed,
That crack and tumble through the universe,
Nature's great organ-hall, where blasts of song
Shiver among her mossy-mantled priests,
And swell across the mountains and the vales,
Thundering at storm-time, murmuring in the calm,
Flowing at day-dawn, rumbling through the dark,
And crashing 'mid the music of the main ;
Stirring the soul's depth like a lofty psalm ;
When, standing here with nature and with God,
How thy full chorus lifts the wanderer !

The Cornish streamer was a rare old man :
Strange stories by the firelight he would tell,
When angry winds went roaring round the rocks,
And not a star looked down upon the snow.
His audience were the petted girl and boy,
And on the oak-stock's end the favourite cat.
Strange stories, bordering on the marvellous:
How once these valleys were brimfull of tin,
Before King Solomon's great fane was built ;
When Jews did smelt within these curious coves ;
And oft a streamer's fortune had been made
By stumbling on a Jew's house wonderful;
Of giant's living in those mighty rocks,
With heaps of pearl, and waggon-loads of gold ;
Of shining creatures coming from the sea,
And making poor men richer far than kings ;
Of horses running swifter than the winds,
And bearing fury comets on their backs ;
Of little pixies, wearing small red cloaks,
And nightly riding timid wights to death ;
Of wizards changing brands to silver bars ;
Of fiery dragons rolling through the air,
Uprising from old Cornwall's copper-caves;
And one dark evening, when the winds were high,
And the fierce lightnings hissed across his shed,
And thunder rumbled up the steep Land's End,
He filled his pipe, and told some cheerful tales.

A passing visit to the poet's widowed mother, who was calmly waiting for her summons to paradise, in a village not far from her son's birth-place, can never be forgotten. The old woman, more than three score years and ten, still retained in her person enough to show that her son John had inherited from her his most marked and expressive features.

She was evidently a woman used to deep communings with herself and the spiritual world. Her voice, while she quietly rejoiced in hope of her heavenly rest, called up the touching verses of one of her son's sweetest lyrics:—

> My mother's voice! it haunts me when
>   I'm sitting in my cot,
> Surrounded with my little ones,
>   The sharers of my lot.
> Their voices chime like music-chords
>   Within my humble bower;
> But this is heard above them all,
>   In sunshine and in shower.
>
> I hear it when the midnight winds
>   Are rushing o'er my head,
> And busy thought drives sleep away
>   From visiting my bed.
> It comes on slumber's downy wings,
>   'Tis blended with my dreams,
> When wandering over unknown lands,
>   Among the crystal streams.
>
> I hear it when the storm is high,
>   And when the winds are still;
> I hear it in the shelter'd vale,
>   And on the storm-beat hill.
> Yes! floating o'er its rocks of heath,
>   That silvery voice I hear,
> Above the ruins of the past,
>   In cadence sweet and clear.
>
> I hear it in the busy throng;
>   I hear it when alone;
> I hear it in the darksome earth,
>   The same melodious tone.
> I hear it when my heart is sad,
>   And when my lips rejoice;
> It floats around me everywhere,
>   That same mysterious voice!
>
> It leads me back when life was new;
>   Tells of those happy hours
> I passed in childhood's sunny vale,
>   Among the opening flowers;
> Brings back again my early home,
>   That home of homes to me,
> Engraven on my heart of hearts,
>   For ever there to be!

> The music of this voice I hear
>   Above the world's rough roar,
> Like whispers from another sphere,
>   Some calm Elysian shore;
> Sweet harp-notes from the lyre of Time,
>   Around me and within;
> They gush with conqu'ring ecstacy,
>   To lure my soul from sin.
>
> I hear it in the moonlight bower,
>   And by the murmuring stream!
> I hear it when spring's earliest flower
>   Smiles in the sun's glad beam.
> In weal, or woe, where'er I be
>   On this revolving sphere,
> Above the thunderings of the world,
>   My mother's voice I hear!

That voice, perhaps, is now hushed—heard no more on earth, except by the poet's own soul's ear. Other voices still live to cheer his home. That home has comforts more befitting his later life than those afforded by the cottage of his boyhood. When his early inspirations came upon him, he " sometimes found himself without pencil or ink; but he was not to be deterred by such a difficulty. Not he, indeed! Were there not blackberries growing on the hedges which lined the mountain-road leading to the mine? John found that blackberry-juice furnished a cheap and ready substitute for ink, and more than one of his idylls was written with the homely and unusual fluid. But his real trials came from the frosts of winter. Then he would sit down in his bed-room, his feet wrapped in his mother's woollen cloak, his writing-desk being a small pair of bellows." Now, however, pen, ink, and desk, are within comfortable reach; and his dwelling is garnished, as a poet's home should be, with the best poetical literature of his country.

CHAPTER XXI.

A KENTISH LYRIC.

He looks abroad into the varied field
Of Nature; and though poor, perhaps, compared
With those whose mansions glitter in his sight
Calls the delightful scenery all his own.

"THIS is Mountfield," said the driver of our comfortable little open carriage, in which for a few miles we had been enjoying the lively pleasures which belong to communion with new scenes in nature. "This is the house," said he, as he drove through the gateway on the road-side. It was in Kent —old Kent, as we had always called it, because it was old enough to have a remarkable history. But now it appeared with as bright and fresh a complexion, and turned upon us a smile as sweet and winsome, as if no years had passed since the Creator first saw its ripeness of youth unveiled. The country was new to us. Our road lay, now through open fields, and now amidst shadowy foliage, fruit plantations, or hop-grounds, or orchards. Everything was giving early and beautiful promise of fruitful life. The hops were putting forth their young vigour, and were already tinging the vineyard-like slopes with green. Many hands were busily employed in tying up the young plants so as to sustain their upward growth; while they seemed as if they were giving us wayside lessons on the importance and necessity of early training and timely aid to young minds in the spring-tide of their life. How many a young plant has failed to rise into fruitful maturity for lack of seasonable help amidst the exposures and weaknesses of its early springing? Happy is the young spirit which submissively allows itself to be gently trained to dependence on Divine strength!

But we were on our way to Boughton, and were on the look out for Mountfield, the home of one whose "Kentish Lyrics" had often given means of expressing our sympathy with nature. We drove up at length before a comfortable-looking villa, built in old English style, and surrounded by sheltering beauties of wood, shrubberies, and flower borders. It was a lovely retreat—a fitting home for a poet. Our mind and heart already claimed an interest in those whom we hoped to meet there. There are some human spirits whose presence seems to hallow the spots on which they breathe; some action of their life, some blessed words from their lips, some ever-living lines from their pens, shed a sacred light upon their country, their birth-place, their dwelling. This was the dwelling of one whom we had learnt to love for the sweet, natural music of his songs; and now we had a curious, indefinable feeling, which, in the anticipation of a first interview, inspired the question, "Will his person answer to our first idea of one whose poetic utterances have been so pleasant to us?" The greeting came. Our previous conceptions were more than realized. It was a calm joy to see Benjamin Gough amidst his own "woodlands:" the agreeably set figure, the well-borne compact head, with its tingings of silver; the good-humoured, thoroughly English face; the eye-sparkle of genius, the play of passing thought over the harmonious features,—all were in happy keeping with the gentle inner circle of his home, and its outward surroundings. What we had enjoyed in our author's Lyrics seemed now to touch us with more lively sweetness, and to come pleasantly upon the heart, as if reflected from everything which distinguished the abode of benevolence, taste, fine feeling, and piety. Who could wonder at the poet of Mountfield sometimes hearing "angel whispers" amidst the quiet scenes of his life, and singing of "angel visits"? How all things are hushed around us, and how still the inner world becomes, while he sings,—

Have you heard an angel's whisper,
  Or the cadence of a hymn,
Sung by a voice celestial,
  Some radiant cherubim?
Once in the lonely woodland,
  Beneath the harvest moon,
Entranc'd, I knelt and listen'd,
  At midnight's solemn noon.

The earth lay round me sleeping
  In undisturb'd repose,
And zephyrs stay'd their breathing,
  And not a sound arose;
The nightingale's sweet trillings
  Of melody had gushed
Upon my ravished ear, but now
  Her warbling voice was hushed.

It was the reign of silence,
  The aspen-leaves were still,
And motionless as death,
  While stars, at their sweet will,
Look'd down in radiance loving;
  So did the full round moon,
While all my thoughts rose heav'nwards
  At that calm midnight moon.

A gentle voice spoke softly,
  In words of peace and love,
Of higher, nobler being
  Awaiting us above;
Of dear ones with the angels,
  Who once were here below,
Waiting till we rejoin them,
  And their high glory know.

Of heaven, where knowledge knoweth,
  And the mind's comprehension
Expands for ever, grasping
  Unlimited extension;
Where God, and life eternal,
  And purity, and joy,
Fill the immortal spirit
  With bliss without alloy.

Then came such strains of melody,
  Ethereal on my ears,
As evermore is echoing
  Along those happy spheres.
Surely the song of angels
  That summer night I heard,
And my inmost soul adoring
  With those high hymns was stirr'd.

> Was it a dream? so holy
>   That night was every thought,
> That woodland was a sacred place,
>   With heavenly blessing fraught.
> And still those angel whispers,
>   And the cadence of those songs,
> Heard on that summer midnight,
>   My memory prolongs.

The tone of these verses calls up recollections of our rambles through the hop-gardens to and from the house of prayer in Boughton. It was while we talked by the way to and from the religious services which we enjoyed together for a time in that sequestered but cheery little town among orchards and gardens, that the poet's religious character was felt to be one which exemplified what has always appeared to us as blessedly possible—the consistent combination of holy delight in "the things which are seen" with pure enjoyment of "the things which are not seen." To our Methodist poet, Creation and Providence and Grace were as one. His tender sympathies and intercourse with nature seemed to be ever sweetly passing into loving converse with inspired truth and "communion of the Holy Ghost." In this the Kentish singer is something like the Psalmist of higher inspiration. David opens one of his sublime hymns (Psalm xix.) with rapturous admiration of the glories of the firmament, the harmonies of day and night, the order and beauty of fixed and revolving worlds, and then passes, without any conscious break of thought, or without apparently interrupting his current of feeling, to the converting power, the teaching wisdom, the enlightening and consoling virtues of God's revealed law. To the Divine psalmist there is the same law above and within. The lesser and greater beauty, the lesser and greater order, the lesser and greater law are all one. The worlds above and the kingdom within bear the same Divine impress; and

> The voice that rolls the stars along
> Speaks all the promises.

In habitually devout recognition of this oneness of God's

government, this unity of Divine law, our poetic friend sometimes shows himself ready, too, to catch the spirit of the old prophetic bard, who so finely indicates the essential connection between the principles on which the great Ruler deals with sinful men and the laws by which He controls material powers; showing that God's manifestations of Himself in the sublime and more awful transactions of nature are not only symbolic of His retributive and corrective administrations among moral agents, but that they are designedly made to take their part in the accomplishment of His moral and saving purposes respecting man. Not only, as David says, are the laws of natural beauty and order one with the published laws of His word, but, as Nahum declares (ch. i. v. 3), His rules for nature's more terrible operations belong to the code of His gracious discipline for human character and life. "The Lord is slow to anger, and great in power, and will not at all acquit the wicked; the Lord hath his way in the whirlwind, and in the storm, and the clouds are the dust of his feet." So our poet sings, as the prophet's paraphrast, with a voice of mingling force and beauty:—

    Oh! wind, terrible wind!
Whence comest thou?—stop and say;
And whither art thou bound to day?
What dost thou mean by that furious shriek,
Like the panther's howl or hyena's yell,
  In some lone jungle where lions wreak
Their wrath, and ring the traveller's knell?

Moaning and groaning like dark sprites intoning
  Horrible dirges for souls that are lost,
Whirling and swirling—new terrors unfurling,
Now with a roar—as a thunder-clap loud.
    The heavens are bowed, by the tempest tost,
      And a black cloud
Spreads o'er the earth like a funeral shroud.

    Oh! wind, terrible wind!
Ethereal express, at high-pressure speed,
  Cyclone—hurricane—gale, all in one!
Rushing on and on, without fear or heed,
  Till thy vengeful work is done.

A KENTISH LYRIC.

      Oh! wind, terrible wind!
Sweeping like lightning on thy path,
Over earth, over sea, with the sword of wrath;
Who can image thy shape, or picture thy form,
Riding upon the wings of the storm?
Raising the ocean surge—riving the rocks—
Chanting thy bass to the thunder's shocks;
With cheeks distended, and wild, fiery eyes,
Piercing the murk of the wintry skies,
Girded with strength, and belted with might,
Rapid as shooting-stars in flight—
      Oh! wind, terrible wind!
Great is thy power, and none may stay,
Or hold thee back on thy stormy way!

      Oh! wind, terrible wind!
Before thee the woodland trees are rent,
   And the gnarly trunks of the ancient oaks
     Are twisted and bent.
The woodman strikes full a thousand strokes
   Ere the forest tree is fell'd,
But the old giant Wind, when he comes for loot,
Grasps the tree and tears it up by the root
   Before his fury is quell'd.
Down to the sea-side follow his track,
And see maiming and slaughter, grim and black,
Mountainous waves, cresty with foam,
Shipwreck and death on the threshold of home;
Signals outflashing, vessels down-crashing,
One on other tost—both to be lost.
Flags of distress—crews upon decks,
The bleak shore strewn with corpses and wrecks—
Oh! wind, put back thy sword to its sheath,
To-night thou hast reap'd a harvest of death!

      Oh! wind, terrible wind!
I would not misjudge thee as though thou hadst sinn'd;
No tyrant art thou, nor despot uncheck'd,
Though forests are fell'd, and navies are wreck'd;
The evil, by men long misunderstood,
He only can turn into infinite good,
    Who doth as He lists,
And holdeth the turbulent winds in His fists.

      Oh! wind, terrible wind!
Trembling I own
Thy voice divine!
God's high behest is thine.
   His will be done!
The zephyr cannot wander through the trees,
Or whisper in the summer breeze,

>   Apart from God.
>   Storms prelude calms;
> And oft the chastening rod
>   Attunes for blessed psalms.
>   So, wind, terrible wind!
>   I will not fear thee more or deem thee wrong.
>   But bow in reverence meet, and find
>   Sweet solace in submission's humblest song.

The taste of our songster is distinctively rural. Nor could such a taste ever be indulged and cultured in more congenial surroundings than those which engirdled the rural songster's home. His characteristic strain of song seemed to be as much the natural music of his chosen retreat as was that of the nightingale which nestled and warbled familiarly by his chamber-window, as if it knew him to be a fellow native of its own choral class. Within comfortable distance of the hop-grounds, orchards, fruit-gardens, and meadow-slopes which immediately surrounded our good poet's home, there was a verdant hill country, in whose leafy retirements we once enjoyed a most delicious ramble with the intelligent, tasteful, and fine spirited members of the Mountfield family.

It was a bright morning. We were a lightsome party, snugly packed in a lightsome open carriage—not a gig, either single or double; nor a barouche; nor a landau; nor a waggonette;—but something that combined all the advantages of all these, without being exactly like either. It is enough to say that it was a Kentish conveyance—on springs, of course. We were the friends and guests of a Methodist psalmist, and might be called a Methodist party. Nevertheless, we were merry; though as yet we had not begun to act on the advice of that inspired man, whose voice sometimes gave out sounds of rich poetic grace, amidst his deep-toned prophet-like utterances. "Is any merry?" said he, "let him sing psalms." Hitherto, however, all our "psalms and hymns and spiritual songs" had been sung within ourselves; and the inward music gave no outward sign, except in cheerful faces, quiet laughs, and happy glances. Some of those who witnessed our starting might have thought, as a fish-wife once did, when she saw a Methodist band of choristers getting into a barge for the purpose of floating up a beautiful river that they might enjoy the music of Handel's choruses among the pensive echoing woods. The good woman expressed her wonderment, as the barge moved off, by exclaiming, "Well, I declare! the Methodists are going to enjoy themselves!" Yes, my good dame! And why not? No people have more right to enjoy themselves than real Methodists; for real Methodists know that genuine Christianity is the happy religion. At all events, we were happy enough in our carriage on our way to the woods. We kept up our gaiety until we reached the top of a hill on the road to Canterbury. Indeed, we might have been taken for Canterbury pilgrims. There had been side-long chat, pleasant bits of word-play; now a story or a tale, and then a scrap from an elect poet to illustrate some passing thought or expressed sentiment. Could the spirit of Chaucer have seen us, or listened to our tangled talk, he might have felt that it is possible for pilgrims to beguile their way in a manner as pleasant as his, but harmless. Our fresh morning joys were damped a little as we reached the summit of the hill, where we were to leave our carriage, and strike into the copse for a woodland ramble. Just then a storm-cloud came rolling down, and we were in danger of being drenched. A neighbouring dwelling, however, furnished the ladies with wrappers, and an enormous gig-umbrella was lent, which might have served to canopy the out-door throne of an eastern despot. Thus equipped, we passed through the shower, and pursued our way among the freshened woods. Our gigantic parachute was now closed, and served either as a pilgrim's staff, or was borne aloft in the style of a furled banner. We were merry again. Our path led us along copsy hill-sides, or

> Down into hollows, where the running brook
> Warbles old tunes from nature's service-book,
> Where, 'midst the willows and the wild-wood flowers,
> The birds are in their bowers.

Or through bending valleys, where scattered cottages looked happy amidst their leafy shelter, with every nook and corner of ground around them made to pay tribute to the table of the rustic household, or to regale their senses with the simple beauty, rich colouring, or delicate perfume of dear old English flowers. We were all happily alive amidst the peaceful life of nature; every ear was open to its whispers, every soul tenderly responsive to its touches. One was soon in enthusiastic pursuit of botanical favourites, another was distinguishing the different air-tones in different leafage, or listening to

> A hallelujah chorus on the trees;

and another quietly enjoying variations of bird-music. By-and-by a shady dell invited us down to emulate each other in pursuit of fern treasures. At length we seemed to hear our poet's voice of challenge:—

> Come, climb with me this hill-side; on the top
> You'll gain a glorious view of land and sea,
> Thousands of acres waving with their crop
> Of ripening corn. The sweet variety
> Of fields and foliage, all in summer sheen,
> And pastures dotted o'er with flocks of sheep
> And herds of cattle. What a lovely scene
> Opens before us! See the river creep
> In silence, like a silvery line of light,
> To where the ships lie in yon ocean bay,
> And the wide world of water is in sight.
> Oh, broad expanse of land! Oh, wondrous sea!
> Here will we sing, O Lord, a psalm of praise to Thee.

All were agreed to reach the summit of a rounded hill which, crowned with clumps of pine, overtopped its neighbours, and looked out over a rich expansion of landscape. There was the old-storied sea-board of Kent. There was the sea, the North Sea, seemingly at rest, still smiling after so many generations of friends and foes had come and gone. There were the strange minglings of land and water which appeared to offer mysterious guardianship to the most populous city of Europe; and there were the rich undulating lands where the first Teuton settlers laid the groundwork of English greatness. Immediately beneath and around, there were the tranquil scenes which were so congenial to the distinctive taste of our poetic friend, and among which he had been used to catch his happiest inspirations. We passed through some of these on our way home. There were successive unfoldings of exquisitely-finished natural pictures of rural life; and these furnished us with themes for pleasant interchanges of thought and feeling when we were once more seated under the poet's roof. The recollections of that day's enjoyable stroll continue to live, and have been made more certainly permanent by him with whose character and gifts they were first associated; for, in response to our subsequent allusions to those charming scenes of Kentish rural life, Mr. Gough's genius and taste pictured for us "A Rural Sketch":—

> Here is a pleasant nook,
> A beautiful recess of country life,
> Sequestered and alone,
> But exquisite in charms unknown.
> Few see it; but on all who look
> It leaves an impress which no after-strife,
> Or wear and tear of travel, can erase,
> While memory holds its place.
>
> A rural homestead, with a field in front,
> Where cows are grazing, and a flock of sheep,
> In rumination or asleep,
> Lie in the shade of an ancestral oak,
> Which for long centuries has borne the brunt
> Of blast and storm, surviving every stroke,
> And smiling now in foliage green and young,
> As when stern Cromwell ruled, and Milton sung.
>
> Then on the greensward, by the cottage door,
> Sweet children gambol, and their merry laugh
> Has nature's truest ring for evermore.
> Yon ancient grandsire, leaning on his staff,
> Watches their sports, and thinks of days of yore,
> When *he* tripped lightly on the self-same green;
> But now he is fourscore,
> In healthful age serene.
> The watch-dog follows, barking as he goes,
> But every utterance chimes with the delight
> Of happy children, as it flows
> Like sunshine, warm and bright.

A flight of pigeons, fluttering to and fro,
Add to the rural scene;
And a pure streamlet, in its crystal flow,
Runs on where bending willows grow
In double ranks, and sings between.

Beside the farm-yard gate old Dobbin stands,
While from the topmost rail
The cock's shrill clarion sounds afar
Athwart the wooded vale,
Answered from neighbour lands.

The cheery sparrows chirp along the eaves,
And swallows twitter on the chimney-top;
A summer rustle is among the leaves,
And snowy blossoms from the hawthorn drop.
The garden smiles beyond with common flowers,
Where pinks and roses hold their rival sway;
Here flames a tall laburnum, golden, gay;
And there an odorous jessamine embowers
A summer-house; while up the thatch and o'er,
An ivy creeps, and round the window clings;
While, in a wicker cage above the door,
A blackbird sings.

Oh, happy nook! Oh, beautiful retreat!
Screen'd from the wintry storm and summer's heat,
Where peace and plenty always are at home,
As generations go and come.
Strangers to fashion, and the dreams of wealth,
Childhood and age alike bring peace and health;
In virtue train'd, their peasant path is trod,
They read their Bible, and they love their God.
Their joys are blooming ever, and increase;
They live contented, and they die in peace.
Heroes may live in marble, misers old
Die midst their glittering piles, and grasp their gold;
But pure enjoyment, springing fresh and rife,
Hallows a cottage and a country life.

Mr. Gough might never have entertained the hope that the lyrics so happily expressive of his own joy amidst the gentle and quiet beauties of Kent would ever tell with sweet and refreshing power upon downcast spirits, amidst the wild and weird scenery of West Cornwall. Yet so it has been. A man and wife once sat pensively side by side at their family hearth at the close of a simple meal. They were silent, and their silence was plaintive. The woman felt that i had cost her some care and pains to furnish the meal which her husband had shared, and she knew that the difficulty was growing from day to day. She was disposed to hide from her companion, as long as she could, the cares that were gathering upon her heart; while her husband, on his part, wanted, if possible, to keep from her sight the shadows which seemed to be falling upon his soul from his darkening prospects. The wife at length broke the silence, by saying—

"We are in want of coal, my dear."

"Coal again!" was the reply. "I don't know what to do! Coal seems a necessity, but I have no means of getting a supply for more than a day or two. We cannot keep pace with advancing prices."

The appearance and position of the saddened couple were such as to allow no outside suspicion that such as they could be distressed for want of fuel. Alas! they belonged to that class whose position has to be kept on comparatively small incomes, and whose incomes have so fixed a limit that their money power can never rise equally with the rise of prices for food and fuel. The silent sufferings of this class have deepened all through the period in which coal masters, miners, and merchants, have seemingly combined to press fortunes for themselves out of the crushed flesh and spirits of their struggling and helpless neighbours.

While, however, the man and his wife were looking at one another, both feeling strongly tempted to indulge hard thoughts about everything and everybody, a happy-looking child ran into the room, crying, "Hark! how my sparrows are singing for their dinner! Can't I have some crumbs for my sparrows—my dear sparrows? They belong to Jesus; and He sends them to our window for crumbs, and lets me feed them for Him, and call them mine, too! Shan't I have some crumbs for them?"

"Yes, darling!" was the response from father and mother in one breath. They had been touched. The gathering hardness had melted, and there were answering glances from moist eyes.

"*We* belong to Him, to whom the sparrows belong," said the wife. "Yes; nor will He leave *us* without our crumbs, any more than he leaves them."

"No," said the softened man; "and He will forgive me for my moment's feeling of doubt. He is able to supply our need: let us trust Him. As the dear child spoke, I thought of what a quaint old writer says, 'It costs the Lord more to keep his sparrows than it takes to keep up all the governments of Europe. And He has always enough still in store for His people.'"

"And I thought," said the wife, "of Mr. Gough's merry, chirping song, 'My Sparrows.' I shall teach our dear child to repeat it. It will help to save us from sorrowful doubt in moments of darkness. Come here, my darling; I am going to tell you a pretty song about your sparrows; and when you have learnt it, you shall sing it to your sparrows, and to us sometimes. Now listen:—

"I am very fond of sparrows,
 And they are fond of me;
For ever bright and cheery,
 And pert and full of glee.
Sparrows never seem in trouble,
 Though all is dark around,
They chirp in storm and sunshine,
 And when snow is on the ground.

When trees are bare in winter,
 And bitter cold benumbs,
They gather round my window,
 And ask me for some crumbs;
And then, just before the sunset,
 In the ancient holly tree,
They hold a choral service,
 As happy as may be.

For countless generations,
 The sparrow has been known;
They built around God's temple,
 And near to David's throne;
And the Blessed One has spoken
 Of sparrows kindly words,
How our heavenly Father careth
 For these joyous little birds.

> They have taken full possession
>   Of my roof and eaves all round,
> And build and hatch their young ones
>   In the freehold they have found.
> I never shoot my sparrows,
>   Or otherwise molest;
> And woe be to the youngsters
>   Who dare to take their nest!
>
> But when the cherries ripen,
>   I'm obliged to use my gun;
> But I only fire with powder,
>   And they cry, 'It's all in fun.'
> So they help themselves to cherries,
>   Until their crops are fill'd,
> And put that down as payment
>   For caterpillars killed.
>
> They chirp at early daylight,
>   And cheer the morning's dawn,
> And chatter in the ivy,
>   And hop upon the lawn;
> And in damp and foggy weather,
>   When I'm apt to mope and sigh,
> As merry as young crickets,
>   'Cheer up, cheer up!' they cry.
>
> Mr. Sparrow sports a black cravat,
>   And seems a trifle proud;
> But he's faithful to his lady love,
>   And too gallant to be cow'd;
> And he scolds and struts, and sharps his bill
>   Upon the old oak bough,
> As if he said, 'If you want to fight,
>   I'll accommodate you now!'
>
> So I'm very fond of sparrows,
>   About my homestead door,
> Waiting till the cloth is shaken,
>   And begging still for more.
> They cannot sing like thrushes,
>   But in buoyant spirits rife,
> They are always brisk and cheerful,
>   And they stay with you for life."

"How strange it is," said an eminent minister to his friend, as they wandered in the suburbs of a smoky city, if haply they might recognise some little vestiges of pure nature; "how strange it is that you, with your passion for rocks, and flowers, and moors, and weird old castles, and the like, should be called to spend your life in cities and great towns! And how strange twenty million other things are that we see and know of! Indeed, what is not strange? All is strange —stranger and stranger I feel it to be, as years march onward. Thank God for the good hope of the final unveiling!"

"Thank God!" was the response; "but you remind me of that admirable woman, John Wesley's mother; she expresses a feeling something like yours, when speaking of her gifted and learned husband: 'Did I not know,' she says, 'that Almighty wisdom hath views and ends in fixing the bounds of our habitation, which are out of our ken, I should think it a thousand pities that a man of his brightness and rare endowments of learning and useful knowledge, in relation to the Church of God, should be confined to an obscure corner of the country, where his talents are buried, and he determined to a way of life for which he is not so well qualified as I could wish.' So every one of us has strange things to test our faith. How little we see of our surroundings, and how much less we know about the interests and relations of our own inner world. And as to control, how much have we over the little things which sometimes give turns of great consequence to our course? We look on, as the transactions of our life pass, just as spectators look from their places upon the movements on the stage; how little they know of the preparations and machinery behind the scenes! How little they know of the thought, the knowledge, the wisdom, the power, the skill, the insight, the foresight, and the secret counsels invisibly engaged in pre-arranging and setting the life of the stage in action, adapting each actor to his place, and preparing each actor's part, and, by combination of agencies, securing as a result the honour of the managing mind, and the best effects upon the senses, thoughts, feelings, and character of those who look on from outside!"

"Then you think that—

> "All the world's a stage,
> And all the men and women merely players:
> They have their exits, and their entrances;
> And one man in his time plays many parts."

"Well, I don't know as to the world; I was not so broad in my allusion. Though I believe the Psalmist had a notion something like the one in your quotation, when he said, 'Surely every man walketh in a vain show; verily they are disquieted in vain.' Does he not mean that men are something like actors? They walk in shadow, in a representation, a kind of living, moving picture. They hum, and strut, and go through their postures; but how vainly! with how little truth in themselves! with how little knowledge of things as they truly are concerning themselves! And with how little insight into the realities of the future! I believe, however, that God is nearer to every man than any man thinks. As to the individual, as well as the multitude, there is One who, though unseen and unthought of by the creatures of His hand, 'had marked out and previously appointed their times, and the limits of their dwelling, that they might seek the Lord, if haply they might feel after Him and find Him.' God's modes of arranging human affairs, and of keeping men in action on the stage of life, can be seen only behind the scenes. He puts men, I think, where they may best secure the true ends of life. And even when in their wilfulness they venture to choose places and circumstances for themselves, He still keeps up His invisible interferences so as to render final salvation possible for them, though by their unholy usurpation of self-government they have wrecked all their mortal interests. God never places men in circumstances which render it necessary for them to ruin themselves; for He 'cannot be tempted of evil, neither tempteth He any man.' But I am leading you and myself into more of the strange things about which you spoke. I merely wished to express my firm belief in the ceaseless superintendence of Divine wisdom and goodness over the minutest things in the life of those who love and trust. I think that the doctrine of Providence in the case of the Christian comes very near to the doctrine of fate. To the loving child of God,

> "All is best, though we oft doubt
> What the unsearchable dispose
> Of highest wisdom brings about,
> And ever best found in the close.

"For my part, He has taught me that it must be mine to secure the calm, abiding conviction that my will puts nothing in the way of Providence; and then to fill the place and time He chooses for me, so as to enjoy a good conscience,—'a conscience bearing witness in the Holy Ghost,'—that I please Him. How often I find myself inwardly humming,—

> "A faithful witness of Thy grace,
> Well may I fill the allotted space,
> And answer all Thy great design;
> Walk in the works by Thee prepar'd;
> And find annex'd the vast reward,
> The crown of righteousness divine."

"Then it is on this principle," it was remarked, in reply, "that you are reconciled to a life in large towns and cities, apparently in such ill-keeping with your taste."

"Yes, of course. And am I not right? It has struck me that one evidence of life in such scenes being best, in my case, for awhile, is to be found in the fact that my taste for nature has been kept fresh throughout, and, indeed, becomes fresher as I approach the time when life in cities will no longer be my calling. I sometimes think that God will set me free for a little while among the scenes with which I have such loving sympathy, that I may plume my wings a moment before my flight to paradise. One benefit I shall have gained by living in the smoky 'wilderness of the people' is, that my opportunities of insight into the artificial, the unsound, and the false, will prepare me, as nothing else can, for the pure enjoyment of natural reality, and simple, free, and healthy life. If you think that life in cities seems a hard lot for one like me, I can conceive of others as having a much harder lot than mine. Suppose that I should have my city discipline through the earlier days of vigour, and God were to release me, and let me finish among the woods and fields, mine would then be the calm joys of the soldier, who, having had his last campaign, settles in his native valley, in the enjoyment of his honours and his pension. But I can think of a man with tastes like mine, born in the country, shut up to business through middle life, in the worst part of a city, retiring with the fruit of his labour into the scenes of his heart's choice, to finish his course amidst the pleasures of undisturbed devotion to nature, books, and religious contemplation. His rest seems certain, and his joy full. He has enough to make him easy, and to free him from care. He may take up the song which our friend Gough teaches such a man to sing, 'At the Door':—

> "Wearied with the long pilgrimage of life,
>   Wayworn, and full of scars,
> Won in victorious strife,
>   In Christ's triumphant wars;
> By age enfeebled, now I sigh for rest,
>   And with my hand upon the palace door
> I wait in patience, longing to be bless'd
>   With peace for evermore
>
> . . . . . .
>
> I have no fear—the summons soon will come,
> And at Christ's palace door I feel at home;
> I think of my past victories, and am glad;
>   I count my scars and shout,
> To know that in God's armour clad,
>   I put my foes to rout.
>
> . . . . . .
>
> Here, then, within sound of their songs,
>   Saint, angel, martyr, cherubim,
>   Who dwell with Him,
>   I lay me down and wait,
> Singing in concert with the countless throngs
>   Inside the gate;
> Full soon the messenger will come;
> Being so near, I will not stray from home,
>   For God is never late.

"But suddenly, when the habits of the retired man have thus ceased to accord with the severer action of life, by a turn in the circumstances of somebody whose fortunes had become linked to his, he loses his all in the world, can no longer stay in the nest which he had built for his old age, and, without resources, except such as those who loved him may afford for his bare sustenance, has to hide himself amidst the shadows of a town population—would not such a case be worse than mine?"

"It would be indeed!—a case to be classed with very strange things that grow stranger and stranger. Well, we must hope that every one upon whom such distress may fall will act on your principle of peaceful submission, and be able to use my words: 'Thank God for the good hope of the final unveiling!'"

Alas, for the changeableness of human things! This last sketch of a hard lot might have been a forecasting vision of our Kentish lyric's case. Nor, when the reality of such a sorrow first threw its shadow over us, could we help thinking that the songster must have been deeply touched by a kind of presentient feeling, and moved to provide a song for himself, "In the Time of Sorrow":—

> In the time of sorrow,
>   Jesus, comfort me;
> Bring the bright to-morrow,
>   Bid the shadows flee.
> O'er the night of weeping,
>   Let Thy mercy dawn,
> And the watch-night keeping,
>   Usher in the morn.
>
> When in sore affliction,
>   Gloomy thoughts increase;
> Breathe the benediction
>   Of Thy loving peace.
> Meet me in contrition,
>   Till I bless the ill;
> Give me sweet submission
>   To Thy perfect will.
>
> Near me in temptation,
>   Conquering Jesus, stand.
> Work Thy full salvation—
>   Snatch from Satan's hand:
> Evermore enduring
>   Through the battle's strife,
> Victory securing,
>   And the crown of life.

A KENTISH LYRIC.

Other things forgetting—
  Things that are behind—
Nought of earth regretting,
  To its pleasures blind;
Towards the prize still pressing,
  Glory in my view,
Jesus, give Thy blessing ;
  Jesus, help me through.

When beside the river,
  Lingering half in fear,
Jesus, then deliver,
  Jesus, then be near.
Let me pass rejoicing,
  With Thy staff and rod,
Hallelujahs voicing
  To my Saviour God.

May the sweet singer "in sorrow," have his "sorrow turned into joy," as he walks home with Jesus!

CHAPTER XXII.

THREE POETIC VOICES FROM THE WEST.

> Yes, 'tis sweet to wake the strains
> Of those we lov'd in former years,
> Who shar'd our pleasure, sooth'd our pains,
> And shed a lustre o'er our tears.
> Whose smiles beguil'd the evil hour,
> As on those tones we fondly hung,
> Which woke each bud of hope to flower,
> And charm'd our sorrows into song.

ON the west side of the communion-table in the Methodist Chapel of Redruth, an ancient town in the midst of the Cornish mining district, and an old honoured centre of Methodist life and action, there is an ornamental niche, containing a memorial urn, on which is written "In memoriam, THOS. GARLAND," with the simple record underneath, "OB 1865. ÆT 61." This is to the memory of one, the intellectual gracefulness of whose countenance, the music of whose voice, and whose harmonies of thought and language are lovingly cherished in the recollections of his native Countymen, and would be thought of with pleasure by all who once saw and heard him either in private or public.

"He used to sit there," said one who knew him, pointing at a front seat in the gallery of the chapel, nearly overlooking the monumental urn. "How often I have seen him there! I used to watch for the play of thought upon that calm, fixed face, though sometimes that play was so delicate as scarcely to be caught. It would come and go as the thought of the preacher found a response in his soul, or as it merely served to suggest a course of thought into which his mind might strike out in a style of its own. How quiet are the deeper workings of Divine truth in some minds! So quiet as scarcely to give a sign that would touch the eye of an observer from without. So quietly did truth act upon the thinking powers, and through them on the heart of the one whose facial muscles seemed always tranquil, as he sat in that seat and listened to the appeals of truth from the pulpit. On one occasion he was seen to lift his hand, and gently, with one finger, take away a tear that was trembling on his eyelid. The deep, full feelings, of which that was the token, found subdued utterance afterwards to the ear of the preacher, as, by invitation, he sat in private chat with Thomas Garland in a room looking out on the still majesty of the western hills, then reposing under evening shadows. That evening chat is still thought of with hallowed pleasure. There were unfoldings of experience which for ever marked the hour as a holy one. It was a blessed period in the spiritual history of a soul afterwards so beautiful in its mode of consecrating its powers to Him who had filled it with peace so gently, and yet so certainly, and with such profound effect. The manner in which that soul expressed the Divine love which had been manifested to it was sweetly in keeping with the style in which the tender affections of some kindred spirits mutually make themselves known; the style of utterance so finely pencilled in one of the early effusions of Mr. Garland's poetic feeling and taste:—

> "There's a language that's mute, there's a silence that speaks,
>   There is something that cannot be told;
> There are words that can only be read on the cheek,
>   And thoughts but the eyes can unfold.
>
> There's a look so expressive, so timid, so kind,
>   So conscious, so quick to impart;
> Though dumb, in an instant it speaks out the mind,
>   And strikes in an instant the heart.
>
> This eloquent silence—this converse of soul—
>   In vain we attempt to suppress;
> More prompt it appears from the wish to control,
>   More apt the fond truth to express.

> And, oh ! the delights in the features that shine,
> The raptures the bosom that melt;
> When blest with each other this converse divine
> Is mutually spoken and felt."

The writer of these lines was about sixteen when he thus proved himself capable of delicately combining music of words and music of feeling. He was born and brought up on a spot surrounded by scenes that might aid the inspirations of genius—scenes amidst which the soul as well as the body seems to breathe a life-giving atmosphere. On the side of one of the somewhat bare hills which range along the north-west coast of Cornwall, and whose seaward slopes end in the grand cliffs and wild crags that ceaselessly echo to the voice of the Atlantic, there is an old homestead with its orchards and lines of elm-trees forming a green patch on the bald slope. The quiet ivy-clad dwelling looks down through its garden foliage on a weird valley with its discoloured stream of mineral water rushing over a bed of pebbles and metallic sand, the sea-gull or the passing rook giving occasional responses to its babbling tones as it passes into the waters of the richly wooded dell that winds its way down to the little romantic harbour of Portreath. Beyond that weird valley, old Cambridge allows the eye to wander over a swell of furzy common, and still beyond, over rounded hills, here and there abruptly sinking into zig-zag hollows; and then, to range along the distant line of undulating heights and grand uplifted old carns keeping watch and ward for ages over the secret depths of subterranean wealth. Amidst these hills and hollows the intellect of our golden-tongued Cornishman first learnt to put its thoughts into form ; here his pen made its earliest trials of skill ; and here his heart had its first lessons of joy and sorrow. To some of the lad's first experiences of repulse from editorial powers, as well as to what he felt of the threatening influence of indulged poetic passion on his early culture of spiritual piety, we probably owe some lines which have enough of poetry in them to warrant hope on the part of a youthful genius :—

And would'st thou wake the minstrel's lyre,
  And pour its swelling notes along?
And gather from each trembling wire
  The moody revelry of song?
Beware! it hath a fatal power,
  That round it like a serpent clings,
And desolates the fairy bower,
  Whose blossoms shade its warbling strings.

Its sounds are first all pure and deep,
  And whisper love and breathe of heaven,
But reckless if its chords thou sweep,
  Thy dust may slumber unforgiven!
And Pleasure's sweet, alluring strain,
  And Passion's wild voluptuous tone,
May give thee that undying pain
  Which is not felt on earth alone.

The poet's wreath of hues divine
  Is from the fairest flowers that blow;
Would'st thou the glittering chaplet twine,
  And bind it round thy honoured brow?
Beware! its colours oft deceive,
  And when their beauty most adorns,
The blooming flowers may fade and leave
  A circlet of the sharpest thorns.

It has become the native custom of cold and severe critics to sneer at the first tender effusions of young poets—their languishing homage to some Delia or Sylvia, their melting sentiment, their fond epithets, their soft imagery, their plaintive appeals, and their submissive devotion to love and beauty; and as such critics, like leaders of fashion, give the cue, all who affect literary taste, like the crowd who follow the given fashion, take up the critical mode, and in turn have their laugh at the juvenile essays of genius to express the first tender yearnings of the youthful heart. But why should the natural affections of our nature be ridiculed in their spring-time, in their earliest unfolding, and in their first essays at expression? It is human to love. God has given man affections, in the pure exercise of which human life finds a secret joy. The young heart feels after something to love; and the language of the awakened feeling is no other than properly belongs to it. Love will never be laughed out of the world; nor will young genius, when first touched by its warmth, ever be persuaded to repress its native outflowings of tender thought and feeling.

If our young Cornishman had never made his first effort to give out his first kindlings in tuneful measure, he might never have gathered power to utter those more mature voices of song which live as evidence of his true poetic gifts, as well as the delicate and warm tone of his affections. Whether his young heart had real cause for plaintiveness at the loss of what it loved and would have clung to, or whether the tenderness of his nature went forth upon the mere conceptions of his genius, one piece, among the remains of his youthful authorship, is finely conceived. The lines are beautiful, passingly beautiful—beautiful in form, beautiful in soul, beautiful in language; so much ease, such naturalness of voice, and all the words falling in such graceful harmony, that it might be the poet's passion itself living, breathing, and speaking "To Isabelle":—

> Yes, years have darkly stolen by,
>   Since on thy neck I fondly hung,
> And drank the fragrance of thy sigh,
>   And caught the music of thy tongue;
> But many a coming year must roll
> Its weight of grief upon my soul,
> Ere time can steal away from me
> One relic memory keeps of thee,
>   My gentle Isabelle!
>
> I've mingled with the festive throng,
>   And drain'd the sparkling wine-cup dry,
> While the ripe thrilling voice of song
>   In echoing volumes rose on high;
> A voice was stealing on the lee—
> A voice unheard by all but me—
> Upon the faintest note it hung—
> Amidst the loudest peal it rung—
>   The voice of Isabelle.
>
> I've been where beauty charm'd the soul
>   With her full starry eyes revealing;
> And love's divinest languor stole
>   Upon the latest chords of feeling;

Even then I saw another stand,
And beckon me with bloodless hand;
And other eyes were on me then—
When will those eyes be bright again?
    My long-lost Isabelle!

'Tis vain that thou should'st thus recall
 The passion naught but death can sever;
Would we had never loved at all,
 Or, having loved, had loved for ever!
But vain the wish; within the tomb
Thy beauty has forgot its bloom;
Thy faithful heart has long been cold,
Within the earth-worm's slimy fold,
    Ill-fated Isabelle!

Then cease to haunt my tortur'd breast,
 With pangs which time can ne'er remove;
Or in the grave I fain would rest
 With thee whom only yet I love.
This is for every wound a balm—
The fiercest storms must end in calm,
And woes, however quick they come,
But sooner speed me to the tomb,
    With thee, my Isabelle.

"Long years had passed," said an old Cornishman, "since I had seen the face and heard the voice of Thomas Garland—that face which had so often charmed me, that voice that so many times had held me in alternations of merriment and silent pleasure. But coming within the reach of him once more, I flung myself into an open carriage, and told the coachman to drive me to Fairfield. Fairfield! what rich memories gather around that woodland retreat! Fairfield! It tells me of table-chat, rich in humour, wit, comical sketches of life and manners, passing criticisms, and portraitures of human character; it tells me of mental freedom amidst the treasures of an elegant library; of readings from Wordsworth, De Quincy, and Lamb, which made one proud of his own language, and happy under the voice of one who knew how to give musical utterance to that language, and could make its power felt. That dining-room, opening at the end into a conservatory, in which a robin sat among the flowers and sang to us while we dined; and looking out in front on a beautiful lawn surrounded by shrubs and wood, and peopled by happy creatures, who moved amidst the sunlight and shade as if they felt they were in their own paradise; and then the old familiar faces at that quiet, hospitable board; all live before me now.

"My poetic host was then in his prime, and as a reader of poetry, in my opinion, the best I ever heard; to my taste, far more enjoyable than any professional I ever listened to. There was a voice of melody; tones rich, clear, and distinct. The very genius of the author himself seemed to be present, breathing his own inspiration into one's soul, until one's whole nature was thrilling under the fascinating charm. The man who read was one who had poetic 'music in himself,' and could therefore do justice to the poets whom he had learnt to enjoy so as now to keep his own poetic gifts in hushed silence. Nevertheless, one could but remember on that bright spring day, amidst the natural beauties and intellectual charms of Fairfield, how the now maturely cultured soul of its owner once sang a youthful song of his own on the opening 'Spring':—

> " 'Tis spring—I know by the soften'd breeze,
>   And the freshening balm 'tis bringing;
> By the buds that are opening among the green trees,
>   And the birds on their branches singing.
> By the flowers around me thickly blooming,
>   And the silver voices through heaven that ring,
> And the sun drawing nearer to herald her coming,
>   'Tis the glad approach of Spring.
>
> She has breath'd on the woods, and their blossoming boughs
>   Are to life and beauty waking,
> She has loosed the floods, and the tingling rill flows,
>   From its fetters gaily breaking.
> The violet and hedge-rose are silently quaffing
>   Her richest showers of clustering dew,
> And through the flying clouds she is laughing
>   With eyes of sunny blue.
>
> The hare o'er the brushwood nimbly flies,
>   The stag through the copse is glancing,
> The lark's sweet melody swells in the skies,
>   And light on her plumage is dancing;

>   The eyes on earth and the stars in heaven
>   Are shining out more vividly bright,
>   And the season's warm glow to the day is given,
>   And her placid smile to the night.
>
>   The earth has felt in its sylvan recesses,
>   Her gladdening influence breathing,
>   And the moonlight groves are with sparkling tresses
>   Her rosy coronal wreathing;
>   And ocean from every shore he laves
>   Has caught up the circling story,
>   Borrow'd her brilliance, and lit by his waves,
>   In a living tide of glory!
>
>   But there is a spot where flowers are springing,
>   Where never I wish to see them spring;
>   And there is a spot where birds are singing,
>   Where music should never its wild notes fling:
>   'Tis over the graves of those who last year
>   Were in health and beauty blooming,
>   But faded away like visions of air,
>   And are in the dark tomb consuming.
>
>   The flowers that wave midst the stillness of death,
>   Lend but a deeper gloom to sorrow!
>   Nor will melody charm the poor sleepers beneath,
>   Till they wake to a glorious morrow:
>   In a land where the hours will eternally bring
>   Pleasures which no rude winter can sever—
>   There is no renewal of summer or spring,
>   For they 'll last for ever and ever!"

Cornwall has long been remarkable for her religious revivals, wide-spread, and sometimes attended by circumstances pregnant with spiritual lessons, and strikingly significant of the Holy Spirit's most gracious modes of dealing with human masses. And whatever may be said by laughers, or philosophers, or doubtful Christians, these revivals always brighten under the test, when judged on the sacred principle, "By their fruits ye shall know them." However mysterious such successive visitations may appear to some, their results are found in the high moral tone, and the deep, religious sentiments, tastes, and habits of the people. The best and largest number of Methodist folk have been revival converts; and that many of the leading minds and largest hearts of the county—men who have left their marks upon the world—

have been among the permanent blessings following such stirring excitements, is enough to show that the movements are Divine. The poetic spirit, whose name is still so balmy; the elegant mind, that so charmed his generation; the fascinating speaker, and the persuasive and cultured writer, who maintained so pure and agreeable an influence over all who knew him, owed that religious life, which hallowed his gifts, to the grace of a Cornish revival. It was during the extraordinary religious excitement which moved all classes through the entire west of the county, in the year 1814, that Thomas Garland, then a lad about ten years old, realized that spiritual change which the blessed Lord has called a new birth. Like many others, however, he afterwards felt himself swayed amidst the conflicts to which he was called, as his physical nature was developed, and as his intellect and heart opened amidst the allurements of the outer world. The distraction incident to warmly-pressed intellectual pursuits, and the consequent fluctuation of the will and the affections amidst the clash of opinion, and the unfolding claims of public life, are finely indicated in a poem on his twenty-second birthday: a piece in which the young poetic genius and the youthful Christian show themselves, by turns, living, breathing, asserting their claims, and giving out their voices in harmony, amidst the contending influences of earth and heaven :—

> Let others hail their day of birth
>   With festal glee, and dance, and song;
> And dedicate its hours to mirth;
>   To me far other thoughts belong.
> To me it tells of pleasures gone,
>   Of hopes that only bloom'd to die;
> And one more year swept wave-like on
>   To thy dark shores, Eternity.
> It asks if o'er my youthful brow
>   No self-accusing thoughts can rise;
> If I have sojourn'd here below,
>   As one whose home is in the skies!
> If I to Heaven can lift mine eye,
>   And smile at death's unconscious sleep?
> My quiv'ring lips yield no reply,
>   I only bow my head and weep.

Lord, I have wander'd far from Thee;
    And though Thy Word sublimely show'd,
Like Israel's pillar'd flame, my way,
    In paths of dark delusion trod;
Have strayed, while Truth's eternal beams
    Around me shone divinely clear,
And thirsted while the gushing streams
    Of living waters murmur'd near.

But now, if like the bird that o'er
    The billowy waste of waters sped,
Nor saw to its wild waste a shore,
    Nor found, where'er she vainly fled,
One bright, green resting spot of earth,
    Back to the ark again I wing:
Oh! wilt Thou not thy hand stretch forth,
    And take the weary wanderer in?

Thou wilt—Thou wilt—even now I feel,
    While bending at Thy pitying throne,
That half the darkness of the veil
    Which hid my soul from Thee, is flown.
And from Thy presence shadowing forth,
    A glimpse of love divine is given,
Eclipsing every charm of earth
    With light that only springs from heaven.

Oh! breathe Thy voice into my heart,
    And let it ever whisper there;
That when from Thee my steps depart,
    Its deep, low tone I still may hear
In all my wanderings, like the shell
    That, torn from Ocean's coral caves,
Retains, wherever it may dwell,
    The music of the murmuring waves.

The traveller on the mountain's height,
    Walks on beneath a cloudless sky,
While lightnings flash beneath his feet,
    And in the vale harsh thunders die.
Such is the Christian's path; below
    He sees the world's wild tempests driven,
But heeds them not; and smiles to know
    They cannot harm, so near to Heaven!

There are some minds of poetic power and taste which never find expression in measured verse of their own from the time when they give themselves to the full joy of companionship with poets of supreme claims. Thomas Garland was one of these; not that he ever ceased to be a poet in spirit, feeling, taste, and language, but he ceased to utter himself in rhyme. Even as a journalist and a reviewer he made it evident, every now and then, that it was possible for prose pages to be instinct with essential poetic life. It was, however, chiefly as a public speaker, preacher, and lecturer that this "golden-tongued Cornishman," as he got to be called, became the poet in prose form. His tuneful genius was most happy when exercised on religious and benevolent themes. The wiping away of that tear from his eye in the chapel at Redruth, near the parish in which he found his last retreat, Fairfield, marked a period of restored consolation in Christ, and of entire sacrifice of his genius and talents to the "truth as it is in Jesus."

"One of his earliest attempts as a public speaker on behalf of Christian missions," says a friend, "at first startled, and then hushed, me into pleasurable wonderment. It was a genuine poet putting his soul into persuasive speech for Christ's sake. This was in a small village chapel among the mines, where the crowded congregation showed how keenly they relished truth when introduced in its native attractions, in language of transparent beauty and powerful simplicity. The gathering and fixing of his hearers' attention on the heavenly Dove brooding on the waters of chaos, and the consequent unfolding of newly-created life, beauty, and order, can never be forgotten; nor have I ever lost the thrilling charm of a sudden transition to the immortal loveliness of the new creation as the result of the same holy Dove's peaceful motion on the dark deep moral chaos of this fallen world. It was prose, pure and energetic; and yet it was poetry, genuine and rich. Never, it seemed to me, was there prose so poetic and yet so manly; so full of musical thought and feeling, and yet so powerful and chaste—'the happy mixture of the serious and the playful, the pathetic and the harmonious, the keen argument and the powerful declamation, all given in language which seemed to have reached its utmost finish, would hold the audience in breathless attention.' It was, indeed, the speech of a poet veiling his poetry in unexceptionable prose. One might be reminded of a passage in his lecture on Robert Hall, as illustrative of his own style. 'To one striking quality of Mr. Hall's style,' says he, ' I must make a pointed advertence. I refer to its musical structure. Great writers are as much *composers* as great musicians. They test the sound of words by a sense as exquisite as that which tries notes of music. They combine words, as the musician blends his notes, into sprightly or solemn movements—into triumphal swells or dying falls. This art is one of the secrets of genius—untaught and incommunicable; and this Hall possessed in perfection. His sermons are magnificent lyrics : each separate paragraph is a melody, and the periods are like bars in a strain of music. I don't know that he ever wrote a line of poetry, nor am I aware whether he had what is called an ear for music; but the divine spirit of poetry colours his prose, and beyond all rules of musical art—

"' His thoughts, involuntary, move
Harmonious numbers.'"

All this would remind one of Thomas Garland's own best public utterances. He was not the divine that Hall was, but his sermons and his lectures were sometimes lyrics, every paragraph of which " was a melody."

How often he showed himself the poet when expressing his happy appreciation of poets. Those who ever heard him talk of Charles Wesley and the Methodist Hymn-Book, and who to any fair extent caught the spirit which breathed in his tuneful sentences, will remember how his claims as a poetic Cornish Methodist were placed beyond a discordant doubt as they heard him say, " The strains which are familiar to every household—the songs with which the mother lulls her infant to slumber on her bosom—the melodies which cheer the traveller on his lonely path, or the ploughman while he turns his furrows, or the miner in his subterranean solitude; the words in which a mourning spirit utters its sorrows, or a happy soul pours forth its overflow of blessedness,—these are in reality the creeds and articles of a community. And so, while Charles Wesley was composing the strains which were to animate our devotional feelings, he was at the same time fixing our doctrinal standards. What solitary truth, precious to the Christian believer, is not vividly displayed in these hymns? Whatever changes may mark the future history of Methodism, we need not apprehend any doctrinal declension. As long as the hymn-book keeps its place in our public worship, our households, and closets, so long will the purity of our faith be guarded by the double defence of the understanding and the affections. At this moment, how many children are prattling these hymns at their parent's knees; how many prayerful spirits are giving utterance to them in their closet silence; what griefs are being lightened, and joys increased by the singing of these sacred melodies! I remember an instance, and my hearers can refer to others, in which a happy soul while singing a verse from one of our hymns passed away to the other world. The song which began on earth ended in heaven; the notes of the Church militant blended with those of the Church triumphant. Death itself was but a bar in the music between the strains of oft-repeated praise and the Song of Moses and the Lamb."

The poetic soul who thus kept in sympathy with the poets of Methodism, seemed to have some sorrowful associations of thought with the quiet leafy grave-yard of his native parish, when he sang—

> But there is a spot where flowers are springing,
> Where never I wish to see them spring;
> And there is a spot where birds are singing,
> Where music should never its wild notes fling.

That spot, however, is now hallowed as the resting-place of his dust; and there, ever since that redeemed dust was deposited in hope, the "flowers" have been "springing" around his tomb, and the "birds" have been "singing" amidst the foliage which shelters and beautifies what, in his early days he called the—

> One sweet resting-place,
> Where mourners find repose,
> And sorrow's children cease to weep,
> Regardless of their woes;
> Where never was an eye impearl'd
> With one unbidden tear,
> Or strain of grief, or tale of woe
> Assail'd the listless ear.

On the day before his comparatively sudden departure from his Fairfield paradise to the paradise above, he was returning from Portreath to his home. A friend who met with him on the way "observed, after he left him, that on ascending the hill he turned and gazed for a considerable time on the fine panorama which there lay outstretched before him—the hills and woods and waters, and the calm, unruffled sea, bathed in the sunshine of a bright summer afternoon." It was the last look of his bodily eye upon that mighty sea. What were his thoughts? Were they in tune with his brother's poetic musings and rhythmical voice, "To the Ocean"? His brother and he were akin in poetic genius and feeling. Both had the spirit of song. Of each, in his own order, it could have been said, he "hath a psalm, hath a doctrine, hath a tongue." And often, lingering on that bold hill-side, overlooking the great deep, have thoughts about the brothers arisen, until it has seemed as if Thomas were standing there, still gazing out on the sun-lighted waters; and as if the voice of Charles Garland were rising into harmony with the murmurs from the rocks, while he sang—

> Hail! mighty Ocean, rolling on
> In everlasting pride and power;
> From clime to clime thy voice hath gone,
> From shore to sounding shore,
> A type of that which cannot die,
> A symbol of eternity!
>
> Thy voice was heard when earth first sprang
> From the primeval chaos forth;
> When morning stars together sang
> The glories of her birth,
> As darkness from his throne was hurl'd,
> And sunlight flash'd upon the world.

And there will yet thy billows roll,
    While distant ages shall decay,
Till the high heavens—a shrivell'd scroll—
    Consume and pass away—
Till Time shall flag his weary wing,
And perish—a forgotten thing!

Time—that hath crumbled to the ground
    The towers that climb'd the far-off sky,
And spread stern desolation round
    Beneath his withering eye—
Hath look'd on thee in still despair,
And never wreak'd his vengeance there!

While mighty changes sweep away
    The fabrics reared by mortal hand—
While thrones are tottering day by day,
    And monarchs throneless stand—
Unbow'd, unsmote by earthly will—
Thou art the rolling ocean still.

Thou wert a wonder evermore,
    Thou art a thing of wonder still;
Scorning the might of human lore,
    The heights of human skill;
With one sublimest mystery fraught,
Deeper than all the depths of thought.

How wondrous, then, in slumbering peace,
    Still as an infant on the breast,
When smiles of blessed tenderness
    Have lull'd it into rest;
With scarce a murmur or a sound
Waking from thy vast regions round!

How wondrous when, in stormy night,
    Thy waves uprear their massy walls;
When thunder from the billow's height
    To distant thunder calls;
And o'er thy face the wingèd blast
Sweeps with first-born fury past!

Yet even he of earthly clay,
    Whose breast the voice of truth inspired—
Whose heart one emanating ray
    Of heavenly light hath fired—
May hear within thy rolling flood
Some echo of the voice of God.

Whose years are boundless, like thy own—
    Whose wisdom seraphs may not name—
Whose thunders roll around His throne,
    Built by the lightning flame—
The depths of whose eternal power
Are soundless and without a shore!

Thou mighty one! thou goest forth
   On thy unwearied way alone,
A journeyer to the ends of earth,
   To distant lands unknown!
Ranging the wastes by man untrod,
And search'd but by the eye of God!

Rich treasures, Ocean, are thine own,
   Diamonds of countless price hast thou,
And brighter gems than ever shone
   On beauty's wreathèd brow;
And studded o'er a thousand caves,
Far down beneath thy sounding waves!

And thou hast greater still than these—
   Greater than even wealth untold—
Thou hast the gorgeous palaces,
   The cities fam'd of old,
On whose high banner once unfurl'd
In silence gazed a raptur'd world.

Where Sodom and Gomorrah stood,
   In grandeur looking o'er the earth,
The billows of thy restless flood
   Are ever rolling forth;
Their turrets high and temples proud
Have found beneath thy waves a shroud!

Yea, greater still—in sleep profound,
   The warrior lies within thy womb;
The mighty ones of earth have found
   In thee an unsought tomb!
And, like a miser, day by day
Thou guardest all thy hidden prey!

Retain thy gems and jewels rare,
   To blaze within thy cavern shrine;
But earth's lost heroes, slumbering there,
   Ocean, were never thine!
Give back, from thine unfathom'd bed—
Thou shalt not keep the mighty dead!

A voice shall wake them from their sleep—
   From thy lone depths the dead shall call;
Heaven's final thunders o'er the deep
   In mighty wrath shall fall!
Roll on, in thy unconquer'd sway,
Thou art the creature of a day.

When suns shall vanish from the skies—
   When stars shall sink in dim decay—
And with a sound of mighty voice,
   Heaven, earth, shall pass away;
The winds that sweep thy swelling wave
Shall sing the dirge o'er Ocean's grave!

The author of these lines had entered on his period of poetic rhyme and rhythm just as his brother Thomas, older by nine years, was passing from his verse-making era to that through which his poetical soul expressed itself with such fascinating power in richly-finished lectures, and speeches, and sermons. Charles Garland, too, after a few years of successful indulgence in songs about "The Stars," and "Wings of the Dove," "Remorse," and "The Last Slumber," with other worthy associates of his hymn "To the Ocean," gave himself to his own style of prose; and, as a journalist, lecturer, and preacher, shows himself, as compared with his departed brother, whose memoirs he has written, the less attractive speaker, the less popular penman, the severer critic, the better-read theologian, and, though without the charms of his brother as a preacher, yet the more profound, discriminating, and full. Original poetic genius in both the brothers gave richness to their sacrifice of all gifts to Christ, and will give lasting impressiveness to their lives. The memory of Thomas is like a bright poem still, and Charles will leave the world more in love with the pure beauty of truth than he found it. Uncertain mortality! The last sentence had scarcely been written, when Charles Garland, too, was gone!

In the course of a chat about books the other day one of the group said, "I picked up a volume of poems this morning, some verses in which acted like an instantaneous charm as my eyes fell on them, opening in a moment some inner chambers of imagery, with pictures of forms and scenes belonging to my childhood, which had been shut up for years, unthought of, as if they never had been. The reappearance of these images was so vivid as to beget a notion that there may be, at times, some mysterious link between a poet's visions and the realities of life in some former generation, as if the poet's genius were a spirit of divination having access into the picture-galleries of one's early memory. The volume of poems was by Charles Lawrence Ford, B.A., and was entitled 'Lyra Christi.' The first piece which caught my attention touched a spring, as I said, and in an instant up came my old grandfather's fireside, he sitting on one hand, as I stood by his knee, and on the other an old favourite called Lawrence, a travelled, talkative neighbour, who had nothing to do but to fill up his old friend's leisure hours with racy tales of his early adventures and later alternations of joy and sorrow. His voice seemed to fall upon my ear just as it did when I listened to him telling my grandfather that one of his elect pleasures in the course of his peregrinations was to watch the play of children of an evening from the window of the inn where, for the time, he happened to be, and to watch them till the shades began to deepen, and the music of their young voices, as the little groups left the ground, melted away in the distance, and lulled him into dreams of his own childhood.

" 'I liked it all the more,' he said, 'because it always seemed to me such a token of our country's happiness and welfare. For you know,' he added, giving his friend a knowing look from his one twinkling eye, 'you know our heavenly Father mentions it as a token of "peace and plenty." What a pretty picture he teaches the prophet Zechariah to draw of a happy city: "There shall yet old men and old women dwell in the streets of Jerusalem, and every man with his staff in his hand for very age; and the streets of the city shall be full of boys and girls playing in the streets thereof." And I like it still the more,' said old one-eyed Lawrence, ' because our blessed Lord himself used to notice it, and liked it so, that He drew lessons from it for the proud and hard-hearted Pharisees. How kindly He must have looked at the "children playing in the market-place;" and their little toy-pipes, and even their mimic sorrows, were dear to Him. Oh, what a difference He could see between their bright young spirits and the dark, disguised, selfish minds of the great doctors!'

"I learnt to love that old traveller, because he loved children; and his talk led me to love *Him*, too, whose interest in children and whose knowledge of them led Him to prefer their company and to place little ones before His disciples as examples of true greatness. The verses which so suddenly called these early impressions into new life are founded on Zechariah's words, as quoted by the old pleasant talker. (Zech. viii. 4, 5). Here they are:—

"My children, pleasant are your voices,
  As the song of merry birds in May!
Earth amidst her sorrows yet rejoices,
  Hearing the glad echoes of your play,
Breaking through the melancholy noises
  Wrung from her sad bosom all the day.

Joyous is your life, that knows no morrow—
  Knows no dark regrettings for the past;
We, along the sober path of sorrow,
  Walk with looks before and after cast;
Ye from beast and bird some wisdom borrow,
  Plucking flowers of pleasure while they last.

Earnest is your way in its pursuing,
  Not with the half-heartedness of men
Now some truth or pleasure feebly wooing,
  Turning from the hollow purpose then;
Weary with this doing and undoing,
  Almost would I be a child again.

Fearless is your speech, untaught to measure
  Fashion's cold proprieties and rules;
Love and hate, and bitterness and pleasure,
  Brook in you no lessons of the schools;
We who weave disguises of our leisure,
  Half, perchance, are wise, and half are fools.

Frozen are our hearts with self-repressing,
  Hiding from our brother all we can;
Yours, at will rebuking or caressing,
  As an open volume all may scan;
Ours may be the gain, but yours the blessing,
  Bearing more the pattern of the man.

Said He not, the meek, the loving-hearted,
  In whose gentle spirit was no guile,
He whose life its sun-like radiance darted,
  Flooding all the nations with its smile,
That the children's mind must be imparted
  Unto all would reach the Happy Isle?

> Teach us, then—for we have need of teachers—
>   Teach us your simplicity to win;
> Preach to us, most golden-mouth'd of preachers,
>   From the temple that ye stand within;
> Sing us songs, most blessèd of God's creatures,
>   While we hear, but cannot enter in.
>
> Show us that of all the visions golden,
>   Woven of that paradise above,
> That of all its treasures new and olden,
>   Angels show the ransom'd as they rove,
> Naught so sweetly perfect is beholden
>   As its childlike confidence and love.
>
> Then, to guileless merriment returning,
>   Charm us from our sorrows by your glee,
> While our forms conventional unlearning,
>   Life untrammell'd in your sports we see,
> In your wilfulness of joy discerning
>   God's great will that all should happy be.
>
> Shaking in the breeze your golden tresses,
>   Singing to the music of the sky,
> Plunging in the thickest green recesses,
>   Laughing at the echo of your cry—
> Every word and every motion blesses,
>   Unawares, the loving One on high.
>
> Laugh, and leap, and shout! the hours are flying!
>   Fill your lap with roses while ye may,
> Reckless of the years before you lying,
>   Seeing not the ending of your day;
> Soon enough will come the time of sighing—
>   Who shall dare to check you from your play?
>
> Oh! my children, ye have left your places;
>   Silence falls with darkness on the strand;
> But the laughing light upon your faces
>   Haunts me still, as if, with influence bland,
> Angels had been here, and left their traces
>   Of the ever young and happy land."

"Some of these verses," it was remarked, "show with beautiful delicacy and instructive clearness the border lines between the simple thoroughness, truthfulness, and purity of happy childlikeness, and the double-faced, double-minded, false-coloured humbug of our mature culture, as we call it; while they indicate the secret of that real greatness which is so lovely and dear to the heart of Him who said, 'Whosoever, therefore, shall humble himself as this little child, the same is greatest in the kingdom of heaven.' "

"Yes," said the first speaker, "and Mr. Ford has given me, over and above, an insight into another secret. He has sweetly explained to me somewhat of the reason why, in childhood, I always seemed to be better and happier when alone among the rocks and sands on the sea-shore than in some other scenes. I see now that the lessons which were instilled into my young soul about the scenes of our Saviour's favourite resorts had associated the sands with His footprints, and the sea with the divine music of His voice, as well as the deep movements of His power. My early love of the sea was hallowed by sympathy with Him whose gentle presence it so often felt. One of the poet's pieces seemed to lead me back to my favourite resort when a child. It was a green flat on the margin of a solitary little lake by the sea, a plot where every step pressed out the grateful perfume of the chamomile-flowers which bespangled it. There, sometimes of an evening, I used to be, when the sky was clear and the moon was full, and nothing broke the stillness but the leap of a fish now and then from the placid water, or the whistle of the sandpiper, or the murmur of waves which the light breeze at times brought up from the neighbouring beach. Happy hours! I seemed to have them over again when I read Mr. Ford's lines on 'Christ by the Sea,' founded on the significant though simple statement, 'And He went forth again by the sea-side':—

> "Thy ways were in the haunts of men—
> The city's lanes, the rustic glen,
> The desert wild, the mountain sod;
> But most the murmur of the sea
> Thy footsteps drew—meet path for Thee,
> O Son of God!
>
> Perchance a brief repose was found
> In that interminable sound,
> Hushing all voices save its own;
> Even as in some o'ercrowded street
> We plunge, and find its noise most sweet,
> Then most alone.

Perchance it was Thy music, played
By hands unseen that o'er it strayed,—
    God's harp of multitudinous roll;
To mortal ears the waves' low moan,
To Thine some heavenly undertone,
        To soothe Thy soul.

For Thou wast weary with the sighs
Of sorrowing earth; men's harsh replies
    Struck, sword-like, through Thy finer sense;
And weary evermore to spend
On hearts that could not comprehend
        Thy love intense.

The wide, unfathomable deep,
Unchanging type that mortals keep
    Of what outlies the bounds of time—
Nearest to infinite—might well
Suit with Thy thought, who couldst not dwell
        Out of that clime.

And haply, at the day's soft close,
When sought Thine own their calm repose,
    This path, alone, Thy footsteps trod,
All night, from mortal hindrance free,
Thy soul outpouring by the sea
        In prayer to God.

The day's hot glare beheld Thee far,
Healing all pains; but eve's cool star
    Still drew Thee to Thy lov'd retreat;
The waters knew Thee—every wave
Waited Thy coming, proud to lave
        His Sovereign's feet.

And if that small blue oval field
Might scarce (thou think'st) occasion yield
    To thoughts more meet for ocean's roll,
Still was that watery strength confined,
Emblem of Him whose form enshrined
        An infinite soul.

'There shall be no more sea'—thus sings
Heaven's final seer—vague sound, that brings
    A harmless, half-regretful sigh.
I would not, in the earth new-dressed,
That aught His sacred feet have press'd
        Should wholly die."

The genius who gave out these utterances cannot strictly be called a Cornishman—he was born in Bath; but he has become naturalized as a resident in the old Cornish town of Camborne, where he has proved himself to be a cultured and efficient tutor of some of the bettermost boys of the county, and where his pupils have learnt to love him as the object of their parents' high esteem. His voice is now a voice from the West, and it is a poetic voice worthy of Methodism; the doubtful voice of a Methodist Quarterly Reviewer notwithstanding. He has been said to be, not a poet, but rather a verse-maker. He who said so, however, can never have read all his verses, or, having read them, must have read them in forgetfulness of what betokens a poet. Who but a poet could have given such soul-music "to children playing," or have called up such spiritual harmonies around the footsteps of "Christ by the Sea"? Who but a poet could so delicately disclose the great secret of his being loved by boys as their tutor as he has done in his lines "To a Wild Rose," founded on Job's words, "As I was in the days of my youth . . . . my glory was fresh in me" (Job xxix. 4—20) :—

> Sweet, simple blossom of the brake,
> I pluck thee for my childhood's sake;
> For in thy slender leaves I know
> A message from the long-ago.
> To me thy opening buds are singing
>   Of a diviner time gone by;
> I hear the happy voices ringing;
>   I see the never-clouded sky;
> I breathe the invigorating air
> Of life inviolate from care.
>
> The natural smile, the thought half-heard,
> The unpremeditated word,
> The fancy wild all rein that spurned,
> The eye that always outward turned,
> The simple taste, the spirit free,
> The fellowship with bird and bee,
> Come back, consociate with thee!
> Oh, rich munificence of time!
>   Oh, freshness of the morning breeze!
> My light step trod some other clime
>   With larger faculties than these;—
> An eye that, by some mystic law,
> Beheld what since I never saw,

> An ear that heard, distinct and near,
> Sounds such as now I cannot hear;
> A mind at ease; a heart that gave
> To leaf, and cloud, and star, and wave,
> A portion of itself, to gain
> A joy without reserve or stain:
> So, gentle blossom of the brake,
> I pluck thee for my childhood's sake.

Nor can the beautiful concentrations of thought, the quiet play of imagination, and the happily-turned allusions of some of his verses "On the Meekness and Gentleness of Christ" fail to secure for him the honour of being classed with truly poetic versifiers. None that can feel the touch of a poet's voice fails to hear such a voice when he reads verses like these about the gentle Jesus:—

> The folded napkin 'mid the earthquake's roar,
>   The blessing as he vanish'd at the board,
> The curl of smoke that rose upon the shore
>   When that disciple said, "It is the Lord";
>
> The kindness, condescending once to share
>   All human needs, but once by angels fed;
> That stooped, unchanged, our common form to wear,
>   And ate and drank, though risen from the dead;
>
> The easy calmness of His latest hour,
>   With noiseless footstep treading up the stair
> Unto His higher room;—all these have power
>   To turn our meanest acts to praise and prayer.

CHAPTER XXIII.

SOME OF THE LATEST SONS OF SONG.

In varied streams benignant Nature leads
Her fostering waters o'er rejoicing meads :
. . . .
So God ordains, to bless His church below,
His Spirit's gifts in varied streams should flow.

A VENERABLE friend, who owed his spiritual life, under God, to Methodism, devoted his lively talents to Christ, consecrating to Him his powers of music and his gift of sweetly flowing and persuasive speech. He excelled as a public speaker. Among his favourite themes were the missionary character, and the wide, various, and accumulative influences of Methodism. One specimen of his aptness in illustration was this : " I have been told," said he, " that it used to be the custom among whalers in the North Seas, to have each ship's name engraven on all its harpoons; so that if one ship first struck a whale and it escaped with the harpoon in it, on its being struck by another ship and captured, it would be acknowledged as the property of the ship whose first harpoon was found in it; according to the rule that a captured whale belonged to those by whom it was first harpooned. And now," said the speaker, " I have no doubt that in ' the time of the restitution of all things,' when all who have been captured for Christ are gathered together, there will be many Christians brought up by other Churches, who will be found to have the Methodist harpoon in them. For all that was happy in the circumstances of their birth and early training;

for all their first good turns of thought, their first heavenward bent of affection, the first discipline of their will; and for all that was best in the process of their preparation for responsible life, many, very many a man will be found indebted to Methodism, though at his latter end he had not borne the name of Methodist. Influenced by unforeseen surroundings in their later course, such Christians have become associated with other communities, by whom they have been held for a time, until, presented at last, they are manifest in their true relation to those by whose instrumentality they received their first impressions of truth and grace."

If the zealous old Methodist speaker had looked about for an exemplar case, he might have thought himself happy, perhaps, in lighting upon one among the deacons of a Baptist Church in Hackney; one who had distinguished himself as a journalist, whose public pen had been, for some years, stirringly employed about the ecclesiastical affairs of Methodism, who had written a "Life of Dr. Adam Clarke," and a spiritual volume of "Familiar Colloquies between a Father and His Children." This is John Middleton Hare, the son of a Methodist preacher of a past generation. Who that has looked at the crowded group of Methodist preachers represented in the old Methodist Book-Room engraving as sitting at a Conference in City Road Chapel, listening to John Wesley, who occupies the pulpit, has not been struck with one fine intellectual-looking face and head among those who are seated in the foreground under the pulpit? It is one of those oval countenances, with a lofty and expanded brow, so often seen among Englishmen of high type. That is the portrait of Edward Hare, whose name is revered to all who are thankful for Methodist preachers like him—men whose preaching has been rich and weighty, and whose pens have equalled their voice in power. John Middleton Hare is this preacher's third son, born at Stockport, June 5, 1804. The foundation of his learning was laid in the Methodist School at Woodhouse Grove, near Leeds. He was one of the first race of scholars there, and was in school companionship with some who have become known as venerable or leading Methodist preachers, and some who have been distinguished in other spheres, such as the late Attorney-General Sir William Atherton.

As a literary man, Mr. Hare began his course in association with the learned printer, James Nichols; and from contributions in prose and verse to Methodist periodicals, he passed to "Leaders" in popular journals; until, having done the heavier work of life in influencing public opinion by his pen, he sought a retreat at Forest Hill, in which he might solace his last days with psalmody and sacred verse. In giving himself to song, "My first object," he says, "has been to assist myself in the acquisition of habits of composure after a somewhat busy, and sometimes turbulent, career; and my second, if without rebuke I may confess so much ambition, to write, if possible, a hymn or two which may at some future time find their way into the hymn-books of the Christian Church." This is an amiable and devout ambition. Nor are there wanting among his numerous verses hymns of sufficient merit to give good hope that the object of his ambition will be realised. He has attempted a lyrical rendering of "The Song of Songs," a long poem on the "Character and Exploits of David," and rhythmical versions of several psalms. Whether these are as likely to live as some of the "Early Christian Songs" which he has given in a versified form, may not be at present clear. But one at least of these hymns will show that he has not failed to reach his own ideal: "It has been my endeavour," he tells us, "to render the original words—or rather, the received version of those words—with as much closeness as possible. . . . Charles Wesley's versification of the *Te Deum* is so far from being a mere rhymed rendering of the piece as it stands in the Prayer-book as to extend to fourteen six-lined octo-syllabic stanzas. . . . Be pleased to bear in mind that I invite no comparison, in poetical success, between my piece and that of Charles Wesley, or of any other writer; but only wish it to be noted, in what degree I have succeeded in preserving the words as well as the sentiment, while putting them, or trying to put them, into smooth and vigorous verse." Charles Wesley's hymn—

>Infinite God, to Thee we raise
>Our hearts in solemn songs of praise—

is, indeed, a grand musical paraphrase of the *Te Deum;* but Mr. Hare has succeeded in a high degree in his close version, given in verse as "smooth and vigorous" as so close a rendering admits. His hymn has life in it—

>Thee, God, we praise; Thou art the Lord,
>Whom all the earth, with full accord,
>>Eternal Father owns.
>Loud raise to Thee the angel throng,
>Cherub and seraph, pauseless song,
>>Low bending from their thrones.
>
>"Holy"—and all, with veiling wing,
>Their faces cover as they sing—
>>"Thrice-holy Lord," they cry:
>"Creation waits Thy sovereign will
>Both heaven and earth Thy glories fill
>>With speechless majesty."
>
>Thee, praise the glorious company
>Who travailed with their Master; Thee,
>>The fellowship of seers;
>Thee, too, the martyrs' noble band,
>With all the Church, in every land,
>>Through the long lapse of years.
>
>Father, to Thee we humbly bow:
>Of majesty unbounded Thou,
>>Eternally the same;
>Nor less Thy true and only Son,
>And Him, the High and Holy One,
>>The Comforter, who came.
>
>To Thee, for Thou art glory's King,
>Regal acclaim, O Christ, we bring—
>>God's everlasting Son;
>Yet, when Thou cam'st to rescue man,
>Didst stoop to all Thy Father's plan,
>>Nor birth of woman shun.
>
>Triumphant o'er the powers of night,
>Thou didst unbar the gates of light,
>>To all believers free.
>At God's right hand Thy lofty seat,
>In Thee Jehovah's glories meet,
>>And perfectly agree.

Thou, we believe, our doom wilt give;
Help, then, Thy servants so to live,
   Bought with most precious blood,
That in the world of endless bliss,
Their ransomed souls, released from this,
   Be numbered with the good.

Thý people save, O Lord, and bless
Thine heritage with fruitfulness;
   Rule, and for ever raise,
Who day by day adore Thy name,
And always magnify its fame
   In ceaseless songs of praise.

Vouchsafe, O Lord, this day to keep
Our thoughts from sin; awake, asleep,
   Thy mercy still abound;
As is our trust, that mercy be!
Lord, I have fixed my hope in Thee—
   Let nought that hope confound!

"We had a beautiful sermon yesterday," said a working man, as his master stood at his side looking on, in one of the workshops of a large foundry.

"What was the text, John?"

"Well now, I'm a poor hand at chapter and verse—it was a long text, a good deal about charity."

"That's too often the way with you Methodists, John. You seem to be satisfied with the flashes of feeling which may pass over you while you listen to the preacher; or with the mere general impression of some good which you carry away with you from the sermon; without taking any devout pains to get a certain knowledge of the thoughts that touched you, or the sacred words, doctrine, or argument, on which the discourse was founded. It ought not to be so."

"What can I do, sir? My memory is so weak."

"Do? Why, do your best to make your memory stronger, especially about things which have to do with your soul's health. You would manage to recollect any bit of knowledge or skill upon which your weekly wages depended. And if the Bible is the word of Him whom you say you love with all your heart, how is it that you know little or nothing about the prophecy, or the psalm, or the gospel, or the epistle out of which your minister brings truth to your soul? You ought to know God's truth better than you know your trade. Your trade is only for a few days' bread, but God's word is for eternal life. You say the text was a long one, and a good deal about charity?"

"Yes, I remember that."

"Well, but charity is that without the experience and practice of which you cannot be a perfect Christian, or get to the Christian's heaven. Now that chapter which the preacher took for his text gives you the rules of charity or love. It was, I suppose, the thirteenth chapter of the First Epistle to the Corinthians. Did it not begin with 'Though I speak with the tongues of men and of angels,' &c., and finish with 'The greatest of these is charity'"?

"Yes, that was it."

"Can't you tell me what the chapter says about charity?"

"No; I can't go through it all."

"But ought you not to be able? Ought you not to be like the old woman who, feeling her own decay, said that she forgot everything now but Jesus? How can you be an example of that charity or love which you profess is the joy of your heart and the rule of your life, if you don't know what its rules are? You ought to take pains to store your memory with such sacred rules, and try to do it prayerfully."

"I wish I could. How shall I manage? It seems hard to work all the verses into my memory."

"Can you recollect verses of hymns better than verses of Scripture?"

"Yes."

"Come, then, I will repeat a hymn to you which contains all that the preacher's long text says about charity, and gives it all very clearly and pleasantly in rhyme. Now listen :—

"'Tis the heart must truly speak:
Though I had an angel's tongue,
What I said, if love were weak,
Would be like a bell that's rung.

What were all that Paulus knew,
  What Isaiah's prophet art?
What the Exiled Seer's view,
  From his charity apart?
Though my faith should never fail,
  And I could the hills remove,
Nothing would it me avail,
  Were I destitute of love.
All my goods the poor may feed,
  In the fire my body burn;
Yet, unless I love indeed,
  This shall yield me no return.
Love long suffereth and is kind;
  Envies not another's good;
Vaunts not with a puffed-up mind;
  Shuns the manners of the rude.
Never seeketh she her own;
  Never into passion breaks;
Is not to think evil prone,
  But each kind allowance makes.
Not in error, but in truth,
  Taketh she her pure delight;
Full of patientness and ruth,
  Hoping, trusting all is right.
Charity shall never fail,
  Though the prophet's eye grow dim,
Tongues no longer aught avail,
  Knowledge vanish like a dream.
Now, indeed, in part we know,
  And in part we prophesy:
When the perfect cometh, lo!
  Like a shadow these shall fly.
When I was a child, I spoke,
  Thought, and understood as one;
When a man, my place I took,
  I with childish things had done.
Through a glass we darkly see;
  Soon will face to face be shown.
Here we know in part; but we
  There shall know as we are known.
Now abide faith, hope, and love,
  Sweet and sacred virtues three;
But her sisters far above
  Shines divinest Charity."

"They are pleasant verses, as you say, sir. I think I could learn them. Whose are they? Can I get them?"

"They were written by a Mr. Hare, the son of a Methodist preacher. You may not be able to get them in print, but I will write them out for you; and if you will learn verse by verse, and then go to the apostle's chapter and pray over it, I think these verses will help you to remember all the words of the long text; and let me remind you that, when St. Paul prays, 'And the very God of peace sanctify you wholly, and your whole spirit, and soul, and body, be preserved blameless unto the coming of our Lord Jesus Christ,' he means, among other things, not only that perfect love to God will enable a man habitually to govern his body, but that, when the Christian's 'spirit' is fully given to Christ, his 'soul,' or intellect, will be properly regulated and fully exercised. Now, as memory belongs to the intellect as well as the thinking power and the imagination, it is a part of holiness to train that memory to be familiar with the truth which saves us. Otherwise, no man's 'soul' can be 'preserved blameless to the coming of our Lord Jesus Christ.'"

If it could be thought that, as the character of vegetation in some way answers to that of the soil, so, on some spots, the surface productions of the soil may symbolize the character of that human life which occupies it, then a man might think that he had lost his way, if, while in search of refined and sanctified genius, he found himself in a neighbourhood where the human dwellings were flanked by hedge-rows fruitful with poison of the "deadly nightshade." Should he, however, find the genius which he sought on such soil, he would be led, perhaps, to wonder at God's modes of distributing His chosen ones, or His way of choosing their inheritance for them. His conclusion might be that, after all, no part of the peopled world, since antediluvian times, may be without some faithful one who, like Noah, is found "perfect in his generation"; or that, as

> There's not a heath, however rude,
> But hath some little flower
> To brighten up its solitude,
> And scent the evening hour;

so not even a wilderness with borders of deadly nightshade but may have its philosopher, its artist, its Christian poet.

It was in a suburb of North London, near what used to be called "Cut-throat Lane," that an inquirer, a few years ago, found the one whom he sought,—one whose face, bearing, and manner, at once gave fair expression to the man's pure gentleness, fine taste, calm and elegant thought, deep spiritual feeling, and richly-toned poetical genius. Never will the friendly chat in that studio be forgotten. The poet was an artist, and he talked critically, devoutly, and gracefully, as, by turns, he went back from his easel to see the effect of one touch and came up again to give another. The palette and pencils were one day laid down, and he threw open a large quarto Bible with very broad margins, and displayed to his companion's eye a series of marginal pencil sketches that seemed to picture the very life of the prophetic words and actions given in the text. "These," said he, "are the results of some years' efforts at realizing the thoughts, visions, life-scenes, and ministry of inspired and historic men, as they ministered each to his own age or generation. My attempts to make myself one with them, and their times and circumstances, almost unfitted me for the realities and duties of my own life; but I am thankful for that comparative ease with which, as the result, I can now enter into the experience of one who says, 'We walk by faith, not by sight.'" His marginal sketches were poems in picture; but his poetical genius gave some of them a musical form too; and now and then an exquisite little poem would prove how deeply the tuneful soul of the artist had gone into the very soul of those ancient men whose forms and actions he had fixed in the margin of his Bible. Among these rare and finely-cut gems of poesy one is uncommon in its theme and of very distinctive beauty. It is founded on the fortieth chapter of Jeremiah, and is entitled "Gedaliah in Mizpah":—

    This evening I walk upon the walls
    Made strong with stones from Ramah, in the day

When Asa fenced them and Baasha fled
For fear of Syria, with his work half done,
Baffled by politic compacts of power.
At noontide I looked down into the well,
Hollow and echoing, sunk in my courtyard
That men might want no water in a siege
(For Asa thought how Rabbah—with the spring
Clasped in its citadel—for two long years
Kept out even Joab); and there seemed to rise
From its dark ring a mist and shade of death,
Which clung about my thoughts, and raised such dreams
As seldom cross my well-attempered soul—
Rising unbidden, as the gods arose,
Precursors of the shape of Samuel,
In that wild cave of Endor—nay, I saw—
Not visibly, but in my hurtling thought,
This Samuel, who—near six hundred years
Back from the present—made his circuit here,
Judging in Mizpah when there was no king.
Then did the kingdom—which the folk would have
Whether or no—spring up. It here has end.
Both root and branch, and all that pleasant vine,
Brought out of Egypt, flourishing so long,
And bearing such sour fruitage, is uptorn
By the strong eagle of war, and planted far
Among the streams of Shinar. Then I saw
The long, slow, wicked living of the kings
Out-tiring God's long-suffering while He sent
Prophets to hew them with His Word's sharp sword,
Hacking the grove and cleaving the high place,
His judgments every morning going forth,
Clear as the sun's uprising—but in vain !
So that even here—two hundred years ago—
Hosea saw the spreading idol-snare
As on the rounded height of Tabor hill—
And I with my own eyes beheld the snare
Still spread—still here—till all Chaldea came,
And, in a sudden storm of blood and fire,
Broke all the kingdom's power, and took the king,
And slew his sons before his very sight,
Then burned his sight away—and here am I,
Charged with the humble remnant of God's own,
The poor, afflicted dressers of the soil,
Not strong enough to drudge in Babylon !
Some scattered forces wander in the field,
And some have gathered to me with their guides,
Johanan, Jonathan, and Ishmael—
Warlike, yet aimless, with no foe to fight
But hunger and a rising discontent,
Which breaks them from their purpose more and more.
This Ishmael, they tell me, has been hired

By Bene-Ammon with no good intent;
And, taking me aside upon the wall,
Johanan bade me note the oily tongue
Of Ishmael, and his lithe and wiry limbs,
His eye both quick and furtive, and his smile,
Which, said Johanan, he had never seen
Except in men who have a thirst for blood;
And, while he talked, again the mist arose
As from my courtyard well—which whispered death;
The mystic veil of life seemed growing thin,
But yet I could not let my ruler's heart
Inherited from good Ahikam's breast,
As his from Shaphan's—noble ancestry!—
Grow timid with suspicions—nor could give
A sanction based on less than act and deed
For staving off my risks with Ishmael's life.
Man judges by a gesture or a look,
God reads the heart, let God defend His own.
This even I have bid him to a feast;
He eats my bread, and if he lift his heel
Against me—as one did against a king,
Whose high-impassioned heart, whatever fault
Were chargeable against it, always scorned
To crouch with little fears and little cares—
Then let him smite, and let me, smitten, die—
Better to die than wrong one honest heart—
Better to die than live and fear to die.

This charming re-embodiment of old Eastern thought, feeling, character, and life, we owe to Mr. James Smetham, one of those examples of devotion to purely spiritual work in the Church which are, it may be feared, getting rare now among modern Methodist laymen; especially rare in its harmonious combination with high qualities and cultured gifts; one with his lot cast amidst a generation of professors, to crowds of whom an apostle might say, "When for the time ye ought to be teachers, ye have need that one teach you again which be the first principles of the oracles of God, and are become such as have need of milk, and not of strong meat." Yet, the poet is one who may be classed with the "perfect, to whom strong meat belongs, and who by habit have their inward senses alive to distinguish and properly estimate both good and evil." He is one, too, who in times when intellectual culture and refinement of taste are allowed so largely to alienate Methodists from the more spiritual and distinctive ordinances of their own community, finds his joy in bringing all the native and acquired graces of his mind and heart to his beloved and successful work as a class-leader. Nor can those who know him fail to see the secret of his spiritual influence and power over the souls who are happily under his leadership. That secret may be found in the pure child-like simplicity of aim which shows itself with such lovely transparency in his hymn on " The Single Wish ":—

> One thing, O Lord, do I desire;
> Withhold not Thou my wish from me,
> Which warms me like a secret fire:
> That I, Thy child, may dwell with Thee,—
>
> Dwell in Thy house for evermore,
> Thy wondrous beauty to behold,
> And make inquiry as of yore,
> Till all Thy will to me is told.
>
> In this pavilion have I hid
> These many years when hurt by sin,
> Or by my angry sorrows chid,
> Or deaf with life's unceasing din.
>
> Blown hither by the blasts of fear,
> Or stooping with the weight of care,
> My feet have hastened year on year,
> With psalm of praise or sigh of prayer.
>
> Fear tells my heart that I may be
> One day an alien from Thy door;
> May cease Thy lovely face to see,
> And hear Thy whispers never more.
>
> This woe hath not befallen yet;
> Shall it, O Rock of Strength! befall?
> Then were my sun for ever set,
> And dropped in that abyss my all!
>
> Tell me this hour shall never come;
> Plant me so deep Thy courts among,
> That I may have my final home,
> And end where I began my song.

"I was the only son of my father," said a minister the other day; "his hope and mainstay amidst the toils and cares of his old age. I knew somehow, from within, that I should be taken from his side. One conviction had been fixed in my mind from very early—life that was, that I should be a preacher of the Gospel. At the same time I had a persuasion equally strong, that no forward step was needed on my part; but that, if I placed nothing in the way, my path would be opened, and I should most certainly be led into my proper place for life. By-and-by, in some way, the thing was put before my father. He opposed it, and so did his friends. Indeed, he refused his consent that any step should be taken to effect my separation from him. There was delay, therefore, until I was taken with fever, and on the abatement of fever was seized with pleurisy. I remember the night when an old physician stood by my bedside. I saw him shake his head. I knew what he thought, but was in perfect peace. My father was told that I should not, probably, live till the morning. Dear old man! I found out afterwards that he had shut himself up with God, and pleaded for my life, vowing that, if I were spared, he would give me up to the work from which he had hitherto withheld me. I saw the light of another day. Disease had been rebuked, and the morning found me fresh and hopeful. That night had been one of 'weeping' to my father; but 'joy came in the morning,' and the old man realized the double joy of feeling, that God had not only heard his prayer, but had accepted the sacrifice of his boy for the service of Christ. Recollections of that night and that following morning will never pass away. In that morning light stood my father and the old physician once more by my bedside—one smiling to see me smile, and the other in wonderment at the startling change, but piously willing to think that my restoration might be, in a great degree, owing to the peace of my soul, allowing the body its utmost advantage of quietness and freedom to rally. My recollections of that scene have become much more fresh and bright since I met with some lines by the Rev. F. F. Woolley, now of Hammersmith, whom I knew long ago, but whom I have not seen for years, and, perhaps, shall never see again in the flesh. How little one can foresee Who would have thought at our interview in earlier life that verses from his pen would have come to brighten my retrospect now, and by their tender beauty and true poetic feeling help, in my evening of life, to deepen my assurance that, to the very end, I shall find it true, ' In the evening weeping endures, and singing in the dawn ; ' or, as our Methodist preacher and songster entitles his song, ' Joy cometh in the morning ' :—

> " The shades of evening deepen fast,
>   Looming along the dreary lea;
> Each sound of rural life is past—
>   The herd's deep low, the rustic's glee,
>   The throstle's song, the hum of bee—
> And silence reigns at last.
>
> Uncheer'd by the dim taper's light,
>   The watcher by the couch of pain
> In the still chamber *feels* the night,
>   And fears her hope hath all been vain;
>   Nor in the gloom dares hope again
> For buoyant spirit bright.
>
> The ever-restless fevered brow,
>   The beautiful and speaking eye,
> The burning lips which whisper low,
>   The rapid breath, the sudden sigh,
>   All tell that loved one soon must die—
> No hope remaineth now.
>
> With slow, soft step she walks the room,
>   Or bends to soothe the weary head ;
> Counting each lazy hour of gloom,
>   And longing that the last were fled—
>   For night seems suited to the dead,
> And to the silent tomb.
>
> And often peering through the pane
>   Her eye looks for a streak of grey
> Along the east, but looks in vain ;
>   The darkness doth not pass away,
>   No tint tells of the coming day—
> Life dawns not on the brain.
>
> But lo ! at length the twilight gleams,
>   The clouds begin to break and fly,
> The morning opes in rosy beams,
>   Unveiling now a beauteous sky,
>   And sheds upon her weary eye
> Its glittering, golden streams.
>
> New life that orient light doth bring ;
>   The blackbird pipes its liquid note,

"The lark is on its buoyant wing,
　Its rich song on the air afloat;
　And every warbler swells its throat
In gleesome carolling.
Hope shineth on the sufferer's bed;
　The listless hand is cooler now,
Softer the eye, and calm the head,
　The flush no more is on the brow,
　The pulse, erst rapid, beateth slow;
The watcher's prayer hath sped!
Fear now hath vanished with the night,
　And hope revives her soul at last;
　Her heart, and eye, and face, are bright;
　Joy cometh with the morning fast;
　Thank God the gloomy night is past!
Thank God for morning light!"

Every man has his own mental and moral inheritance. Family physical types are kept up, if not immediately from one to another in the family line, yet making their appearance again in clear distinctiveness after more or less of interval. But mental and moral features, too, are mysteriously perpetuated; and much of suffering as well as comfort may be the lot of one generation, coming as a sort of bequeathment from another that was before it. It does not follow, however, that a man must be a poet because his father was before him. Though sometimes the original poetic genius and elemental powers that were possessed and put forth with untrained energy by a father, may show themselves in the son more richly developed, and harmonized under circumstances of culture. So it would appear to be from the public utterances and poetic effusions of one, at least, among living Methodist songsters.

It was on a Whit-Monday, about seventy years ago, that the little village of Denby in South Derbyshire was all astir. The Benefit Club was to turn out, and march to church. There was a mustering of old flags. Every man proudly handled his newly-painted staff. Flute and fiddle, triangle, bagpipes, and drum, were attuned. The ranks fell in. The band struck up; and then,

　　　With motion like clock-work, they all move along,
　　　First right leg, then left, as the bell goes ding dong.

All at last were in their places at church. There was to be the usual sermon from the parson, who was nothing loath to dispense his guinea's worth; for temporalities were of more importance to him than such spiritual matters as he thought might be left to those who knew more about them. His Whit-Monday sermon was, perhaps, more valuable than many others in his stock, as it served every year, and every year was again paid for by the club. All were on the look out for the homily, now become so well known; when, lo! even thoughts of the club dinner were interrupted by the announcement of a new text, and by the opening of a new sermon. What could this mean? The text, too, was remarkable—"Be not righteous over much; neither make thyself over wise; why shouldest thou destroy thyself?" The problem was soon solved. It was a sermon against the Methodists. The club was warned and exhorted to beware of the over-righteous people whose teachings and practice were declared to be dangerous to soul and body, Church and State; tending most certainly to self-destruction. There was one Methodist in the club upon whom the discourse had anything but a soothing effect. And as the club passed out in order before the parson, who, at the close of the service, stood in the porch to give them his smile, this young member confronted his pastor, and cried at the top of his voice, "If Satan, sir, had taken the pulpit this morning, he would have preached as you did!" "Who are you?" was the angry response, "who are you, who presume to call a clergyman in question?" "Sir!" replied the other, "if some one did not speak, surely the very stones would cry out!" The parson left the field. At this crisis, when there might be some fears that the young zealot's conduct would cost him dismissal from his master's service, for he was a farm-servant, the very master himself, recovering a little from the bewilderment into which the parson's discourse had thrown him, walked up, and said, "Benjamin, if you'll tell 's what that text really means, we'll all stop and hear you." It was too good a chance for Benjamin, who was, in fact, a Methodist local preacher. He took his stand on the church steps. He was no more in apparent social position than farmer Abel's man; but to unseen observers he was really more. There he stood, with his long face, which told how used he was to pondering; his high, round brow, showing its signs of power beneath his black hair, combed in straight primitive fashion; his large Roman nose, and his eye—verily his eye—there was but one —his flashing brown eye. The power of that eye was felt by a person, who says, " I heard him preach once. His text was, 'Upon one stone shall be seven eyes.' And I thought as I looked up at him and met his gaze, 'And sure enough you've got one of them!'" But now that eye threw its light around from the church steps upon the congregated club, standing with their banners and staves, and hushed band, willing even to delay their dinner, that they might have a sermon from one of themselves. The text was the parson's own. And now the preacher lifted up his strong, well-modulated voice, and with firm articulation, fervent gravity, logical expertness, vigorous and quaint style, he held the crowd in deep, silent attention, while he showed that "over-much righteousness is necessarily a righteousness pushed too far in one direction; that the over-much righteousness which tends to self-destruction is self-righteousness, showing itself in various ways—in straining towards a self-imposed standard of righteousness in one's own strength, instead of frankly accepting the righteousness of the Gospel; an over-done, hollow, outward righteousness, paying 'tithe of mint, anise, and cummin;' an over-much righteousness in one's own conceit, needing no repentance, not submitting to the righteousness of God; the worst instance of overdoing in one direction, which is undoing in another." This was the first Methodist sermon ever heard in Denby. And this preaching genius was Benjamin Gregory, the father of a genius, scholar, theologian, preacher, writer, Christian poet, still living to bless Methodism with his consecrated utterances in prose and verse. Surely, if the hallowed employment of poetic gifts on the part of the son gives pleasure to the poetic spirit of a glorified parent, one may think of the old preacher in paradise, setting his son's grand and beautiful psalms to music, and finding his joy deepened while singing such metrical renderings from the Psalter as this, on the first seventeen verses of the eighteenth Psalm:—

> I love Thee from my inmost heart,
>   O Lord! my strong munition:
> My sunlit castle crag, Thou art,
>   My God, my foe's perdition;
>   Redeemer, Rock of rest,
>   Broad buckler, crowning crest,
>   My horn of victory,
>   My tower heaven-high,
> My song, and my salvation.
>
> For death's wild waves came roaring round,
>   And Belial's bands assailed me,
> I sunk in hell's black horrors drown'd,
>   My struggles nought availed me;
>   Death had me in his net,
>   He drew it tighter yet;
>   My suffocating cry
>   Was lifted up on high—
> It rose unto the Temple.
>
> Then the earth shook and trembled sore,
>   Started her strong foundation;
> The monarch mountains shrunk before
>   Jehovah's indignation;
>   Uprose the pillar'd smoke,
>   Fire from His mouth outbroke,
>   And the charred cedars blazed;
>   Earth's ruin glowed and glazed
> Beneath the stooping heavens.
>
> Upon a cherub strong He flew,
>   The solid blackness bore Him;
> The wingèd wings His chariot drew,
>   And cleft the gloom before Him:
>   Thick darkness was his shrine,
>   Around Him tempests twine,
>   Clouds His pavilion spread,
>   And canopy o'erhead;
> Hail-storms are his outriders.
>
> As from mid-gloom His glory shone
>   The reverent clouds retreated,
> Hurling huge stones my foes upon,
>   And bolts in fury heated.

> Hark! O'er the hush of fear
> His battle-shout I hear!
> Peal over peal it rolls,
> Hailstones and hissing coals
> From the rent heaven outshaking.
>
> He sent out arrows fast and far,
> And my fierce foes He scatter'd;
> With lightnings from His rushing car
> Their serried ranks He shatter'd.
> Old Ocean felt His breath,
> And struck with shivering death,
> He gathered up his waves,
> Laid bare his oozy caves
> To the world's gaping centre.
>
> Deep down among the startled dead
> His melting eye hath found me;
> His angels sped to raise my head,
> His arm I felt around me.
> From the devouring foam
> His heart received me home,
> And my strong enemies
> Let go their helpless prize—
> For He hath over-matched them.

The departed father of Benjamin Gregory, the author of this fine rendering, entered the ranks of the Methodist ministry in 1799, and became remarkable among remarkable contemporaries, such as Jabez Bunting, Robert Newton, and Daniel Isaac. He was born at Little Eaton, near Derby, November 25, 1772; where, very early, he manifested his native poetic quaintness of turn by issuing a popular nursery-rhyme, suggested by the monotonous music of the church-bells, and, perhaps, the growing numbers of spoiled, or, as he would say, *marred* children:—

> Ring 'em, ding 'em; bells at Eaton,
> Crying children must be beaten;
> Beaten i' th' house, beaten i' th' yard,
> All because they are so *marr'd*.

This nursery-rhymester's parentage was not favourable to Methodism; his father being parish clerk, and his mother a Unitarian. But under Methodist preaching his heart was changed, and his mental powers developed, until he became proof against Church influence, powerful against the Socinian

Antichrist, and so distinguished as a preacher that, after thirty years' work in the Methodist Itinerancy, he was welcomed back and honoured in " his own country " as an able minister of Jesus Christ. He had poetic genius as well as pulpit power. Of this he has left evidence in a single published sermon on the " Death of the Princess Charlotte," and in a small volume, entitled, " Short Poems on various Religious Subjects." His pulpit power has been inherited, enriched, and beautified, by his son, the editor, of the *City Road Magazine;* and in that son he has an elegant and cultured representative of his poetic genius and power. None will doubt this after they have caught the spirit and felt the music of that son's metrical version of the forty-second Psalm:—

> As the chased hart on the mountains,
>   Peering backward wistfully,
> Panteth for the far-off fountains,
>   So my soul, O God, for Thee!
> For the living God it thirsteth;
>   When shall I again appear
> Where salvation's current bursteth
>   From Thy presence fresh and clear?
>
> Tears have been my only diet,
>   Sole refreshment of my nights,
> Whilst upon my dumb disquiet,
>   Still the scornful question smites,
> "Where is *now* thy God, thy 'Glory'?"
>   Brooding thus my soul I pour,
> Telling it the silent story
>   Of my blessedness of yore.
>
> To God's house I marchèd singing,
>   'Mid the Sabbath-keeping throng,
> With our praise the city ringing,
>   As we slowly stept along.
> O, my soul, why thus dejected?
>   Why disquieted in me?
> Hope in God; His smile reflected
>   On my face again shall be.
>
> O, my God, my spirit sinketh;
>   Yet will I remember Thee;
> From the land whose exile drinketh
>   Jordan's separating sea;

From old Hermon's shadows lonely,
  And from Mizar's darkened hill,
I will think upon Thee only—
  I will think upon Thee still.

Deep to deep the signal shouteth,
  Wave to wave roars wild reply,
And Thy answering tempest spouteth
  From the chasms of the sky:
All Thy billows have gone o'er me;
  Yet the Lord will soon command
His own guardian Love before me,
  Like the glory-cloud, to stand.

All day long His hand shall shade me,
  All the night His song shall cheer,
And my prayer to Him who made me
  Shall delight His willing ear:
Th' my free expostulation
  Unto God, my Rock, shall be,
Why hast Thou, my sworn Salvation,
  In my woes forgotten me?

Why go I in scornèd sorrow,
  Bow'd beneath the tyranny
Of Thy foes, till conscience borrow
  Tauntings of the enemy?
As a poison-pointed arrow,
  Fiery dart, bone-bruising rod,
Sword-point piercing joints and marrow,
  Comes the taunt, "Where's now thy God?"

O, my soul, why thus dejected?
  Why disquieted in me?
Hope in God; His smile reflected
  On my face again shall be.

INDEX.

		PAGE
A giant flower, &c.	*Emma Tatham.*	8
A lily of the vale without a spot	*Do.*	8, 9
Author of Being, Source of Light	*S. Wesley, Senr.*	34
A Steward once, the Scripture says	*Do.*	50
Angels, where'er we go, attend	*C. Wesley.*	59, 60
As o'er fair Cloe's rosy cheek	*John Wesley.*	79
Arise, my soul, arise	*C. Wesley.*	118
Away with our sorrow and fear	*Do.*	145
Ask not who ended here his span	*Gambold.*	166
All hail the power of Jesu's name	*Ed. Perronet.*	182
"A Descriptive and Plaintive Elegy on the Death of the late Rev. John Wesley"	*Oliver.*	239, 240
"A Penitential Soliloquy"	*Byrom.*	248
As through mid-air the sweeping current blows	*A. Bulmer.*	271
Awake, my muse, and swell the votive lay	*Treffry, Junr.*	287
As some bright cloud, by evening's sunlight painted	*Do.*	299
Amidst the wonders Islington can boast	*S. Drew.*	315
Accept, dear Mary, on thy natal day	*Do.*	315
"A Psalm of Prophecy"	*J. Sutcliffe.*	327
And light I saw like to a flowing river	*Dante.*	366
"A Christian seeking to be useful"	*W. M. Bunting.*	381
"Among the Mountains"	*Do.*	383
"A Christmas welcome to divers sparrows," &c.	*Do.*	384
A poor old crow, with wounded wing	*Do.*	385
Almighty God, whose hand of power, &c.	*E. Tatham.*	403
Art thou created for a sinner's sight	*Do.*	410
Ah, meet me at the portal of the grave	*Do.*	409
"Angel whispers"	*B. Gough.*	435
"A Rural Sketch"	*Do.*	443
All the world's a stage	*Shakespeare.*	449
A faithful witness of Thy grace	*C. Wesley.*	450
"At the Door"	*B. Gough.*	45
And would'st thou wake the minstrel's lyre?	*T. Garland.*	457
As the chased hart on the mountains	*B. Gregory.*	479
"Apology for the enemies of music"	*C. Wesley.*	92
"A Retrospect"	*Do.*	153
"Anti-Empiricus"	*J. W. Thomas.*	393

		PAGE
Before this beauteous world was made	S. Wesley.	34
Behold the Saviour of mankind	Do.	38, 39
Beneath, a sleeping infant lies	S. Wesley, Junr.	51
But should the bold usurping spirit	C. Wesley.	57
Bound in chains of hidden night	Do.	58
But, oh, thou man of God	Berridge.	193
Beneath this solitary shade	Brackenbury.	254
Bible, Verses on	A. Bulmer.	271
"Blessings," A hymn	Do.	279
Be thou rich or poor	E. Tatham.	401
Bathed in the ruddy light	J. Harris.	422
Come, neighbours, with your sticks and stones		13
Commit thou all thy griefs	J. Wesley, from Gerhardt.	108
Come, Thou everlasting Lord	C. Wesley.	121
Come, O thou Traveller unknown	Do.	155
Come hither, ye whom from an evil world	Gambold.	165
Children of the heavenly King	Cennick.	199
Come, O my God and King	W. Darney.	214
Come, immortal King of Glory	Oliver.	222
Careless content	Byrom.	246
Come, Saviour Jesus, from above	Do. from Bourignon.	247
Companions of Thy little flock	Lady Huntingdon.	263
Christ, He sits on Zion's hill	Bourne.	333
"Covenant Hymn"	W. M. Bunting.	377
Come, let us use the grace divine	C. Wesley.	378
Come, Holy Ghost, all quickening fire	Do.	382
"Christian Heroism"	J. Harris.	422
Come, climb with me	B. Gough.	442
"Christ by the Sea"	C. L. Ford.	674
"Character and Exploits of David": A Poem	M. Hare	480
"Conversion Hymn"	C. Wesley.	86, 87
Dear mother, you were once	Hetty Wesley.	67
Death in the pot! 'tis always there	C. Wesley.	152
Dear Jesus, cast a look on me	Berridge.	190
Devotion! holiest offspring of the skies	McNicoll.	318
"Divina Comedia"	Dante.	364
Down into hollows where the running brooks	B. Gough.	441
"Epistle concerning Poetry"	S. Wesley, Sen.	38, 351
"English bards," &c.	Byron.	38, 351
England, Verses to Christian	A. Bulmer.	276
Enoch, the seventh, walked with God	Bourne.	334
"Edwin; or, Northumbria's Royal Captive"	J. Everett.	450
"Early Christian Songs"	M. Hare.	480
Epitaph	C. Wesley.	89
Eupolis' "Hymn to the Creator"	S. Wesley.	34
From whence these dire portents	S. Wesley, Junr.	54, 55
Farewell to the world	Hetty Wesley.	77

INDEX.

		PAGE
Father of all, whose powerful voice	*J. Wesley.*	98
Father of everlasting grace	*C. Wesley.*	148
"Festival Songs"	*Do.*	147
For thousand, thousand mercies new	*A. Bulmer.*	279
Far be it from me I should choose	*E. F. A. Sergeant.*	282
Farewell, ye scenes where desolation reigns	*S. Drew.*	309
For her on the morn of her birth	*W. M. Bunting.*	369
"Good Friday Hymn"		39
Great Power, at whose Almighty hand	*Hetty Wesley.*	76
God of faithful Abraham, hear	*C. Wesley.*	123
Guide me, O Thou great Jehovah	*Williams.*	177
Glory to God on high	*James Allen.*	215
God bless the king	*Byrom.*	250
Gloomy cloud, that, low'ring low	*A. Bulmer.*	273
God's Love	*E. Tatham.*	401
"Gertrude of Wyoming"	*Campbell.*	430
"Gedaliah in Mizpah"	*James Smetham.*	486
"Gloria in Excelsis"	*Williams.*	177
Henceforth may no profane delight	*Byrom, from Bourignon.*	10
Hide me by Thy presence, Lord	*C. Wesley.*	25
Here she beholds the chaos dark	*Pope.*	28
"Hymns and Sacred Poems"	*J. & C. Wesley.*	34, 162, 97, 194
Hail, Father, whose creating word	*S. Wesley, Junr.*	53, 54
His eyes diffuse a venerable grace	*Emilia Wesley.*	60
How happy is the pilgrim's lot	*J. Wesley.*	102
How shall a slave released	*C. Wesley.*	116
How full of heaven his latest word	*Do.*	172
"Hymn of Praise to Christ"	*Oliver.*	230
"Hymn to the God of Abraham"	*Do.*	232
Hail, thou once despised Jesus	*Bakewell.*	258
"Hymns, A Collection of"	*Lady Huntingdon.*	263
High on Thy heavenly seat	*A. Bulmer.*	269
Hail, holy record of supernal love	*Do.*	271
Heaven, to thy hands the lamp, &c.	*Do.*	276
Hail, Lord of angel-hosts above	*J. Bustard.*	332
"Hymns for Camp-meetings"	*Bourne.*	335
"Hymns for Children"	*J. Everett.*	337
"Hymn of Thanksgiving for Preservation," &c.	*Do.*	337
How glorious the mount to behold	*Do.*	339
"Hymns for. Pastors and People"	*S. Dunn.*	340
He had written much blank verse	*Byron.*	352
He who foresaw the ruin of mankind	*J. W. Thomas.*	354
"Hymn of Paradise"	*Do.*	358
Hail, sweet musician	*J. Harris.*	413
Hast ever seen a mine?	*Do.*	421
Hail to thee, little flower	*Do.*	428

	PAGE
Hail to thee, mountain birth-place	*J. Harris.* 429
Haunt of the sea-bird	*Do.* 431
Have you heard an angel's whisper?	*B. Gough.* 436
Here is a pleasant nook	*Do.* 443
Hail, mighty ocean	*C. Garland.* 450
"Hosannah to the Son of David"	*Williams.* 177
In a mean cot, composed of reeds,	*S. Wesley.* 31
If highest worth in beauty's bloom	*Hetty Wesley.* 62
If blissful spirits condescend	*Do.* 62, 63
I am an implement that's common	*Do.* 67
If e'er thou did'st in Hetty see	*Do.* 71
Integrity needs no defence	*J. Wesley.* 80
In age and feebleness extreme	*C. Wesley.* 89
In Thine utmost indignation	*Do.* 150
I am content, I do not care	*Byrom.* 244
It was a fearful night when fell Despair	*A. Bulmer.* 271
In what soft numbers shall my muse	*Treffry, Senr.* 292
I love the dawnings of the beautiful	*McNicoll.* 321
I had a dream, which was not all	*J. W. Thomas.* 347
In the beginning!—yes	*Do.* 348
In the worst inn's worst room	*Pope.* 351
It was at Oxford, as I said	*J. W. Thomas.* 360
"Il Paradiso"	*Dante.* 365
In Wensley Dale there lies a village	*E. Tatham.* 399
I'm fond of travelling old deserted	*J. Harris.* 412
I ask Thy heavenly guidance	*Do.* 424
I'm very fond of sparrows	*B. Gough.* 446
In the time of sorrow	*Do.* 452
I love Thee from my inmost heart	*B. Gregory.* 495
Jesus, Thou art my righteousness	*C. Wesley.* 114
Jesus, lover of my soul	*Do.* 131—134
Jesus, the name high over all	*Do.* 141, 142
Jesus, accept the grateful song	*Do.* 142
Jesus, Thy blood and righteousness	*J. Wesley, from Zinzendorf.* 194
Jesus, my all, to heaven is gone	*Cennick.* 196
Jerusalem divine	*Rhodes.* 212
Jesu, touch this heart of mine	*Byrom.* 250
Jesus, at Thy command I go	*Brackenbury.* 254
Joy to thine opening eye	*J. Harris.* 427
Joy cometh in the morning	*F. F. Wooley.* 491
Kent Sunday Schools	*J. Bustard.* 330
Let thy mind's sweetness have its operation	29
Lo! from the borders of the grave	*Whitfield.* 173
Leaning on Thy loving breast	*Berridge.* 193
Lord, I Thy messengers receive	*Brackenbury.* 253
Long his flight the avenging angel	*A. Bulmer.* 272

INDEX.

		PAGE
"Life"	McNicoll.	322
"Litanies and Confessions"	J. Sutcliffe.	325
Let my lamp at midnight hour	Milton.	345
"Lament of Mary Queen of Scots"	J. W. Thomas.	353
"Lays from the Mine, the Moor," &c.	J. Harris.	416
"Love of Home"	Do.	415
Little music-breathing lyre	Do.	416
"Land's End"	Do.	430
Let others hail their day of birth	T. Garland.	462
"Lyra Christi"	C. L. Ford.	470
My God, I love Thee, not because	Hymns A. & M.	15
My fortunes often bid me flee	Hetty Wesley.	55, 56
Methinks I see you striving all	S. Wesley, Junr.	64
Men of true piety, they know not why	C. Wesley.	92
My name be on the children? No	Do.	152
"Martyrdom of Ignatius: a Tragedy"	Gambold.	165
Make the extended skies your tomb	Hervey.	169
My heart and voice I raise	Rhodes.	209
"Messiah's Conquest"	W. Batty.	217
"Messiah's Kingdom"	A. Bulmer.	270, 276
"More than meets the eye"	McNicoll.	321
Missionary hymn	J. Sutcliffe.	329
Mount Tabor	J. Everett.	337
"Ministry of Angels"	W. M. Bunting.	374
My mother's voice! it haunts me	J. Harris.	432
"My Sparrows"	B. Gough.	446
My children, pleasant are your voices	C. L. Ford.	472
"Maggots"	S. Wesley.	27—29
"Mitre, The"	E. Perronet.	183
Mirth, Vain: A hymn	Berridge.	193
No matter how dull the scholar	C. Wesley.	15
No fiction shall guide my hand	S. Wesley, Junr.	64, 65
No—wert thou as thou wast	C. Wesley.	85
No trumpet was blown	Treffry, Junr.	302
Now through the aisle	J. W. Thomas.	360
O Thou whose poetry and love	E. Tatham.	5
O let my heart in tune be found	Watts.	14
O tarry not, your Lord obey	Old Baptist H.B.	15
Oh, she's dead!—but she's gone, &c.	Anon.	17
Or worn by slowly rolling years	S. Wesley, Junr.	47, 48
Oppressed with utmost weight of woe	Hetty Wesley.	74
O Lord, I bow my sinful head	J. Wesley.	81
O God, my God, my all Thou art	Do., from the Spanish.	104
O for a heart to praise my God	C. Wesley.	119
O'er the gloomy hills of darkness	Williams.	178
"Occasional Verses, Moral and Sacred"	Ed. Perronet.	182
O Father, let Thy kingdom come	Berridge.	189

O, dear Redeemer, who alone	*Wm. Batty.*	217
Our hearts and hands to Christ we raise	*Oliver.*	230
Oh, thou God of my salvation	*Do.*	237
O'er thy much-loved infant's urn	*Treffry, Senr.*	290
Oh, the river! oh, the river	*S. Dunn.*	340
On Sinai's lofty steep, where Moses stood	*J. W. Thomas.*	349
Oh, how shall the sinner perform	*C. Wesley*	379
Oh, happy day that fixed my choice	*Doddridge.*	379
O God, how often hath Thine ear	*W. M. Bunting.*	379
Oh, for my Master's generous mind	*Do.*	381
Oh, never could my Master seek	*Do.*	386
Oh, that thou had'st a soul, sea-bird	*E. Tatham.*	406
On sweeps the war-fiend	*J. Harris.*	426
Oh, wind! terrible wind!	*B. Gough.*	438
"On the Meekness and Gentleness of Christ,"	*C. L. Ford.*	477
One thing, O, Lord, do I desire	*J. Smetham.*	489
Poor harmless Wesley, let him write again	*Dunton.*	39
Publish, spread to all around	*C. Wesley.*	92
Peace my heart, be calm, be still	*Do.*	121
Permit me to foretell thy doom	*Ed. Perronet.*	185
Praise God, my soul, whose wondrous love	*R. Rodda.*	204
Paraphrase, Poetic, on John iii. 8	*A. Bulmer.*	275
"Peace, all is peace!" th' expiring warrior said	*Treffry, Junr.*	291
"Pleasures of Devotion"	*McNicoll.*	322
"Psalms and Hymns"	*J. Sutcliffe.*	326
"Peace Poems"	*J. Harris.*	426
Psalm eighteenth	*B. Gregory.*	495
Psalm forty-second	*Do.*	497
Quoth Christ, No sparrow falleth to the ground	*W. M. Bunting.*	384
Righteous God, whose vengeful vials	*C. Wesley.*	140
Ready for my earthen bed	*Do.*	153
Rome, its Fall, Verses on	*A. Bulmer.*	272
"Reflections on St. Austell Church-yard"	*S. Drew.*	311, 312
Ring 'em, ding, 'em; bells at Eaton	*B. Gregory, Senr.*	496
Sweet are the uses of adversity	*Shakespeare.*	27
Surely when Prometheus climb'd	*S. Wesley, Senr.*	29
Sweet recreation barr'd	*Shakespeare.*	30
She graced my humble roof	*S. Wesley, Senr.*	31, 32
Spirit of faith, come down	*C. Wesley.*	116
Saviour of all, what hast Thou done	*Do.*	127
So many years I've seen the sun	*Gambold.*	163
Since all the downward tracts of time	*Hervey.*	167
Send help, O Lord, we pray	*Berridge.*	186
"Sion's Songs"	*Do.*	191
Sacred Poetry on Old and New Testament	*Brackenbury.*	255
Sparkling and silent, save where	*Adeline.*	277
"Saul of Tarsus"	*Treffry, Junr.*	302

		PAGE
"Scripture Themes in Rills and Streams"	*J. Bustard.*	331
"Salvation for All"	*H. Bourne.*	336
"Save Some"	*S. Dunn.*	342
"Sinai"	*J. W. Thomas.*	349
Stiff in opinions, always in the wrong	*Dryden.*	351
She sate upon the vessel's deck	*J. W. Thomas.*	356
Solomon's Song, English version	*Do.*	356
Saviour, to whom my strain I bring	*W. M. Bunting.*	375
"Sea Bird"	*E. Tatham.*	405
Shakespeare's Birthday	*J. Harris.*	422
"Spring"	*T. Garland.*	468
Sweet, simple blossom of the brake	*C. L. Ford.*	476
"Song of Songs"	*M. Hare.*	480
"Short Poems on various Religious Subjects"	*B. Gregory, Senr.*	497
"Select Psalms"	*C. Wesley.*	150
"Short Hymns on Select Passages	*Do.*	151
Though now there seems one only, &c.	*French.*	6
There's bread and fish for you and me		12
'Tis like the precious ointment		13
The race is not for ever got		13
To lie in shady cloister mew'd	*Shakespeare.*	15
The snuff-box first provokes	*S. Wesley, Junr.*	30
"The Life of Christ:" A Poem	*S. Wesley, Senr.*	32
The Father's image He, as great	*Do.*	34
The morning flowers display their sweets	*S. Wesley, Junr.*	48
The Lord of Sabbath let us praise	*Do.*	52
'Twas owing to his friendly care	*Hetty Wesley.*	66
The period fast comes on when I	*Do.*	68
Though sorer sorrows than their birth	*Do.*	74
"The Resignation"	*Do.*	76
"The Man of Fashion"	*C. Wesley.*	85
Thou God of harmony and love	*Do.*	94
'Tis done! The Sovereign will's obey'd	*Do.*	96
"To a Friend in Love"	*Gambold.*	162
"The Mystery of Life"	*Do.*	163
Thou who a tender parent art	*Whitfield.*	174
To what compare thy fertile womb	*Edward Perronet.*	183
Thou dear Redeemer, dying Lamb	*Cennick.*	195
The God of Abraham praise	*Oliver.*	232
The pensive dove whene'er his mate	*Do.*	240
Turn again, my children, turn	*Brackenbury.*	255
The blessed Jesus is my Lord	*Lady Huntingdon.*	265
Then, hapless man, the soil that gave	*A. Bulmer.*	270
Thou who hast in Sion laid	*Do.*	275
Tropical plain	*Adeline.*	278
The desert spread around me	*Do.*	278
These eyes have seen a tender mother	*S. Drew.*	307
There shall I bathe my weary soul	*Watts.*	318
The perfect man has faith in God	*S. Dunn.*	341
"The Beginning"	*J. W. Thomas.*	348

L L

INDEX.

		PAGE
"The Cross Anticipated"	J. W. Thomas	354
"The Bridal Week"	Do.	357
True love is light from heaven	Do.	357
The reverend gentleman his text	Do.	361
"The Trilogy"	Do.	365
"To a Mother on her Birthday"	W. M. Bunting.	369
The clamour of the crowd is spent	Do.	376
"The Christian's Chamber"	Do.	386
"The Mother's Vigil"	E. Tatham	390
They were angels come	Do.	390
"The Dream of Pythagoras"	Do.	393
'Twas but a dream	Do.	394
To yet another lesson, I became	Do.	395
The mother watched with love's	Do.	400
"Tempest Hymn"	Do.	402
"To Die"	Do.	409
The babe dies peacefully in its mother's arms	Do.	409
"To Music"	Do.	409
"To the White Rose"	Do.	409
"To the Passing Month"	J. Harris.	413
"To the Hawthorn"	Do.	413
"To the Thrush"	Do.	413
"To the Skylark"	Do.	413
The earth is fair with fields	Do.	415
"The First Violet"	Do.	417, 428
"The Mother's Teaching"	Do.	417
The springs of hope	Do.	422
There's a language that's mute	T. Garland.	455
"To Isabelle"	Do.	458
'Tis spring—I know by the soften'd	Do.	460
The one sweet resting-place	Do.	467
"To the Ocean"	C. Garland.	467, 470
"The Stars"	Do.	470
"The Last Slumber"	Do.	470
Thy ways were in the haunts of men	C. L. Ford.	474
"To Children Playing"	Do.	476
"To a Wild Rose"	Do.	476
The folded napkin 'mid the earthquake's roar	Do.	477
Thee, God, we praise	M. Hare.	481
'Tis the heart must truly speak	Do.	483
This evening I walk upon the walls	J. Smetham.	486
"The Single Wish"	Do.	489
The shades of evening deepen fast	F. F. Wooley.	491
Upborne aloft on venturous wing	J. Wesley.	82
"Union Version of the Psalms"	J. Sutcliffe.	326
Unsaved, O Lord, Thy people are	S. Dunn.	342
Unbounded source of joy	J. W. Thomas.	358
"Vision of Judgment"	Byron.	352
"Vale of Siddim"	J. W. Thomas.	357

INDEX.

507

		PAGE
Where shall I lay my weary head?	C. Wesley.	7
When Israel, by God's command		13
Why dost thou hold thine hand aback		13
What sudden blaze of song	Keble.	41
While Butler, needy wretch	S. Wesley, Junr.	51
While sickness rends this tenement	Hetty Wesley.	77
Where shall my wondering soul begin?	C. Wesley.	87
With poverty of spirit bless'd	Do.	89
When my sorrows most increase	Do.	127
Worship, and thanks, and blessing	Do.	137
When young, and full of sanguine hope	Do.	154
What art thou, Love?	Gambold.	163
When snows descend, and robe	Hervey.	170
When I tread the verge of Jordan	Williams.	176, 177
We sing to Thee, thou Son of God	Cennick.	198
What!, though no objects strike	Byrom.	248
We soon shall hear the midnight cry	Huntingdon.	266
Within my hand is a little lyre	E. F. A. Sergeant.	280
Why looks my father on that lettered stone	S. Drew.	308
What is the soul? and where does it reside?	Do.	312
What is our life? ofttimes we ask	McNicoll.	322
When in the round of giddy life	J. Sutcliffe.	325
Why do the Gentile nations rage	Do.	327
"Walking with God"	H. Bourne.	334
Within our isle, along our shores	J. Everett.	337
What fair one from the desert do we meet	J. W. Thomas.	357
"War of the Surplice"	Do.	360
When on death's lone bed I lie	W. M. Bunting.	387
"White Roe of Rilston"	Wordsworth.	398
Without, the angry elements	J. Harris.	417
Who hastes to heap up gold shall find	Do.	425
"War Fiend"	Do.	426
Wearied with the long pilgrimage of life	B. Gough.	451
Wings of the dove	C. Garland.	470
Ye monsters of the bubbling deep		14
Ye sons and daughters of the Lord	H. Bourne.	336
Yon mountain altars	W. M. Bunting.	383
Yes, years have darkly stolen by	T. Garland.	458
Zion, arise and shine	J. Sutcliffe.	329

INDEX TO NAMES AND PLACES, &c.

	PAGE
"Account of Christian Perfection," Song about	119
Act of Uniformity	24, 26
Acland, Sir Thomas	383
Adeline, Mrs. Sergeant	277, 278, 279, 280, 283
Addington Square, Margate	405
Allen, Mr. James	215, 217
Alnwick—Abbey—Castle	336
"A Life Lesson," by J. Drew	305
A Jack-Tar's Maxim	27
"A Tobacco Pipe," by S. Wesley	29
Annesley, Dr.	32
American Improvements on Watts	14
"Athenian Gazette"	32
Atterbury, Bishop	49
Athlone, Ireland	197
Associations of the Wesleys, Curious	96
"Arminian Magazine": its Editorship	238
Ancoats Hall, Manchester	275
Arthur, King, his Castle	294
Alan, River, Cornwall	294
"As You Like It," New Act in	355
Ambleside	363
A Very Pretty Stick	17
Axminster	20
Atlantic Ocean	203, 430
Aysgarth, Yorkshire	398
Badcock, Boatman in the Patagonian Mission	117
Bardsley, Samuel	208
Bakewell, Mr. John	234, 257, 259, 260, 261
Bath	475
Baptist Church in Hackney	478
Batty, Lawrence	216
Batty, Giles	216
Batty, Wm.	216, 217
Batty, Christopher	216, 217, 218
Batty, Alice	217
Beveridge, Bishop	13
Belcher, Dr.	14

INDEX TO NAMES AND PLACES, ETC. 509

	PAGE
Bereaved Infidel Saved	124
Bedfordshire	184
Berridge, Rev. John	186, 187, 189, 190, 192
Bedford Family	393
Bourne, Hugh	333, 334, 335
Bourignon, Madame	10, 246
Bohemian Brethren	42
Blundell Grammar School, Tiverton	50, 51
Blundell, Peter	50
Blackwell, the London Banker	95, 107
Blind Young Man at Tewkesbury	129
Birstal, Happy Death at	144
Bolton, Lancashire, Last Visit of J. Wesley	157
Bideford, Devon	169
Bolingbroke, Old, Lincoln	252
Boston's "Four-fold State"	257, 259
Bishopsgate Street, London	327
Bloomsbury, London	393
Bolton Abbey, Yorkshire, 397—Castle	398
Bishop's Dale, Yorkshire	398
Boughton, Kent	435, 437
Brady and Tate	13
Brinkhill, Lincoln	31
Bray, Mr., Moravian	86, 243, 245, 248
Brewster, Rev. Mr.	146
Bristol, 155, 226, 227—Channel	294
Bradford, Wilts	227, 229
Brackenbury, R. C., Esq.	252, 253, 254, 257
Brailsford, Derby	257
Brownwilley Hill, Cornwall	294
Bryant, Rev. John	296
Brougham Castle	363, 364
Brougham, Lord	364
British Museum	393
Buckinghamshire	75
Burnup Field	181
Bulmer, Mr. Joseph	268
Bulmer, Mrs. Agnes	268, 270, 273, 275, 276
Bunting, Thos. Percival	368
Bunting, Rev. W. M.	268, 288, 289, 303, 368, 370, 372, 373, 377, 382
Bunting, Dr. Jabez	368, 380, 496
Bunyan's, John, "Pilgrim"	314
Bustard, Rev. John	330, 332
Burden Moor, Yorkshire	398
Byron, Lord	1, 2, 3, 352
Byrom, Dr.	18, 242, 243, 246, 249, 250, 252
Catholic Christianity	2
Carfax Conduit, Oxford	26
Carter, Mrs. Elizabeth	75
Cares at Night	104

INDEX TO NAMES AND PLACES, ETC.

	PAGE
Canterbury	183, 184
Calvin, John	192, 343
Catherine Hall, Cambridge	216
Carnmarth, Cornwall	219
Carvosso, William, 235—Saintly wife of	235
Callington, Cornwall	235
Campbell, the Poet	430
Cambridge	243
Camelford, Cornwall	293, 294, 295
Camel, River	294
Caxton Press	314
"Catechism of Christian Religion," by Rev. J. Sutcliffe.	326
Camp Meetings, Origin in England	335
Camborne, Cornwall, 340, 417, 422, 475—Exciting Scene in	341
Caledonian Forest	363
Carnbrae, Cornwall	418, 419, 420, 421
Cæsar, Julius	419
Catherston, Dorset	24
Cambridge Farm, Cornwall	456
Cennick, John	194, 195, 196, 197, 199
Centenary Hall, London	327
Church of England Doggrel	15
Chimes and Rhymes	17, 18
Charles II.	21, 22
Charmouth, Dorset	24
Charwell River, Oxford	25
Christchurch, Oxford	164
"Christian World Unmasked," by Berridge	193
Cheerful Piety, by Berridge	193
Cheapside, London	195
Chester City	236
Chancery Lane, London	324
Cheshire	335
Chevy Chase	336
Chaucer	441
Charity, Story about	483
Charlotte, Princess, Sermon on Death of	497
City Road Chapel, London	479
"City Road Magazine"	497
Clayton, Rev. Wm.	161, 249
Clare Hall, Oxford	187
Clarke, Dr., of Bradford	229
Clarke, Dr. Adam	236, 309, 339, 343, 479
Cleveland, Yorkshire	398
Clowes, Wm.	335
Coach Travel	21
Coke, Dr.	314
Coke's, Dr., Edition of "Wesley's Life of Christ"	33, 34
Commentary, by Rev. J. Sutcliffe	326
Confession, a Lesson on	57
Covent Garden Theatre	92

INDEX TO NAMES AND PLACES, ETC. 511

	PAGE
Cornish Minister and Old Woman	147
Cornish Hills	414
Cornwall 168, 207, 230, 235, 294, 339, 340, 414, 415, 444, 456, 461	
Cornish Mines and Miners, 200—Cornish Britons	294
Cork, City	230
Collinson, Agnes	268
Congleton	335
Consecrated Places	372, 373
Conversion on London Bridge	373
Covenant, Renewal by Methodists	378
Coleridge	382
Coutts, Miss Burdett	385
Contented Miner	423, 425
Critic of Redruth	208
Crosse, Mr., of Bradford	325
Cyrus, Travels of, by Raynal	393
Dales-Green, Stafford	335
Dante	364, 365
David, Psalmist, 437, 438—Queerly Versified	13
Dawson, Wm., Anecdote of	181
Darwin, Dr.	29
Darney, Wm.	213, 214, 215
Darwin, Robert, of Epworth	58, 59
Dartmouth, Lord	264
Devonshire, 383—A Hymnist, 12—North	119
Devonport	389
De Quincey, Mr.	459
Delamotte, Mr.	216
Denby, Derby, 492, 496, 494—Shire	257, 492
Deal, Kent	331
Delany, Mrs.	81
Donnington Park	268
Dorset	20, 23, 26
Doddridge, Dr.	379
Dorchester Grammar School	26
Dolcoath Mine, Cornwall	422, 423
Dublin	95, 155, 198
Dryden, John	359
Dunton, the Publisher and Author	29, 32
Duncombe Park, Yorkshire	350
Duncombe, Mr.	75
Drew, Samuel	305, 306, 307, 308, 312, 313, 314, 317
Dundee	320
Dunn, Rev. S.	339, 340, 341, 342, 343
Earthquake in London, 138—Thoughts on, by Wesley	139
Eamont, River	363
Eaton, Little, Derby	496
Elchester, Young Methodist of	130
Eden, River	363
Edward IV.	419

INDEX TO NAMES AND PLACES, ETC.

	PAGE
Edgware, Middlesex	75
Egbert, King	294
English Lakes	363
Epworth	43, 55, 58, 61
Epworth Singers	40, 41, 44, 51, 55, 62
Essay on Godhead of Christ, by J. Sutcliffe	326
Everton, 187, 192—Revival at	188
Everett, James	337, 338, 339, 326, 343
Ewood	215
Exe, River	53, 359
Exeter College, Oxford	26
Exeter, 20, 359—Bishop of	360
Family Life of C. Wesley	122
"Farther Appeal," by J. Wesley	249
Falmouth, Cornwall	305, 430
Fal, River	289
Fairfield, Cornwall	459, 464, 467
"Familiar Colloquies," by M. Hare	479
Fetishism, Christian	372
Fletcher, John, of Madeley	186, 239, 257
Foxall, Cheshire	237
Foundry, Moorfields	250, 260
Fordhays, Stafford	334
Foundling Hospital, London	393
Ford, C. L.	470, 472, 474
Forest Hill, London	480
Frith Street, London	73, 75
Franklin's "Way to Wealth"	314
Gambold, John	161, 162, 163, 164, 166
Gawksholm	215
Garland, Thos.	454, 455, 459, 462, 463, 465, 467, 470
Garland, Charles	467, 470
German Psalmody	42, 43
German Ocean	75
Georgia	81, 105
Gerhardt, Paul, 108 Illustrations of	110, 111
Gell, Dr., on the "Pentateuch"	152
Geake, Mr. and Mrs.	235
George III. and Lady Huntingdon, 264, 265—his Queen	266
"Gentleman's Guide to English," by J. Sutcliffe	326
"Geological Essays," by J. Sutcliffe	326
Gould, Mr.	131
"Gospel Magazine"	182
Goodman, Dr. John	343
Gough, Benjamin	435, 443, 444, 446, 451
Goldsmith, Oliver	197
Granvill, Mary	81
Grimshaw, Rev. Mr.	139, 140, 325
Grenville, Sir Bevil	169
Green, John	217

INDEX TO NAMES AND PLACES, ETC.

	PAGE
Green, Miss	231
Greenwich	259
Grange House	275
Gregory, Benj., Senr.	493, 494, 496
Gregory, Benjamin	496, 497
Gumby, Colonel	250
Gwennap, Cornwall, 107—Pit	148, 219
Harrington, Lincoln	31
Harper, Mrs.	55
Hall, Mr.	85
"Harlequin Preacher at Covent Garden"	93
Haworth, Yorkshire	139, 140, 213, 215, 325
Haslam, Mr., of Markland Hill	158
Hardingston, Northants	166
Hartland, Devon	167, 168, 169
Hawley Square, Margate	212
Hayle, Cornwall	284, 285, 286
Handel, 393, 441—His Music	389
Harris, John	413, 418, 422, 423, 425, 426, 430
Hall, Robt.	465
Hackney	478
Hare, Mr. Middleton	479, 480, 481, 485
Hare, Rev. Edward	479
Henry, Matthew, Commentary	152
Hervey, Rev. James	161, 166, 168, 169, 171
Hervey, Wm.	172
Heptonstall	215
Henry III. of England	252
"Hermit of Warkworth"	331
Helmsley, Yorkshire, 349, 350—Castle	350, 351
Helston, Cornwall	427
High Street, Oxford	26
Highman, Mr.	75
Hicks, Rev. Mr.	187
Highgate Rise, London	382
Honiton	20
Hopkey, Sophia Christiana	81
Holy Club, Oxford	161
Horn, Rev. John	252
Holland	254
Holland, Mr. J., of Sheffield	337
Holmcote, Devon	383
Holborn Hill, London	392, 399, 401, 402, 403
Hudibras	51
Huntingdon, Countess of, 177, 183, 184, 189, 192, 262, 263, 264, 265, 266, 268	
Hulne Abbey	336
Hymns of Methodist Poets	11
"Hymns, Ancient and Modern"	15, 91
Hymn-making on Horseback	88, 89

	PAGE
Hymns for a Family	120
Hymns for the Brotherhood	128
Hymn of a Young Mother	173
Indiana, U.S., Pilgrim Preacher of	103
Ingham, Benjn.	161, 174, 215, 217
"Immortality of the Soul," by J. Sutcliffe	326
Ireland	139, 230
Islington, London	242, 243, 245
Isaac, Rev. D.	496
Ivey, Mr.	295
Jabbok River	155
Jackson, the Painter	317
Jackson, Rev. Thos.	330
Jenyns, Soame, Works of	133
Jordan, River	155
Johnson, Dr. Samuel	66, 393
Keith, Scotch Family	337
Kent	211, 212, 442, 444
Kexborough, Yorkshire	210
Kendal	218
Kersal-cell, Manchester	249
Kentish Town, London	382
Kirk of Scotland Doggrel	15
Kirton, Lincoln	43
Kirkham, Betsy	81
Kirkham, Robert	81
Kirk, Rev. J.	155
Kingswood	155, 197
Kilkhampton, Cornwall	168
Kingston, Northants	187
Kidsgrove, Stafford	335
Kirby Moorside, Yorkshire	351
Kynance Cove, Cornwall	416
Laud, Archbishop	26
Lambert, John, of Epworth	64
Lampe, Mr., Musician, 92, 93—Death and Elegy	96
Lancashire	215
Langson, Mary	237
Law, Wm.	241
Lacy, Mr. Jeremiah	259
Lanteglos, Cornwall	294
Langstrothdale Chase, Yorkshire	398
Lady in a West of England Paradise	407
Land's End, Cornwall	430
Lamb, Charles	459
Lawrence, Mr., Story of	471
Leyburn, Yorkshire	80
Lee, Elizabeth, of Nottingham	145
Leeds	224

INDEX TO NAMES AND PLACES, ETC. 515

	PAGE
Leoni, Dr.	234
Lincolnshire	43, 211, 252
Lincoln College, Oxford	27
Limerick	230
Little Britain, London	242, 248
London, 26, 230, 242, 295, 314, 326, 392, 397, 400, 401, 408—From, to Oxford on Foot, 25—Houses and Streets, 393—Bridge	373
Loman, River, Devon	53
Lomas, John, of Manchester	131
Lombard, Rev. Daniel	294
Locke, John	314
Louth, Lincoln	31
Luther	42, 43, 192
Lynton, Devon	383
Master Singers	42
Marazion, Cornwall	100
Manchester, 131, 242, 274, 275—An Infidel in	124
Martyn, Tune	133
Margate	212, 404
Maidenhead, Kent	303
"Magazine, Imperial"	314
Malcolm's Cross	336
Mary of Scots	356
McNicoll, Rev. David	317, 318, 319, 322, 323
Methodism	2, 9, 16
Methodists, their Principles	8
Methodist Magazines, Ancient and Modern	12, 270
Methodist Club, 242—Hymn-book, 465—Book-room	479
Methodist Doggrel	15
"Meditations," Hervey's	167, 171
Mevagissey, Cornwall	339
"Measure for Measure," New Scene in	355
Milton, his Hymns, 11—Sonnets	348
Minnie Singers	42
Middleham, Yorkshire	398
Miner's Remarkable Escape	111
Mount Edgcumbe, Cornwall	126
Moravians	162
Montgomeryshire	225
Montgomery, James	234, 270, 337
Moorfields, London	250
Modred, King Arthur's Nephew	294
Mow Cop, Stafford	335
Mountfield, Kent	434, 435, 440
Murray, Grace	81
Musician's Hymn	94
Music, Heavenly	389
Mystic Hymnists	42
Newington Green, London	26
Newcastle	95, 337

	PAGE
Nelson, John, on St. Hilary Downs	100, 101, 325
Newfoundland	146
Nectan, St., Abbey, Devon	168
Newlyn, Penzance	204
Newby Cote, Yorkshire	216
Newton, Cornwall	289
Newton, Rev. Robt.	330, 496
Newgate, 402—Street, London	402
Nichols, Mr. Jas.	480
Night of Weeping	490
Normanby, Marquis	31
Nottinghamshire, 43—Nottingham	139, 145, 295, 298
Northern Wolds	44
Norwich	183
Norfolk	211, 230
Norman Isles	254
North Sea	442, 478
Nye, Mr.	287
Olives, Mount of	386
Oliver, Thos.	220, 225, 228, 229, 234, 235, 237, 238, 239, 258
Orphan House, Newcastle	337
Oral Hymnology	12
Owen, Dr. John	25
Oxonian, a Young	360
Oxford, Lord	49
Oxford, 25, 179, 243—Lincoln College	161
Oxfordshire	211, 326
Parting Scene between Fletcher and Berridge	187
Paine, Tom	314
Patagonian Mission	117
Perronet, Edward	180, 181, 183, 184
Perronet, Charles	180
Perronet, Vincent	180
Penkridge, Persecution at	180
Penzance, Cornwall, 204, 301—Bay	201
Pearce, Mr. Richard	228, 229
Penrith, 365—Castle	363
Penhill, Yorkshire	398, 399
Pin Mill Brow, Manchester	275
Poetry, What is It?	17
Poets of Methodism, Classified	19
Pope, 49, 311, 351—Dunciad, 28, 38, 351, 352—Villa	312
Ponsanooth, Cornwall	235
Portsmouth	256
Polwhele, Parson	314
Portreath, Cornwall	456, 457
Presbyterian Doggrel	15
Pressgang and Quaker	201
Providential Escape of a Young Miner	202
Pretender, The, 250—In Manchester	249

INDEX TO NAMES AND PLACES, ETC. 517

	PAGE
Primitive Methodists, their Origin	334
Preacher, Soon Made	. 371
Puncheston, Pembroke	164
Quaker, an Old Dutch, in Dublin	. 95
Quaker Lady and John Harris	. 425, 426

Raithley Hall, Lincoln 252, 253, 254
Redruth, Cornwall, 206, 207, 212, 219, 328, 454, 464—Wesley's
   Room, in, 106—Letter from 107
" Reflections in a Flower Garden," by Hervey . . . 170
Reading, Berks . . . 196
Redmire, Yorkshire . . . 398
Redbourne, near St. Albans . . 408, 409
Revivals, Religious . . 461
Rhodes, Benjamin . 208, 209, 210
Ripley, Yorkshire . . . 88
Rich, Mrs., of Covent Garden . . 92, 93
Rich, Mr. R., his House . 92, 93
Rievaulx Abbey, Yorkshire . 352, 354
Richard of York . . . 398
" Rounders," Methodist . 201
Rodda, Richard . 203
Roundhouse at Redruth 207
Robinson, the Hymnist . 266
Rochester . . 326
Russell Square, London . 393
Russell Family . . 393

Sarah, the Dying Sunday-school Girl . 38
Sancreed, Cornwall . . . 203
Sandemanian Faith . . 175
Saul, King, at Endor . 271
Saurin's Sermons, by J. Sutcliffe . . 326
Scott, Walter . . . 1, 2, 371
Scotland 211
Scotch William, the Lion 336
Scotch Lakes . . . 363
Settle, Yorkshire . . 216
Sevenoaks, Surrey . . 286
Sergeant, Mrs. . . 277, 278, 279, 280, 283
Sergeant, E. F. A. . . . 280, 282
Sermons on Regeneration, by J. Sutcliffe . . 326
Sermon, High Church . . . 361
Sermon to a Village Club . . 493
Sherborne, Dorset . . . 330
Shakespeare Quoted . . . 15, 27, 30, 393
Shannon, River . . 146, 147
Sheffield 331
Short-hand Lessons on a Verse . . 246
Singing of Early Methodists, 90—Decline of . . 91
Singer, Female, at Vermont . . 132
Smetham, Mr. James . . . 488

	PAGE
Smith, Dr. George	417
Solomon Versified	13, 18
South Ormsby, Lincoln	31, 55
Soho Square, London	73
Song of a Working Father	174
Southey, Poet	352
"Speedwell," Patagonian Mission Ship	118
Spanish Hymn, by J. Wesley	104, 106
Spilsby, Lincoln	252
Sparrows, Story about	445
St. Paul's Experience and Gifts	3, 4
St. Mary's, Oxford	26
St. Peter's, Tiverton	54
St. Hilary Downs, and Wesley Adventures	100, 101
St. Just, Cornwall	101, 203
St. Agnes, Cornwall	219
St. John, Family	252
St. Blazey, Cornwall	308
St. Austell, Cornwall	289, 306, 316
St. Saviour's Grammar School, Southwark	373
St. Albans	408
Sternhold and Hopkins	13
Stepney	26
Stanmore, Middlesex	75
Stuart, House of	249
Staffordshire	334
Storm at Night in London	402
Stockport	479
Sunday School Teacher's Death	47, 48
Supernatural Disturbances, Epworth	57, 58
Suffering Triumphant in a Cottage	126
Surrey	286, 295
Sussex	212
Sutcliffe, Rev. Josh.	324, 328
"Sweet Auburn," Goldsmith's	198
Swaddlers	198
Swift, Dean	246
Tatham Family	399
Tatham, Emma, 391, 393, 397, 398, 401, 403, 404, 408, 411—	
Quoted,	5, 8, 9
Tate and Brady	13
Taylor, Isaac	58
Tamar River	126
Thomas, Rev. J. W.	347, 355, 359, 364, 365
Tewkesbury	129
Teuton Settlers	442
Terra del Fuego	118
Tin-washers' Song	113
Theobald's Road, London	393
Tinner, a Seeker of Signs	115

INDEX TO NAMES AND PLACES, ETC. 519

	PAGE
Tintagel Castle, Cornwall	. 294
"The Immateriality, &c., of the Soul," by S. Drew .	312
Tiverton, Devon	50, 53, 55, 229
Trent River	43
"Theron and Aspasio," by Hervey .	. 171
Toplady, Rev. A.	. 239, 259
Treffry, Rev. R., Senr.	289, 290, 291, 293, 294, 303
Treffry, Rev. R., Junr.	286, 288, 289, 294, 301
Treffry, Mrs. R.	. 303
Tregony, Cornwall	289
Truro, Cornwall	. 293
Truscott, Rev. F.	295
"Travels of Cyrus," by Raynal	. 393
Tunes for Methodist Hymns, by Lampe	95
Tunbridge Wells	. 287
Tunstal	335
Twickenham	. 312
United Methodist Free Churches	338
Ulswater Lake .	. 363
Vermont, America	. 131, 133
Veryan Bay, Cornwall	. 289
Virgil Quoted against a Shrew .	88
Virginia, Young Man of .	. 133
Villiers, Duke of Buckingham .	351
"View of the Kingdom of Christ," by Williams	. 178
War Song, Spiritual .	. 13
Watts, Isaac	14, 155
Walpole, Robert	. 49, 50
Wales, South, 164—Adventures on the Way to	. 110
Walsall	136
Waterford, 230—Cathedral and Bishop of	. 231
Watson, Rev. R.	236
Warburton, Bishop	241, 242
Wesley, John, 1, 7, 15, 16, 23, 29, 34, 44, 55, 57, 60, 73, 75, 78, 82, 84, 86, 97, 98, 100, 104, 106, 119, 135, 139, 141, 151, 153, 155, 157, 158, 161, 162, 166, 171, 179, 180, 183, 187, 194, 196, 197, 204, 219, 220, 229, 232, 238, 239, 241, 242, 243, 245, 246, 247, 249, 250, 253, 254, 262, 268, 320, 325, 326, 328, 337, 344, 378, 398, 448	
Wesley, Charles, 1, 6, 7, 25, 33, 34, 44, 57, 66, 84, 85, 86, 88, 89, 90, 92, 93, 95, 98, 115, 117, 120, 125, 128, 135, 139, 141, 147, 150, 151, 155, 158, 161, 162, 172, 180, 181, 183, 197, 198, 214, 215, 224, 245, 246, 248, 249, 250, 378, 465, 466, 480	
Wesley, Samuel, Senr., 351, 352—Quoted, 13—Alluded to, 26, 27, 29, 30, 31, 32, 34, 40, 44, 52, 82	
Wesley, Bartholomew	22, 23, 24, 26
Wesley, John, Senr.	. 23, 24, 26
Wesley, Samuel, Junr.	. 30, 44, 45, 46, 49, 51, 52, 53
Wesley, Matthew	. 66
Wesley, Susannah	. 32, 44, 45, 46, 448

	PAGE
Wesley, Susannah, Junr.	44, 45, 68
Wesley, Emilia	44, 55, 57, 58, 59, 60
Wesley, Mary	44, 61, 62
Wesley, Mehetabel	44, 62, 66, 67, 70, 75
Wesley, Anne	44, 64, 65
Wesley, Martha	44, 65, 66, 85
Wesley, Kezia	44, 66, 85
Wesley, Mrs. C.	124
Wesley Family, their Seat	22
West Street Chapel, London	60, 92, 257
Wedding, Remarkable	121
Wednesbury	136, 138
Wensley Dale, Yorkshire	398, 399
West Witton, Yorkshire	398, 399
Weymouth	24
Westmoreland	398
Westminster, 258—School, 46—Abbey	51, 52, 53
Whitfield, Geo., 90, 161, 166, 172, 173, 177, 199, 210, 226, 227, 241, 268	
Whitaker, John	314
Wharf, River	397, 398
Whitehall, London	257
Whalers, Old Custom among	478
Whit-Monday Sermon to a Club	492
Winterborn-Whitchurch, Dorset	24, 26
Whitelamb, John	61
Williams, Mr., of Patagonian Mission	117
"Widow Indeed," her Last Song	175, 176
Williams, Wm., the Hymnist	176, 177, 178
Williams, Mr., of Kidderminster	90, 91
Wilmot, Lord	22
Wood, Rev. Robert, and Crystal Palace	145
Wood, Mr. James	275
Worth, Rev. Wm.	236
Wordsworth, Wm., 272, 459—On the Rainbow	273
Woodhouse Grove, near Leeds	479
Wooley, Rev. F. F.	490
Wroote, Lincoln	55, 61, 64
Wright, Mrs.	55
Wright, Mr.	70, 72, 78
Wrestling Jacob, Sung at Bolton	158
Wrigley, Francis	328
Yorkshire	44, 213, 295, 397
Yore Valley and River, Yorkshire	398
Zinzendorf, Count	165, 241
Zetland Isles	343

www.ingramcontent.com/pod-product-compliance
Lightning Source LLC
Chambersburg PA
CBHW031946290426
44108CB00011B/695